Cyber Security Policies and Strategies of the World's Leading States

Nika Chitadze
International Black Sea University, Georgia

A volume in the Advances in Digital Crime, Forensics, and Cyber Terrorism (ADCFCT) Book Series

Published in the United States of America by
        IGI Global
        Information Science Reference (an imprint of IGI Global)
        701 E. Chocolate Avenue
        Hershey PA, USA 17033
        Tel: 717-533-8845
        Fax: 717-533-8661
        E-mail: cust@igi-global.com
        Web site: http://www.igi-global.com

Library of Congress Cataloging-in-Publication Data

Names: Chitadze, Nika, 1969- editor.
Title: Cyber security policies and strategies of the world's leading states
  / edited by Nika Chitadze.
Description: Hershey, PA : Information Science Reference, 2023. | Includes
  bibliographical references and index. | Summary: "This book is essential
  for government officials, academics, researchers, NGO representatives,
  mass-media representatives, business sector representatives, and
  students interested in cyber warfare, cyber security, information
  security, defense and security, and world political issues. With its
  comprehensive coverage of cyber security policies and strategies of the
  world's leading states, it is a valuable resource for those seeking to
  understand the evolving landscape of cyber security and its impact on
  global politics. It aims to identify, prevent, reduce, and eliminate
  existing threats and provide readers with a comprehensive understanding
  of cyber security policies and strategies used by leading countries
  worldwide"-- Provided by publisher.
Identifiers: LCCN 2023022597 (print) | LCCN 2023022598 (ebook) | ISBN
  9781668488461 (hardcover) | ISBN 9781668488508 (paperback) | ISBN
  9781668488478 (ebook)
Subjects: LCSH: Computer security--Government policy--Case studies. |
  Cyberspace operations (Military science)--Case studies.
Classification: LCC QA76.9.A25 C91916 2023 (print) | LCC QA76.9.A25
  (ebook) | DDC 005.8--dc23/eng/20230717
LC record available at https://lccn.loc.gov/2023022597
LC ebook record available at https://lccn.loc.gov/2023022598

This book is published in the IGI Global book series Advances in Digital Crime, Forensics, and Cyber Terrorism (ADCF-CT) (ISSN: 2327-0381; eISSN: 2327-0373).

British Cataloguing in Publication Data
A Cataloguing in Publication record for this book is available from the British Library.

All work contributed to this book is new, previously-unpublished material. The views expressed in this book are those of the authors, but not necessarily of the publisher.

For electronic access to this publication, please contact: eresources@igi-global.com.

Advances in Digital Crime, Forensics, and Cyber Terrorism (ADCFCT) Book Series

Bryan Christiansen
Southern New Hampshire University, USA
Agnieszka Piekarz
Independent Researcher, Poland

ISSN:2327-0381
EISSN:2327-0373

MISSION

The digital revolution has allowed for greater global connectivity and has improved the way we share and present information. With this new ease of communication and access also come many new challenges and threats as cyber crime and digital perpetrators are constantly developing new ways to attack systems and gain access to private information.

The **Advances in Digital Crime, Forensics, and Cyber Terrorism (ADCFCT) Book Series** seeks to publish the latest research in diverse fields pertaining to crime, warfare, terrorism and forensics in the digital sphere. By advancing research available in these fields, the **ADCFCT** aims to present researchers, academicians, and students with the most current available knowledge and assist security and law enforcement professionals with a better understanding of the current tools, applications, and methodologies being implemented and discussed in the field.

COVERAGE

- Digital Surveillance
- Information Warfare
- Vulnerability
- Database Forensics
- Identity Theft
- Criminology
- Telecommunications Fraud
- Malware
- Network Forensics
- Computer Virology

IGI Global is currently accepting manuscripts for publication within this series. To submit a proposal for a volume in this series, please contact our Acquisition Editors at Acquisitions@igi-global.com or visit: http://www.igi-global.com/publish/.

Titles in this Series

For a list of additional titles in this series, please visit: www.igi-global.com/book-series

Exploring Cyber Criminals and Data Privac Measures
Nuno Mateus-Coelho (Lapi2s, Copelabs, Lusófona University, Portugal) and Manuela Cruz-Cunha (Polytechnic Institute of Cavado and Ave, Portugal)
Information Science Reference • © 2023 • 324pp • H/C (ISBN: 9781668484227) • US $275.00

Modeling and Simulation of Functional Nanomaterials for Forensic Investigation
Allah Rakha (Department of Forensic Medicine/Medical Jurisprudence, University of Health Sciences, Pakistan) Anam Munawar (Department of Forensic Medicine/Medical Jurisprudence, University of Health Sciences, Pakistan) Virat Khanna (Department of Mechanical Engineering, Maharaja Agrasen University, India) and Suneev Anil Bansal (Department of Mechanical Engineering, Bharat Institute of Engineering and Technolog, India)
Information Science Reference • © 2023 • 378pp • H/C (ISBN: 9781668483251) • US $250.00

Handbook of Research on War Policies, Strategies, and Cyber Wars
Fahri Özsungur (Mersin University, Turkey)
Information Science Reference • © 2023 • 463pp • H/C (ISBN: 9781668467411) • US $315.00

Global Perspectives on the Psychology of Terrorism
Nika Chitadze (International Black Sea University, Georgia)
Information Science Reference • © 2023 • 330pp • H/C (ISBN: 9781668453117) • US $215.00

Aiding Forensic Investigation Through Deep Learning and Machine Learning Frameworks
Alex Noel Joseph Raj (Shantou University, China) Vijayalakshmi G. V. Mahesh (BMS Institute of Technology and Management, India) Ruban Nerssison (Vellore Institute of Technology, India) Ang Yu (Carolina University, USA) and Jennifer Gentry (Carolina University, USA)
Information Science Reference • © 2022 • 273pp • H/C (ISBN: 9781668445587) • US $250.00

Dark Web Pattern Recognition and Crime Analysis Using Machine Intelligence
Romil Rawat (Shri Vaishnav Vidyapeeth Vishwavidyalaya, India) Shrikant Telang (Shri Vaishnav Vidyapeeth Vishwavidyalaya, India) P. William (Sanjivani College of Engineering, Savitribai Phule Pune University, India) Upinder Kaur (Akal University, Talwandi Sabo, India) and Om Kumar C.U. (School of Computer Science and Engineering (SCOPE),Vellore Institute of Technology, India)
Information Science Reference • © 2022 • 281pp • H/C (ISBN: 9781668439425) • US $250.00

IGI Global
PUBLISHER of TIMELY KNOWLEDGE

701 East Chocolate Avenue, Hershey, PA 17033, USA
Tel: 717-533-8845 x100 • Fax: 717-533-8661
E-Mail: cust@igi-global.com • www.igi-global.com

Table of Contents

Detailed Table of Contents

Chapter 1
The Role and Place of Cyber Warfare and Cyber Security in the World: Past, Present, Future 1
    Nika Chitadze, International Black Sea University, Georgia

Computer security, cyber security, or information security is the protection of computer systems and control points of networks from intrusion, unauthorized use, or damage to hardware, software, and electronic data, as well as from destruction and disruption of the services they provide to users. This area is becoming more and more important as a result of increasing dependence on computer systems, the internet, and wireless networks such as Bluetooth and Wi-Fi. Because of its complexity, in terms of politics and technology, cyber security is also one of the main challenges in modern life.

Chapter 2
The Main Historical Stages of the Development of Cyber Space 18
    Irakli Kervalishvili, Georgian Technical University, Georgia

Technologies and the threat of harmful activities using them are developing in international politics. The age we live in is a daily routine of technological revolutions, and with new technologies are born powerful and more flexible both defensive and offensive mechanisms. Cyber attacks have become an inseparable part of our lives, accompanying all military wars. Today, wars are fought using hybrid components. Cyberwar as an event began with the invention of the computer and the Internet.

Chapter 3
Information War as a Result of the Information-Technological Revolution 34
    Salome Mikiashvili, Cyber Security Bureau, Georgia

In the chapter, different aspects related to the information war and cyber warfare of Russia-Ukraine war and the China-Taiwan relations are analyzed. In general, information warfare (WW) (as opposed to cyber warfare, which attacks computers, software, and control systems) is a concept that includes the use of combat space and the management of information and communication technologies (ICT) to achieve the goal. Information warfare is the manipulation of information trusted by the target, without the knowledge of the target, so that the target makes decisions against its interests but in the interests of the one who wages the information war. As a result, it is not clear when the information war begins and ends and how strong or destructive it is.

Chapter 4

C. V. Suresh Babu, Hindustan Institute of Technology and Science, India
P. M. Akshara, Hindustan Institute of Technology and Science, India

Security challenges are faced by every single country on this planet. These threats can occur through violent non-state habitats, any organized group of criminals, economic threats, disasters, or native citizens. In ancient wars, nations used physical forces and weapons as a tool to acquire regions, resources. Whereas, in the future, a wide range of technologies like automated weapons, drones, and cyber warfare may come into action. A single person can control an army of computers, and the person behind the actions can go unidentified. The surging need for the use of computers has greatly imposed an effect on the military. Unlike traditional warfare, where large mobilizations of military forces were involved, in modern warfare, integration with latest innovations in military forces like guided munition systems, explosives, and nuclear weapons are brought into use. As a result, there rises an inevitable need to acquire insight into the field of cyber military technology. This chapter mainly aims to analyse the nation's virtual threats and asymmetric military challenges.

Chapter 5

C. V. Suresh Babu, Hindustan Institute of Technology and Science, India
S. Kowsika, Hindustan Institute of Technology and Science, India
M. Sai Tejaswi, Hindustan Institute of Technology and Science, India
T. R. Janarakshani, Hindustan Institute of Technology and Science, India
S. Mercysha Princy, Hindustan Institute of Technology and Science, India

Cyberbullying is a huge problem online that affects young people and adults. It can lead to accidents like suicide and depression. There is a growing need to curate content on social media platforms. In the following study, the authors used data on two different forms of cyberbullying, hate speech tweets on Twitter, and ad hominem-based comments on Wikipedia forums. The authors use machine learning-based natural language processing and textual data to build models based on cyberbullying detection. They study three feature extraction methods and their four classifiers to determine the best method. The model achieves an accuracy of more than 90 degrees on the tweet data and more than 80 degrees on the Wikipedia data.

Chapter 6

Szde Yu, Wichita State University, USA

Information warfare is one crucial aspect of cyber security. Unlike physical targets, such as network systems or electronic devices, information warfare is aimed at manipulating what people believe to be true and thereby swaying public perceptions. A more organized and advanced form of information warfare is called cognitive warfare. It is a psychological strategy intended to gradually influence the targeted public's belief, opinion, and perception about a subject, such as an event, a politician, a government, or an ideology in general. This chapter discusses the tactics commonly used in cognitive warfare. Using the China-Taiwan relationship as an example, this chapter illustrates how such warfare is carried out.

Chapter 7

The concept of fifth dimension operations is conceptually based on adding the five-dimensional, holistic approach to warfare that uses the three dimensions of land, sea, and aerospace but also incorporates the temporal and cyber dimensions of warfare. In more recent times, the concept of fifth dimensional operations, as a concept under military operations, has taken a wider scope than its original information operations background, focusing on the advanced space-time manipulating capabilities cyberspace offers. This development was begun as early as 1996 in regards to advanced battlespace and cybermaneuver concepts.

Chapter 8

In the 21st century, activities in cyberspace rose and developed significantly. New security dynamics aftermath of the Cold War have led to a shift in the world's power structures. Non-state actors (corporations, organizations, and individuals) now can reflect strategic global power due to modern information and communication technologies. Collective defense in cyberspace might be more challenging considering the nature of the virtual dimension which accomplishes two factors. They pledge the signatories to resist a shared threat, and as a result, are designed to dissuade possible aggressors. They stand at the nexus of law and strategy, as well as the junction of war and peace because of their dual objectives. But with hybrid threats on the rise, some have begun to wonder if the mutual aid provisions established in the North Atlantic and EU treaties still apply in the context of the current security situation.

Chapter 9

In this chapter, the main concept of cyber security strategy and policy of several states in the field of cyber defense policy are discussed and analyzed. This factor allows the authors to make a comparative analysis of the cyber security strategies of such states and organizations as NATO, the European Union, the USA, Estonia, Lithuania, and Georgia. Particularly, there are analyzed appropriate documents in the field of cyber security and cyber defense taking into account the current realities in world politics.

Chapter 10

The chapter reviews the main aspects of the Russia-Ukraine war on the example of the information policy carried out within the framework of the mentioned war between the USA and Russia. In particular, the information policy of the US on the one hand, which is aimed at protecting the independence and territorial integrity of Ukraine and providing democracy enlargement, and on the other, the disinformation policy of Russia, which aims to mislead the international and primarily the Russian public, are discussed.

Chapter 11

Mukesh Shankar Bharti, Jawaharlal Nehru University, India

This chapter aims to discuss the EU's cyber security strategy and how its policy is capable of restricting cybercrime in Europe. The study explains the role of EU Member States in dealing with cybercrime in this region. This research draws on qualitative comparative analysis to examine various EU initiatives to tackle cybercrime issues in Europe. Furthermore, this chapter discusses the core literature of primary and secondary resources through an empirical approach. Since globalisation reached its highest level across the world, the question of cyber security has emerged as a key area of multiple cooperation between the global actors. Cybercrime is now a complex issue among the global actors to restrict its expansion. The EU also started cooperation with Asian, American, and African countries on cybercrime issues. Finally, this chapter suggests that cybercrime is the central area of cooperation between the global actors to restrict it which is dangerous for humanity.

Chapter 12

Tamari Bitsadze, International Black Sea University, Georgia

This chapter first examines the European Union's cyber security strategy and then analyzes the common principles of the member states in this regard. The authors discuss the European Union's role in the advancement of cyber security. In addition, the chapter reviews the EU Convention on Cybercrime. Most importantly, they discuss the impact of the most important and relevant issue, the Russia-Ukraine war, on the EU's cyber security strategy and investigate what changes and challenges the ongoing conflict in Ukraine has brought to the EU's cyber security strategy.

Chapter 13

Tamar Karazanishvili, International Black Sea University, Georgia

Cybersecurity threats are one of the main national security, public safety, and economic challenges every nation faces in the 21st century. The Russia-Ukraine War becomes a defining feature of the US national cyber security strategy too. The purpose of this chapter is to analyze the increasing role of cybersecurity in US politics. It is evident that US cybersecurity strategies at a national level seems to be increasing across multiple sectors too. The chapter analyses Trump's and Biden's national cyber security strategies and challenges. It deals with different initiatives of both presidential administrations and the implications on national security of the country. The chapter focuses on the measures taken by US politicians in strengthening cybersecurity at a national level and combating both state or non-state-sponsored cyber threats.

The most important details in this text are that Russia could make a military impact through cyber operations, but this was not exposed due to limitations created for Russia, the protection system of Ukraine, and support from partners. Russian cyber strategies and objectives regarding Ukraine have been addressed in the same direction as Ukraine space, and the method of collection of intelligence was the main objective for Moscow in the process of the Russia-Ukraine war, but it also had minimal benefits for the aggressor. Additionally, Russia appears to rely on non-cyber sources of target intelligence, despite previous thoughts which said that Russia used malware against the Ukrainian positions. In general, cyber-policy has both positive and negative sides, but it has a very negative impact in the case of Russia's war against Ukraine.

In the modern world, transferring data into digital format, electronic commerce, social media, and receiving public services through online platforms are very relevant. The more states become dependent on cyberspace, the more reasons and means hostile actors have for cyberattacks, stealing and distorting information, and paralyzing systems. We must keep in mind that cyber security is not only about computer programming and information technology. Cyber security is a vital part of national security, as cyber-attacks target people, public opinion, and public and business sectors. China is indeed quite an aggressive cyber actor, but there is another, non-democratic state that has much greater economic-technological resources, ambition, and aspiration for cyber expansionism.

This chapter aims to analyze the cybersecurity policies and strategies of the United States and China, representing democratic and authoritarian regimes, respectively. The study explores the key roles played by cyber security policies, legal frameworks, and international relations in these countries. By examining these aspects, the authors discern the disparities between cyber security policies in democratic and authoritarian regimes. The chapter highlights the diverse approaches employed to ensure cyber security and the challenges faced by both countries in countering cyber threats and safeguarding their national interests.

Preface

The development of digital technologies has covered all areas of human life. The technological revolution, which has brought great benefits to humanity, has increased cyber risks in the virtual space. Currently, the geographical borders of the state do not represent a barrier to cyber attacks. Malicious cyber activities can be carried out covertly from anywhere in the world, by a person or groups of people from home, through a computer, without requiring special, expensive resources. It can have the same devastating effect as conventional warfare.

The speed of technology development has completely changed the international security landscape. The world is faced with massive cyber challenges. Cyber security is a global challenge that transcends state borders and requires collective international cooperation. Even though the world's leading countries, members of the European Union, and the alliance are trying to deal with cyber threats independently, none of the states has been able to effectively fight against cyber challenges. The fight against cybercrime at the international level is possible only with the collaboration of countries, with a collective approach.

The social and economic well-being, health, and life of each citizen significantly depend on ensuring the security of information systems and electronic services. Cyber-attacks have a great impact on all sectors of the economy, hinder the proper functioning of the economic space, reduce public trust in electronic services, and threaten the development of the economy using information and communication technologies. Against the background of global cyber threats, when cyber-attacks, cyber-espionage, cyber-terrorism, and disinformation are being carried out daily, the development, implementation, and development of new defense mechanisms is an important issue. It should be noted that NATO plays an important role in this direction and, together with the European Union, represents a kind of security umbrella for both member and partner countries.

Every century has its problems. In the 21st century, the events taking place in cyberspace have become the most dangerous events - many people, private companies, and state institutions are affected every day. Billions of dollars are already being spent on defense.

For example, if we consider the documents of the world's strongest military-political alliance, NATO, we can note that in all the concepts and doctrines of the North Atlantic Alliance, it is emphasized that based on the basic principles, none of its member countries should be forced to rely only on their forces. The strategy of the alliance allows each member state to realize national security goals through collective methods.

All leading countries in the world have a national cyber security strategy, which is a determining factor of state policy. The national security strategy aims to identify, prevent, reduce, and eliminate existing threats.

Cyberwar, as a global issue, cannot be a subject of research in one direction. Moreover, it will not be possible to resist this event unequivocally. There are many factors to be considered here - the essence of cyberwar, analyzing the history of the origin and development of cyberwar, identifying the causes and contributing factors, defining terminologies related to cybercrime, classifying viruses and cyberattacks, detecting international organized hacker groups, assessing threats from their side and developing security mechanisms, computer programs and Classification of their structure, programming languages and description of their purpose, study and definition of the basics of the Internet and network, presentation of various strategies of unauthorized entry into the computer system, description of the facts of cybercrime directed against people, definition of various options for improvement of legislation about cyberspace in the form of recommendations.

The development of technology has not changed the priorities in matters of state defense in the same way as during the Second World War - the main tactical strikes are aimed at energy facilities. Currently, the most serious cyber-attacks occur in the fuel and energy complex, followed by the financial sector. The digital world has contributed to the emergence of new types of threats. As we have already mentioned, not all types of cyber attacks can be considered in terms of cyber war. Although we have defined what is cyberwar and what is a cyberattack, it is still difficult to qualify cyberwar because most of the facts on a global scale are based on assumptions. Traces often lead to one of the aggressor states, but often there is no evidence. We discuss cyberwars and technical characteristics based on various studies, we analyze - when does it start, how did it transform, what is its role in the production of conflicts, and so on. It is an important fact that many states not only conduct cyber espionage, intelligence, and investigation but also create cyber warfare capabilities themselves. At the end of the 20th century, no one could have imagined that a real war would become an extension of a war created in a set dimension, or vice versa, that unreal space would merge with real space. Perhaps, no one could have imagined that a dimension would emerge that would be almost impossible to control, and boundless, humanity would face an invisible threat. When we try to explain the transformation of cyberwarfare, we must identify what is changing it all. This is mostly related to the improvement of cyber attack technologies and the creation of malicious hacking strategies, programs, or viruses. Therefore, we must distinguish the types of attack: there are passive and active cyberattacks, and passive attack involves traffic analysis and monitoring of vulnerable communications. During an active attack, a hacker attacks protected systems.

It can be seen in physical tools like computers, cables, mobiles, etc. Tools interact in the virtual and non-real realms. It helps to wage war from one part of the world to another part of the world, and the perpetrator cannot always be identified. Cyberwarfare often represents a conceptual framework related to the traditional conduct of war - involving a show of force, physical harm, and violence. As time passes, it becomes more and more important to define what type of cyberattack should be called a cyberwar. These types of definitions are important when dealing with issues related to cyber warfare, which sometimes involve kinetic and sometimes non-kinetic attacks. It should be discussed The difference between a cyber attack and a cyber war - worldwide there have been many attempts to accurately define the essence of cyber war at the conceptual level, for example, the "Tallinn Guide" was created under the leadership of NATO's "Cyber Defense Cooperation Skills Center" - where the violations of law used in cyber wars are discussed according to the laws of international law. However, it is not a political, official document of NATO. The difficulty in this case is that nation-states and non-state actors do not always follow the law. Some Experts think that some topics in the "Tallinn Guide" are general, superficial, and incompatible with the theoretical definitions of cyberspace, and need to be refined. For example, in the "Tallinn

Manual", cyberwar is equated with a cyberattack - it is said to be an offensive or defensive operation that can cause human death, injury, or destruction of objects.

In our opinion, this definition excludes psychological pressure during cyber operations or cyber intelligence. The main drawback of this definition is considering cyber war and cyber attack as one term. Also, the aforementioned definition excludes cyber operations that may aim to destabilize the financial system of states. In this case, the cyber attack does not result in death or physical destruction.

The results of the book's research can be useful to cyber security specialists, hybrid warfare analysts, and organizations interested in cyber security. It can be used for persons interested in further research, and specialists in the field.

The practical significance of the research lies in the possible use of its results during the activities carried out for the development of the legislative framework in the field of national security. Studies and recommendations can be used by the governments of different countries to determine the main directions of the country's security strategy.

The book will provide theoretical and practical assistance to academic circles, the public-political sector, and persons interested in these issues. The materials of the book can be used in civilian and military higher education institutions; During the teaching of social sciences, international relations, and other subjects, for the preparation of lecture courses, in the process of carrying out scientific projects and research on the issues of the mentioned topic. The presented work will also be of great help to undergraduate and graduate students of the university.

Discussing and analyzing each chapter of the book, it should be pointed out:

Chapter 1, "The Role and Place of Cyber Warfare and Cyber Security in the World: Past, Present, Future," presents the analysis of the main aspects related to conducting Cyber Warfare and working out the preventive mechanisms, which should be determined in the framework of Cyber Security strategy. In general, together with other topics it is the role of Cyber Warfare and Cyber Security in world politics within the different periods.

The second chapter, "The Main Historical Stages of the Development of Cyber Space," mentioned information technology development during the period of modern history and how technological revolutions and scientific-technical progress have affected Cyber Space and Cyber Security issues.

Chapter 3, "Information War as a Result of the Information-Technological Revolution." analyzes various aspects related to information warfare and cyber warfare, using the example of the Russian-Ukrainian war and Sino-Taiwanese relations. In general, information warfare (MI) (as opposed to cyber warfare, which attacks computers, software, and command and control systems) is a concept that involves the use of battlespace and the management of information and communications technology (ICT) to achieve an objective. Competitive advantage over an opponent. Information warfare is the manipulation of information trusted by the target, without the target's knowledge, so that the target makes decisions against its interests, but in the interests of the one waging the information war. As a result, it is unclear when the information war will begin and end, and how strong and destructive it will be.

Chapter 4, "Virtual Threats and Asymmetric Military Challenges," explained that every country on the planet faces security challenges. These threats can arise through violent non-state environments, any organized group of criminals, economic threats, natural disasters, or indigenous citizens. In ancient wars, people used physical force and weapons as a tool to seize regions and resources. Whereas, a wide range of technologies such as automatic weapons, drones, and cyber warfare may come into play in the future. One person can control an army of computers, but the person behind the action may remain unknown.

The growing need to use computers has greatly impacted the military. Unlike traditional wars, which involved large mobilizations of military forces, modern warfare uses the latest innovations in the military, such as guided munition systems, explosives, and nuclear weapons. As a result, there is an inevitable need to understand the field of cyber warfare technologies. This chapter mainly focuses on analyzing the country's virtual threats and asymmetric military challenges.

In the fifth chapter, "Framework for Detection of Cyberbullying in Text Data Using Natural Language Processing and Machine Learning," the author presents an analysis, according to which Cyberbullying is a significant problem online that affects young people generation. This can lead to such tragic events as suicide and depression. There is a growing need for content curation on social media platforms. In the following research, it has been used data on two different forms of cyberbullying: hate tweets on Twitter and comments based on advertorials on Wikipedia forums. Furthermore, the three feature extraction methods and their four classifiers to determine the best method have been studied and researched.

Chapter 6, "Cognitive Warfare: A Psychological Strategy to Manipulate Public Opinion," concerns the fact, that cognitive warfare is a psychological strategy designed to gradually influence the target audience's beliefs, opinions, and perceptions about a subject such as an event, politician, government or ideology in general. The second part of the chapter discusses tactics commonly used in cognitive warfare. Using Sino-Taiwan relations as an example, this chapter shows how such a war is fought.

The next, seventh chapter, "The Fifth Space of Warfare and Confrontation," discusses that the Fifth Dimension Concept of Operations is conceptually based on the addition of a "five-dimensional, holistic approach to warfare that uses three dimensions: land, sea, and aerospace, but also includes time and the cyber dimensions of war."

Regarding Chapter 8. "Collective Cyber Defense: Legalization of Cyberspace," the researcher emphasizes that in the modern period, activities in cyberspace have significantly increased and developed. New post-Cold War security dynamics have led to a shift in global power structures. Non-state actors (corporations, organizations, and individuals) can now reflect strategic global power thanks to modern information and communication technologies. Collective defense in cyberspace may be more challenging given the nature of the virtual dimension, which is driven by two factors. They oblige the signatories to confront a common threat and, as a result, are designed to dissuade possible aggressors. They stand at the intersection of law and strategy, and the intersection of war and peace, because of their dual goals. However, with the rise of hybrid threats, some have begun to question whether the mutual assistance provisions established in the North Atlantic Treaty and the EU treaty apply in the context of our current security situation.

Chapter 9, "Cybersecurity Strategies: International Experience," discusses and analyzes the basic concepts of cybersecurity strategy and policy of several states in the field of cyber defense policy. This factor allows for a comparative analysis of the cybersecurity strategies of such states and organizations as NATO, the European Union, the USA, Estonia, Lithuania, and Georgia. In particular, relevant documents in the field of cybersecurity and cyber defense are analyzed taking into account the modern realities of world politics.

Next is Chapter 10, "The War in Ukraine and the United States-Russian Information War: Comparative Analysis," which examines the main aspects of the Russian-Ukrainian war using the example of information policy carried out within the framework of the mentioned war between the United States and Russia. In particular, the US information policy, on the one hand, aimed at protecting the independence and territorial integrity of Ukraine and ensuring the expansion of democracy, and on the other,

Russia's disinformation policy, aimed at misleading the international and primarily the Russian public, is being discussed.

Chapter 11, "EU Cybersecurity Strategy: Cybercrime Governance and Challenges in Europe," has the purpose of examining the EU's cybersecurity strategy and how its policies can limit cybercrime in Europe. The study explains the role of EU member states in combating cybercrime in the region. This study uses a qualitative comparative analysis to examine different EU initiatives to address cybercrime issues in Europe.

Chapter 12, "EU's Cyber Security Strategy Before and During the War in Ukraine," also concerns the European Union and first examines the European Union's Cybersecurity Strategy and then analyzes the general principles of member states in this regard. We discuss the role of the European Union in promoting cybersecurity. In addition, the article discusses the EU Convention on Cybercrime.

Chapter 13, "Understanding US Cyber Security Policies During Donald J. Trump's and Biden-Harris' Administrations," explains that cybersecurity threats are one of the major national security, public safety, and economic challenges facing every country in the 21st century. The Russian-Ukrainian war is also becoming a defining feature of US national cybersecurity. The purpose of this chapter is to analyze the increasing role of cybersecurity in US policy. Because this is becoming one of the main issues of national security of the country. And U.S. cybersecurity strategies at the national level appear to be expanding across many sectors. This chapter analyzes Trump's and Biden's national cybersecurity strategies and challenges. It examines the various initiatives of both presidential administrations and their impact on the country's national security. The Chapter focuses on measures taken by U.S. policymakers to strengthen cybersecurity at the national level and combat state and non-state-sponsored cyber threats.

Chapter 14, "Russia's Aggressive Cyber Policy During the Russo-Ukrainian War," highlights the fact that Russian cyber strategies and goals regarding Ukraine were viewed in the same direction as the Ukrainian space, and the method of intelligence gathering was Moscow's main goal during the Russo-Ukrainian war. war, but this also brought minimal benefit to the aggressor. Additionally, Russia appears to be relying on non-cyber secure sources of targeted intelligence, despite previous thoughts suggesting Russia used malware against Ukrainian positions. In general, cyber policy has both positive and negative sides, but in the case of Russia's war against Ukraine, it has a very negative impact.

Chapter 15, "China's Cyber Security Policy and the Democratic World," determined main principles and approaches related to cyber security in China and should be done by the democratic community to take into consideration the national interests of China first of all in the field of Cyber policy.

Chapter 16, "Analysis of Cybersecurity Strategies in Democratic and Authoritarian Regimes: A Comparative Study of the United States and China," aims to analyze the cybersecurity policies and strategies of the United States and China, representing democratic and authoritarian regimes, respectively. The study examines the key roles played by cybersecurity policies, legal frameworks, and international relations in these countries. By examining these aspects, we can discern differences between cybersecurity policies in democracies and authoritarian regimes, especially in the US and China. The document highlights the variety of approaches used to achieve cybersecurity, as well as the challenges both countries face in countering cyber threats and protecting their national interests.

Taking into consideration the above-mentioned factors, it should be pointed out that the novelty of the book and its contribution to the development of the academic disciplines, Cyber Warfare, Cyber Security Strategies, and Cyber Defense is connected with the fact, that the book " Cyber Security Policies and Strategies of the World's Leading States" for the first time have been presented the combination of the topics, related to the Cyber War, including war between Russia and Ukraine and Comparative analysis of the Cyber Security strategies of the leading countries of the world, modern development of the world (for example topics on globalization, role, and place of the states, etc.) and different, particularly - political, military, security, information, socio-economic, environmental, etc. threats and challenges before the international security and ways for those problems resolution.

Nika Chitadze
International Black Sea University, Georgia

Acknowledgment

In the framework of the working over the book, *Cyber Security Policies and Strategies of the World's Leading States*, I would like to express my special gratitude to *Ms. Joselynn Hessler* – Managing Editor of Book Development, IGI Global for her assistance and attention within the different stages in the framework of the book preparation Process.

At the same time, I would like to dedicate a special thanks to each author of the chapters – citizens of the different countries and representatives of the different nationalities, who took to the Heart the global problems of our planet related to cyber warfare and implemented very important research in favor of development academic discipline – Cyber Security. So, without the contributions of experienced scholars it would be impossible the publishing of the book.

I am too much thankful to my native – International Black Sea University and its Administration, Academic and Administrative personnel for establishing for me an excellent scientific environment and great atmosphere during working over the book.

Introduction

The main purpose of the book is to discuss about main aspects related to Cyber Security, by taking into account the cyber security strategies of the world's leading states.

In general, cybersecurity is the process of using security measures to ensure the confidentiality, integrity, and availability of data. The system administrator ensures the protection of assets, including data on a local network of computers and servers. In addition, the buildings themselves and, most importantly, the personnel are taken under protection. The purpose of cybersecurity is to protect data (both during transmission and/or exchange and in storage). Countermeasures may also be applied to ensure data security. Some of these measures include (but are not limited to) access control, staff training, auditing and reporting, risk assessment, penetration testing, and authorization requirements.

Chapter 1
The Role and Place of Cyber Warfare and Cyber Security in the World:
Past, Present, Future

Nika Chitadze
International Black Sea University, Georgia

ABSTRACT

Computer security, cyber security, or information security is the protection of computer systems and control points of networks from intrusion, unauthorized use, or damage to hardware, software, and electronic data, as well as from destruction and disruption of the services they provide to users. This area is becoming more and more important as a result of increasing dependence on computer systems, the internet, and wireless networks such as Bluetooth and Wi-Fi. Because of its complexity, in terms of politics and technology, cyber security is also one of the main challenges in modern life.

INTRODUCTION

The development of digital technologies has covered all areas of human life. The technological revolution, which has brought great benefits to humanity, has increased cyber risks in virtual space. Currently, the geographical borders of the state do not represent a barrier to cyber attacks. Malicious cyber activities can be carried out covertly from anywhere in the world, by a person or groups of people from home, through a computer, without requiring special, expensive resources. It can have the same devastating effect as conventional warfare.

The speed of technology development has completely changed the international security landscape. The world is faced with massive cyber challenges. Cyber security is a global challenge that transcends state borders and requires collective international cooperation. Even though the world's leading countries, members of the European Union, and the alliance are trying to deal with cyber threats independently,

DOI: 10.4018/978-1-6684-8846-1.ch001

none of the states has been able to effectively fight against cyber challenges. The fight against cybercrime at the international level is possible only with the collaboration of countries, with a collective approach.

At a time when many countries are constant targets of cyberattacks, information-psychological operations of the aggressor Russia, and a strong disinformation campaign by the Kremlin and its allies, the role of cyber security and the development of cyber capabilities in the national security policy of various countries is vital. The country's sovereignty, territorial integrity, and stability are achieved through integration into the democratic world. Although significant research has been conducted in the field of cyber security, because cyberspace is a new challenge of an unpredictable nature, which is becoming increasingly complex and large-scale with the rapid development of digital technologies, it can be said that the underlying causes of Countries cannot unite to fight cybercrime with all their might. What prevents them from cooperating on a global level? What methods can different countries deal with modern cyber challenges, which will become even more complex and unmanageable in the era of smart technologies, artificial intelligence, and quantum computers (Svanadze, 2015)?

Cyber Security: Taking Social Media and National Security as an Example

Mass media could always play a certain positive or negative role in any country's national security issues and have a certain impact on it, the main thing was just in which direction? who and where and how it would use traditional media. In the last decade of the beginning of the XXI century, the use of social media became very popular and useful. The means have changed, while the goals and objectives, as well as the questions above, have remained the same. Media means still have the same influence on national security as traditional media, only all this has accelerated in time, events are developing and spreading faster. Social media began its existence in the 21st century in the USA, and it is developing here with geometric progression. As of 2010, there were approximately two billion social media users, nearly a third of the planet's total population. In the first stage of development, between 2000 and 2005, social media was widespread in countries with high technologies, where the indicator of the index of democracy is quite high. Since 2005, social media has started to spread in relatively underdeveloped countries, where the index of democracy is relatively low, and in some places, it does not exist at all. This fact greatly affects not only the national security of the country but also regional and in many cases international security. Traditionally, social media refers to such well-known social networks as Facebook, LinkedIn, MySpace, Twitter, YouTube, Flickr, WordPress, Blogger, Typepad, LiveJournal, Wikipedia, Wetpaint, Wikidot, Second Life, Del.icio.us, Digg, Reddit, Lulu (Lindsay, 2011).

The number of users of social networks is increasing day by day. Its rapid global spread is facilitated by the features of social media, important for the user, such as operationality, rapid transfer of information and the possibility of two-way communication, cheapness, etc. Sh. Constant growth of users. However, social media has both positive and negative sides. Its misuse can adversely affect the national security of the country. However, at the same time, social media can bring a positive effect on the country, it can be used to achieve strategic or tactical goals, work on threats and prevent them in time. Social media is developing very quickly, and it is necessary to constantly monitor geo-political, geo-economic, or other types of processes by the state. As a whole, this complex process will allow us to avoid external threats and their impact on domestic events. It can be said that social media is used quite successfully by international criminal groups, including terrorist organizations. Potentially adversarial countries and alliances do not hesitate to use social media in their interests to achieve their goals. It is necessary to know how and to what extent social media can help the state prevent threats and protect strategic interests. It is necessary to properly use the opportunity of social media, however, it is necessary to take into account the fact that the rights of the user as a person should not be violated. In many countries, social media are studied by journalists for some reason, and journalists learn the competence of the issue, when this topic, based on its relevance, content, and busyness, represents the subject of international relations, and international security research. Before we start discussing the main issue, to create a clear idea, let's talk a few words about the definition of social media, its definition, difference from traditional media, and the user categories of social networks. We will also talk about the information war and the role and place of social media in this war.

Definition of Social Media and Comparison With Traditional Media

What is social media in general? It's been nearly a decade since social media hit the Internet, and news like this usually spreads at lightning speed. The spread and use of social media have outpaced the process of its study, which has become the main reason for heated debates and differences of opinion among opponents. It can be said that the issue has not been studied to the end, not enough studies have been conducted and there is no unified opinion about it, therefore the definition of social media in general. For example, the US Congressional Research Service (CRS) analyst Bruce Lindsay defines social media as follows: "The term social media refers to Internet links that allow people to interact, share resources and information. Social media includes discussion forums, blogs, chat rooms, YouTube channels, LinkedIn, Facebook, and Twitter. Access to social media can be accessed via computer, as well as through smartphones, cellular connections, and text messaging on cell phones." Strategic communications expert and Oklahoma State University professor Bobby Lewis define social media as "Internet tools like blogs, YouTube, Flickr, MySpace, and Facebook that allow the average person to create content to share with a global audience. The interactive nature of these media has changed from one-way distribution of mass media to two-way dialogue. As mentioned above, there is no single established opinion on the exact definition of social media, and to dwell on it would take us a bit too far, but in the end, I will save the consulting firm Burston-Marsteller's version of the description of social media, namely "it is a switch where people make discoveries read and share news, information, and content, including text, video, photo, and audio." In short, we can say that social media is a means of connection and communication that can be achieved in cyberspace, which functions operationally based on technological devices (Internet, mobile phones, computers, etc.) and has software (Facebook, Twitter, MySpace, LinkedIn, YouTube, etc.) platform.

With the help of all mentioned, users can:

- Communicate with each other;
- Sharing of different types of content (video, photo, audio, etc.);
- Creation of network associations (professional, religious, cultural, acquaintances, political, etc.);
- Defining and developing social identity (Lewis, 2010).

Social media, unlike traditional mass media, have a very high level of interactive interdependence between users. Traditional media are one-way disseminators of information, while social media users are both information receivers and creators and disseminators. When comparing traditional and social media, the latter is more dynamic, personal, and interactive. It is also characterized by the promptness and the speed of spreading information around the world, time and space are unacceptable for it, it is simple and cheap. When using social media, the user can create, activate and manage his profile in the virtual space, establishing his place in the unreal world.

Social Media User

Social media users can be divided into several categories. First of all, these are ordinary individuals who use such means of social media as information and content exchange - sharing, communication, and raising personal identity using social networks. Social media allows individuals to satisfy almost all of their needs, except physiological (eating, drinking, sleeping). And this increases the user's dependence on various social networks, in many cases, such dependence is already compared by specialists to dependence on alcohol, narcotic substances, and coffee.

According to 2011 statistics, social media users are:

- 75% of Internet users have their profile;
- About 40% have access from a mobile phone, which they use actively;
- People over 55 use only their computers;
- Women use social media more often than men;
- The age of active users of social networks is 18-35 years (Svanadze, 2015).

According to the Center for Strategic Studies in The Hague, the penetration of social media into our daily lives is increasing, and it is expected to increase even more shortly. The rapid increase in the level of social penetration in public life depends on several factors, among which ease of access to the network and a higher degree of trust play a major role. These factors are increasing and the number of users of social networks will increase accordingly.

Individuals can use a social network not only for personal purposes but also for other interests, for example, to create a group with their peers in the field of interest to them. A group created in a social network is a potential user and it is managed by one or more members of the group, on behalf of all the people who join it. In many cases, social network groups serve the personal interests of a small circle, which can be both existential and public. Specialists have already issued a warning to the user about showing more attention and caution in the process of working with social networks.

Social Media and Information Warfare

Before we talk about the role and place of social media in the information war, let's see what is an information war, what methods are used and what are its main characteristics. According to the definition of the United States Department of Defense, Information War (IW) or as it is also called Information Operations (IO) - is an action aimed at maintaining one's information system to prevent unwanted penetration from the outside, to violate the country's defense capability. At the same time, this is an action aimed at paralyzing the opponent's information system to gain an advantage over the latter. However, there is another kind of definition, namely IW/IO is referred to as an adversary or another country's population and military personnel, through the dissemination of information, and psychological influence, to gain political and military advantage. With such a definition, IW/IO is often referred to as "information-psychological warfare". During IW/IO production, the main method used is to spread disinformation or to spread information containing the necessary context. Similar methods allow changing public opinion on certain events. IW/IO production is mainly characterized by:

- information impact can be carried out both against the background of an information boom and during an information vacuum;
- traditional and social media, as well as mail and rumors, are used as means;
- Informational impact contains distorted facts and the object surrounds itself with the emotional background of the information acceptable to the broadcaster;
- Both the population as a whole and individuals are considered objects of informational influence. The objects of individual influence are the ruling persons of the country (president, prime minister, ministers, politicians, state or public figures, top managers of companies, etc.) and its main goal is to make them make the desired decision. And in the case of the population, there is a massive impact on consciousness, which can be considered an analog to psychotherapy;
- It is not necessary to use psychoactive means (blackmail, intimidation, physical influence, bribery, etc.) during informational influence, although the event can be carried out in a complex manner (Burson-Marsteller, 2010).

Social media tools are actively used during IW/IO production. When using it, organized groups try to gain an advantage over their opponent, and become more competitive. Social media can become an effective IW/IO tool because it allows its users to:

1. Provides important results from a strategic and tactical point of view:
   a. Operates within the domain (cyberspace), unlike traditional military types (land, sea, air).
   b. In size and scope, in contrast to traditional warfare.
   c. In addition to the military, social society (ethnic, religious, professional, and cultural) is accepted as objects.
2. It is possible to achieve the goal with minimum financial expenses.
3. Achieving significant results without any control and monitoring, as well as the possibility of investigation.
4. Asymmetric conflict management, in particular, affects small and medium-sized groups when the real target is a larger group or the state as a whole.

Conducting informational warfare using social media can have different characteristics, depending on the nature of the organized group (terrorist or criminal group, state, company, etc.) and the task set before them. This can be divided as follows:

1. Cyber-war (cyber-attack) - "the action of a state-nation aimed at penetrating the computer network of another state, to cause damage to it or to completely disable it" (Richard Clarke, USA national security expert) or in other words, to say that it is a complex of offensive measures carried out in cyberspace by one or more states, and directed against another state or a non-state entity of the international level;
2. Cyber-terrorism, which is used by terrorist organizations in cyberspace and is directed against the national security of the country;
3. Anti-cyber-terrorism, used against terrorist organizations and carried out in cyberspace;

4. Cybercrime, used by various criminals or transnational groups, during which cyberspace is used for theft, information theft, fraud, etc. Sh. Their objects can be both individuals and large companies. Its purpose is to obtain economic profit;

5. Anti-cyber crime, which includes protective measures by state law enforcement or private individuals and companies against cyber criminals. Here it can be noted that specialists and experts separate cyber-attack as separate issue, and distinguish it from cyber-war. However, it should also be noted that in many cases it is very difficult to distinguish cyber-war from cyber-attack, as yet, in fact, the boundary between these two commandments is not established, and the criteria by which one or the other action should be evaluated are not specifically defined. Social media can be used by domestic and international criminal groups to directly threaten national security (Svanadze, 2015).

Such groups include:

- National subversive groups (Marxist-Leninist groups, anarchists);
- National and transnational criminal groups (Mafia, Yakuza, Triad, Camorra);
- Terrorist organizations;
- Multinational companies with their financial means;
- Companies with foreign capital;
- Extra-parliamentary opposition groups (right-wing extremists, xenophobic groups);
- Religious sects;
- Hacker groups;
- Other state and national military-political, as well as financial unions;
- Associations, foundations, and non-profit organizations;
- Non-governmental and international organizations;
- Political organizations and trade unions;
- State institutions. Social media tools are evolving rapidly and are spreading around the world wherever there is internet access (Svanadze, 2015).

This fact allows for the formation and creation of unknown groups of a new type and different in their activities, whose real goals and aspirations are not known until a certain time, and it may contain a certain danger, which needs some time to study. All this hurts national security. Therefore, this topic is a subject of constant research and study. Also, it can be said that there is a need for constant monitoring of social media, although the rights of individuals should not be violated and should be within the limits defined by the constitution.

National Security

Before we start talking about specific threats, let's say a few words about what is national security, what does it include and what does it protect, as well as which state structures protect national security? There are many definitions of national security, of which we present several options, namely:

1. National security - it is the protection of the vital interests of individuals, society, and the state from external and internal threats, ensuring the stable development of the country;

2. National security - this is the ability of the nation, taking into account the minimal threat to the basic values of the existing situation, to meet the needs necessary for self-establishment and self-preservation;
3. National security - this is stability that can be maintained for a long period, at the same time, existing threats can be assessed and identified to neutralize them in time;
4. National security - this is a set of officially accepted views of state strategy and goals, which ensures the protection of individuals, society, and the state from external and internal threats of a political, economic, social, military, informational, technogenic, ecological or other nature, taking into account the available resources and capabilities (Chitadze, 2016). Taking into account the given definitions, national security includes and consists of the following components:
    ◦ State security;
    ◦ Public security;
    ◦ technogenic safety;
    ◦ environmental safety;
    ◦ political security;
    ◦ military security;
    ◦ economic security;
    ◦ energy security;
    ◦ information security;
    ◦ Personal safety.

Ensuring national security is a combination of political, economic, social, military, healthcare, and law enforcement measures aimed at ensuring the normal life of the nation and the timely prevention of possible threats. Its main task can be considered to be the establishment of a citizen's stable economic situation, protection, and development of the well-being of the citizens of other countries. Ensuring national security includes:

- protection of state and public order;
- ensuring sovereignty and territorial inviolability;
- ensuring political and economic independence of the nation;
- ensuring the nation's health;
- protection of public order;
- fight against crime;
- Ensuring technogenic safety and protection from natural disasters (US Government, 2010).

All available resources of the state are complexly involved in the protection of national security, although its protection is mainly provided by the army, intelligence, counterintelligence services, law enforcement, and healthcare structures. Threats created by the use of social media to national security Social media can have both positive and negative effects on a country's national security. The higher the level of informatization of the country, the higher the risk factors, are directed against the country's strategic interests and goals. Similar threats to national security can be posed through the use of social media. Terrorist Organizations Social media tools will be used more and more actively by terrorist organizations. In this way information exchange and communication, dissemination of ideology, recruitment process, and training is produced. Today, the most active social media tools are used by Islamist-jihadist terrorist organizations. For example, Al-Qaeda often uses Facebook and YouTube channels to recruit "Islamic fighters" and spread fundamentalist Islamic ideology, as well as try to gain more and more followers, especially in the West. In addition, social networks are actively used to exchange information and advice between terrorist organizations. Through social media, and the Internet in general, terrorist organizations disseminate extremist materials and ideas, allowing them to recruit without any intermediaries.

In addition, social media tools are used to achieve propaganda goals, in particular, to spread information and relevant materials about successful terrorist activities, thereby sowing panic among the population. In addition, disinformation materials of various natures and information about carrying out a terrorist attack, the goal of which is also panic, are being spread. At this time, in addition to the population, the object of the alleged attack may be a specific person, financial institution, political organization, or large company. According to US research services, some terrorist organizations use social media to spread deliberate lies during or immediately after a natural disaster to overstate the impact and delay the country's response. According to the US Army, social media tools can be used by some terrorist organizations to target computers and mobile equipment. In addition to the distribution of propaganda materials, especially infected programs are sent through social networks, mainly using Facebook and YouTube channels, which disrupt the user's equipment (US Department of Defense, 2011). The best and most successful use of social media can be considered al-Qaeda, namely Anwar al-Awlaki, who developed an entire strategy for the dissemination of desired information, propaganda, and recruitment through the Internet. He was killed on September 30, 2011, in Yemen, by US special forces. Anwar al-Awlaki's "successful" ideological operation can be considered the killing of 13 American servicemen and the wounding of 43, which took place in the US, on a military base, on the way to Iraq, by Major Nidal Hassan of the US Army, under the influence of propaganda spread by al-Awlaki's social network. in front, Nidal Hasan was a psychologist by profession and conducted psychological training courses for the military (US Department of Defense, 2011).

Criminal Organizations

Criminal organizations use social media to support their illegal activities. Such illegal business can be either the dissemination of information (for example, child pornography, spreading viruses, stealing personal information of a person, etc.) or traditional activities (for example, drug smuggling, trafficking, money laundering, transfer of stolen documents, corporate espionage). Criminal gangs can be in one place, a group of people gathered locally who know each other personally, or individuals scattered in different parts of the world who have only virtual contact with each other. Such groups are held e. year By moderators, who are equipped with special management rights, they can kick out less active members, or "promote" good performers. The criminal network in social media is getting bigger and bigger. War According to research conducted by NATO, future conflicts will arise in an environment characterized by the active use of the latest information and communication technologies, including social media (Svanadze, 2015).

At the same time, during military operations, it conducts supporting events through social media. For example, the two recent conflicts between Israel and Lebanon. In 2006, during the second conflict, Hezbollah conducted several IW operations through social media, in particular, using YouTube to publish some video and photo materials they wanted, in response to which Israel released counter-information using the same social media during future conflicts (Svanadze, 2015). Protest Movements and Revolutions New technologies, and in particular social media tools, play a very important, and in many cases, decisive role in the organization of protest movements and revolutions. In such a case, social networks are used by revolutionary groups for mass demonstrations, for their coordination and stimulation of action, as well as for tactical and operational management of protest demonstrations. If we take into account the fact that social media is developing faster and faster, then with taxation it can be said that the number of protests and revolutions will increase accordingly. According to Stratfor analysts, social media is a tool that allows revolutionary groups to reduce the costs of event organization, participation, recruitment, and training. Studying the protests in Tunisia and Egypt revealed that:

- the role of social media in stimulating and managing the population in protests has greatly increased;
- Along with the mobile phone, the speed of action and the area of distribution have increased;
- Due to the cheapness, the revolutionary movement has the opportunity to act more autonomously, it does not depend on foreign finances at all;
- little or no censorship;
- Protests and revolutionary changes occur in countries where there is strict censorship of traditional media by the state or private companies (Svanadze, 2015).

At this time, social media is a unique opportunity for the population to fight against the existing regime, as well as to protect their freedom of speech and rights. Misuse of Social Media by Government Officials The publication of confidential and classified material through social media is increasingly common, causing serious harm to national security. Freedom of expression and communication should stop where confidential material is concerned. State structures are increasingly actively using social media in their activities, during which it is possible to unintentionally spread classified material. Therefore, to reduce the risks, it is necessary to constantly inform government officials about the correct use of social networks and to raise the security culture. Possibilities for national security protection Social media tools can be used by state structures, both defensively and offensively, to protect national security. In particular, defensive measures include prevention, warning, crisis management, counter-propaganda, and offensive measures include influence, propaganda, and lies. Constant monitoring of social media by intelligence services allows us to obtain advanced information about existing and future threats to national security, and to prevent them in time. The continuous process of monitoring also allows us to determine the short-, medium- and long-term political, economic, and military perspectives, to make an accurate assessment of events, and to make the most correct conclusions.

The stability of national security is highly dependent on each component of international security. Today, one of the main components in the world is the threats coming from cyberspace, whether it is a cyber war or a cyber attack, or various types of cyber crimes, which may put the national security and strategic interests of the country in danger. Therefore, to prevent similar threats and reduce risks, it is necessary to take appropriate steps toward cooperation on the part of major player states, thus maintaining a certain balance of action in cyberspace. Bilateral negotiations between the United States and Russia are nearing completion, which will contribute to the reduction of threats, transparency, and mutual coordination in cyberspace. Threats from cyberspace, as well as nuclear threats, will be fed into a secure communication channel through which mutual warnings and information exchange will take place. This will help to imagine the correct picture of the incident and excludes e. year The subject of "false alarms" where a third party may be involved or misled each other which could lead to hostilities or other major catastrophes, including nuclear war. Such an agreement is a step forward, firstly in the matter of protecting the national security of the two countries, and then in the international security of the whole world. Since the negotiations are between two great powers, which are large, may play a decisive role in the issue of world security (US Department of Defense, 2011).

Social Networks: Democracy or Security?

The rapid development of the Internet has given rise to enormous economic and social opportunities. As of 2012, there were more than two billion social media users, almost a third of the planet's total population (Chitadze, 2016). According to existing studies and observations, the expansion of the Internet network has a directly proportional effect on the global indicator of gross domestic product, which contributes to the growth of competition and the creation of new markets. Global commerce in the Internet space means an annual turnover of eight trillion US dollars, and the financial losses caused by cyber criminals reach one trillion US dollars a year. The number of Internet users is increasing every day (for example, Google's daily user has reached one billion), and its rapid development has given rise to such serious problems that significantly reduce the value of the advantage of the positive part of using Internet and threaten the full use of the opportunities of cyberspace. Developed countries have the opportunity to innovate the future of information technology, but at the same time, they and the whole world face the danger that every know-how can also bring great harm. New information technologies provide considerable opportunities to the criminal world and terrorist organizations. They use social networks to cheat, blackmail, steal ideas, spread ideology, corporate or industrial espionage, etc. Sh. Advances in information technology are also being misused by repressive governments and authoritarian regimes. In particular, they restrict their civil rights, prohibit freedom of speech, and prevent the dissemination of information that is easily accessible to others. For example, in the period before the presidential elections in Russia, to paralyze the opposition forces, cyber attacks were carried out on their blogs. And in Turkey, access to Facebook and other social networks was temporarily closed during the election period. The creation of new technologies in cyberspace has also given rise to the concept of "cyber war", which involves states and alliances destroying each other's infrastructure and inflicting maximum damage. Threats emanating from social networks can cause great harm to the world's civilized world, and they directly threaten national or international security. Therefore, the civilized world is trying to preserve the enormous possibilities of the Internet, not to hinder the innovative development of information technologies, not to violate human rights, and at the same time, in the background of all this, to protect security at all levels as much as possible. When thinking about security, we constantly face certain incompatibilities, which in turn raises the dilemma question - more democracy or proper security? That is, where do democratic principles end and where does security begin, be it national or international? The government of every country is concerned with making the right choice between these two concepts and establishing a certain balance between them. In authoritarian countries, the government tries to control user access and activity on social networks. However, it must be said that similar problems have arisen in democratic countries, especially after the "Arab Spring", "Occupy Wall Street" and massive demonstrations in London (Svanadze, 2016). Everything was organized by bloggers through social networks. All the speeches caused great concern and fear in the West that the protests would not take on a larger scale, would not grow into a political one, and would not be used by the ultra-left opposition forces. The West faced a serious problem. In particular. Social networks, which cover a very large part of society, are well used for destabilizing purposes, for internal political, economic, or social temperature control. Because of this, the whole community of the world is looking for ways to use social networks correctly. Monitoring and imposing control on social networks by the authorities is perceived as a violation of human rights, when non-imposition may cause serious threats. This fact presents a kind of dilemma to the governments of this or that country, which try to solve the problem in their way, which in many cases ends in vain. For example, the statement made by the Prime Minister of Great Britain, David Cameron, about the establishment of state control and monitoring of social networks caused great public dissatisfaction, and based on democratic principles, the government was also forced to make concessions. Studies by American scientists show that controlling social networks has been quite easy, which is directly related to the structure of the network itself and its homogeneity. To achieve the desired result through a social network, it is necessary to spread the necessary information to only 20 percent of the users of the network (Svanadze, 2015). However, it should be noted that even with this method, a person's free choice and means of expression of will are somewhat limited. In fact, through the social network, information is provided to the user in a certain form, which is directly related to the occurrence of an acceptable result and leads to the achievement of the desired goal, in which the user of the network unknowingly "helps" you. This too can be considered one of the methods of establishing control over social networks. It is quite difficult to solve the problem related to the rights of a person as a user of social networks. This right is granted to a person by the constitution, various charters, and international acts, and its violation is completely unacceptable based on the principles of democracy. Governments of all countries with a high or average democracy index avoid violating it or even partially restricting it because it would be a politically unprofitable move for them. That is why political leaders in many cases connect the process of misuse of social networks with national and international security, and the strategic interests of the country, which often becomes the reason for the government's attempt to implement unauthorized covert monitoring and control of social networks. This is where democracy ends and its values are limited. However, it is also important to take into account that civil awareness related to the country's security issues and the correct use of social networks by citizens should be raised in order not to cause any kind of damage to the country's strategic interests (Clarker, 2010).

SOURCES AND TYPES OF CYBER THREATS.

Entities Fighting Cyber Threats

There are many ways to define the term "cyberspace". Each of them gives its definition. However, in all definitions, it is defined that "cyberspace" is an interconnected complex of information and technological infrastructure, which includes global Internet and telecommunication networks, computer systems, as well as embedded processors, servers, and control devices used in various industries. With the development of new technologies, the threats that cause great harm to cyberspace and its users are increasing. The state and governmental organizations are primarily concerned with ensuring national security, and protecting critical information and information infrastructure from interference by both foreign states and non-governmental entities and groups to avoid information theft and/or transfer, network damage, and/or destruction. A real threat to the security of the state is cyber-attacks aimed at destroying such vital infrastructure as telecommunication networks, power generation, and oil refining capacity systems, as well as power supply, financial, healthcare, and transportation systems. Cyber threats and their types that threaten cyberspace and the integrity of information infrastructure systems, in general, are discussed below. Also shown are the sources of origin from which the given cyber threats originate. The second part of the paper discusses those international and regional level entities that fight against cyber threats and try to protect cyberspace and information infrastructure systems from cyber criminals (Buckland, 2010).

Sources and Types of Cyber Threats

One of the main problems in the fight against cybercrime is the fact that it is often very difficult to accurately identify not only the direct perpetrators but also their location or the country from which the attack was launched. Therefore, a criminal or a group of criminals can easily hide not only their participation in the organization of a cyber attack but also identify themselves as other network users or remain anonymous altogether. The sources of cyber threats are representatives of the state and private sector, as well as organizations and individuals of various types and brands. According to the materials of the House of Control of the United States, the sources of cyber threats can be qualified as follows, namely:

State - intelligence services of foreign countries use computer technologies for information gathering and espionage. Similar actions by intelligence services can be directed against both friendly and hostile countries or non-state entities. A state, using its intelligence services, carries out cyber attacks against potential adversary states with the aim of disinformation, destabilization, intimidation, or large-scale cyber warfare. It is also noteworthy that the security and rights of individuals are often violated. In particular, the special services of the state may resort to such actions, using which the personal data of citizens is intercepted, stolen, and used. In many cases, similar actions take place without the sanction of the relevant court bodies and proper democratic control:

Corporations - Engaged in industrial/corporate espionage and/or subversive activities, in which they often use hackers and organized crime groups. Companies, corporations, and other representatives of the private sector may also violate human rights by collecting and analyzing an individual's data, or in some cases by sharing that data with government authorities or other interested parties;

Hacking - There was a time when hacking into networks or hacking programs was associated with gaining authority in the hacker community or petty hooliganism. Nowadays, the picture has been radically changed, in particular, the actions of the majority of hackers are criminal. Before, hackers needed to know special skills in the field of computer technology to hack the network, but now it is enough to download the appropriate instructions and protocols from the Internet and use them to organize a cyber attack on a selected site. Because of this, it has become easier for users to carry out a cyber attacks. Hacker services are used not only by corporations and companies but also by intelligence or other special services;

Hacktivists - the term "hacktivism" (hacktivism) originated from the combination of two words "Hack" and "Activism" and it refers to a new phenomenon of expression of social protest, which is a peculiar synthesis of social activism expressed in protest against something and hacking, which is directed to certain websites or vs. postal services. To achieve their political goals, hacktivists tend to damage or disable some websites;

Cyber saboteurs from among disgruntled network users - generally, disgruntled users are a serious threat, as they are familiar with the workings of the system and can use this knowledge for destructive purposes. For example, to damage the system or steal confidential information. According to the United States Federal Bureau of Investigation (FBI), the ratio of the possibility of organizing a cyber attack by system users and external sources is 2:1 (Buckland, 2015);

Terrorists - try to put important infrastructure objects out of order, destroy them altogether, or use them for their purposes. Their actions seriously threaten the national security of countries, cause massive human casualties, weaken the economy, as well as harm the morale of society and reduce their credibility towards the government. Not all terrorist organizations and groups possess sufficient knowledge and technical means to carry out an effective cyber-attack, although there is a theoretical assumption that they may acquire similar knowledge and capabilities, or seek the services of organized crime representatives for assistance;

Botnet-Internet - A bot in a botnet is a program that is secretly installed in the computer device of the victim/object, which allows the criminal/criminal to perform certain actions using the resources of the infected computer. This type of hacker infects a large number of computers with their programs, the resources of which are then used to coordinate a cyber attack, as well as to send "spam", phishing, and other malicious activities. Similar networks are an object of illegal trade;

Phishers - these are individuals or small groups that use phishing technologies to steal personal details and resell information for a fee. Phishers often use spam and spyware to achieve their goals;

Spammers - natural or legal persons who massively send unsolicited e-mails with hidden or false information, the purpose of which is to carry out a cyber attack on specific organizations using phishing and spyware programs; Internet bot - this is a special program that automatically and/or according to a given task performs the same actions as an ordinary user. year Obtaining login and password Spyware and malicious software developers - natural or legal persons who have criminal intentions to carry out cyber-attacks on computer users;

Pedophiles - this category is increasingly actively using the Internet to distribute child pornography, as well as using social networks and Internet chats to meet potential victims. As a rule, all types of the above sources of cyber threats are actively used not only by the criminal world but also by state intelligence or other types of special services, depending on the purpose of solving the set task and achieving the goal. In the same materials of the United States House of Control, the types of cyber threats are also discussed, namely: Data integrity During cyber-attacks, hacking methods can be used, the purpose of which is to destroy the integrity of data or to distort and make changes to it (Buckland, 2010). Subtypes:

- Propaganda and disinformation - entering/disseminating incorrect data or making changes to existing data to destabilize ruling regimes on the territories of foreign states, to influence the results of political processes or commercial activities;
- Intimidation - the purpose of attacks on web pages is to force the user (both a government official and a natural or legal person) to delete or change the site's content/policy;
- Destruction - the permanent and deliberate destruction of data to cause damage or harm to foreign countries or competitors. In particular, similar attacks can be carried out in parallel with other actions during a larger-scale conflict. Access As a result of a cyber attack on the system, the legitimate user of the system faces such conditions that he cannot enter the system and no longer has access to the resources offered by the system, or such access is complicated.

Subspecies:

- Foreign information - carried out attacks, as a result of which it is impossible to open access to public and private sector services. In particular, information sites of mass media and state or private structures; • Internal information - implementation of a local attack on the network of the state and private sector (United States Government Accountability Office, 2009).

For example, local attacks on energy and transport management systems, electronic banking sites, operational management systems, corporate services e-mail, rescue services, etc. Sh. Confidentiality Cyber-attacks can target sources of confidential information and are mainly carried out for criminal purposes. Subspecies: Government officials carrying confidential information and key figures in large corporations are often the victims of cyber attacks.

In particular, it is not only

- Espionage - obtaining information on the part of corporations, companies, and firms about the current and future activities of their competitors. State participation in espionage activities directed against foreign countries and natural or legal entities;
- Theft of personal data - the implementation of phishing or similar attacks, the purpose of which is to trick the user into revealing his data, such as bank accounts. sending viruses that copy and download data from the user's personal computer;
- "Identity theft" - refers to the theft of the user's details. Trojans and similar programs are used to steal personal data;
- Searching for information in the international network - to obtain various types of information, in particular, personal data, information retrieval technologies from open sources are used;
- Scams - often carried out using spam, which is distributed through e-mail.

The most famous type of such machination is e. year "Nigerian Letters 419". Here we can consider the schemes of machinations that steal confidential information but also infringe on the personal information of similar persons, to blackmail them in the future. It got its name because it developed especially in Nigeria, where it first took local and then international dimensions. It is worth noting that this existed before the advent of the Internet and its distribution was carried out by ordinary postal services, and with the emergence of new technologies and the Internet, "Nigerian letters 419" took on a global scale. Offers users to pay in advance for non-existent services and goods (United States Government Accountability Office, 2009).

Entities Fighting Cyber Threats

One of the main problems in combating cyber threats is the fact that most information and communication networks are owned by the private sector, while the government is responsible for their security. It should be noted that the participation of the private sector in the process makes it much more difficult to protect networks and ensure their security. Both groups, the government, and the private sector have different interests and goals, which reduce the effectiveness of cyberspace protection. This process becomes even more complicated when the issue takes on a global nature, in the solution of which international norms and existing subjects play a major role. The latter can play the role of a certain catalyst in this process, aimed at perfecting and harmonizing both the national and international legal framework, which refers to the legal prosecution of cybercriminals, data storage, and protection, as well as the principles of ensuring network security and prompt response to cyber attacks. It should also be noted that with a similar approach to the issue, it is possible to identify weak and vulnerable areas in information systems, as well as the partnership between state and private sector entities in the fight against cybercrime. At the international level, important legal acts have been adopted to combat cyber threats, such as UN General Assembly Resolutions No. 55/6348 of December 4, 2000, and No. 56/12149 of

December 19, 2001 "Fighting the use of information technology for criminal purposes", April 1-2, 2008, in Strasbourg The document "Basic principles of joint work of law enforcement agencies and Internet providers in the field of combating cybercrime" adopted at the world conference "Cooperation against cybercrime" (Svanadze, 2015). At the regional level, recommendations of the European Council No. R (89) 9 "Combating computer crimes" should be noted. One of the main subjects of the fight against cybercrime is the network user. Therefore, it is necessary to involve them in educational activities that will help the users to better understand such things as computer manipulations, theft of personal details, crimes on the Internet, Internet ethics, and others. Below are some of the main entities involved in the fight against cyber threats, namely:

International and regional organizations

- Asia-Pacific Economic Cooperation Working Group on Telecommunications and Information;
- European Agency for Network and Information Security;
- NATO's Joint Center for Advanced Methods of Cybernetic Protection;
- Association of South-Eastern Countries;
- Organization of economic development and cooperation;
- Group for operational response to emergencies in computer networks;
- Internet Management Forum;
- International Union of Electrical Connections;
- Internet community;
- Internet Corporation for Assigning Names and Numbers;
- Civil initiative Internet - policy "Meridian";
- G7 Lyon Group, Subgroup on High-Tech Crimes, United Nations, Council of Europe (Svanadze, 2015).

Non-governmental organizations

- rights protection organizations;
- various funds;
- Analytical centers.

Sectoral organizations

- Anti-phishing working group;
- Research and analytical center of domain name services in functional issues;
- Working group to combat the maliciousness of transmission of messages in systems;
- Sectoral Consortium for Strengthening Internet Security;
- Institute of Electronics and Electrical Engineering Engineers;
- transport organizations;
- Other sectoral organizations related to critical infrastructure management. State
- Ministries of Foreign and Internal Affairs, Ministries of Transport, Finance, and Justice, intelligence and other special services, police divisions/departments, operational security divisions/departments, special divisions/departments in cyber security issues;
- Electronic Incident Response Teams (CERT).

For example, organizations providing security for the management of airports and air transportation, for example, "Data Exchange Agency" of the Ministry of Justice of Georgia Private sector

- Special companies for providing security on the Internet;
- software creators/developers;
- manufacturers of systems, servers, devices;
- hosting - providers;
- Companies that trade goods on the Internet.
- Individuals owners and users of personal computers (Svanadze, 2015).

CONCLUSION

As already mentioned, there are many variants of the definition of cyberspace and information space. Each of them gives us its definition. However, all definitions define "cyberspace" as an interconnected complex of information and technological infrastructure, including global Internet and telecommunication networks, computer systems, and embedded processors, servers, and control devices used in various industries.

In the modern period, along with the development of technologies, the threats that may affect cyberspace, information space, and its users are increasing. The state and its subordinates are primarily concerned with ensuring national security, and cyber security is a key part of national security, and its protection is one of the main duties of each state so that the state adheres to security norms and does not harm.

Threats to national security include cyber-attacks and fake news aimed at misleading the public and destroying vital infrastructure such as telecommunications networks, power generation, and oil refining capacity systems, as well as power supply, financial, healthcare, and transportation systems.

Cyber security and information security are such elements of national security and e-governance, without which the state cannot function.

The main task of cyber security is to protect cyberspace.

Internet users must have information about the risks associated with using the Internet space and the protection of their rights.

The use of computer systems and the Internet has a special place in the work of many countries and organizations, therefore their work interruption or any kind of damage seriously affects any process that the said organization, company, or state structure carries out.

As mentioned earlier, the Internet and computer systems are used to manage various infrastructures. Military and satellite systems, communication channels, water, gas, electric and nuclear energy, oil extraction, and processing infrastructure elements. Damage or failure of any of them will cause serious damage to both the company and the state.

Cybercrime against individuals, which includes various crimes such as publishing child pornography, cyber pornography, harassment of a natural person using a computer, trafficking, distribution, publication, and distribution of obscene material, including pornography and indecent exposure, is one of the most important cyber crimes. Cyber harassment is a different cybercrime. Different types of harassment can happen in cyberspace or through the use of cyberspace, it can be sexual, racial, religious, or otherwise. Cybercrimes against individuals include e-mail abuse, defamation, hacking, hacking, fraud, child pornography, and threatening behavior.

Cybercrime against property, which includes destroying someone else's property, using malicious viruses or programs to destroy someone's property, intellectual property crime, computer system hacking, spreading viruses, cyber trespassing or trespassing, and internet theft.

In my opinion, talking about cyberspace and information space and threats is an inexhaustible issue. The more technology develops, the more "opportunities" are created in terms of the variety of threats.

REFERENCES

Buckland, B., Schreier, F., & Winkler, T. (2010). *Democratic Governance Challenges of Cyber Security DCAF Horizon.* Working Paper Series. Retrieved from: http://genevasecurityforum.org/files/DCAF-GSF-cyber-Paper.pdf

Burson-Marsteller. (2010). Social Media Check-up: a Burson – Marsteller Evidence-Based Tool. Academic Press.

Chitadze, N. (2016). *Political Science.* International Black Sea University.

Clarker, A. (2010). Cyber War: The Next Threat to National Security and What to do About it. Harper Collins.

Lewis, B. K. (2010). Social Media and Strategic Communication: Attitudes and Perceptions Among College Students. *The Public Relations Journal, 4.*

Lindsay, B. (2011). *Social Media and Disasters: Current Uses, Future Options, and Policy Considerations.* Congressional Research Service.

Svanadze, V. (2015). *Cyberspace and Cybersecurity Challenges (Collection).* Institute of Public Affairs of Georgia.

US Department of Defense. (2011). *Department of Defense Strategy for Operating in Cyberspace.* Arlington Country.

US Government. (2010). National Security Strategy 2010. Author.

KEY TERMS AND DEFINITIONS

Cyber Security or Information Technology Security (IT Security): Is the protection of computer systems and networks from attack by malicious actors that may result in unauthorized information disclosure, theft of, or damage to hardware, software, or data, as well as from the disruption or misdirection of the services they provide.

Cyber Space: A concept describing a widespread interconnected digital technology.

Cyber Warfare: The use of computer technology to disrupt the activities of a state or organization, especially the deliberate attacking of information systems for strategic or military purposes.

Information Security: Sometimes shortened to InfoSec, is the practice of protecting information by mitigating information risks. It is part of information risk management.

Chapter 2
The Main Historical Stages of the Development of Cyber Space

Irakli Kervalishvili
Georgian Technical University, Georgia

ABSTRACT

Technologies and the threat of harmful activities using them are developing in international politics. The age we live in is a daily routine of technological revolutions, and with new technologies are born powerful and more flexible both defensive and offensive mechanisms. Cyber attacks have become an inseparable part of our lives, accompanying all military wars. Today, wars are fought using hybrid components. Cyberwar as an event began with the invention of the computer and the Internet.

INTRODUCTION

Internet space and related processes in the last decade Rapid development, as well as the number of users in a short period Colossal growth led to the creation of new state entities The need for development. All countries are trying to be as efficient and flexible as possible and the establishment of a sophisticated organizational structure that Provides critical information infrastructure as much as possible protection, will take effective measures aimed at cyber security on provision, will also protect the person's personal as much as possible information and existing databases. First of all, in all countries, The government considers this issue as a matter of national security one of the important constituent parts, and therefore similar subjects A large part is present in the Ministries of Defense and Internal Affairs, or Under the supervision of intelligence, security or other special services.

Such entities have a short history of existence. Actually, no There was no experience and every country developed individually the given issue. It can be said that the state in the field of cyber security If the creation of private entities and their future development is based on the precedents that arose in the Internet space and are generally related to the need to protect cyberspace. Therefore, parallel to the

DOI: 10.4018/978-1-6684-8846-1.ch002

given field State or private sector entities are constantly being conducted in the process of organizational structure development.

How was the computer created?

This did not happen with one stroke of the hand - it is based on the development of computing technologies. In the 20th century, the effective work of science led to a technological revolution. For example, paper, magazines, newspapers, books, cinema, and television have become available like never before. This was followed by computers and the Internet. It may seem unbelievable, but the first computer occupied a large room and could only calculate numbers. This is the period when the calculator does not exist. At the beginning of the 20th century, scientists invented an electronic lamp, which was used to amplify the signal of a radio receiver. In the 1940s, the idea to use electronic lamps to make a computer came up. During the Second World War, scientists tried to develop technologies. However, scientists have been thinking about creating a calculating machine for centuries - for example, in the 19th century, the question arose of making such a device that would not only calculate numbers but also solve the entire mathematical problem. The first attempt was made by Cambridge University professor, Charles Babbage, in 1791-1871. The attempt was unsuccessful. The failure gave Charles Babbage more incentive, in 1834 he began work on a calculating machine called the Analytical Engine. This machine was supposed to solve all the problems that mathematicians and engineers solved. The machine was equipped with a central processing unit, memory, and punch cards. Significantly, Charles Babbage's machine could handle twenty-digit numbers. The machine had to work without human intervention. That punch cards were used to control calculating machines was a prophetic idea. This idea was developed in 1804 by the French inventor Joseph Marie Jacquard by automating the loom (HC, 2023).

Scientists faced a new task - creation and development of programming. July 19, 1843 is recognized as the date of creation of the first program. Ada Augusta, the daughter of the famous English poet George Gordon Byron, who was Grad Lovelace's wife, made a big contribution to the creation of the program. On July 19, 1843, Augusta created the first program for calculating Greek numbers. At that time, the machine could perform not only arithmetic calculation, but also logical operations. This became possible after (in 1847) the English mathematician George Boole created the theory of logical expressions and called it "Boolean Algebra" (EU-Startup, 2019).

The contribution of the Georgian scientist Giorgi Nikoladze (1888-1931) is worth noting. Before Nikoladze's invention, all arithmometers that existed were mechanical, and during his stay in France, he studied the existing arithmometers and invented a new electronic calculator, which was called "direct multiplication electronic arithmometer". It differed from other calculators with an electronic distributor. American and European companies were immediately interested in this invention, but he refused to cooperate with them and left for his homeland, made a model of an arithmometer in Georgia, which was then sent to an exhibition in Moscow. Unfortunately, Giorgi Nikoladze did not hesitate to clarify the documentation of the entire construction of the arithmometer, he died suddenly in 1931 (RMI, 2019).

It has long been recognized that the first computer was created in 1945 by American physicists John Eckhart and John Mouch, whose name was ENIAK (Electronic Numerical Integrator and Computer). However, this story turned out to be wrong - although "Enyak" is the first computer in the world, the designers of which are Eckert and Mouch, they made a great contribution to the development of computing techniques, but they did not think of the working principles of the first computer. These principles were established in 1937, and the first attempt at a computer by John Atanasovis, a Bulgarian physicist working in Ames, Iowa, and his assistant Clifford Bettis, nicknamed "ABC", was completed in 1942. At this time, only the peripheral part remained. However, due to World War II, it could not be put into operation. In 1973, a dispute began between two large companies, the first regarding the copyright of computer assembly. 135 court sessions were held. It was finally proven that in 1940, Atanasov invited Mouch, showed him the manuscripts, explained and explained the principles of the computing device. And then Mucci was able to create what is called the first computer. However, we can confirm that Atanasov is the creator of the first computer (Smithsonian Magazine, 2013).

A computer is a fast-acting system automatically controlled by a program. An electronic machine whose main purpose is to store, process and transmit large amounts of information. Today, it all seems more diverse, but the basic functions of the computer have not changed. As years pass, the number of computers increases and improves. Thanks to technological advances, the possibilities in all technical systems have increased - in mobile phones, cars, and various household and business devices.

In 1974, the first personal microcomputer "Altair" was created. Its manufacturer was MITS, a company founded by Ed Robertson. The microcomputer "Altair" was an assembly kit, it did not have a keyboard and a monitor. Data input was carried out using switches placed on the front panel. The BASIC interpreter of this computer was created by the company "Microsoft" founded by Bill Gates. In 1977, several more personal computers were released - Tandy, Commodore, and Apple II. One of them is Apple, which was created by two young friends - Steve Jobs and Steve Wozniak. Before the creation of the computer (in 1976), they founded the company Apple Computer, for which they used one of the bedrooms of Jobs's parents' apartment as their office. The computer they created was distinguished by good design and reliability and was also the first in the world to have color graphics. The creation of this model turned out to be so successful that in 1980 the income of Apple Computer reached 117 million dollars. In 1979, a modified model of Apple II was released - Apple II Plus. It was more refined than the previous model. VisiCalc, the first "electronic life" program created for the Apple II Plus, made this computer a serious tool for small business accounting production (Lemelson, 2020).

COMPUTERS ARE DIVIDED INTO GENERATIONS

The first-generation - computers were assembled with lamps, as well as electron-beam tubes. Such cars existed from 1950-1957. "Enyak" weighed 27 tons, consisted of 18,000 lamps, and occupied an area of 200 m2. A lot of programmers and engineers were needed to make the computer work. The performance capacity was 10-15 thousand arithmetic operations per second, which is very small compared to today's computer. Memory was presented on a magnetic level. These were experimental devices, created to test various theoretical ideas. It is important that parallel to "Enyak", a computer IBM was secretly produced in Great Britain, which could decode the codes. That's why it was kept secret. It is already a known fact that it was used in Germany during the First and Second World Wars. The mathematical method of decoding codes was created by a group of professional mathematicians, which included Alan Turing. In 1943 in London M. Newman and F. Flowery invented the machine "Colossus", which consisted of 1500 electronic lamps. In 1937, mathematician Howard Aiken developed a project to create a large calculating machine. IBM president Thomas Watson invested 500 thousand dollars in this case. Thus began the design of the Mark-1. The product was released in 1939 under the name of IBM.

In 1955, the Ferrant firm released the Pegasus computer, in which the concept of general-purpose registers found application. Later, the US Navy officer (admiral), programmer, Grace Hopper created the first compiler for the computer - a program that translated a program written in human-readable language into machine language. This made the programming process much easier. Historically, the founders of the first computer are Claude Shannon, the developer of information theory, mathematician Alan Turing, the developer of programming and algorithm theory, and John von Neumann, the author of the construction of computing devices. The first generation computers are: "Enyak", "Ural-2", "Strela", M-20, etc.

The second generation - since 1958, the development of electronic equipment, which means the appearance of semiconductor elements, led to the development of computers, that is, the creation of second-generation computers. The lamp was replaced with a faster and more reliable transistor. These machines had memory on magnetic coils, which were small rings capable of storing double information. Unlike the previous generation, this generation was more reliable and faster. Its size, scope of use, number of people, and energy also decreased. It was used to solve various economic and statistical problems. It is believed that the contribution of the second-generation computer was great in solving scientific and technical tasks. What we call an operating system today was first used in the second-generation computer. Also, during this period, programming languages were created: COBOL, FORTRAN, and ALGOL. Second generation computers are: M-220, BESM-4, URAL-14, MINSK-2, MINSK-4, etc.

The third generation - in 1964, IBM introduced a six-module device. Computers were connected through an operating system and had a unified command system. In 1957, Robert Noyce, who later founded Intel, invented a perfect method by which several tens of transistors and all the connections were placed on one plate. This scheme was called "chip". In 1968, the first computer with a chip was released, and in 1970, Intel began selling the chip. In the same year, Intel began assembling a central processor with a similar chip. This was the period of the emergence of the first micro-processor - Intel-4004. The use of chips significantly increased the speed of third-generation computers, which meant 80-100 thousand arithmetic operations per second. In the same period, a disk was created, i.e. a disk-type memory and an information input-output device, which was called a "display". A disk, or external memory, is designed to store information that can be used multiple times. It was during these years that IBM began to release computers, both small and large, and at that time the most powerful, expensive computers.

The same period is associated with the creation of such an important global network as "The Internet". Also, the operating system Unik and the programming language "C" appeared, all of which had a huge impact on the software world and continue to do so today. Third generation computers are: EC-1022, EC-1035, CM-2, CM-4, EC-1055, etc.

Fourth generation - computers released in 1975-1985 belong to the fourth generation. However, there are other considerations, because the level of computer development at that time was not so high. Importantly, since the beginning of the 1980s, thanks to the advent of personal computers, computer technology has become available to the public.

Fifth generation - In 1982, a program for building computers was created in Japan. According to this program, in 1991, completely new types of computers should be released, which would be focused on solving artificial intelligence tasks. The main task of computers would not be to store and process information, but knowledge (Business to Business, 2016).

The Creation of the INTERNET

In 1957, the Soviet Union launched an artificial satellite into Earth orbit. This fact was considered by the United States Defense Agency as a high mark of the technological achievements of the Soviet Union. They thought that in the event of a large-scale war, the Americans would need a reliable system of information transmission. One of the drawbacks of other existing systems was the control center, the place where the entire system would fail if it was disconnected. Therefore, it was necessary to create a network that would not have a single control center and the system would work smoothly when any segment was disconnected. This goal was followed by the establishment of the Advanced Research Projects Agency, known as ARPA. This was where the initial concept of the Internet was developed. The idea of creating the Internet belongs to the American military, and American universities were able to implement the idea. After that, the next version of the Internet was created - ARPANET (History, 2010).

First Internet Connection

On October 29, 1969, the first connection between two computers included in the ARPANET was made. They were 640 kilometers apart. The first computer was located at the Stanford Research Institute, and the second computer was located at the University of California, Los Angeles. Charlie Klein attempted to connect to the computer at the Stanford Research Institute and transfer the data, and Bill Duvall monitored the data transfer process at Stanford. During the first activation, only three characters could be sent, the character was LOG, and the entire message was LOGON, that is, the command to enter the system, but the network was disconnected, and it was restored only after an hour and a half. The next attempt was successful. This was followed by the development of Internet networks in various European countries like the USA. In 1973, the first non-American organizations, Great Britain and Norway, became involved through the transatlantic cable, making the network international. In 1983, the existing global network was called the "Internet" and ARPANET represented a large part of it. At first, it was only possible to send and receive information via the Internet. This turned out to be a great step forward. Until then, it was possible to send and receive large amounts of information only through fax. Sending and receiving a multi-page text by fax is associated with many difficulties. This is easily possible with the Internet. Also, it is possible to send one document to several places at the same time on the Internet, but this is impossible with fax. The original Internet is very different from today's Internet, at that time people only exchanged information with each other (Computer History Museum, 2009).

It was like this until the scientist Tim Berners-Lee presented the concept of the web in 1989 at the Cern laboratory in Europe, which is, known to us as "www" (World Wide Web). but also the posting of information by the user. This is how web pages were created, which today are of great importance for the branding of both news agencies and many companies. It is worth noting that Tim Berners-Lee did not believe in the creation of this concept and made his invention on a larger scale, connecting web pages with links so that the user can easily move to another page. Tim Berners Lee didn't patent his invention, he gave it to humanity, and that's why we internet users visit different websites without any charge (CERN, 2020).

In 1990, thanks to a new invention, it became possible to connect to the Internet via a telephone line (Dialup access). This made using the Internet easy and accessible to everyone. Today, there are many ways to connect to the Internet - satellite connection, telephone, cellular connection, special fiber optic line (wifi), and others. It is known that the number of Internet users increased to 50 million in the first five years. Since 2010, it has become possible to use the Internet from the International Space Station (Network Security, 2020).

This is a short history of the process called the technological revolution, which has led to many good and dangerous events - the development of mass social networks, the creation of malicious websites, the continuous regime of viruses and massive fraud, cyber-terrorism, cyber-crime, and cyber-war.

Cyberspace - was first used in 1982 in an extensive article. Cyberspace refers to everything connected to the Internet. Cyberpunk is a subgenre of science fiction, the term was first used in the late 1960s and early 1970s in "New Wave" science fiction novels. Cybersecurity - the first use of this word can be found in scientific literature in 1989. Cybercrime - There are many forms of crime: financial, fraud, cyberbullying, theft, and any crime committed on the Internet. Cyberdefense (Cyberdefense) - this word is the same as cyber security, it is the detection, prevention, and response of cybercrime. This is more often the case with military and government systems. Cyberops (Cyberops) - cyber operations, include cyberspace and are carried out both technically and non-technically. Cyberdelic (Cyberdelic) - refers to art, recreation, or impressionistic experiences that are carried out at the expense of active use of the Internet. Cyborg - Technically a combination of cybernetics and organism, it means something made up of robotic parts.

Cybrarian - cyber librarian, in short - Cybrarian, is a researcher who mainly uses the Internet for information. Cybernauts (Cybernauts) - A cybernaut is a person who creates sensory and virtual reality devices.

Cybercrime, cyberwar, cyberterrorism, cyberattacks, and similar events are part of today's existence (Alpine Security, 2020).

The First Virus Written by 15-year-old Richard Skrentas during winter break on January 30, 1982, this virus is considered the first large-scale self-propagating personal computer virus. Skrentas pranked his friends with various computer tricks, although no one would have imagined such a thing. His "Elk Coner" virus, which was 400 lines long, disguised itself as an Apple boot program. The author himself called this virus a little joke. He later served as CEO of search engine startup Blekko, acting CEO of IBM Watson, and partnered with social engagement platform Magnify Progress. Linkedin recommended Richard Skrentas, saying, "Fear this man and his army of cyborgs." It is known that the term "computer virus" was first used in a security seminar in 1983 (Deffere, 2019).

Cyber attacks started before most people had computers. The first hacking attack was carried out in 1971 and was completely harmless, more of an experiment than a damaging cyber attack. Bob Thomas made history with the program he created, which is considered a "computer worm". It was not malicious at all and displayed a message on every infected screen: "I'm a creeper, catch me if you can" (History of Information, 2020).

As for the damaging cyber attack, it was carried out in 1989 by Robert Morris, his program significantly slowed down the early Internet. Thus, the first DoS attack in history was carried out in 1989. Morris explained that the attack was done to fix security flaws such as Unix sendmail and weak passwords. This attack caused a split in the Internet at the time and lasted for several days (Wired, 1989).

The same year marked a terrible day in history when Joseph Pope created the first ransomware attack. used a malware called the -AIDS Trojan that was sent through his email. Pope hoped to extort money from people with this program (Panda Security, 2018).

As for the biggest cyber attack, it was carried out in 1982, still during the Cold War, when the US Central Intelligence Agency somehow found a way to disrupt the operation of the Russian Siberian gas pipeline - without bombs, missiles, or other explosive devices. America's Central Intelligence Agency caused a gas pipeline explosion using computer system code. The explosion was so large that it could be seen from space (Vidisha, 2019).

In 1999, Microsoft Windows 98 was released, and a completely new generation of technology became available worldwide. The increase in computer usage has helped the proliferation of software and security systems. Windows has released many patches and commercial products. In addition, many companies have released anti-hacking software for home computer use (Microsoft, 1999).

What is the situation we have today and what problems did the technological revolution put us in front of? Humanity has no right to be complacent - the fact is, the more computer technologies rise to greater heights, the more danger will be created by cybercriminals. When researching the topic, cyber war, as an event, must be divided into several directions: first - assimilation and use of technological achievements; Second - development and use of propaganda methods.

In this regard, everything is in the palm of your hands, cyber attacks are increasing and improving every year, as early as 2006, Russian Business Network (RBN) started using malware for identity theft, and since 2007, RBN has completely monopolized online identity theft. By 2007, their virus, called the Storm Worm, was running on about one million computers and sending millions of infected e-mails every day. In 2008, cyber attacks shifted from personal computers to the systems of government institutions. On August 27, 2008, NASA confirmed that the "Storm worm" had been found on laptops aboard the International Space Station.

We can't say for sure, but three months later, the Pentagon's computers were allegedly hacked by Russian hackers. Then there were the financial institutions, on December 25, 2008, there was an attack on the State Bank of India (Lewis University, 2020).

Russia has carried out and is still carrying out combined military and cyber attacks against Georgia and Ukraine, using various components of hybrid warfare. The Kremlin did not change the Soviet methodology, only the technologies. If we consider the issue in terms of the crimes committed by Russia and which are still "uncommitted", probably everyone will admit that we are dealing with an unpredictable state in this regard. Nevertheless, the leading countries of the world are obliged to make the actions of this unpredictable country a unified system and resist.

To make our reasoning about Russia more thorough, we can cite as an example - the 2008 Russia-Georgia war, when the largest cyber attack was carried out by Russia on the websites of the Georgian state, television, and news agencies. We can cite an example of the Russia-Ukraine war in 2014, where the military war was accompanied by various components of the hybrid war, the so-called Use of unrecognized tweets, and cyber-attacks on government agencies. A few years later, namely in 2017, the internal system of the Cabinet of Ministers of Ukraine was the victim of a hacker attack, the Vice-Prime Minister of Ukraine, Pavel Rozenko, wrote about this on Twitter and published a picture:

"Ukraine's Cabinet Secretariat appears to have been the target of a hacker attack, the network is currently down" (Independent, 2017).

At that time, not only the Cabinet of Ministers of Ukraine was the object of the hacker attack, but also the energy companies and the National Bank were working with interruptions. Media holding "Lux", Kyiv Metropolitan, Post of Ukraine, New Post, and others were the victims of the cyber attack. Among the targets was the Boryspil airport system, through which it is possible to delay flights.

The Theory of Cyberwar and Its Place in Modern World Politics

Everything that exists has both a theoretical and a practical direction. When we talk about cyberwar, we must first explain what phenomenon we are dealing with. It is the use of digital attacks by one country against another country (computer viruses or hacking cyber attacks) to damage, disable or destroy the computer infrastructure.

Regarding the term "cyber war", there are different opinions among experts. Some argue that the term "cyberwar" is a misnomer, as no cyberattack to date can be described as "war". Another group of experts believes that this is an appropriate name because a cyber attack causes physical damage to people and things in the real world.

Is a cyber attack considered a war? It depends on many factors - what they do, how they do it, and how much damage they do to the target object. Attacks must be qualified as significant in scale and severity. Attacks by individual hackers or hacker groups are not considered cyberwar unless the state is assisting or directing them. Nevertheless, the virtual world is still vaguely represented in the direction of cyber attacks. Some states support hackers to carry out damaging activities, this is a dangerous but common trend.

For example, cyber crooks who destroy bank computer systems to steal money are not considered cyber warfare, even if they are from another country, but state-sponsored hackers do the same thing to destabilize another country's economy.

There is also a difference between target and scale: defacing an individual company's website is not considered cyberwar, but disabling missile defense systems at an air base is. In this case, what weapon the attacker uses is important. For example, firing a missile at a data center would not be considered cyber warfare, even if the data center contained classified government records. Using hackers to spy or steal data does not constitute cyberwarfare, and it qualifies as cyber espionage. There are many dark holes in cyber warfare, but not all attacks can be considered cyber warfare (Ranger, 2018).

Although there are differing opinions on how to define "cyber war" as a term, today many countries, such as the United States of America, Russia, Britain, India, Pakistan, China, Israel, the Islamic Republic of Iran, and North Korea have already Have cyber capabilities for both offensive and defensive operations.

Cyber war is becoming an increasingly common and dangerous phenomenon of international conflicts. The fact that there are no clear rules for cyberwar means that virtual space may become uncontrolled shortly. In cyber warfare, most of the time, computer systems are not the ultimate target, it aims to manage real-world infrastructure, such as airports, and power grids, because such infrastructure is important to all countries. At the push of a button, they can close airports, metro stations or cut off electricity.

There are many scenarios of cyber warfare. We live in an age where you may wake up one day and find your bank account has been compromised because some hacker wanted it that way. In case of mass attacks, it is possible to cause chaos in any country.

There are three main methods of cyber warfare: sabotage, electronic espionage, i.e. stealing information from computers using viruses, and attacking power networks. The third, perhaps the most alarming, involves a cyber attack on critical infrastructure (Lewis University, 2020).

Governments are increasingly realizing that modern society is highly dependent on computer systems - from financial services to transportation networks. Therefore, stopping these systems by hackers using viruses or other means can be as effective and damaging as a traditional military campaign using armed forces, weapons, and missiles.

Unlike traditional military attacks, cyber attacks can be launched from any distance. It is also possible that there will be no trace and no evidence at all. Governments and intelligence agencies fear that digital attacks against critical infrastructure, banking systems, or power grids, will allow attackers to bypass a country's traditional defenses. Therefore, all countries strive to improve computer security.

In 2012, hackers hired by the government of the Islamic Republic of Iran gained complete control of the Bowman Avenue Dam in New York. The most high-profile example of a cyber attack on critical infrastructure is the "Stuxnet" computer virus attack that halted Iran's nuclear program by disabling centrifuges used to separate nuclear material. This incident caused great concern because Stuxnet was suspected to be adapted to attack SCADA systems as well. SCADA systems are used by many critical infrastructure and enterprise industries in Europe and the USA.

Such an attack was recorded in Germany in 2014, which caused great damage to a steel plant - a cyber attack caused the shutdown of furnaces. The attackers used social engineering techniques (ages, 2020).

Historical Aspects of the Transformation of Cyber War: Spatial Characteristics of Military Conflicts

The development of technology has not changed the priorities in matters of state defense in the same way as during the Second World War - the main tactical strikes are aimed at energy facilities. Currently, the most serious cyber-attacks occur in the fuel and energy complex, followed by the financial sector. The digital world has contributed to the emergence of new types of threats. As we have already mentioned, not all types of cyber attacks can be considered in terms of cyber war. Although we have defined what is cyberwar and what is a cyberattack, it is still difficult to qualify cyberwar because most of the facts on a global scale are based on assumptions. Traces often lead to one of the aggressor states, but often there is no evidence. We discuss cyberwars and technical characteristics based on various studies, we analyze - when does it start, how did it transform, what is its role in the production of conflicts, and so on. It is an important fact that many states not only conduct cyber espionage, intelligence, and investigation but also create cyber warfare capabilities themselves. At the end of the 20th century, no one could have imagined that a real war would become an extension of a war created in a set dimension, or vice versa, that unreal space would merge with real space. Perhaps, no one could have imagined that a dimension would emerge that would be almost impossible to control, and boundless, humanity would face an invisible threat. When we try to explain the transformation of cyber warfare, we must identify what is changing it all. This is mostly related to the improvement of cyber attack technologies and the creation of malicious hacking strategies, programs, or viruses. Therefore, we must distinguish the types of attack: there are passive and active cyberattacks, passive attack involves traffic analysis and monitoring of vulnerable communications. During an active attack, a hacker attacks protected systems. This is mostly done by viruses (DiGiacomo, 2017).

THE CONCEPT OF CYBERWAR AND THE INTERNATIONAL SECURITY SYSTEM OF THE 21ST CENTURY

We see physical tools like computers, cables, mobiles, etc. Tools interact in the virtual and non-real realms. It helps to wage war from one part of the world to another part of the world, and the perpetrator cannot always be identified. Cyberwarfare often represents a conceptual framework related to the traditional conduct of war - involving a show of force, physical harm, and violence. As time passes, it becomes more important to define what type of cyber attack should be called cyber war. These types of definitions are important when dealing with issues related to cyber warfare, which sometimes involve kinetic and sometimes non-kinetic attacks. Above, we have already discussed the difference between a cyber attack and a cyber war - worldwide there have been many attempts to precisely define the essence of a cyber war at a conceptual level, for example, the "Tallinn Manual" was created under the leadership of the NATO "Cyber Defense Cooperation Skills Center" - where the violations of the law used in cyber wars are discussed according to the laws of international law. However, it is not a political, official document of NATO. The difficulty, in this case, is that nation-states and non-state actors do not always follow the law. We think that some topics in the "Tallinn Guide" are general, superficial, and incompatible with the theoretical definitions of cyberspace, and need to be refined. For example, in the "Tallinn

Manual", cyberwar is equated with a cyberattack - it is said to be an offensive or defensive operation that can cause human death, injury, or destruction of objects (Ranger, 2018).

In our opinion, this definition excludes psychological pressure during cyber operations or cyber intelligence. The main drawback of this definition is considering cyber war and cyber attack as one term. Also, the mentioned definition excludes cyber operations that may aim to destabilize the financial system of states. In this case, the cyber attack does not result in death or physical destruction.

When we talk about the concept of cyber war and touch on the issue of security, we must consider it in the context of the North Atlantic Alliance - security and cyber defense are directly related to NATO. NATO member countries discussed the need to strengthen defense against cyber attacks for the first time at the 2002 summit in Prague. Since then, cyber security has become an important component of NATO's agenda. In 2008, the first cyber defense political document was adopted. Since 2012, the process of cyber security integration in the NATO defense system has been actively underway. At the Wales Summit in 2014, the Allies made cyber defense a key part of collective defense, stating that a cyber attack could trigger the use of Article 5 of the NATO treaty on collective defense. At the Warsaw Summit in 2016, NATO member states recognized the security of information and communication networks as one of the main areas of defense and agreed that NATO must defend itself in cyberspace as effectively as it does on land, sea, and air. NATO's main partner in the field of cyber security is the European Union, with which the alliance signed a technical agreement on mutual assistance and cooperation in February 2016 (RIAC, 2016).

One of the main issues discussed at the Warsaw summit was how to best allocate resources to cyber security - acknowledging that large resources were needed to tackle the problem. Also, there were questions about how much money had to be spent, and what would be the minimum level of investment. For example, as of 2014, the Pacte Défense Cyber budget in France included €1 billion for cyber defense. In 2016, the UK announced that it would allocate £1.9 billion to bolster its cyber security program (Reuters, 2014).

At the Brussels summit in 2018, the Allies agreed to create a new Cyberspace Operations Center. Given the common challenges, NATO and the EU are strengthening cooperation in the field of cyber defense, especially in the exchange of information. Joint training and research are conducted (NATO, 2018).

The merit of the United States of America, which spares no efforts to develop new regulations related to cyber security, and also spares no money, is worth mentioning. Spending in the US budget related to cyber security is increasing every year, in 2015 the Barack Obama administration allocated 14 billion dollars officially, and then it was reported that much more would be spent (CNet, 2015). Worldwide defense spending is increasing day by day, but US finances are impressive. It is already known that by 2021 this field will be funded with 18.8 billion dollars (Homeland Security, 2020). Back in 2007, the United States Air Force created a Cyber Command, which existed until the end of 2008, and then these functions were transferred to the Air Force Space Command (EU Law Handbook, 2020).

In May 2011, the United States published its strategy for the defense of cyberspace, which is based on a model of cooperation with international partners and the private sector. Events should be held in seven directions:

1. Economy - attraction of international standards and innovations, open and liberal market;
2. Protection of the national network - increasing security, reliability, and sustainability;
3. Legal side - expansion of cooperation and legal norms;
4. Military field - readiness for modern security challenges;

5. Governmental Internet network - expansion of efficiency and versatility of government structures;
6. International development - organization of security, development of international competencies, and economic prosperity;
7. Freedom on the Internet - Supporting privacy and freedom of citizens (The White House, 2020).

How many types of concepts can exist in today's world? In addition to the fact that the US, the European Union, and NATO have important concepts, all countries have their national action plans, the most noteworthy is the new strategic concept approved at the Lisbon Summit in 2010 (NATO, 2011), according to which the United States of America has established a cyber command. It was a response to Russia's actions. Whether or not Vladimir Putin came to power, he approved a new doctrine of information security (ITU, 2020), whose strategy was to give the government control rights over information and media networks. Putin also signed a legislative amendment giving the tax police, the Ministry of Internal Affairs, the Kremlin's parliamentary and presidential security services, the border guard, and the customs service the same powers that only the Federal Security Service had.

On December 18, 2017, the first "National Security Strategy" (National Security Strategy, 2017) of US President Donald Trump was published, which was based on strategic documents such as the "National Defense Strategy" of the US Department of Defense. The strategy is based on four important national interests:

1. To protect the American people and the American way of life;
2. The growth of American prosperity;
3. Keeping the peace;
4. Increasing the influence of America.

Chapter 3 is interesting, with the title: "Maintaining peace through force", where claims are made against two states - Russia and China:

"For the United States of America, Russia is perceived as an existential threat. Russia is trying to restore the status of a great power and create its spheres of influence near the borders. Its goal is to weaken the influence of the USA and withdraw allies and partners. The growth of nuclear arsenal and military strength, as well as the desire to expel the US from the Indian and Pacific regions, the attempt to change the order in the region and establish the desired economic rules are perceived as threats from China" (US Embassy in Georgia, 2017).

In the textbook - "Cyber Dragon - China's Information Warfare and Cyber Operations", authored by researcher Dean Cheng, he notes that over the past centuries, Chinese leaders have analyzed that the most important thing is technological development, which helps China to improve its position on a global scale. They realized the importance of controlling information as one of the most powerful elements in maintaining power. Cheng also focuses on the development of types of warfare:

"The development of technologies has affected both the economy and society, as well as the nature of war. Historically, as war developed, mankind developed swords, spears, and other types of "cold weapons", i.e. replaced them with rifles, grenades, machine guns, etc. And today, at the expense of the development of technology, humanity has gone from "hot weapon" to "soft power" (Cheng Dean, 2017).

Therefore, the title of Chapter 4 of the new US strategy states directly, bluntly:

"Increasing America's Influence", where special emphasis is placed on America's role, influence, and active participation in international institutions. If existing institutions and rules require modernization, the United States will lead this process," the document states (US Embassy in Georgia, 2020).

When Donald Trump's strategy talks about increasing America's influence, it is noticeable here how the White House is facile with international relations, although it is difficult to say how much it will be realistic when we are dealing with Russia, for which politics and ethics, fulfillment of promises and justice are very far away.

CONCLUSION

Cyberspace and cybersecurity are becoming increasingly important due to the growing reliance on computer systems, the Internet, and wireless networking standards such as Bluetooth and Wi-Fi, as well as the growth of smart devices and various devices that make up the "Internet of Things".

Due to its complexity, both in terms of politics and technology, cybersecurity is also one of the major challenges in today's world. How did it all start? We will look at the history of cybersecurity from its inception to the present day.

The 1970s: ARPANET and Creeper

Cybersecurity began in the 1970s when researcher Bob Thomas created a computer program called Creeper that could traverse the ARPANET, leaving a trail wherever it went. Ray Tomlinson, the inventor of e-mail, wrote the Reaper program that harassed and removed Creeper. Reaper was the very first piece of anti-virus software and the first self-replicating program, making it the first computer worm.

The 1980s: Birth of Commercial Antivirus

1987 marked the birth of commercial antivirus, although there were competing claims to be the innovator of the first antivirus product. Andreas Lüning and Kai Figge released their first antivirus product for the Atari ST, which also released Ultimate Virus Killer in 1987. Three Czechoslovakians created the first version of NOD antivirus in the same year, and in the US, John McAfee founded McAfee. and released VirusScan.

The 1990s: The World Goes Online

As the Internet became public, more people began posting their personal information online. Organized crime saw this as a potential source of income and began stealing data from people and governments via the Internet. By the mid-1990s, network security threats had grown exponentially, and firewalls and anti-virus programs had to be mass-produced to protect the public.

The 2000s: Threats Diversify and Multiply

In the early 2000s, criminal organizations began to actively fund professional cyberattacks, and governments began to crack down on the crime of hacker attacks, issuing much harsher sentences to the perpetrators. Information security has continued to evolve as the Internet has grown, but unfortunately, so have viruses.

2021: The Next Generation

The cybersecurity industry continues to grow at the speed of light. Statista predicts that by 2026 the global cybersecurity market will grow to $345.4 billion. Ransomware is one of the most common threats to any organization's data security and is predicted to continue to grow.

REFERENCES

Allianz. (2016). *Cyber attacks on critical infrastructure*. Retrieved from: https://www.agcs. allianz.com/news-and-insights/expert-risk-articles/cyber-attacks-on-critical-infrastructure. html#:~:text=Cyber%2Dattacks%20against%20critical%20infrastructure%20and%20key%20manufac-turing%20industries%20have,against%20ICS%20and%20corporate%20networks

Business to Business. (2016). *The five generations of computers*. Retrieved from: https://btob.co.nz/business-news/five-generations-computers/

CERN. (2020). *CERN Accelerating science, "A short history of the Web - Where the Web was born"*. Retrieved from: https://home.cern/science/computing/birth-web/short-history-web

Cheng, D. (2017). Cyber dragon, inside China s information warfare and cyber operations. In The Changing Face of War. Praeger.

CNet. (2015). *Obama asks for $14 billion to step up cybersecurity - The president urges Congress to pass legislation that would strengthen the country's hacking detection system and counterintelligence capabilities*. Retrieved from: https://www.cnet.com/news/obama-adds-14b-to-budget-for-stepped-up-cybersecurity/

Computer History Museum. (2009). *October 29, 1969: HAPPY 40TH BIRTHDAY TO A RADICAL IDEA!* Retrieved from: https://computerhistory.org/blog/october-29-1969-happy-40th-birthday-to-a-radical-idea/

Council of Europe. (2018). *Guide to European Data Protection Law*. Retrieved from: https://rm.coe.int

Dawkins, J. (2022). *What's in a Name? The Origin of Cyber*. Retrieved from: https://alpinesecurity.com/blog/what-is-the-origin-of-the-word-cyber/

Deffere, S. (2020). *1st computer virus is written, January 30, 1982*. Retrieved from: https://www.edn.com/1st-computer-virus-is-written-january-30-1982/

DiGiacomo. (2017). *Active vs Passive Cyber Attacks Explained*. Retrieved from: https://revisionlegal.com/internet-law/cyber-security/active-passive-cyber-attacks-explained/

Embassy U. S. in Georgia. (2017). *National Security Strategy of the United States of America*. Retrieved from: https://ge.usembassy.gov/ka/2017-national-security-strategy-united-states-america-president-ka/

EU-Startup. (2019). *Who was Ada Lovelace? The life of the woman who envisioned the modern-day computer.* Retrieved from: https://www.eu-startups.com/2019/10/who-was-ada-lovelace-the-life-of-the-woman-who-envisaged-the-modern-day-computer/

Gartner. (2018). *Gartner Forecasts Worldwide Information Security Spending to Exceed $124 Billion in 2019.* Retrieved from: https://www.gartner.com

Ge, T. V. (2020). *Georgian Public Broadcaster, "At the closed session of the UN Security Council, the USA, Britain and Estonia talked about Russia's cyber attacks against Georgia."* Retrieved from: https://1tv.ge/news/gaero-s-ushishroebis-sabchos-dakhurul-skhdomaze-ashsh-ma-britanetma-da-estonetma-saqartvelos-winaaghmdeg-rusetis-kibertavdaskhmebze-isaubres/

HC. (2023). *Charles Babbage Analytical Engine Explained: Everything You Need To Know.* Retrieved from: https://history-computer.com/Babbage/AnalyticalEngine.html

History. (2019). *The Invention of the Internet.* Retrieved from: https://www.history.com/topics/inventions/invention-of-the-internet

History of Information. (2010). *The Creeper Worm, the First Computer Virus.* Retrieved from: https://www.historyofinformation.com/detail.php?id=2465

Independent. (2017). *Ukraine cyber attack: Chaos as a national bank, state power provider, and airport hit by hackers, Russian energy firms and Danish shipping company also hit by hackers.* Retrieved from: https://www.independent.co.uk/news/world/europe/ukraine-cyber-attack-hackers-national-bank-state-power-company-airport-rozenko-pavlo-cabinet-computers-wannacry-ransomware-a7810471.html

ITU. (2000). *Russian Federation, "Information Security Doctrine of the Russian Federation."* Retrieved from: https://www.itu.int/en/ITU-D/Cybersecurity/Documents/National_Strategies_Repository/Russia_2000.pdf

Lemelson. (2020). *Steve Jobs.* Retrieved from: https://lemelson.mit.edu/resources/steve-jobs-steve-wozniak

Lewis University. (2020). The history of cyber warfare – infographic. *The New Face of War: Attacks in Cyberspace.* Retrieved from: https://online.lewisu.edu/mscs/resources/the-history-of-cyber-warfare

Magazine, C. (2021). *The History of Cybersecurity.* Retrieved from: https://cybermagazine.com/cyber-security/history-cybersecurity

Magazine, S. (2013). *The Brief History of the ENIAC Computer.* Retrieved from: https://www.smithsonianmag.com/history/the-brief-history-of-the-eniac-computer-3889120/

Morgan, S. (2017). *Editor-in-Chief, "Cybersecurity Ventures", 2017 Cybercrime Report.* Retrieved from: https://cybersecurityventures.com/2015-wp/wp-content/uploads/2017/10/2017-Cybercrime-Report.pdf

NATO. (2011). *NATO's new strategic concept: A comprehensive assessment.* Retrieved from: https://www.econstor.eu/bitstream/10419/59845/1/656748095.pdf

NATO. (2018). *Brussels Summit Declaration - Issued by the Heads of State and Government participating in the meeting of the North Atlantic Council in Brussels on 11-12 July 2018*. Retrieved from: https://www.nato.int/cps/en/natohq/official_texts_156624.htm

Network Security. (2023). *Dial-up Internet Access*. Retrieved from: https://www.networxsecurity.org/members-area/glossary/d/dial-up-access.html

News, M. (1999). *Microsoft, "Strong Holiday Sales Make Windows 98 Best-Selling Software of 1998"*. Retrieved from: https://news.microsoft.com/1999/02/09/strong-holiday-sales-make-windows-98-best-selling-software-of-1998

Rapid 7. (2020). *Malware Attacks: Definition and Best Practices*. Retrieved from: https://www.rapid7.com/fundamentals/malware-attacks/

Reuters. (2020). *France to invest 1 billion euros to update cyber defenses*. Retrieved from: https://www.reuters.com/article/france-cyberdefence-idUSL5N0LC21G20140207

RIAC. (2016). *NATO's Cyber Defense Evolution - NATO's New Digital Wall*. Retrieved from: https://www.nato.int/docu/rdr-gde-prg/rdr-gde-prg-eng.pdf

RMI. (2023). *Professor George Nikoladze*. Retrieved from: http://www.rmi.ge/person/nikoladze/

Security, H. (2020). *Department of Homeland Security Statement on the President's Fiscal Year 2021 Budget*. Retrieved from: https://www.dhs.gov/news/2020/02/11/department-homeland-security-statement-president-s-fiscal-year-2021-budget

Security, P. (2018). *Ransomware: Screen Lockers vs. Encryptors*. Retrieved from: https://www.pandasecurity.com/mediacenter/malware/ransomware-screen-lockers-vs-encryptors/

Steve, R. (2018). *What is cyberwar? Everything you need to know about the frightening future of digital conflict*. Retrieved from: https://www.zdnet.com/article/cyberwar-a-guide-to-the-frightening-future-of-online-conflict/

The White House. (2011). *International Strategy For Cyberspace, "Prosperity, Security, and Openness in a Networked World"*. Retrieved from: https://www.hsdl.org/?view&did=5665

Varonis. (2020). *110 Must-Know Cybersecurity Statistics for 2020*. Retrieved from: https://www.varonis.com

Vidisha, J. (2019). *America's Hidden Stories tackles the CIA's alleged involvement in the Trans-Siberian Pipeline explosion of 1982*. Retrieved from: https://meaww.com/americas-hidden-stories-busting-myth-cia-involvement-trans-siberian-pipeline-explosion-1982

White House. (2017). *United States of America, "National Security Strategy"*. Retrieved from: https://www.whitehouse.gov/wp-content/uploads/2017/12/NSS-Final-12-18-2017-0905.pdf

Wired. (2011). *July 26, 1989: First Indictment Under Computer Fraud Act*. Retrieved from: https://www.wired.com/2011/07/0726first-computer-fraud-indictment/

KEY TERMS AND DEFINITIONS

Cyber Warfare: Involves the actions by a nation-state or international organization to attack and attempt to damage another nation's computers or information networks through, for example, computer viruses or denial-of-service attacks. RAND research provides recommendations to military and civilian decision-makers on methods of defending against the damaging effects of cyber warfare on a nation's digital infrastructure.

Cyberspace: Refers to the digital realm of computer networks, the Internet, and other forms of electronic communication. It is a virtual space where individuals and organizations can interact and share information globally, regardless of physical location. The term combines the words "cybernetics" and "space," describing the idea of a virtual space connected through technology.

History of Cyberspace: Is linked to the development of computers and the Internet. After Gibson's coinage of the term, it quickly gained popularity. It was used to describe the interconnected global network of computers and the information and communication that flowed through them. The term cyberspace was also used to describe the virtual world of online communities, where people could interact and form relationships without ever physically meeting. However, before computers existed, many philosophers raised the idea of an alternative reality. In his "Allegory of the Cave," the Greek philosopher Plato mentions that people live in an alternate reality and can only access the true reality through mental training and education. Rene Descartes, a French philosopher, argued that a demon showed people a false reality and that people can see the true reality by thinking.

Chapter 3
Information War as a Result of the Information– Technological Revolution

Salome Mikiashvili
Cyber Security Bureau, Georgia

ABSTRACT

In the chapter, different aspects related to the information war and cyber warfare of Russia-Ukraine war and the China-Taiwan relations are analyzed. In general, information warfare (WW) (as opposed to cyber warfare, which attacks computers, software, and control systems) is a concept that includes the use of combat space and the management of information and communication technologies (ICT) to achieve the goal. Information warfare is the manipulation of information trusted by the target, without the knowledge of the target, so that the target makes decisions against its interests but in the interests of the one who wages the information war. As a result, it is not clear when the information war begins and ends and how strong or destructive it is.

INTRODUCTION

Information is everything. When states go to war, information operations including data manipulation and data misuse are one of the keys to achieving their goals. Even in peacetime governments conduct cyberspace operations to support democratic norms and principles while others, surveil and target to destroy for their success and interests. Information warfare has enormous political, technical, operational, and legal implications for the military. Therefore, here we will try to define IW, identify potential military uses and applications, and explain different types of information warfare.

Information warfare means the use of information or information technology during a time of crisis or conflict to achieve or promote specific objectives over a specific adversary or adversaries. Information warfare (IW) has recently become of increasing importance to the military and the intelligence community.

Technology plays a crucial role in information warfare, as it enables actors to spread disinformation, manipulate public opinion, and conduct cyberattacks on a massive scale. One of the most significant

DOI: 10.4018/978-1-6684-8846-1.ch003

developments in recent years has been the emergence of social media platforms, which have become key battlegrounds for information warfare. Social media enables actors to disseminate information rapidly and target specific demographics with tailored messages.

This has been used by actors to spread disinformation, sow division, and manipulate public opinion.

In addition, the development of artificial intelligence and machine learning has given actors the ability to automate disinformation campaigns, making them faster, more efficient, and more difficult to detect. This has created new challenges for defenders, who must continually adapt their tools and techniques to keep pace with attackers.

On the defensive side, technology has also enabled the development of advanced cybersecurity tools and techniques to detect and respond to cyberattacks. These include tools for threat intelligence, network monitoring, and incident response.

Overall, technology has played a central role in shaping the landscape of information warfare, and it will continue to do so in the future. It is important for all actors, including governments, tech companies, and civil society, to work together to address the challenges posed by information warfare in the digital age.

According to Martin Libicki, information warfare occurs in the following forms: 1) warfare in the sphere of command and control; 2) intelligence 3) electronic warfare; 4) psychological warfare; 5) hacker warfare; 6) economic-information warfare; 7) cyber warfare (Libicki, 1995). All of these forms are connected, especially hacker warfare and cyber warfare which are not completely disjunctive.

Command and Control Warfare is a military strategy that applies information warfare on the battlefield to separate the command structure of the opponents from the units they command intelligence deals with the collection and analysis of various types of information including political, economic, technological, trade, etc., and then use this information to benefit one's interests.

Electronic warfare is also defined as a military activity that involves the use of electromagnetic and targeted energy in terms of dominating and managing events in the electromagnetic spectrum and terms of an electronic attack on the enemy and its combat systems.

Psychological warfare involves the use of information against the human mind. Psychological operations have had a serious impact on the war. Bot accounts that have been spreading misinformation about covid-19 were later spreading fake news about the war. There are numerous cases of psychological terror during the Russia-Ukraine war: Threatening messages were sent to soldiers; they were told to flee or otherwise be killed. Facebook accounts of militaries have been hacked, messages were sent using their names saying they surrendered and calling other soldiers to act the same way. but Facebook detected Russian state actors conducting psychological operations and deleted their accounts.

A hacker attack is usually aimed at congestion and changing the content of the attacked website. Because of their functional and physical characteristics, computer systems represent an ideal target for attackers.

In a global context, the" conflict" of the economic and intelligence services is constantly present, around confidential information that would be used against its competitors in the interests of its companies. This "conflict" essentially constitutes economic (or industrial) espionage (Damjanović 2017).

TECHNOLOGIES USED IN THE WAR IN UKRAINE

On February 24, 2022, the Kremlin tried to seize Kyiv in a so-called "Special Military Operation" intended to force regime change in Ukraine. One year has passed since the large-scale invasion of the

Russian army in Ukraine. Thousands of Ukrainian civilians have died in the war. Millions of Ukrainians were forced to leave their homes.

According to UN figures, more than 8,000 civilians have died as a result of the war. About 14,000,000 people were forced to leave their homes.

Tens of thousands of houses, administrative buildings, educational and medical institutions, and critical facilities have been destroyed in the cities and villages of Ukraine.

According to the General Staff of the Armed Forces of Ukraine, the Russian occupation forces carried out almost 5,000 rockets and about 3,500 airstrikes in one year. Also, up to 1,100 drone strikes.

Ukraine and Russia do not specify the number of killed military personnel. According to intelligence data from Western countries, including Great Britain, about 200,000 Russian soldiers have been killed and wounded since the invasion of Ukraine. The loss of Ukraine is likely to be the same (Radio Tavisupleba, 2023).

In war, the defender typically enjoys certain advantages, including a superior knowledge of battlefield terrain and communication networks. During this invasion, Russian forces are reported to have suffered a breakdown in military comms, which led to a reliance on Ukrainian SIM cards, and a subsequent vulnerability to interception, jamming, and geolocation.

During the opening phase of the war, one group of hackers may have played a strategic role in helping the Ukrainian government to survive. Working with Belarusian dissidents, they compromised Belarusian railway signal control cabinets (which still ran Windows XP) to sabotage Russian military deployments. Train traffic was reportedly "paralyzed" for days, which was believed to have contributed to the vulnerable 40-mile convoy north of Kyiv" (Geers, 2022).

According to Keneth Geers, The hacktivist collective Anonymous said it defaced or knocked offline numerous Russian government and media sites,

the Russian MoD, and hacked Russian television to display war footage from Ukraine. One unit, Squad 303, sent tens of millions of text messages to Russian phone numbers to provide Russian citizens with real information about the war. Hackers defaced a Russian space research website and leaked files they claimed to be from Roscosmos.

As claimed by the author The website Distributed Denial of Secrets posted over 6 million Russian and Belarusian documents, allegedly from the Russian government, military, intelligence, economic, and media domains. For example, there were 360k files from Roskomnadzor, the agency responsible for monitoring, controlling, and censoring Russian mass media. Due to the ongoing war, a disclaimer reminds researchers that some of the documents could be fabricated, altered, or might even contain malware.

Cyberattacks and Satellites

Hours before the Russian invasion of Ukraine, Russia launched the cyber-attack, more specifically a series of denial of service DDoS attacks and trojan horse wiper malware which was later identified by Microsoft as "FoxbLade". The Trojan horse aimed to paralyze Ukraine's command and control centers and shut down the internet. This Cyberattack is known as the ViaSat hack, as Russia launched a Cyberattack, modems of satellite operator VIASAT" S KA_SAT network in Europe were also disabled. This was a large-scale attack but the consequences of the attack were not as destructive as expected because of Ukraine's partnership with international tech companies including Microsoft and Cloudflare because they moved their infrastructure into the cloud. Meanwhile, the anonymous hacker group declared cyber war on the Russian government, so FSB decided to create National Coordination Center for Computer

Incidents (NCCC) and classified the threat level as "critical" as there were clear warning messages and a lack of resources to withstand the attacks.

Meanwhile, the director of RETN Ukraine Olena Lutsenko declared that approximately 1350 cyber-attacks were registered in the first half of 2022, in the end of the year total number was 2194. 22% of Fiber network was damaged and new types of viruses have been identified (Lutsenko, 2023).

25-thousand-star link terminals have been deployed and 5 thousand Star link satellites were sent after the war started. Internet helps citizens to stay connected with their friends and family in the hard times of war and it also aids Ukraine's defensive coordination. Satellite imagery has a vital role in providing open-source information about troop movements, keeping Ukrainian military communications networks operational, and looking up military build-ups of the adversary.

Artillery and Missile Systems

Russia is using different types of artillery and missile systems, including rocket launchers, and ballistic missiles, to shell Ukrainian-held territory and targets. "By October 2022, more than 4,000 base stations, 60,000km of fiber-optic lines, and 18 broadcasting antennas had been seized, damaged, or destroyed, according to Ukraine's Special Communications Service." (Tech inform, 2023).

Ukraine is using advanced intelligence and software for example, software by a US tech company is assisting the Ukrainian military's targeting of Russian tanks and artillery. "Software assists targeting by visualizing an army's positions with detailed digital maps taking in feeds from commercial satellites and social media. Thermal imaging technology further enhances the capabilities of digital targeting" (Tech informed, 2023).

Electronic Warfare

The main objective of electronic warfare is to disrupt radar systems and communications. There have been detected numerous cases of GPS interference Both Ukrainian and Russian militaries had used electronic warfare to jam Russian communications.

Drones

UAVs are actively used in Russia Ukrainian war for intelligence, reconnaissance, and surveillance and for purposes of targeting enemy positions. Drones are simple, most of the drones are commercial ones. Both countries have developed counter-drone systems to find the enemy's UAV and neutralize it. Drones have different features some of them carry laser-guided bombs and they target vehicles.

other technologies used in the war are consumer technologies and applications as well as VR and 3d holograms. Some applications serve to allow civilians to upload the geolocation of different Russian military assets or report troop movements. To" prepare for the conflict, the Ukrainian military has used virtual reality (VR) training systems to simulate combat scenarios and train soldiers in tactics and procedures. This type of training allows soldiers to practice in a safe and controlled environment before deploying to the front lines" (Tech informed, 2023).

Russian Cyber-attacks have not been as impressive as it was expected. The whole world expected to see cyber-attacks on critical infrastructure, coordinated with kinetic military operations. We offered a few possible explanations for that, the scariest being that they are saving the most potent attacks for the

United States. President Biden has repeatedly warned about this, most recently saying, "It's coming." Another reason might be the resistance power of the adversary that Russia didn't expect.

UNEXPECTEDLY BETTER UKRAINIAN CYBER DEFENSE

U.S. and international partners have been bolstering the cybersecurity of Ukraine. Foreign investment in Ukrainian cyber security led to major improvements in the country's cyber posture. Ukraine has moved its critical infrastructure to the cloud, which bolstered its digital resilience. As the Ukrainian government states, no data has been lost or damaged so far because the existing backups are on the cloud. Ukraine's innovation in endpoint security and threat intelligence has been very effective in the process of developing Ukrainian cyber defenses" (Carnegie, 2022).

OPSEC Fog of War Obscure Full Picture

To understand how Russian Cyber Operations, work we have to rely on Ukrainian government announcements, cybersecurity companies, and media outlets, but sources are not sharing much information which creates a "Cyber fog of war". To prevail the uncertainty analysts should offer good assessments and the need to reassess over time (Carnegie, 2022).

U.S. Acknowledges Cyber Help to Ukraine

- "We've conducted a series of operations across the full spectrum; offensive, defensive, and information operations" NSA director and Cybercom Commander General Paul Nakasone, speaking to sky news in Tallinn, June 1, 2022.
- $45 Million Cyber defense aid in 2022 (Sky News, 2022).

What military gains have cyber-attacks yielded and by what means?

Experts have divided opinions about the effectiveness of Russian cyber-attacks in Ukraine. Part of experts believes that Russia has conducted serious cyber operations in Ukraine and that these operations have had a huge impact on the trajectory of the war. But not everyone agrees with the abovementioned theories, according to experts' Russian Cyber operations had very little impact and provided little benefit to Russia and they failed to achieve any goals by using cyber fires (Bateman, 2022).

While experts have paid a lot of attention to cyber-attacks most of them forgot to shift their attention to the intelligence collection part, which supports Russia's interests in war. Intelligence collection was a serious part of Moscow's wartime cyber operations. Ukraine's national cybersecurity agency has reported that "enemy hackers" carried out 242 "information gathering" operations during the first four months of the war (Bateman, 2022).

But it all started a lot earlier for example in 2015 and 2017 US officials accused Russia of repeatedly recording and leaking sensitive, high-level phone convos between Washington and Kyiv." Russia's Cyber espionage, like its HUMINT activities, and at least six Russian "advanced persistent threat" actors and at least eight malware families to grew in the run-up to war.

Just a couple of days before an actual invasion Cyber operations shifted to denial of service attacks. Attacks were targeted against intelligence and governmental agencies. White House announced that by technical evaluation of the attack Denial of Service operation was linked to Russia's main intelligence Directorate GRU.

Cyber operations shifted again after the physical invasion of Ukraine, this time ISAAC wiper targeting the governmental agencies, which was followed by the well-known ViaSat hack which resulted in the loss of communication systems on which the military relied.

It is conceivable that cyber intelligence collection might have sometimes provided unique targeting information—for example, revealing a hidden dependency or vulnerability. There are a few known cases where Russian cyber operators plausibly fed intelligence to missile targets.

Russian cyber doctrine emphasized intelligence, subversion, and psychological warfare rather than combat integration.

The GRU has been Russia's lead provider of cyber fires in the Ukraine war. Microsoft stated in December that all "destructive attacks against Ukrainian targets in support of the Russian war effort have been the responsibility of" GRU-associated actors. Although part of the military, the GRU is a national-level element that specializes in intelligence, subversion, and assassination; This may help explain why the GRU succeeded in executing a strategic cyber campaign (ViaSat and early wipers) to coincide with the initial invasion but has subsequently failed to show much tactical coordination with Russian units on the ground (Bateman, 2022).

The concentration of cybersecurity capability and international support that Ukraine possesses presents an obstacle for even a determined and powerful adversary like Russia.

End-point security and threat intelligence had a huge impact on Ukrainian cyber defenses. Threat intel from Western governments provided cybersecurity support to Ukraine and exposed the malicious activity of Russia

Similarities Between Ukraine and Taiwan

Comparisons have been made between Taiwan and Ukraine; predictions are made that Taiwan might become the next Ukraine. Comparisons are made according to the power asymmetry that exists between China and Taiwan and Russia and Ukraine. However, there are many structural similarities too, which deserve to be examined.

Two major geopolitical fault lines are formed today due to competition between the US-led maritime alliance and great continental powers (China and Russia). One fault line is in Eastern Europe, and the other is in East Asia. Both countries are under cross pressure from the maritime alliance and continental power. Together with other lesser powers on the fault lines, Ukraine and Taiwan need to take a strategic position between the two camps. There is a finite number of feasible positions that the lesser countries can choose from junior partner, hedger, and pivot.

Both countries are economically linked to great continental power but dependent on the maritime alliance for security. both countries have historical and cultural ties for a larger share of the population Russia and Ukraine share the same language (Yu-Shan Wu, 2022).

China is a significant danger with its growing cyber-attack capabilities, which the US strategic community, including the lawmakers, seems to focus on.

According to a report released by a congressional advisory commission, the United states sees a huge threat in China's focus on the development of its cyber capabilities, espionage capabilities, and cyber warfare over the past years.

The report says that the country has achieved this transformation by reorganizing its cyber policymaking institutions, developing sophisticated offensive cyber capabilities, and perpetrating cyber espionage to steal foreign intellectual property at an industrial scale. Plus, China has an asymmetric advantage because it doesn't play by the same rules. States' increasing reliance on cyberespionage efforts, promote its national security interests by controlling cyberspace.

The report also says that Beijing's cyber operations are sophisticated. Beijing is using advanced tactics and often relies on vulnerability exploitation and third-party compromise to infiltrate victims' networks. forced technology transfers, the theft of U.S. intellectual property, and market access restrictions have raised serious concerns in the united states. The report is recommending that Congress "should consider legislation to immediately suspend China's permanent normal trade relations treatment" (Graham, 2022).

China's information warfare against Taiwan is also raising serious concerns. Taiwanese President Tsai Ing-wen describes the information assault against Taiwan as "cognitive warfare tactics".

"A Chinese People's Liberation Army official publication openly outlines its priority for information warfare, describing it as taking a central role over conventional military strength. It postulates that warfare is evolving away from the mechanized battle to information assaults, stating, "Information age warfare depends mainly on information to subdue an enemy (Bastian, 2022).

The Question We Should Be Addressing Right Now Is Whether Taiwan Will Become the Next Ukraine

Experts argue that there are many deterrence factors for Xi to not become the next Putin. One of which is that China is way more integrated into Global Economy than Russia. According to a distinguished fellow with the China Program at the U.S. Institute of Peace, Dr. Andrew Scobell China largely pretends to be playing by international norms. In terms of leaders, Xi Jinping, the leader of China likes to project the image of a global statesman who is part of the world, abides by world norms, and largely plays by the rules. Putin, by contrast, likes his bad-boy image. Those are some key differences, between Russia and China. According to Scobell as far as Ukraine and Taiwan, both are the object of irredentist claims by Russia and China, respectively. And yet, Ukraine is outside of NATO. It doesn't have any de jure or de facto allies. Taiwan doesn't officially have any allies but it has close security ties with several countries, including the United States. From China's perspective, in any military operation against Taiwan, they assume that the U.S. will come to Taiwan's aid. But clearly, in Ukraine, Putin understood that no country, including the United States, would come to its aid (United States Institute of Peace, 2022).

There is an ongoing tension between China and Taiwan, and there have been instances of what can be described as "information warfare" between the two sides.

In recent years, there have been reports of Chinese state-sponsored information and cyber-attacks targeting Taiwanese government agencies and businesses, as well as efforts to spread misinformation and propaganda through social media and other channels. Taiwan has responded by strengthening its cybersecurity capabilities and implementing measures to counter disinformation.

There have been numerous reports and allegations of China engaging in cyber warfare against not only Taiwan but the United States and other world-leading cyber powers too. Chinese state-sponsored hacking groups have been accused of stealing sensitive information from US government agencies, military contractors, and businesses.

In recent years, there have been high-profile cyberattacks attributed to Chinese hackers, including the theft of personal data from millions of US government employees in 2015 and the Equifax data breach in 2017. There have also been reports of Chinese hackers targeting US infrastructure, including power grids and transportation systems.

The U.S. government had been preparing a report on Chinese Malicious cyber activities. CISA, NSA, and FBI released an advisory to provide the top Common Vulnerabilities and Exposures (CVEs) used since 2020 by the People's Republic of China. The report is the result of analytic efforts between CISA, the U.S. Department of Defense (DoD), and the Federal Bureau of Investigation (FBI). Reports describe Chinese malicious cyber activities and the tools used by state-sponsored actors. Report scans activities starting from 2019. Those identified activities were:

People's Republic of China State-Sponsored Cyber Actors Exploit Network Providers and Devices of Chinese Gas Pipeline Intrusion Campaign, 2011 to 2013 (Cybersecurity & Infrastructure Security Agency, 2022).

INFORMATION WARFARE AND TECHNOLOGICAL ADVANCEMENTS

There is a growing argument that throughout history, wars have been characterized by revolutionary technological discoveries that cause "waves" of socioeconomic changes. Each wave is marked by a significant technological advancement that fundamentally changes the way societies function and interact, leading to significant geopolitical shifts and conflicts.

The current wave, often referred to as the "informational wave," is characterized by digitalization, computers, and information technologies. These technologies have had a profound impact on every aspect of society, from communication and commerce to governance and warfare.

In the context of warfare, information technologies have had a significant impact on the way militaries operate and interact with each other (Paulo Fernando Viegas Nunes, 1999).

New technologies have greatly impacted information warfare in several ways, both positive and negative. Here are some of the most significant impacts:

1. Speed and Reach: New technologies have increased the speed and reach of information dissemination, making it possible to spread information quickly and widely. Social media platforms, for example, allow individuals and groups to rapidly disseminate information to a large audience, potentially causing misinformation to spread at a faster pace.
2. Anonymity and Pseudonymity: New technologies have made it easier for individuals and groups to remain anonymous or use pseudonyms when spreading information. This makes it harder to track the source of the information, making it easier to spread disinformation and propaganda without being held accountable.
3. Artificial Intelligence and Machine Learning: The use of AI and machine learning has made it easier for information warfare actors to create convincing fake content, such as deep fakes and manipulated images, that can be used to spread disinformation and propaganda.
4. Cyberattacks: New technologies have also made it easier for information warfare actors to launch cyberattacks against their targets, including hacking, data breaches, and other cybercrimes.
5. Countermeasures: On the positive side, new technologies have also enabled the development of more effective countermeasures against information warfare, such as advanced algorithms that can detect fake news and disinformation, and tools that can trace the source of online content.

Information warfare encompasses attacks on command and control systems, operational security, cyberwar, and electronic warfare. Hacking, information-based warfare, and even psychological warfare.

Information warfare has become the new post-Cold War era national security catchphrase. Information warfare in its broadest sense is a struggle that involves the communications process, a struggle that began with the advent of human communication and conflict.

FRAMEWORK FOR THE USE OF INFORMATION WARFARE WEAPONS

The question of conflict or warfare is not only a physical but also a psychological issue. Information operations can be divided into offensive IO (e.g., computer network attack, command and control warfare, special information operations), civil affairs, public affairs (media warfare), and defensive IO (e.g., physical security, computer network defense, and counter-propaganda) (Huhtinen & Rantapelkonen, 2002). Information superiority means the simultaneous joint operation with all aspects of information operation. For example, the lack of a defensive IO aspect can put at risk offensive IO. Without civil affairs or public affairs capabilities there are risks at achieve success in offensive and defensive IO (National Defence College, Finland, 2008).

States are becoming dependent on information infrastructure, the information infrastructure itself consists of networks, communications, and information systems. Technological advances are creating new vulnerabilities. Given this reality, states need to ensure the safety and protection of their information infrastructures.

Defensive Information Warfare (IW) refers to the use of strategies, techniques, and technologies to protect against cyber-attacks and other malicious activities aimed at compromising the confidentiality, integrity, and availability of critical information assets.

Defensive IW includes various measures such as firewalls, intrusion detection and prevention systems, anti-virus and anti-malware software, encryption, access controls, and incident response plans. These measures are designed to prevent, detect, and respond to cyber threats and attacks in real time, ensuring that critical information remains secure and available.

Defensive IW is essential for organizations and governments to protect their sensitive and critical information assets from cyber threats, espionage, and other malicious activities. With the increasing frequency and sophistication of cyber-attacks, defensive IW has become a critical aspect of cybersecurity, and organizations need to invest in the right tools, technologies, and personnel to protect their information assets effectively.

United States seeks to protect its critical infrastructure with the use of DIW. The United States is investing in information defense to ensure that American computer and information systems will not be compromised because inadequate information security can allow enemy nations to proactive war techniques against the United states. over the past three years, 246 ransomware attacks have struck U.S. government organizations at an estimated cost of $52.88 billion. Ironically, while most ransomware attacks are about just that – holding data for ransom until it's paid – the goal of most of these attacks on cities, states, and counties was not to steal data but to halt processes, interrupt services and cause disruption (SunGard, 2021). One of the latest examples of a large-scale attack is in march 2023 when CISA and FBI reported that a U.S. federal agency was targeted by multiple attackers, including a Vietnamese espionage group, in a cyberespionage campaign between November 2022 and January 2023. Hackers used a vulnerability in the agency's Microsoft Internet Information Services (IIS) server to install malware. The alert does not mention which or how many federal agencies were affected (CSIS, 2023).

While a successful defense may not win a conflict, an unsuccessful defense can make subsequent operations of any sort difficult, if not impossible. Better defenses must be engineered if we are to retain the integrity and reliability of our information systems (Anita D. DeVries,1997).

Offensive Information Warfare (IW) refers to the use of information and communication technologies to attack, exploit, or disrupt the information assets of an adversary, to gain a strategic advantage in a conflict or competition.

Offensive IW includes various tactics such as hacking, phishing, social engineering, and malware deployment. It is aimed at gaining unauthorized access to an adversary's information systems, stealing or modifying sensitive data, disrupting critical services, or spreading false information to influence the adversary's decision-making process.

Offensive IW is often employed by nation-states, intelligence agencies, and other malicious actors to achieve their political, military, or economic objectives. It is a complex and sophisticated activity that requires significant resources, expertise, and planning.

Effective covert offensive information warfare can grant states to foresee rival operations and impair their systems. Offensive warfare can impair combat capabilities by discarding command control and intelligence. A clear example of information warfare would be when "In Iraq, during Desert Storm, the central telephone exchange in Baghdad was among the first targets engaged in the war campaign. Even before the telephone exchange was attacked, anti-aircraft radars were targeted and eliminated by Army Apache helicopters. The United States poked out their radar eyes and severed their wireless nerves; thereby eliminating the acquisition of information and the ability to communicate information.

The offensive cyber operations are typically conducted by governments, intelligence agencies, or state-sponsored entities. For readers, the thesis provides some examples of offensive cyber operations:

One of them is Stuxnet: Stuxnet is one of the most well-known examples of offensive cyber operations. It was a highly sophisticated computer worm that targeted Iran's nuclear program. Stuxnet specifically aimed at disrupting and damaging centrifuges used for uranium enrichment

Stuxnet was created to take advantage of vulnerabilities in the industrial control systems (ICS) employed at Iran's Natanz nuclear plant. It was aimed at the Programmable Logic Controllers (PLCs) that regulated the operation of uranium enrichment centrifuges. Stuxnet caused the centrifuges to malfunction and spin at unforeseeable speed by manipulating the PLCs, resulting in physical damage and lowering the overall efficiency of the enrichment process.

The worm's complexity was significant, as it exploited numerous zero-day vulnerabilities, used rootkit capabilities to mask its existence, and could spread through USB devices. The intricacy and specificity of Stuxnet revealed a high level of expertise and resources, leading many experts to conclude that it was created jointly by the US and Israel, albeit no official confirmation has been provided.

Stuxnet represented a significant milestone in the realm of offensive cyber operations, showcasing the potential for cyber weapons to impact physical infrastructure and disrupt critical systems. Its discovery brought global attention to the growing field of cyber warfare and highlighted the need for enhanced cybersecurity measures in critical infrastructure sectors. (Zetter, 2014)

Another notable example of offensive cyber attack was NotPetya: NotPetya was a destructive cyber attack that occurred in 2017. It initially masqueraded as ransomware, but it quickly became apparent that its primary purpose was to cause widespread damage and disruption. NotPetya affected numerous organizations worldwide, primarily in Ukraine, and caused significant financial losses.

NotPetya mainly affected organizations in Ukraine, including government agencies, banks, and critical infrastructure sectors. However, it quickly spread to other states, impacting organizations globally. Some of the affected organizations included shipping company Maersk, pharmaceutical company Merck, and the Chernobyl nuclear power plant.

The malicious software standing behind NotPetya used several propagation techniques, including exploiting a vulnerability in the Windows operating system called EternalBlue, which was also used in the WannaCry ransomware attack that occurred earlier in 2017. Once inside a network, NotPetya employed advanced techniques to move laterally and infect other systems, encrypting files and rendering them inaccessible.

NotPetya caused significant financial losses for affected organizations due to the disruption of operations, downtime, and recovery efforts. Estimates suggest that the total financial impact reached billions of dollars.

While the attack was initially attributed to criminal actors seeking financial gain, subsequent investigations and analysis revealed that it was likely a state-sponsored operation with the objective of causing widespread damage and disruption. The attack further highlighted the potential impact of cyber attacks on critical infrastructure and the need for robust cybersecurity measures to mitigate such threats. (Greenberg, 2018)

Operation Aurora: Operation Aurora was a series of cyber attacks discovered in 2009 that targeted major technology companies. The attacks were attributed to state-sponsored actors from China and aimed to steal intellectual property and gain unauthorized access to sensitive systems.

The attack started with a spear-phishing email campaign that enticed workers of the targeted firms to click on a malicious link, allowing the attackers to obtain access to the targeted network. The attackers then moved laterally across the network, gaining access to sensitive data and exfiltrating it back to the attackers' command and control infrastructure.

The major goal of Operation Aurora was to steal intellectual property and trade secrets from the firms targeted. The attack was a huge success, with a substantial amount of vital information stolen. The incident also revealed the potential for cyber espionage to have an influence on national security and the global economy.

In response to the attack, many of the affected companies implemented stricter cybersecurity measures, and the US government increased its focus on cybersecurity issues, leading to the development of new cybersecurity policies and initiatives. The attack also raised concerns about the role of state-sponsored hacking in international relations and the need for stronger international norms and agreements around cyber espionage. (Council on Foreign Relations, 2010)

"Moonlight Maze: Moonlight Maze was a series of cyber attacks discovered in the late 1990s. The attacks targeted various U.S. government agencies and defense contractors. It was one of the earliest examples of a large-scale cyber espionage campaign, and its origins were suspected to be linked to Russia."

Since the term "maze" connotes intricacy and breadth, the attacks were given the moniker "Moonlight Maze" after it was discovered that an attacker's server contained a directory with the name "moonlight".

Moonlight Maze stood out for a number of reasons. Prior to other well-known occurrences like Titan Rain and Operation Aurora, it is regarded as one of the early examples of a significant cyber espionage campaign. The attackers, who are thought to be state-sponsored, acquired illegal access to many computer networks and exfiltrated a sizable amount of sensitive material over an extended period, from 1996 to 1997.

The attackers that employed Moonlight Maze are still unknown, specifically.

While the evidence pointed towards Russia at the time, attribution in cyberspace can be challenging, and definitive proof is often elusive.

Moonlight Maze did however raise questions about the likelihood that nation-states might use cyberattacks to carry out espionage and obtain sensitive data.

The incident led to significant improvements in the cybersecurity posture of the United States, including the foundation of institutions like the U.S. Cyber Command and a greater focus on information security across all government departments. In addition, Moonlight Maze acted as a wake-up call for numerous businesses, emphasizing the requirement for strong defense mechanisms and pro-active cybersecurity measures to protect crucial systems and data. (Industrial Cybersecurity Pulse, 2022)

Olympic Games (Stuxnet follow-up): Olympic Games, also known as Operation Olympic Games, was a follow-up to the Stuxnet operation. It involved the joint efforts of the United States and Israel to develop and deploy malware, including the Stuxnet worm, to disrupt Iran's nuclear facilities. According to reports, the United States and Israel collaborated to sabotage Iran's nuclear program via Operation Olympic Games. Beyond Stuxnet, other cyber weapons and tactics were used in the operation.

Even though Operation Olympic Games' most well-known element was Stuxnet, it's essential to realize that the operation as a whole included a wider range of cyber capabilities and goals. According to reports, these operations lasted for a number of years and involved other cyberattacks targeting Iran's nuclear infrastructure.

It's important to note that information concerning Operation Olympic Games and its specifics is still secret, and that the majority of public knowledge about the operation is based on media accounts and anonymous sources (Security&Defence, 2020).

Operation Cloud Hopper: Operation Cloud Hopper was a large-scale cyber espionage campaign attributed to APT10, a Chinese state-sponsored hacking group. The operation targeted managed IT service providers (MSPs) to gain unauthorized access to their clients' networks and steal sensitive information.

A huge-scale cyber espionage operation known as Operation Cloud Hopper, commonly referred to as APT10 or Stone Panda, was initially identified in 2016. The operation targeted managed IT service providers (MSPs), using them as an entry point to enter the networks of their clients without authorization. Operation Cloud Hopper's main goal was to steal confidential data and intellectual property from numerous businesses and organizations.

Operation Cloud Hopper deployed a staged attack approach. The attackers first gained access to the MSPs' computer systems by frequently employing spear-phishing emails or taking advantage of software flaws. Once within the MSPs' networks, they carried out reconnaissance, increased their level of access, and proceeded laterally to enter the networks of their customers.

The discovery of Operation Cloud Hopper led to a coordinated response from law enforcement agencies, and governments to address the threat. Attributing the campaign to APT10 and raising awareness about the tactics used by the attackers helped organizations bolster their defenses and implement measures to detect and prevent such intrusions (Giles, 2017).

The attackers managed to access several organizations, including governmental bodies, technological companies, energy companies, and others via hacking the MSPs. The stolen material was mostly concerned with sensitive company information, trade secrets, and intellectual property.

These examples illustrate the range and impact of offensive cyber operations. However, it's important to note that attribution in the cyber realm can be challenging, and sometimes multiple actors or groups may be involved in a single operation

Theoretically, if you can functionally disrupt or destroy an opponent's information, computer information systems, or infrastructure control systems using information warfare, you may sever the head from the body of the snake by isolating the leadership from the rest of the nation or armed forces. You can win a victory without the physical destruction of national assets (Anita D. DeVries,1997).

CONCLUSION

The military in industrialized nations has become increasingly dependent on its communication systems and electronic equipment. The superiority of modern weapon systems is basically because they transfer their data quickly across the battlefield.

"Information-based technology attacks are extremely easy to execute. The means are relatively cheap, easy to smuggle, virtually undetectable, and hard to associate. All this, along with the vulnerability of civilian communication networks (which are extremely attractive to terrorists), affords information warfare actions a prominent place in the terrorist arsenal (Paulo Fernando Viegas Nunes, 1999).

Information warfare technologies, precision fire technologies, and the fusion of a host of other technologies are also likely to transform the way we conduct warfare in the future.

Information warfare technologies, such as cyber warfare and electronic warfare, can disrupt or disable an adversary's communication systems, command and control infrastructure, and critical infrastructure. This can give a significant advantage to a military force that has superior information warfare capabilities.

Precision fire technologies, such as guided missiles and smart munitions, enable military forces to target and destroy enemy assets with greater accuracy and efficiency, reducing the risk of collateral damage and civilian casualties.

The fusion of other technologies, such as artificial intelligence, unmanned systems, and advanced sensors, can enhance situational awareness, improve decision-making, and provide a competitive edge on the battlefield.

The use of these emerging technologies in warfare could lead to more efficient, effective, and precise military operations. However, they also raise ethical, legal, and moral concerns and may require new rules and regulations to ensure their responsible use.

Just as the Industrial Age led to concepts of mechanized warfare and mass destruction of the enemy's war-making resources, the information era is leading us to concepts of domination of "information systems" to ensure the attainment of military objectives.

The root cause of war is ultimately human behavior and the complex web of motivations and emotions that drive it. Political leaders, nation-states, and non-state actors may engage in wars or conflicts for a variety of reasons, including fear, revenge, hatred, and greed, among others.

While technology and other factors may play a role in the conduct of war, ultimately it is human behavior and motivation that underlie the root causes of conflicts. But technology has indeed changed traditional thought processes on military effectiveness in several ways.

Technology has made it possible for smaller militaries to be more effective than larger ones. In the past, the size of the military was often seen as an indicator of its strength. However, with the advent of advanced weapons systems, smaller militaries equipped with cutting-edge technology can be more effective than larger ones with outdated equipment.

Technology has changed the nature of warfare. In the past, wars were often fought with large numbers of troops and a focus on land-based combat. However, with the development of air power and advanced weapons systems, wars can now be fought with fewer troops and a greater focus on precision strikes.

Technology has changed the way militaries communicate and coordinate with each other. The use of advanced communication systems has made it possible for militaries to share information and coordinate their actions in real time, making them more effective in combat.

Technology has made it possible for militaries to conduct operations remotely. Drones and other unmanned vehicles can now be used to carry out reconnaissance and even attack targets without putting troops in harm's way. This has not only made militaries more effective but has also reduced the risk of casualties.

Technology has changed traditional thought processes on military effectiveness by making it possible for smaller militaries to be more effective, changing the nature of warfare, improving communication and coordination, and enabling remote operations.

While technology can provide militaries with advanced weapons systems, communication tools, and other capabilities, it cannot solve all the problems associated with war. The conduct of war requires both science and art, as well as Good leadership, and a deep understanding of the political, social, and economic factors that drive conflict.

REFERENCES

Bastian, A. A. (2022). *"Foreign Policy" China Is Stepping Up Its Information War on Taiwan.* https://foreignpolicy.com/2022/08/02/china-pelosi-taiwan-information/

Bateman, J. (2022). *Carnegie, Russia's Wartime Cyber Operations in Ukraine: Military Impacts, Influences, and Implications.* https://carnegieendowment.org/2022/12/16/russia-s-wartime-cyber-operations-in-ukraine-military-impacts-influences-and-implications-pub-88657

Conger, K. (2022). Ukraine Says It Thwarted a Sophisticated Russian Cyberattack on Its Power Grid. *New York Times.* https://www.nytimes.com/2022/04/12/us/politics/ukraine-russian-cyberattack.html

CSIS. (2023). *Significant Cyber Incidents.* https://www.csis.org/programs/strategic-technologies-program/significant-cyber-incidents

Cybersccurity & Infrastructure Security Agency. (2022). *China Cyber Threat Overview and Advisories.* https://www.cisa.gov/china

Damjanović, D. (2017). *Types of Information Warfare and Examples of Malicious Programs of Information Warfare; Dragan Z.* https://www.researchgate.net/publication/320254033_Types_of_information_warfare_and_examples_of_malicious_programs_of_information_warfare

DeVries Anita, D. (1997). *Information Warfare and Its Impact on National Security.* https://irp.fas.org/eprint/snyder/infowarfare.htm

ESET Research Jointly Presents Industroyer2 at Black Hat USA With Ukrainian Government Representative. (2022). https://www.eset.com/int/about/newsroom/press-releases/events/eset-research-jointly-presents-industroyer2-at-black-hat-usa-with-ukrainian-government-representativ/

Fleming, J. (2022). The Head of GCHQ Says Vladimir Putin Is Losing the Information War in Ukraine. *Economist.* https://www.economist.com/by-invitation/2022/08/18/the-head-of-gchq-says-vladimir-putin-is-losing-the-information-war-in-ukraine

Geers, K. (2022). *Computer Network Operations during the Russian Invasion of Ukraine.* Academic Press.

Howell O'Neill, P. (2022). Russian Hackers Tried to Bring Down Ukraine's Power Grid to Help the Invasion. *MIT Technology Review.* https://www.technologyreview.com/2022/04/12/1049586/russian-hackers-tried-to-bring-down-ukraines-power-grid-to-help-the-invasion/

Industroyer2: Industroyer Reloaded. (2022). https://www.welivesecurity.com/2022/04/12/industroyer2-industroyer-reloaded/

KA-SAT Network Cyber Attack Overview. (2022). *Viasat.* https://news.viasat.com/blog/corporate/ka-sat-network-cyber-attack-overview

Lewis, A. J. (2022). *Cyber War and Ukraine.* Center for Strategic and International Studies. https://www.csis.org/analysis/cyber-war-and-ukraine

Nunes, P. F. V. (1999). *Information Warfare by Captain.* https://www.airuniversity.af.edu/Portals/10/ASPJ/journals/Chronicles/nunes.pdf

Scobell, A. (2022). *Comparing Russia-Ukraine to China's Aggression Toward Taiwan.* https://www.usip.org/publications/2022/03/andrew-scobell-comparing-russia-ukraine-chinas-aggression-toward-taiwan

SkyNews. (2022). *US military hackers conducting offensive operations in support of Ukraine, says head of Cyber Command.* https://news.sky.com/story/us-military-hackers-conducting-offensive-operations-in-support-of-ukraine-says-head-of-cyber-command-12625139

Ukraine Conflict: Cyberattacks, Frequently Asked Questions. (2022). CyberPeace Institute. https://cyberpeaceinstitute.org/news/ukraine-conflict-cyberattacks-frequently-asked-questions/

Volz, D., & McMillan, R. (2022). In Ukraine, a 'Full-Scale Cyberwar' Emerges. *Wall Street Journal.* https://www.wsj.com/articles/in-ukraine-a-full-scale-cyberwar-emerges-11649780203

Wu, Y.-S. (2022). *Ukraine and Taiwan: Comparison, Interaction, and Demonstration, Adrian Chiu Cross-Strait, History, International relations, Security, Taiwan-Ukraine.* https://taiwaninsight.org/2022/04/04/ukraine-and-taiwan-comparison-interaction-and-demonstration/

Zetter, K. (2022). *Viasat Hack 'Did Not' Have Huge Impact on Ukrainian Military Communications, Official Says.* Zero Day. https://zetter.substack.com/p/viasat-hack-did-not-have-huge-impact

Zhora, V. (2022). *Digital Peace Now.* https://digitalpeacenow.org/stillvulnerable-viktor-zhora/

Chapter 4
Virtual Threats and Asymmetric Military Challenges

C. V. Suresh Babu

🆔 https://orcid.org/0000-0002-8474-2882

Hindustan Institute of Technology and Science, India

P. M. Akshara

Hindustan Institute of Technology and Science, India

ABSTRACT

Security challenges are faced by every single country on this planet. These threats can occur through violent non-state habitats, any organized group of criminals, economic threats, disasters, or native citizens. In ancient wars, nations used physical forces and weapons as a tool to acquire regions, resources. Whereas, in the future, a wide range of technologies like automated weapons, drones, and cyber warfare may come into action. A single person can control an army of computers, and the person behind the actions can go unidentified. The surging need for the use of computers has greatly imposed an effect on the military. Unlike traditional warfare, where large mobilizations of military forces were involved, in modern warfare, integration with latest innovations in military forces like guided munition systems, explosives, and nuclear weapons are brought into use. As a result, there rises an inevitable need to acquire insight into the field of cyber military technology. This chapter mainly aims to analyse the nation's virtual threats and asymmetric military challenges.

INTRODUCTION

Cyberattacks on military networks and their systems are referred to as virtual military threats. These evil attacks are imposed by hackers, hacktivists, terrorists, or opponent countries. Threats may consists of phishing attacks, malware infections, denial of service attacks and data theft. Virtual threats may highly harm a nation's military operations by threatening the confidentiality, integrity and availability of sensitive information and infrastructure. Countries undergo various security issues. It may be both in the real world and the virtual world. Off late attacking through virtual world is exponentially increasing.

DOI: 10.4018/978-1-6684-8846-1.ch004

The evolving crisis is that every gadget can turn into a weapon on a virtual battlefield for which the loss may be felt in the real world. Virtual threats to the military may include stealing sensitive information from the system by introducing malicious code and phishing techniques etc., dignitaries can be compromised to reveal confidential information to unauthorized parties, supply chain attacks, and IoT attacks (Suresh Babu, 2023).

To bring about a change in the prevailing unsecured system, blockchain technology can be merged with military forces like ammunition, and nuclear weapons, and bringing the entire network under blockchain can make things more secure. By applying blockchain in supply chain systems, ammunition can be tracked and information like production date, manufacturing location and storage location could be managed and recorded securely in such a way thereby making it hard for the attackers to sniff the data.

Secondly, the proliferation of nuclear weapons along with terrorism and computer technologies increasingly leads to the risk of virtual threats. Blockchain when integrated with nuclear weapon technology can bring about a solution to this problem. This chapter will provide suggestions and techniques to put a stop to the virtual threats through blockchain technology.

In today's world, employment of big armaments and ammunition for wars are outdated strategies to conquer one's nation. Cyberwarfare is the developing trend where every computer under the internet becomes a weapon. So there arises an urge for the government to protect each and every device from the attackers. Cyber-attacks on military systems can affect seriously on weapon systems, disrupt communication routes, and steal confidential data. Military enterprises must do the needful cybersecurity measures which includes firewalls, intrusion detection systems, and encryption protocols to guard against asymmetrical and virtual military attacks (Suresh Babu & Srisakthi, 2023). Cyber hygiene training for employees can also help to reduce the risk of invasions. Defined practises must be created in order to minimise damage and swiftly restore activities following a cyber-attack. As days move by there is an increasing need for military to invoke technologies like artificial intelligence, blockchain technology and internet of things etc. Invocation of blockchain technologies in military programme can build meticulously secure environment.

RATIONALE BACKGROUND

A military system without threats is ideal, but it is unlikely to be achieved due to the constant evolution and adaptation of cyber threats. However, if we make the assumption that a military system is completely immune to cyberattacks, it would look very different from the military systems we currently have. In a system free from cyber threats, military organisations could confidently share and access sensitive information across numerous networks without worrying about unauthorised access or data breaches. This might lead to a more collaborative and successful military where commanders seek for accurate and perfect facts to make wise decisions. Military systems wouldn't need regular cybersecurity updates or ongoing cyberattack monitoring if there were no cyberthreats. This might really free up resources and labour to focus on other fundamental military operations. It's crucial to remember that this perfect situation is unlikely to occur in reality but Military systems need to be created to resist and adapt to cyberthreats since they will never go away. This study provides a more practical methodology can be improved the network safety posture of military frameworks, utilising the most recent innovations and best practises to reduce the risks of digital hazards.

LITERATURE REVIEW

Problem Statement

The rising usage of automated, highly sophisticated, and computerized equipment in the military increases the productivity of the defence system. At the same time, there is an increased risk that this equipment can be hacked or misused. The advancement in technologies has its own pros and cons. Any kind of miserable casualties will impose a severe effect on the nation. Thus, there arises an urge to secure the cyber defence system. Despite attempts to safeguard military systems, it is challenging to remain ahead of possible attacks due to the continuously shifting cybersecurity threat landscape. The blockchain technology has the capability to fundamentally transform how defence systems work, particularly in the sectors of security, logistics, and supply chain management. The decentralization and transparency of blockchain technology may provide a more secure and efficient method for the defence industry to conduct transactions and communicate information. Despite its potential benefits, integrating blockchain technology into military systems is not without challenges. One of the main issues is the demand for compatibility with existing systems and legacy technologies. Additionally, there are security concerns with blockchain technology, particularly with regard to data privacy and cyberattacks (Sudhan & Nene, 2017).

The necessity for strong cryptographic algorithms has grown as a society depends more and more on digital communication and commerce. Elliptic Curve Cryptography (ECC), a contemporary and popular cryptographic technique, has a number of benefits over more established algorithms like RSA and Diffie-Hellman. ECC acceptance does not, however, come without difficulties. The lack of knowledge and education regarding ECC among practitioners is one of the key issues, which has caused its acceptance to be slower than that of other cryptographic methods. Concerns exist regarding ECC's possible weaknesses as well, notably with regard to installation and key management. This type of cryptography promises a faster and a secure way of encryption. The paper claims ECC as a way that is more standardized than other public key encryption algorithms. ECC has gained popularity in recent years due to various factors like speed, security, key size, key distribution, and post-quantum security (Amara & Siad, 2011).

Existing literature mostly focuses on specific security aspects, such as agent authentication or access control, without providing a holistic view of the security landscape for mobile agents. This study aims to provide a comprehensive overview of the current state of knowledge on mobile agent security. The paper covers different security threats, such as confidentiality, integrity, availability, and non-repudiation, and discusses various solutions proposed in the literature to address these threats (Lauter, 2004).

The potential for blockchain technology to completely transform a variety of sectors has captivated a lot of attention in multiple domains in recent years. The implementation of blockchain technology is not without difficulties, though (Suresh Babu & Das, 2023). In particular, there are unresolved issues that must be resolved if blockchain technology is to reach its full potential. The goal of this study is to present a complete review on blockchain technology's challenges and current solutions that could be provided. The article discusses numerous facets of blockchain technology, including its fundamental structure, consensus procedures, and industrial applications. The study also explores several methods put out in the literature to meet open problems, including scalability, interoperability, and security (Khan & Salah, 2017b).

Blockchain technology has emerged as a useful tool for facilitating safe and transparent transactions in a variety of businesses. Despite this, there is still a dearth of knowledge about the fundamental ideas, advantages, and potential drawbacks of blockchain technology (A Critical Review of Concepts, 2020).

Consecutively, the article (Ghimire et al., 2021) Sharding-Enabled Blockchain for Software-Defined Internet of Unmanned Vehicles in the Battlefield researches unmanned i.e. Automated vehicles as it is becoming increasingly prevalent in modern warfare, and there is a growing need for secure and efficient communication and coordination among them. Blockchain technology has emerged as a potential solution to this problem, providing a secure and decentralized platform for communication and data sharing. However, existing blockchain systems are not designed to handle the scale and complexity of communication among unmanned vehicles on the battlefield.

Military applications are particularly suited for consortium blockchain technology in particular since it enables several organisations to work together on a single blockchain network while yet preserving control over their own data. But there isn't much research on the application of consortium blockchain technology for passing military messages (R & Kavitha, 2020).

Blockchain technology has been hypothesised to contribute to the security of IoBT (Internet of battlefield) by providing a decentralized, hacker-proof platform for data transfer and storage. Despite being frequently used for business applications, permissioned blockchain technology's suitability for IoBT security has not been thoroughly investigated. Usability is a critical factor in the acceptance of new technologies since it has a substantial impact on the system's effectiveness, efficiency, and user satisfaction. This article's goal is to evaluate the suitability of permissioned Blockchain for IoBT security (Buenrostro et al., 2019b).

The purpose of the article (Sharikov, 2018) is to investigate the possible dangers that nuclear weapons, cyberattacks, and AI represent. Nuclear weapon systems are progressively integrating artificial intelligence (AI), raising concerns about the possibility of cyberattacks that might jeopardise the safety and security of these weapons. The risk of autonomous decision-making is increased by the employment of AI in nuclear weapon systems, which might accelerate and expand nuclear assaults. Using AI simultaneously opens up additional attack vectors and weaknesses that might be used by bad actors (Sharikov, 2018b).

The current status of blockchain technology is examined, along with its numerous uses in supply chain management, digital identification, voting, and energy management. This study aims to provide a comprehensive survey of the use of blockchain technology in modern applications. The paper reviews the applications of blockchain technology which includes supply chain management, digital identity, voting, and energy management (Krichen, Ammi, Mihoub, & Almutiq, 2022). This paper aims to provide a comprehensive survey of the use of blockchain technology in modern applications. The purpose of this study is to investigate the use of blockchain technology in the development of military strategy from a resource-based view of capabilities. The article explores the advantages of blockchain for the military, including improved security, accountability, and transparency. The report also looks at blockchain technology's drawbacks and restrictions in the military sector, including interoperability, scalability, and legal concerns. The theoretical foundation for examining the possibilities of blockchain in the military arena is the resource-based view on capabilities (Chedrawi & Howayeck, 2018b).

METHOD SECTION

The research on analysis of virtual and asymmetrical military challenges targets to bring about a solution to all the existing problems faced by defence system in using the latest technologies. Many other researches also have been carried out to solve several issues. This process of a literature review entails a methodical and exacting approach to finding, examining, and synthesising pertinent literature on issues in cyber defence systems.

Employability of Blockchain Technology in Defense Applications

This paper deeply analyses the need of blockchain in military applications. Military operations are a wide range of processes starting from key generation, transmission, analysis of mission-critical data, and so on. These processes are done to ensure high level integrity, confidentiality, and application of data. The fundamental ideas of blockchain are taught in-depth along with its variations. The network-enabled military operations (nemo) model is used to simulate military operations that are made possible by networks. A military operation is referred to as a network-enabled operation that uses advanced network technology and communication systems to improve the mission's efficacy. The ability to share information and plan actions in real time gives military units that deploy network-enabled operations (neo) a significant advantage over their opponents. Satellites, communication networks, sensors, and computer systems are just a few of the technology that Neo uses to quickly gather, process, and disseminate information. As a result, military forces can operate more effectively during complicated operations, react swiftly to changing circumstances, and make quicker and better-informed judgments. Another significant advantage of neo is the capacity to have a more distributed command and control structure. Military units are capable of communicating and coordinating their activities without relying on a centralized command (Sudhan & Nene, 2017).

Elliptic curve cryptography and its applications:

This paper mainly aims to give a clear-cut visualization of the algorithm of elliptic curve cryptography. This type of cryptography promises a faster and a secure way of encryption. The paper claims. ECC provides a combination of security, efficiency, and flexibility that makes it a popular choice for a wide range of applications in cryptography. In the modern era, important research is emerging in the field of data security over weakly secured networks. ECC differs from RSA its quicker evolving capacity by providing an alternate way to the cryptographic algorithm (Amara & Siad, 2011).

Blockchain solutions, and open challenges:

The rapid growth of the internet of Things (IoT) has gained a huge demand in society. The article reviews and categorizes the security issues pertaining to the IoT layered architecture, as well as networking protocols, communication, and management, as well as presents and surveys major IoT security issues (Suresh Babu, 2023). Additionally, a summary of the requirements for IoT security, including current threats, attacks, and novel approaches, is provided. According to Khan (2017), IoT security threats take advantage of flaws in a variety of components, including software, physical devices, network components, applications/interfaces, and firmware. In an IoT paradigm, users interact with these parts through protocols that may also have their security measures removed. In order to achieve a particular level of security, the security threats' countermeasures address the vulnerabilities of this interaction at various layers. The paper further overviews the requirement for incorporating blockchain with IoT. Blockchain innovation has been anticipated by business and mainstream researchers to be a troublesome innovation that will essentially affect how IoT gadgets are made due, controlled, and most vitally, got. The part of the exposition that examines blockchain's true capacity as a significant empowering innovation for conveying serviceable security answers for the present complex IoT security issues. IoT security concerns are taxonomized and categorized according to their layering, as well as the solutions employed to mitigate these vulnerabilities. Future paths outlining potential fixes for unresolved IoT security issues are also discussed. The main contributions of the article are a parametric examination of security risks and their correlation with potential IoT solutions (Khan & Salah, 2017b).

A Critical Review of Concepts, Benefits, and Pitfalls of Blockchain Technology Using Concept Map

The design and development of conceptual frameworks to create more dependable, transparent, as well as efficient digital systems was the primary focus of this study article by (Iyolita, Munim, Oishwee, Islam, & Muhammad, 2020). Blockchain has a wide range of advantages, it also has some drawbacks. In order to offer a fair knowledge of blockchain, the goal of this research is to comprehend the features of blockchain, its present usage, recognized advantages, and potential hazards. As a result, this research offers an overview of the most recent research investigations done in the field of blockchain. Additionally, we create a series of idea maps to give a comprehensive understanding of blockchain technology for its effective and effective usage in the development of future technological solutions. The goal of this research is to present a fundamental understanding of blockchain in order to improve its successful application in the creation of the next technological solutions. This research provides a series of concept maps to offer an in-depth description of blockchain, all feasible aspects of blockchain, and the link between the qualities, advantages, and disadvantages of blockchain in order to achieve this goal. This paper shows a precise mapping between the specified advantages, dangers, and usage context (R & Kavitha, 2020).

Sharding-Enabled Blockchain for Software-Defined Internet of Unmanned Vehicles in the Battlefield

This study discusses the advancing technology used in military applications to provide significant strategic advantages in addition to fully automating battlefield operations and surveillance systems. To ensure the success of the mission, all UVs in IoUV collaborate as a coordinated network to exchange information, increasing context awareness, risk assessments, and response times. This article presents a perspective on the coordination of programming characterized IoUV (otherwise called expanded 5g) with blockchain innovation for a tactical situation. For further developed network security and the executives in IoUV, programming characterized IoUV powerfully designs the organization settings and gives network perceivability. Sharding is a course of separating an enormous information base into more modest and easier hubs. A sharding-empowered blockchain is proposed to resolve the issue, where shards of lightweight UVs hold the essential number of excavators/evaluators to handle the difficulties when a digger is obliterated or harmed in fight. Be that as it may, present blockchain innovation isn't adaptable (Ghimire et al., 2021).

Military Message Passing Using Consortium Blockchain Technology

The consortium blockchain technology is suggested on "message passing technology" in the HPBC military communications system. There's a confidential way in which military messages an data are conveyed and transmitted. So there are high chances for the data to be tampered and modified or it can be leaked to the wrong hands. So this paper analyses the current message passing technology in the defence system. To provide a much more secure environment, the military message passing using consortium blockchain technology was suggested by (K.R. & M., 2020) the emerging blockchain technology has a decentralized infrastructure. Almost every industry, including finance, energy, cloud computing, communications, and many more, uses this technology. Military message passing utilises blockchain, which provides message security by preventing alterations to data stored in blocks. A permission-based blockchain is necessary, meaning that each and every user must be authorised. In the present pow algorithm system, distributed consensus is the major problem. In order to increase the precision of CMB measurements by minimising numerous types of noise and systematic errors, the research considers the usage of HPBC methods. The authors suggest many options for increasing precision, including optimising the architecture of CMB sensors, enhancing the methods for processing CMB data, and creating fresh statistical techniques for cosmic parameter estimation (R & Kavitha, 2020).

Evaluating the Usability of Permissioned Blockchain for Internet-of-Battlefield Things Security

The study "fast cosmological parameter estimation from CMB anisotropies with neural networks" puts forth a fresh approach for calculating cosmological parameters utilising measurements of the cosmic microwave background (CMB) and machine learning methods. Based on the CMB data, the authors describe a neural network-based method that can quickly estimate the likelihood of various cosmological parameter values. Numerical simulations and data analysis are traditional techniques for calculating cosmic parameters. Due to the suggested method's speed, broader parameter spaces may be explored and big CMB data sets can be analysed more effectively. The authors demonstrate that, compared to conventional approaches, their neural network methodology can predict cosmological parameters, such as the Hubble constant and the quantity of dark matter, precisely and with a substantially shorter calculation time. The accuracy and speed of parameter estimates in those disciplines might be increased by applying their approach to more cosmological data sets, such as galaxy surveys. In conclusion, the research offers a potential new method for parameter estimation in the area of HDPC, which may assist to speed up the development of our understanding of the universe. In this work, the authors have integrated hyper ledger sawtooth, a permissioned blockchain, into the context of IoBT and assessed its performance to see if it has the ability to meet the performance requirements of the IoBT ecosystem. The metric data would assist in recommending the ideal parameter set, network setup, and blockchain usability perspectives in an IoBT environment using various testing parameters (Buenrostro et al., 2019b).

Artificial Intelligence, Cyberattack, and Nuclear Weapons: A Dangerous Combination

The article examines the analysis and interpretation of geographical patterns in CMB data using hierarchical Bayesian modelling. The authors provide a statistical model that takes into consideration the intricate spatial correlations and noise properties of the CMB data while also permitting the insertion of extraneous data, such as previously acquired cosmic parameter knowledge. The Planck satellite mission data are analyzed using the model, and the outcomes are contrasted with those attained using conventional analytic techniques. The article recommends that the proposed various leveled Bayesian displaying approach could have significant applications in the field of HDPC, especially with regards to enormous scope studies of the CMB. The authors say that the method could make it possible to analyze these data sets in a more effective and precise way, which would help us learn more about the universe's properties and how it has changed over time. Additionally, they suggest that the approach could be utilized with additional spatial data sets, such as those utilized in military applications like satellite imagery analysis (Sharikov, 2018b).

Blockchain for Modern Applications: A Survey

The article discusses the architecture, consensus mechanisms, and future trends of blockchain-based applications. This article titled "a survey of blockchain-based applications: architecture, consensus, and future trends" published in the journal sensors. The authors of the report presented their conclusions after conducting a thorough review of research papers on blockchain-based applications. The article also addresses the potential advantages and difficulties of using blockchain technology in a variety of industries, including banking, healthcare, and supply chain management. Understanding the uses of blockchain is essential since it is a relatively new technology that has the potential to destroy a number of industries and enterprises. Blockchain is a type of digital ledger that may be used to track, confirm, and manage data and transactions. It is decentralised, transparent, and secure. It is possible for individuals and organisations to think about how they may utilise technology to enhance operations, boost transparency and accountability, and improve security and privacy by understanding the numerous uses it has. If investors and entrepreneurs are aware of how blockchain is being used, they may be better able to spot prospective use cases and business prospects. Knowing the blockchain's limitations and difficulties can help guide the creation of more robust and useful blockchain solutions.

This article examines the use of blockchain in great detail, including how it is used in blockchain architecture, financial transactions, healthcare, information systems, wireless networks, the Internet of things, smart grids, government services, and the military and defense (Krichen, Ammi, Mihoub, & Almutiq, 2022).

The Role of Blockchain Technology in Military Strategy Formulation, a Resource Based View on Capabilities

The essay discusses how military strategy may be developed using blockchain technology. The authors the military a unique resource that will help them better their skills and operations. Argue that blockchain technology may provide significant advantages to military organisations by promoting secure and transparent data interchange, bolstering decision-making procedures, and enhancing supply chain management. According to the authors, blockchain technology can provide The authors provide several examples of how blockchain technology may benefit military operations. By creating a secure and transparent record of all transactions, blockchain technology, for instance, may improve supply chain management. As a result, there will be fewer errors, fraud, and corruption will be stopped, and logistical operations will be more effective. Blockchain technology may improve information and data sharing between military agencies by creating a secure and decentralised platform. The central claim of the paper is that blockchain technology has the potential to completely transform military operations by providing a unique set of capabilities. The authors do concede, however, that there are a number of barriers to the military's use of blockchain technology, including the requirement for substantial infrastructure and operations. By creating a secure and transparent record of all transactions, blockchain technology, for instance, may improve supply chain management (Chedrawi & Howayeck, 2018b).

RESULT

This literature review summarises the findings and conclusions drawn from the analysis and synthesis of relevant literature. The results section includes the key findings and themes identified from the literature. Firstly an overview of blockchain in defence applications is mentioned which enhances the force's agility and reactivity, boosting its effectiveness in dynamic, rapidly changing environments. Overall, network-enabled military operations have had a substantial impact on how modern militaries plan and execute their missions. By exploiting cutting-edge network technology and communication systems, military units can operate more effectively, efficiently, and precisely, ultimately achieving their objectives with fewer casualties and less collateral damage. Secondly, The research focuses on expressing the essential concepts behind blockchain technology using concept maps in order to make the greatest use of blockchain in developing technology. A few idea maps are offered, outlining the characteristics, advantages, and drawbacks of blockchain technology. This study also provides a foundational understanding that will make it easier for future academics to incorporate blockchain into the creation of advanced technology solutions. A comprehensive grasp of how the qualities, benefits, and drawbacks relate to one another enables better utilisation of Blockchain. The importance of Blockchain Technology in Military Strategy Development is then discussed. As a result of this analysis, errors can be reduced along with fraud and corruption. Blockchain technology may improve the information and data sharing between military agencies by creating a secure and decentralised platform. However, the development of Blockchain suggests significant growth in any Defence Budget and necessitate the development of a defence strategy based on available resources in order to meet the demands of the changing environment. Then the paper focusses on the challenges on blockchain which concludes by stating that IoT devices are insecure and incapable of defending themselves (khan, 2017). The main causes of this include limited IoT device resources, immature standards, and a lack of secure hardware and software design, development, and implementation.. The variety of IoT resources is also impeding efforts to define a strong worldwide strategy for protecting the IoT layers. Elliptic curve cryptography is an algorithm that is far better and more advanced than other algorithms and helps to keep data safe. The paper summarizes that a secure way of encryption can be achieved by using even smaller keys of ECC and also explains the mechanism of the algorithm. The paper targets to provide the entire concept of elliptic curve cryptography. This concept can be implied in military systems to securely communicate between networks. The next paper that is reviewed is based on securing unmanned vehicles in battlefield. In order to offer IoUV with consistent wireless connectivity, certain participating UVs serve as wireless stations. The suggested structure intends to improve communication between the various units on the battlefield, as well as to strengthen trust and responsibility. To infer, the paper deeply focusses to provides an idea to the build the security of unmanned vehicles (IoT). The performance of an IoBT platform with Blockchain integration depends heavily on the properties of the underlying network, such as topology, connection bandwidth, jitter, and other communication parameters. "Hierarchical Bayesian modelling for spatial analysis of cosmic microwave background data" is the title of an article published in the journal "journal of defense modeling and simulation (Buenrostro et al., 2019b). From another paper which demonstrates the cons of Artificial intelligence, cyberattack, and nuclear weapons, we can conclude that AI, cyberattacks, and nuclear weapons are a dangerous combination, thereby highlighting the need for careful consideration of the potential risks and consequences of advanced technologies in the context of national security. It is important to establish clear guidelines and regulations to ensure that these technologies are used in a responsible and safe manner. Pitfalls of blockchain technology using concept map focuses on presenting the core ideas behind blockchain technology through concept maps for the best possible use of blockchain in advancing technology. In order to characterize blockchain technology in a more systematic approach, including its potential characteristics, projected advantages, and potential hazards, this research is a thorough literature review. A few idea maps are offered, outlining the characteristics, advantages, and drawbacks of blockchain technology. This study also provides a foundational understanding that will make it easier for future academics to incorporate blockchain into the creation of advanced technology solutions. A comprehensive grasp of how the qualities, benefits, and drawbacks relate to one another enables better utilization of blockchain (R & Kavitha, 2020).

METHODOLOGY

Synopsis of Blockchain

Blockchain technology is contemplated as a technology that has created revolution in the transactional relations and even behaviours also. Blockchain is considered to be a transitional, transactional, and transparent mode to exchange blocks of data(information) in such a way that it viable to access by collaborators(stakeholders) in a decentralized manner. This blockchain technology has a major contribution to the global digitalization. The purpose of the bitcoin blockchain was to create a decentralized digital currency that would enable people to deal securely and directly without the use of middlemen like banks or financial institutions. Here the transactions are verified to maintain the anonymity and privacy of users through a process called mining, where the network nodes are completed to solve a mathematical problem and new blocks are added to the blockchain. The creation of blockchain marked a significant milestone in the development of decentralized technologies and set the foundations for other blockchain-based systems. Entrepreneurs started looking for ways to leverage blockchain technology outside of cryptocurrencies. As a result, blockchain-based solutions for several applications, including supply chain management, voting processes, and identity verification, smart contracts, healthcare, logistics, non-fungible tokens(nfts), government, media were created. Developers are working to implement an interoperable blockchain system that can communicate with one another other thereby increasing the greater integration and overall efficiency and security of the technology.

Blockchain is a distributed ledger technology that enables to maintain a secure, tamper proof and a transparent database. Firstly, a transaction is initiated. In order to initiate a transaction, digital signatures are created using their private key and its sent it to the network. The transaction details consist of the public address of sender, public address of recipient and the amount of cryptocurrency being transferred. Consecutively, the transaction is verified. The network's nodes (computers linked to the blockchain) check the transaction to make sure the sender has enough money and that the transaction is valid. The transaction is added to a pool of unconfirmed transactions after it has been validated. Thirdly, the block has to be created. In order to validate the transactions in the pool, miners (special nodes on the network) compete to solve a challenging mathematical challenge. The network certifies the solution that the first miner broadcasted, and it then adds the verified transactions to a new block. Then the block has to be validated. The new block is verified by other miners on the network to make sure the transactions and the solution are genuine. A permanent record of the transaction is made when a block is added to the chain of blocks and determined to be legitimate. Then, the block is propagated and each node updates its version of the blockchain to incorporate the newly added block. This is followed by the consensus mechanism which consists of the full of protocols, rewards and concepts that allows network of nodes to agree on the state of blockchain. Likewise, data or blocks of information can also be transferred securely in military prospectus hen integrated with blockchain technology. There are several models of the network in blockchain. The Merkle tree is the foundation of blockchain technology. It is a form of mathematical data structure that is made up of hashes of multiple data blocks and is used to summarise all the transactions in a block of data. Furthermore, it offers rapid and secure content verification across a large body of data. It also helps to confirm the accuracy and completeness of the data. Bitcoin and Ethereum both use the Merkle trees structure. Merkle tree is also known as hash tree.

Significance of Blockchain

Blockchain technology has emerged as a significant tool for overcoming the digital age's trust and transparency concerns. The distributed nature of the blockchain enables a trust mechanism to be constructed via big data-supported encryption algorithms, enabling intelligent trust-building even in circumstances of knowledge asymmetry. This implies that each node along the chain holds the same information, and all blockchain data is verified, accounted for, stored, maintained, and sent using a distributed methodical framework. One of the most significant advantages of blockchain technology is its resistance to tampering. When data is submitted to the blockchain, it becomes permanent and cannot be erased or changed. The blockchain stores data in a chain of blocks with a timestamp, adding a temporal dimension to data and improving its verifiability and traceability. This resistance to tampering and trackability ensures the integrity of data on the blockchain.

Another important aspect of blockchain is its openness and lack of trust. Blockchains' operating rules and data information are transparent to all nodes, lowering fraud risks and middleman costs and enabling reliable data transfer in an untrustworthy network. The blockchain is also jointly maintained by utilising an economic incentive system to guarantee that all nodes participate in the data block verification process. The consensus process chooses selected nodes to add new blocks to the chain, providing blockchain technology self-maintenance and lowering network operating and maintenance expenses. The programmability of the blockchain enables users to develop powerful smart contracts, currencies, and other decentralised applications. It offers a versatile script code framework that enables users to connect blockchain technology with current technologies and apply it in a variety of scenarios. Finally, to withstand external assaults and prevent data tampering and forging, the blockchain employs asymmetric encryption to encrypt data and consensus processes such as proof-of-work consensus. In comparison to traditional security approaches, blockchain technology provides greater security and indestructibility. Blockchain technology is quickly gaining traction, with potential applications in banking, supply chain management, healthcare, and other fields. Blockchain technology in finance can allow quicker and more secure transactions, removing the need for middlemen, lowering costs, and promoting financial inclusion. Blockchain technology may improve traceability, minimise fraud risks, and increase efficiency in supply chain management. Blockchain technology in healthcare can enable safe exchange of medical information, minimise fraud concerns, and improve privacy (Zhu et al., 2020).

In conclusion, the blockchain technology's distributed nature, tamper-resistance, transparency, collective maintenance, programmability, and security enhancement make it a powerful tool to overcome the challenges of trust and transparency in the digital age. Its adoption is growing rapidly, with potential applications in various sectors. The blockchain technology's benefits include faster and more secure transactions, enhanced traceability, reduced fraud risks, improved efficiency, and secure sharing of medical records. As the technology evolves, its potential applications will continue to expand, bringing greater benefits to society (Zhu et al., 2020).

Problem Statement

Weakened military systems generate a severe impact on the security systems of a nation. The army performs hundreds of operations to secure the nation. Unstable military systems will lead to destruction of peace and stability. A vulnerable cyber defence system can handicap the entire nation. The military database holds various sensitive information starting from personnel records, operational data, equipment information, logistics data, training and educational data to highly confidential details regarding nuclear forces.

Information is essential in the military industry. Storage and handling of these information play a vital part in the in the military systems. Data interception issues like data manipulation for information warfare, tampering with crucial data. Data modification in the military refers to unauthorized changes to sensitive military data, which can have serious consequences. Here are some of the data modification issues that can occur in the military:

- Tampering with military's crucial data: if sensitive military data is modified, it can jeopardize mission success. Tampering is one of the worst security breaches. Even a change in the coordinates of the data can lead to casualties.
- Data manipulation for information warfare: adversaries may modify military data to spread disinformation and manipulate public opinion. This can be a form of information warfare, which can undermine trust in military operations and decision-making.
- Data manipulation for cyberattacks: adversaries may modify military data to launch cyberattacks against military systems and networks. For example, they could modify data to exploit vulnerabilities in military software or hardware.
- Insider threats: insider threats refer to the risks posed by authorized personnel, including military personnel, contractors, and third-party vendors who may have access to sensitive military data. These insiders can modify military data for personal gain or as part of an insider attack.

To mitigate the risks of data modification, the military must implement strong access controls, data encryption, and monitoring systems to identify and prevent unauthorized changes to sensitive military data. Additionally, the military should conduct regular security assessments and training for personnel to ensure they are aware of the risks of data modification and how to prevent it. Secondly, authorization and authentication issues may lead to providing access to unauthorized person and denying access to authorized person. The inability to give access to an authorized user is called an access control failure or access denial. This can occur for various reasons, such as incorrect authentication credentials, system errors, network connectivity issues, or intentional access control policies. Access control failure can be a serious security concern, as it can prevent legitimate users from accessing the resources they need while allowing unauthorized users to gain access to confidential information or systems. To prevent access control failure, it is important to implement robust authentication and authorization mechanisms, monitor system logs for suspicious activity, and regularly review and update access control policies. Authorization issues in military security refer to situations where individuals are granted access to information, systems, or resources beyond their clearance level or scope of responsibility. Such issues can arise due to errors in the authorization process or intentional breaches of security protocols by insiders.

In the military context, authorization issues can have serious consequences, as they can compromise sensitive information and disrupt operations. For example, unauthorized access to classified information could lead to leaks or espionage, while unauthorized access to military equipment could result in theft. To prevent authorization issues, the military employs restrict the access control policies and procedures that are created to ensure that only authorized individuals are granted access to sensitive information, systems, or resources. These policies and procedures include background checks, security clearance processes, access control lists, and identity management systems.

In addition to these technical measures, the military also conducts consistent security awareness training for personnel to teach them about the importance of security protocols and the risks of unauthorized access. It is also essential to have a system of monitoring and auditing to detect and respond to any suspicious activities.

Overall, authorization issues in military security pose a significant threat to national security and must be addressed through a combination of technical controls, training, and monitoring.

Effects of Artificial Intelligence on Military

Depending on how things are used and sent, simulated intelligence can be both a danger and a resource for the military. The military might be placed in risk by computer-based intelligence in the accompanying ways:

1. **Cybersecurity:** Cyberattacks become almost certain as the foundation and military activities become more reliant upon computerized innovation. Malware and hacking instruments in view of man-made brainpower could be utilized to break into military organizations and stop tasks.
2. **Autonomous weapons:** Without the assistance of a human operator, it is possible to program AI-powered weapons systems to make decisions about targets and engagement on their own. This raises moral concerns regarding the possibility of accidental or deliberate harm to common people or non-warriors.
3. **Failure to withstand man-made intelligence attacks:** AI can be used to launch cyberattacks as well as defend against them. However, if an adversary has access to an artificial intelligence framework, they may actually use it to launch their own attacks or disrupt military operations.
4. **Blunder and predisposition:** Computer-based intelligence frameworks are only as objective and accurate as the data they are based on. If biased or inaccurate data is used to train an ai system, it may make poor decisions that could hurt military operations.
5. **Changing careers:** As AI technology advances, it may eventually replace human soldiers in certain roles, which could lead to job losses and social unrest.

Blockchain With Elliptic Curve Cryptography

The combination of blockchain technology and elliptic curve cryptography (ECC) can have significant applications in the military sector. For logging and tracking military assets and transactions, blockchain technology can offer a safe and open system. A tamper-proof record of their exchanges and secure communication amongst military members are further benefits.

Figure 1. Applications of AI in defence

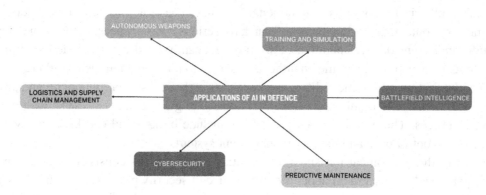

Public key cryptography of the elliptic curve variety offers more security with smaller key sizes than other encryption techniques. It may be used to encrypt sensitive data, authenticate users, and protect conversations. In the military, the combination of blockchain and ECC can be used for secure communication, data encryption, and secure storage of sensitive information. It can also be used to authenticate military personnel and provide secure access to restricted areas and equipment. Furthermore, blockchain can be used to create secure supply chains for military equipment, ensuring that all components and materials are tracked and verified for authenticity. This can help to prevent counterfeit equipment from entering military supply chains and ensure the safety of military personnel.

Overall, the combination of blockchain and ECC can provide significant benefits in terms of security, transparency, and efficiency in military operations. However, it is essential to note that the execution of these technologies requires careful consideration of their potential risks and limitations, particularly in terms of scalability and usability in a military context.

Elliptic Curve Cryptography (ECC)

ECC is a compliant cryptographic approach for use in a variety of sectors and applications since it has received approval from several regulatory agencies, including as NIST, ISO, and ETSI. Future predictions indicate that ECC will become much more common as technology develops.

Algorithm

Elliptic curve cryptography (ECC) is a public key cryptography technique that is used for secure communication over the internet. The algorithm used in ECC involves the following steps:

- Key pair generation: Creating a public-private key pair is the first stage in the key pair generating process. While the user keeps the private key a secret, others can access the public key.
- Elliptic curve parameter selection: The user must choose an elliptic curve that fulfils a number of mathematical requirements, including the curve's non-singularity and high prime order.
- Key agreement: When two users wish to communicate securely, they exchange public keys and use those keys to run the elliptic curve method to compute a shared secret. Then, messages are encrypted and decrypted using the shared secret.

- Encryption and decryption: To encrypt a communication, the sender creates a ciphertext by using the shared secret and the recipient's public key. The recipient uses the shared secret and their private key to decode the message in order to retrieve the plaintext message.
- ECC is also a viable option for digital signatures. The recipient validates the signature using the sender's public key and the message after the sender signs it with their private key.

ECC has several advantages over other public key cryptography techniques, such as RSA. ECC provides the same level of security as RSA, but with much smaller key sizes, making it faster and more efficient. Additionally, ECC is resistant to quantum computing attacks, which are a threat to many other cryptography techniques. One of the main advantages of ECC over other public-key cryptosystems is that it offers the same level of security with smaller key sizes. This makes it particularly attractive in military applications where size, weight, and power constraints are critical considerations. Additionally, ECC is resistant to attacks from quantum computers, which makes it an attractive option for military applications where long-term security is a concern (Yadav, 2021).

ECC has been implemented in a variety of military systems, including secure communication systems for ground and airborne platforms, secure data transfer systems for unmanned aerial vehicles (UAVs), and secure network protocols for battlefield communication systems.

Overall, ECC has proven to be a reliable and secure method for military applications, providing strong encryption and efficient computation, making it an ideal solution for secure communication and data transfer in the military domain.

Internet of Things (IoT)

The internet of things (IoT) is a network of physical objects, gadgets, automobiles, buildings, and other items that are outfitted with sensors, software, and network connectivity to collect and exchange data. The Internet of Things (IoT) allows devices to communicate with one another and with other systems, ushering in new levels of automation, efficiency, and convenience. IoT has the potential to transform

Figure 2. Elliptic curve cryptography

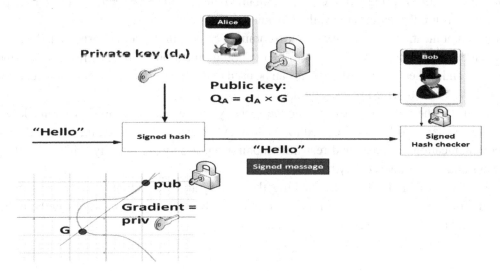

many aspects of our life, including smart cities and homes, healthcare, and industrial automation. Connecting equipment to the internet allows for remote monitoring and control, which increases production, reduces costs, and improves safety.

For instance, IoT-enabled sensors may be used to track the temperature and humidity of crops, assisting farmers in optimising their yields. IoT devices can also be used in the healthcare industry to track patients' health condition and notify medical professionals of any anomalies. The expanding usage of IoT, however, also prompts worries about security and privacy. A danger of unauthorised access, hacking, and data breaches exists as more and more devices are connected to the internet. Furthermore, the enormous amounts of data produced by IOT devices may be used for surveillance or other illegal activities (Suresh Babu & Yadavamuthiah, 2023).

IoT designers and producers must prioritise security and privacy in their plans and include strong encryption and authentication protocols in order to allay these worries. Additionally, consumers must be aware of the dangers posed by IoT devices and take precautions to protect their devices and data.

Overall, the internet of things has the potential to change how we live and work, but in order to ensure its safe and ethical usage, it is crucial to address security and privacy issues.

Blockchain Integration With IoT

IoT and blockchain are two potent technologies that may be used in military applications to improve efficiency, dependability, and security. The following are a few ways that blockchain and IoT can be applied to the military:

Supply chain management: To move and distribute supplies and equipment, the military employs a sophisticated supply network. In order to make sure that the correct materials are delivered to the right location at the right time, blockchain and IoT may be used to track the movement of commodities and equipment in real time. IoT sensors may gather information on the location, temperature, and state of a product, and blockchain technology can safely store and distribute this information.

Asset management: the military has a large number of assets, such as vehicles, aircraft, and weapons, that need to be tracked and maintained. Blockchain and IoT can be used to monitor the condition and usage of these assets, ensuring that they are maintained and repaired as needed. This can help reduce downtime and ensure that assets are available when needed.

Secure communication: the military needs to communicate securely, both internally and with external partners. Blockchain and IoT can be used to secure communication channels, ensuring that messages are encrypted and authenticated. IoT sensors can be used to monitor communication channels and detect any anomalies or unauthorized access attempts.

Cybersecurity: the military faces many cybersecurity challenges, including cyberattacks and data breaches. Blockchain and IoT can be used to enhance cybersecurity, by providing secure data storage, secure communication channels, and real-time monitoring of network activity. This can help prevent cyberattacks and detect any security breaches.

Overall, blockchain and IoT can be used together in military applications to enhance security, reliability, and efficiency. As these technologies continue to advance, their applications in the military are likely to expand and become even more sophisticated.

Securing Unmanned and Automated Vehicles Used in Battlefield (Ghimire et al., 2021)

The defence system's security of automated unmanned vehicles is a major concern because of the potential dangers posed by cyberattacks or other forms of unauthorized access. These vehicles can be made to be more secure in the following ways:

- **Encryption:** Encryption is the process of encoding data so that only authorized parties can read it. Encrypting data transmissions between unmanned vehicles and other defence network systems can significantly reduce the risk of interceptions and unauthorized access.
- **Control of Access:** Automated vehicles can be confined in access through access control components, guaranteeing that the main approved people approach the vehicle's information and frameworks. This can be done with strong authentication methods like biometric or multi-factor authentication (Suresh Babu, 2023).
- **Deployment of Firewalls:** Firewalls can prevent unmanned vehicles from gaining access to external networks. By deploying firewalls at the network's perimeter, the system can monitor and filter incoming traffic and prevent unauthorized access to the unmanned vehicle's system.
- **Intruder detection systems (IDS):** Using IDS systems, any attempts at unauthorized access or unusual system activity can be detected and reported to the operators. Cyberattacks can be avoided and the unmanned vehicle's system is protected by this.
- **Consistent maintenance and patching:** The unmanned vehicle's software and systems can be patched and maintained frequently to prevent vulnerabilities that could be exploited by cybercriminals. It is essential to regularly update the product and make repairs in order to maintain the security of the automated vehicle's frameworks.
- **Actual Insurance:** Unmanned vehicles can be physically secured with the help of access controls, monitoring cameras, and secure storage facilities. Physical security measures can reduce physical threats like theft or sabotage as well as unauthorized access to vehicles.

In most cases, including computerized automated vehicles in the security framework is essential for maintaining the security and sufficiency of military operations. By executing the recently referenced security frameworks, the bet of unapproved access and computerized attacks can be restricted, ensuring that robotized vehicles stay a safeguarded and strong asset for military undertakings.

CONCLUSION

A nation's national interests, including its residents, framework, and regional honesty, are shielded by its tactical security. Protecting a nation's sovereignty and territorial integrity from external threats like hostile foreign powers, terrorist organizations, and cyberattacks is the responsibility of the military.

Additionally, military security is required for global peace and stability. Through diplomatic and military efforts, nations can prevent aggression and promote peaceful conflict resolution. Because it makes it safe for businesses to operate and for trade to take place, military security also helps the economy grow. Without military protection, a nation's population and economy could suffer significantly from external threats. Subsequently, military security should be given main concern as a component of a bigger system for public safety. This chapter analyses the virtual and asymmetrical military challenges faced by a nation and provides new suggestions along with detailed review of existing methodologies to build a secure military system.

FUTURE SCOPE

Future scope of this chapter may involve in providing security measures for space-based technologies such as satellites and space-based sensors, to support and real-time intelligence for the ground operations Future military technology is anticipated to be characterised by increased automation, accuracy, and speed, with a focus on enhancing the efficacy and efficiency of military operations. To ensure that these technologies are applied ethically and in conformity with international law, however, is extremely essential.

REFERENCES

A Critical Review of Concepts, Benefits, and Pitfalls of Blockchain Technology Using Concept Map. (2020). *IEEE Journals & Magazine.* Https://ieeexplore.ieee.org/document/9056816

Amara, M., & Siad, A. (2011). Elliptic Curve Cryptography and its applications. *International Workshop on Systems, Signal Processing and their Applications.* 10.1109/WOSSPA.2011.5931464

Aste, T., Tasca, P., & Di Matteo, T. (2017). Blockchain technologies: the foreseeable impact on society and industry. *IEEE Computer, 50*(9), 18–28. doi:10.1109/MC.2017.3571064

Asvija, B., Eswari, R., & Bijoy, M. B. (2021). Security Threat Modelling With Bayesian Networks and Sensitivity Analysis for IAAS Virtualization Stack. *Journal of Organizational and End User Computing, 33*(4), 44–69. doi:10.4018/JOEUC.20210701.oa3

Bond, J. A. (1996). *Peacetime foreign data manipulation as one aspect of offensive information warfare: Questions of legality under the united nations charter article.* doi:10.21236/ADA310926

Buenrostro, E., Rivera, A. O. G., Tosh, D. K., Acosta, J. C., & Njilla, L. (2019b). Evaluating Usability of Permissioned Blockchain for Internet-of-Battlefield Things Security. Military Communications Conference. doi:10.1109/MILCOM47813.2019.9020736

Chedrawi, C., & Howayeck, P. (2018). The role of blockchain technology in military strategy formulation, a resource based view on capabilities. *Researchgate.* Https://www.researchgate.net/publication/330346994

Eswaran, P., Gray, J. N., Lorie, R. A., & Traiger, I. L. (1976). The notions of consistency and predicate locks in a database system. *Communications of the ACM, 19*(11), 624–633. doi:10.1145/360363.360369

Ghimire, B. K., Rawat, D. B., Liu, C., & Li, J. (2021). Sharding-Enabled Blockchain for Software-Defined Internet of Unmanned Vehicles in the Battlefield. *IEEE Network, 35*(1), 101–107. doi:10.1109/MNET.011.2000214

Jafari, S., Vo-Huu, T. D., Jabiyev, B., Mera, A., & Farkhani, R. M. (2018). Cryptocurrency: A challenge to legal system. *Social Science Research Network*. doi:10.2139/ssrn.3172489

Johnsen, T., Zieliński, Z., Wrona, K., Suri, N., Fuchs, C., Pradhan, M., Furtak, J., Vasilache, B., Pellegrini, V., Dyk, M., Marks, M., & Krzyszton, M. (2018). Application of IoT in military operations in a smart city. In Military Communications and Information Systems Conference. doi:10.1109/ICMCIS.2018.8398690

Kamara, S., & Lauter, K. E. (2010). Cryptographic cloud storage. In *Springer ebooks* (pp. 136–149). Springer nature. doi:10.1007/978-3-642-14992-4_13

Khan, M. A., & Salah, K. (2017b). IoT security: Review, blockchain solutions, and open challenges. *Future Generation Computer Systems, 82*, 395–411. doi:10.1016/j.future.2017.11.022

Kitchin, R., & Dodge, M. (2019). The (in)security of smart cities: vulnerabilities, risks, mitigation, and prevention. *Journal of Urban Technology, 26*(2), 47–65. doi:10.1080/10630732.2017.1408002

Krichen, M., Ammi, M., Mihoub, A., & Almutiq, M. (2022). Blockchain for Modern Applications: A Survey. *Sensors (Basel), 22*(14), 5274. doi:10.339022145274 PMID:35890953

Lauter, E. (2004). The advantages of elliptic curve cryptography for wireless security. *IEEE Wireless Communications, 11*(1), 62–67. doi:10.1109/MWC.2004.1269719

Maftei, A., Lavric, A., Petrariu, A., & Popa, V. (2023). Massive Data Storage Solution for IoT Devices Using Blockchain Technologies. *Sensors (Basel), 23*(3), 1570. doi:10.339023031570 PMID:36772609

Mcabee, A., Tummala, M., & Mceachen, J. (2019). Military intelligence applications for blockchain technology. In *Proceedings of the . . . Annual hawaii international conference on system sciences*. doi:10.24251/HICSS.2019.726

Miloslavskaya, N., & Tolstoy, A. (2019). Internet of things: information security challenges and solutions. *Cluster Computing, 22*(1), 103–119. doi:10.1007/s10586-018-2823-6

R, K. B., & Kavitha, M. (2020). Military Message Passing using Consortium Blockchain Technology. In *International Conference on Communication and Electronics Systems*. doi:10.1109/ICCES48766.2020.9138014

Rid, T. (2012). Cyber war will not take place. *Journal of Strategic Studies, 35*(1), 5–32. doi:10.1080/0 1402390 2011 608939

Shaikh, J., Nenova, M., Iliev, G., & Valkova-Jarvis, Z. (2017). Analysis of standard elliptic curves for the implementation of elliptic curve cryptography in resource-constrained e-commerce applications. In *2017 IEEE International Conference on Microwaves, Antennas, Communications and Electronic Systems (COMCAS)*. doi:10.1109/COMCAS.2017.8244805

Sharikov, P. A. (2018b). Artificial intelligence, cyberattack, and nuclear weapons—A dangerous combination. *Bulletin of the Atomic Scientists, 74*(6), 368–373. doi:10.1080/00963402.2018.1533185

Srinivas, J., Das, A., & Vasilakos, A. V. (2020). Designing secure lightweight blockchain-enabled rfid-based authentication protocol for supply chains in 5g mobile edge computing environment. *IEEE Transactions on Industrial Informatics, 16*(11), 7081–7093. doi:10.1109/TII.2019.2942389

Sudhan, A., & Nene, M. J. (2017). Employability of blockchain technology in defence applications. In *International Conference Intelligent Sustainable Systems*. 10.1109/ISS1.2017.8389247

Suresh Babu, C.V. (2023). IoT and its Applications. Anniyappa Publications.

Suresh Babu, C. V., Akshayah, N. S., et al. R. (2023). IoT-Based Smart Accident Detection and Alert System. In P. Swarnalatha & S. Prabu (Eds.), Handbook of Research on Deep Learning Techniques for Cloud-Based Industrial IoT (pp. 322-337). IGI Global. https://doi.org/10.4018/978-1-6684-8098-4.ch019

Suresh Babu, C. V. & Das, S. (2023). Impact of Blockchain Technology on the Stock Market. In K. Mehta, R. Sharma, & P. Yu (Eds.), Revolutionizing Financial Services and Markets Through FinTech and Blockchain (pp. 44-59). IGI Global. https://doi.org/10.4018/978-1-6684-8624-5.ch004

Suresh Babu, C. V. & Srisakthi, S. (2023). Cyber Physical Systems and Network Security: The Present Scenarios and Its Applications. In R. Thanigaivelan, S. Kaliappan, & C. Jegadheesan (Eds.), Cyber-Physical Systems and Supporting Technologies for Industrial Automation (pp. 104-130). IGI Global. https://doi.org/10.4018/978-1-6684-9267-3.ch006

Suresh Babu, C. V. & Yadavamuthiah, K. (2023). Precision Agriculture and Farming Using Cyber-Physical Systems: A Systematic Study. In G. Karthick (Ed.), Contemporary Developments in Agricultural Cyber-Physical Systems (pp. 184-203). IGI Global. https://doi.org/10.4018/978-1-6684-7879-0.ch010

Transformations Through Blockchain Technology. (2022). In *Springer eBooks*. doi:10.1007/978-3-030-93344-9

Yadav, A. (2021). Significance of elliptic curve cryptography in blockchain IoT with comparative analysis of RSA algorithm. In *2021 international conference on computing, communication, and intelligent systems (icccis)*. doi:10.1109/ICCCIS51004.2021.9397166

Zheng, Z., Xie, S., Dai, H., Chen, X., & Wang, H. (2017). An overview of blockchain technology: architecture, consensus, and future trends. In *International congress on big data*. doi:10.1109/BigDataCongress.2017.85

Zhu, S., Zhang, X., Ju, Z. Y., & Wang, C. C. (2020, April 1). A study of blockchain technology development and military application prospects. *Journal of Physics: Conference Series*, *1507*(5), 052018. Advance online publication. doi:10.1088/1742-6596/1507/5/052018

Chapter 5
Framework for Detection of Cyberbullying in Text Data Using Natural Language Processing and Machine Learning

C. V. Suresh Babu
https://orcid.org/0000-0002-8474-2882
Hindustan Institute of Technology and Science, India

S. Kowsika
https://orcid.org/0009-0000-7095-8992
Hindustan Institute of Technology and Science, India

M. Sai Tejaswi
Hindustan Institute of Technology and Science, India

T. R. Janarakshani
Hindustan Institute of Technology and Science, India

S. Mercysha Princy
Hindustan Institute of Technology and Science, India

ABSTRACT

Cyberbullying is a huge problem online that affects young people and adults. It can lead to accidents like suicide and depression. There is a growing need to curate content on social media platforms. In the following study, the authors used data on two different forms of cyberbullying, hate speech tweets on Twitter, and ad hominem-based comments on Wikipedia forums. The authors use machine learning-based natural language processing and textual data to build models based on cyberbullying detection. They study three feature extraction methods and their four classifiers to determine the best method. The model achieves an accuracy of more than 90 degrees on the tweet data and more than 80 degrees on the Wikipedia data.

DOI: 10.4018/978-1-6684-8846-1.ch005

1. INTRODUCTION

Cyberbullying is a type of bullying or harassment that occurs through digital platforms, particularly social media. Cyberbullying manifests in different forms such as sharing or spreading derogatory and hurtful messages, images or videos, spreading rumors, making threats and so on. Social media has given rise to cyberbullying as it provides anonymity to cyberbullies, enabling them to reach a larger audience with their harmful messages.

Identifying cyberbullying on social media is essential to prevent and address the negative impact it can have on victims. While traditional bullying often takes place in person and can be observed by others, cyberbullying takes place in a virtual world and can be more difficult to detect. However, there are some methods you can use to identify and deal with cyberbullying on social media.

One method for identifying cyberbullying via virtual entertainment is through computerized apparatuses that dissect client produced content like posts, remarks, and messages. Patterns of malicious behavior, such as harassing or threatening messages, can be identified using these tools, which make use of machine learning and natural language processing algorithms. Such apparatuses can hail dangerous substance for additional consideration by human mediators or policemen.

Another way is to encourage viewers to report cyberbullying when they see it. Social media platforms may offer reporting features that allow users to report harmful content or behavior for review. Reporting mechanisms are essential tools for detecting cyberbullying that otherwise goes unnoticed. Some platforms also have features that allow users to block or mute other users. This is useful for cyberbullying victims who want to avoid exposure to even more harmful content.

Additionally, educators and parents can play a role in detecting cyberbullying by monitoring children's social media activities and looking for signs of bullying, such as: B. Changes in behavior or mood, withdrawal from social activities, or unwillingness to go to school. It is important for parents and educators to speak openly to children about cyberbullying and to provide resources and support when they are being bullied.

In summary, awareness of cyberbullying on social media is an essential part of preventing and combating the negative effects of cyberbullying. Through the use of automated tools, reporting mechanisms, and personal oversight, we can work together to create a safer and more positive online environment for all of our users.

2. LITERATURE REVIEW

2.1. Define the Problem

Addresses several key issues related to cyberbullying, including its definition, prevalence, and harmful effects on individuals' mental health and well-being. Cyberbullying is a form of online harassment that involves various behaviors such as spreading rumors, threats, and harassment. As technology and social media use have become more prevalent, cyberbullying has become a pervasive problem with serious consequences, including anxiety, depression, and even suicide. One approach to predicting cyberbullying in social media involves using machine learning techniques to identify posts, messages, or comments that contain content that could be considered cyberbullying. The overall accuracy and robustness of the model can be enhanced by employing an ensemble learning strategy, which entails training multiple machine learning models on distinct subsets of data and combining their predictions. In order to protect users and prevent online harassment, it is crucial to develop a model that can accurately identify instances of cyberbullying.

Another critical issue related to cyberbullying is its prevention. A systematic review of cyberbullying prevention programs is a rigorous research methodology that involves identifying, evaluating, and synthesizing existing literature on intervention frameworks used to prevent cyberbullying. This review aims to assess the effectiveness of different interventions and identify gaps in current research that may help inform future interventions and strategies. Understanding the causes and effects of online harassment is also crucial to developing effective strategies to prevent and mitigate its harmful effects. The issue of the influence of social norms and personal beliefs on young people's cyberbullying behavior is a complex issue that requires a multifaceted approach to understand and address.

Cyberbullying in the workplace is another issue with serious negative consequences for individuals and organizations. Some strategies for addressing this issue include developing clear policies and guidelines for online behavior, offering training and education for employees and managers, creating a supportive and inclusive work culture, and implementing technology solutions to monitor and prevent cyberbullying.

The paragraph also highlights several studies that address different aspects of cyberbullying, including cultural factors that may contribute to cyberbullying perpetration and victimization among adolescents, the relationship between perceived parenting styles and adolescent cyberbullying behaviors, and the impact of cyberbullying on mental health among college students.

Overall, the paragraph emphasizes the importance of addressing cyberbullying through a comprehensive and proactive approach, including developing effective prevention strategies, understanding the underlying causes and consequences of cyberbullying, and implementing technology solutions to monitor and prevent online harassment (Hasan & Shah, 2020).

2.2. Literature Searing

The prevalence and impact of cyberbullying have become a growing concern in recent years, particularly among young people. As a result, there has been a significant increase in research on cyberbullying prevention and intervention strategies. One approach that has gained attention is the use of ensemble learning models, which can effectively detect cyberbullying behavior in online communication. Ensemble models have been found to achieve higher accuracy than single models and can handle imbalanced data sets commonly found in predictive cyberbullying tasks. Ensemble learning has been used with machine learning algorithms like Random Forest, Gradient Boosting, and Stacking. Combining these models with feature selection and data augmentation can make them even better.

In addition to the detection and prevention of cyberbullying, research has also explored the broader impact of online harassment and cyberbullying on individuals, particularly young people. A comprehensive literature review of this topic requires a systematic search of relevant databases, such as PubMed, Web of Science, and Scopus, using appropriate keywords and search terms. Inclusion and exclusion criteria are applied to identified studies, and the search process is documented and reported according to PRISMA guidelines to ensure transparency and reproducibility.

Other areas of research on cyberbullying include the influence of social norms and personal beliefs on youth behavior, organizational culture and productivity, and the relationship between cyberbullying and mental health among college students. Literature searches for these topics involve searching relevant databases and journals using appropriate keywords, analyzing the methodology, results, and limitations of identified studies, and synthesizing the findings. Overall, the literature on cyberbullying suggests the need for effective prevention and intervention strategies, particularly given the rapid development of technology and social media platforms. More research is needed to fully understand the complex nature of this issue and to develop evidence-based approaches to addressing it (Thomas et al., 2020).

2.3. Summaries

Cyberbullying is a growing concern in today's society, particularly among young people who are increasingly reliant on digital technology and social media platforms. The ease of anonymity offered by these platforms makes it easier for individuals to engage in online harassment, intimidation, and rumor spreading. This behavior can have serious negative consequences, including anxiety, depression, and even suicide. The impact of cyberbullying is not limited to young people, as it also affects individuals in the workplace. To combat cyberbullying, researchers have explored various prevention and intervention strategies. Using ensemble learning methods to predict cyberbullying behaviors is one such strategy. Group learning includes preparing numerous AI models on various subsets of information and consolidating their forecasts to work on the general precision and heartiness of the models. It has been demonstrated through research that ensemble learning techniques are capable of accurately identifying cyberbullying behaviors, handling imbalanced datasets, and outperforming single models.

The literature on cyberbullying prevention intervention frameworks shows that combining ensemble models with other techniques such as feature selection and data augmentation can further improve the performance of cyberbullying detection models. This evidence-based approach can help identify gaps in current research and inform future interventions and strategies to address the problem of cyberbullying.

However, the field of predicting social media cyberbullying using machine learning algorithms still faces various limitations and ethical concerns, including bias and privacy issues that require further research and development. Additionally, the negative impact of cyberbullying on victims' mental health and academic performance is significant. Interventions and prevention strategies are needed to address this problem and raise awareness of the possible long-term consequences for both victims and perpetrators. The impact of cultural values, norms, and beliefs on online behavior has also been explored, with research showing potential differences in cyberbullying rates between different cultural groups. Parenting practices have also been shown to influence young people's moral thinking and online behavior, highlighting the need for informed interventions to prevent and combat cyberbullying.

Victimization of cyberbullying can be difficult for young people to self-report for fear of being targeted. However, research suggests that online communication patterns and personal/environmental factors influence victimization. Cyberbullying can have negative consequences such as social isolation and psychological distress, highlighting the need for interventions to support affected youth. Regulation of education, support systems, and social media platforms is needed to address the negative impact of cyberbullying on adolescent mental health. The dark side of social media is that it can negatively impact mental health, particularly with the rise of cyberbullying. The use of social media platforms where cyberbullying is common has been shown to have far-reaching effects on the psychological well-being of victims.

Overall, addressing the problem of cyberbullying requires a multi-pronged approach that includes awareness, prevention, and intervention strategies. The emergence of new forms of bullying online and facilitated by technology highlights the need for a multi-faceted approach involving parents, schools, and technology companies. This approach must be informed by evidence-based research and data-driven techniques such as ensemble learning to effectively combat cyberbullying and protect young people from its negative consequences (Wu et al., 2020).

2.4. Define the Argument

The issue of cyberbullying is a serious problem affecting individuals of all ages, but especially young people. The ease of anonymity offered by digital technology and social media platforms has made it easier for individuals to engage in online harassment, leading to negative psychological effects and a decline in productivity and social connection. Cyberbullying prevention programs have been argued to be important in promoting a safe and healthy online environment for all.

One effective approach to predicting cyberbullying in social media is the use of ensemble learning techniques. Ensemble learning models can effectively combine the strengths of multiple machine learning models and reduce their weaknesses, thus improving prediction accuracy. Additionally, tasks designed to predict cyberbullying often involve imbalanced datasets, in which positive cases (cyberbullying cases) are rare compared to negative cases. Ensemble learning models can deal with such imbalances and minimize false positives.

To develop effective measures to prevent online harassment and protect social media users, cyberbullying prevention programs have been designed. These programs aim to identify effective strategies to prevent, mitigate, and mitigate the harm caused by cyberbullying. By using a systematic and evidence-based approach, effective interventions can be identified and implemented to reduce the prevalence and impact of cyberbullying. Harmful social norms and personal beliefs help perpetuate cyberbullying and online harassment, but interventions that challenge these attitudes and promote positive values can help reduce their prevalence. Cultural factors may also play a significant role in cyberbullying perpetration and victim (Kohn et al., 2020).

2.5. Detailed Argument

The thorough justification for employing ensemble learning techniques to anticipate cyberbullying on social media includes a number of elements. First off, cyberbullying and online harassment are serious problems that have a negative impact on both individuals and communities. For the safety and wellbeing of social media users, it is essential to accurately recognize and prohibit such conduct. It has been demonstrated that using ensemble learning models, numerous machine learning algorithms can be combined to produce predictions that are more accurate than those made using individual models. This is crucial in cyberbullying prediction problems because they frequently include unbalanced datasets with few positive occurrences. Such imbalances can be managed, and false positives can be reduced, through ensemble learning models. Moreover, combining ensemble models with other methods like feature selection and data augmentation might enhance the effectiveness of cyberbullying detection (Sahin, 2020).

2.6. Drafting

There are various processes involved in creating a prediction model for cyberbullying on social media using ensemble learning techniques. The dataset must first be gathered and preprocessed, which involves data cleaning and labelling. A training set, a validation set, and a testing set are created from the dataset. To generate distinct models, several machine learning algorithms are then trained on various subsets of the training data. The final prediction model is created by combining several models using ensemble learning strategies like bagging or boosting. Metrics including accuracy, precision, recall, and F1-score are used to assess the model's performance. Techniques for feature selection and data augmentation can be used to enhance the performance of the model. In order to forecast instances of cyberbullying in social media postings, messages, and other content, the final model is then applied (Jones et al., 2021).

2.7. Communicate the Findings

Cyberbullying, online harassment, and self-disclosure are just a few of the many factors that need to be taken into account when assessing the impact of social media on mental health. This is a complicated issue. Communication of research findings should emphasize the negative impact of cyberbullying on mental health and the need for effective prevention and intervention strategies. Machine learning algorithms can predict cyberbullying on social media, improving the safety of online communities. Effective cyberbullying prevention programs should incorporate a combination of methods, including education, support, and intervention, to reduce the prevalence of cyberbullying. The relationship between online harassment and cyberbullying requires effective prevention and intervention strategies to address these issues (Suresh Babu & Srisakthi, 2023).

Culturally sensitive interventions are required to prevent and address cyberbullying among young people from diverse cultural backgrounds because cultural factors play a significant role in its perpetration and victimization. The perceived parenting styles of adolescents can have a significant impact on their moral standards and online behavior, leading to cyberbullying and victimization. Effective communication of research findings can raise awareness and promote action to prevent cyberbullying and protect the mental health of adolescents (Stylianou et al., 2021).

3. REQUIREMENT ANALYSIS

3.1. Data Collection

The first requirement is to gather a lot of information about cyberbullying. This can be accomplished by extracting personal attack comments from Wikipedia forums and hate speech tweets from Twitter using scraping tools.

3.2. Data Preprocessing

Once the data is collected, it needs to be preprocessed to remove unnecessary information, such as stop words, punctuations, and special characters. The data needs to be converted into a standardized format suitable for analysis.

3.3. Feature Extraction

The process of selecting the most relevant cyberbullying features from textual data is called feature extraction. Bag of Words (BoW), Frequency Inverted Document Frequency (TF-IDF) and Word Embeddings are the three feature extraction options.

3.4. Machine Learning Algorithm

Selecting a machine learning algorithm that accurately classifies the text data is the next step. To determine the most effective strategy, four classifiers like Naïve Bayes, Logistic Regression, Decision Trees, and Support Vector Machines should be investigated.

3.5. Model Training

The preprocessed data ought to be used to train the chosen machine learning algorithm. The hyperparameters should be adjusted in accordance with the model's optimization in order to boost performance.

3.6. Model Evaluation

Metrics like accuracy, precision, recall, and F1-score should be used to evaluate the model's performance. To ensure that the model does not overfit the data, it should be tested on a different test set.

3.7. Deployment

Once the model is trained and evaluated, it should be deployed on a suitable platform where it can be used to detect cyberbullying in real-time.

4. SYSTEM SPECIFICATION

4.1. Programming Language

Python is the preferred programming language for this project as it has a wide range of libraries and tools for natural language processing and machine learning.

4.2. Libraries

The following libraries should be used in the project:

i.   Pandas and Numpy for data preprocessing and analysis
ii. Scikit-learn for machine learning algorithms
iii. NLTK for natural language processing
iv. Gensim for word embeddings
v.   Matplotlib and Seaborn for data visualization

4.3. Database

A database is not required for this project as the data can be stored in CSV or JSON format.

4.4. User Interface

A simple user interface can be developed using Flask or Django frameworks, where users can input text data and get a result of whether it contains cyberbullying or not.

4.5. Deployment

The model can be deployed on a cloud platform such as AWS or Google Cloud Platform. The API can be created using Flask or Django and deployed on the platform. The users can access the API through a web or mobile application.

5. SYSTEM ARCHITECTURE

Figure 1. System architecture

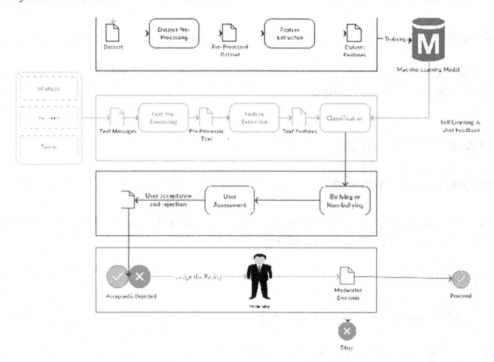

6. PROPOSED SYSTEM

The following study builds a model based on the detection of cyberbullying in textual data using natural language processing and machine learning, using data from two different types of cyberbullying: Twitter hate tweets and attacks based on personal forum comments from Wikipedia. The classifier cannot classify text data, so it must be converted to numeric data. Each record (a tweet or comment in this case) can form a vector that can be used for rendering. The following project investigates three feature extraction techniques: TF-IDF, Word2Vec, and Bag of Words.

7. INDUCTIVE LOGIC

A "bottom up" method of reasoning is used in inductive logic. This indicates that the agent here takes specific data and makes it more general in order to gain a complete understanding. This is demonstrated by an agent's natural language processing of L.e., in which it organizes words into categories. A noun, verb, article, etc., and afterward deduces the importance of that sentence.

7.1 Representing Knowledge Using Rule

Using rules to express what must happen or does happen when certain conditions are met is one way to represent knowledge.

IF...THEN... statements are typically used to express rules, such as:

IF A THEN B This has a logical meaning that is comparable to the following:

In this statement, A is referred to as the antecedent, and B is the result.

The subsequent usually takes the form of an action or a conclusion when rules are expressed.

To put it another way, the typical function of a rule is to instruct a system, such as an expert system, on what to do in particular circumstances or what conclusions to draw from a set of inputs regarding the current circumstance.

A rule can typically have more than one antecedent, which is typically combined using either AND or OR (which is logically equivalent to the operators A and V). In general, the antecedent of a rule employs an operator to compare an object with a possible value. The s in the Zoo Animals rules base are summarized in first-order logic (Suresh Babu, 2022).

8. IMPLEMENTATION

Modules

i.   User
ii.   Admin
iii. Data Preprocessing
iv.   Machine Learning Results

9. MODULES DESCRIPTION

9.1. User

A "bottom up" method of reasoning is used in inductive logic. This indicates that the agent here takes specific data and makes it more general in order to gain a complete understanding. This is demonstrated by an agent's natural language processing of L.e., in which it organizes words into categories. A noun, verb, article, etc., and afterward deduces the importance of that sentence.

9.2. Admin

Admin can use his login information to log in. Registered users can be activated by the admin. Only the user can access our system after it has been activated. The whole set of data is viewable by admin in the browser. The administrator can view the calculated Accuracy, Precision, Recall, and F1-Score based on the algorithms by clicking the Results link on the webpage. When the execution of all algorithms is finished, the admin can view the page's overall accuracy.

9.3. Data Preprocessing

For data preprocessing, the Natural Language Toolkit (NLTK) is utilized. Tokenization of text patterns, the removal of stop words from the text, and other tasks call for NLTK.

- **Tokenization:** The input text is divided into separated words and words that are added to the list during tokenization. To begin, Punkt Sentence Tokenizer is utilized to insert tokenized text into sentences (Jones et al., 2021). The sentences are then tokenized into words using four distinct tokenizers:
  - i.   Whitespace Tokenizer
  - ii.   Word Punct Tokenizer
  - iii. Treebank Word Tokenizer
  - iv.   Punct Word Tokenizer
- **Lowering Text:** It brings down every one of the letters of the words from the tokenization list. Example: Before and after lowering "Hey There," respectively.
- **Removing Stop words:** The most significant aspect of the preprocessing is this. In the data, stop words are useless words. NLTK makes it easy to get rid of stop words. Stop words like "t," "https," and "u" are removed from the text at this point.
- **Wordnet lemmatizer:** Wordnet lemmatizer links a word's synonyms, meaning, and many more to the same word.

9.4. Machine Learning Results

The cleansed data is divided into 60% training and 40% test according to the split criterion. After that, the dataset is subjected to four machine learning classifiers, such as logistic regression (LR), linear SVC, random forest classifier (RF), and MLP classifier. In my findings, I calculated and displayed the classifiers' accuracy. It is possible to identify the best classifier as the one with the highest accuracy.

10. OUTPUT SCREENSHOTS

Figure 2. Home page

Figure 3. Register form

Figure 4. Admin login page

Figure 5. Admin home page

Figure 6. Activate user

Figure 7. Login page

Figure 8. User home page

Figure 9. View data

Figure 10. Preprocessed data

Figure 11. ML results

Figure 12. Prediction results

11. FUTURE WORK

The application of machine learning algorithms brings a hopeful method for detecting cyberbullying within social media platforms. Large sets of user-generated content can be utilized in training the algorithms, to recognize negative patterns like the use of offensive language, harassment, or threatening messages.

One potential route for detecting cyberbullying with machine learning techniques is to create more advanced models that have the capability to recognize delicate patterns of cyberbullying, including subtle forms such as microaggressions or passive-aggressive behavior. These models could also consider contextual factors when analyzing messages, such as the sender-receiver relationship, message frequency, and timing (Suresh Babu et. al. 2023).

One possible approach is to apply machine learning techniques to recognize the attributes of cyber-bullies themselves. These techniques can help identify shared demo graphical and behavioral features or patterns that precede or coexist with cyberbullying. This knowledge could potentially be used to create more effective preventive measures or interventions against cyberbullying.

Machine learning algorithms have the ability to be utilized alongside other techniques, such as human moderation or reporting mechanisms. These algorithms have the potential to recognize problematic content for further assessment by human moderators or provide automated feedback to users who may be involved in cyberbullying.

In general, machine learning algorithms have the potential to enhance our capability of identifying and stopping cyberbullying on social media. As the field advances, we can anticipate more advanced models and approaches for detecting and dealing with this critical issue.

12. CONCLUSION

Cyberbullying is serious and can lead to incidents such as suicide and depression. Therefore, its spread must be controlled. Therefore, it is very important to detect cyberbullying on social media platforms. With more data and better disaggregated user information available about other forms of cyber-attacks, social media cyberbullying detection can be used to engage in these activities. You can block users who try. This paper proposes a cyberbullying detection architecture to deal with this situation. He described the structure of two types of data: hate speech data from Twitter and personal attack data from Wikipedia. For hate speech, natural language processing techniques have proven effective, using basic machine learning algorithms with an accuracy of over 90 degrees. For this reason, the BoW and Tf-Idf models give better results than the Word2Vec models. However, it is difficult to detect personal attacks with the same model (Suresh Babu et al., 2023).

In fact, these comments often make no sense at all. It can be learned using one of the three methods of job selection, but it is done in the same way. The Word2Vec model using feature context was found to be effective for both datasets and, when combined with layered recognition, produces similar results for a relatively small number of features. As seen in the nature of the changes.

REFERENCES

Alshawi, S. H., Alrodhan, W., & Alarifi, A. (2020). Predicting Cyberbullying on Social Media Using Machine Learning Algorithms. *IEEE Access : Practical Innovations, Open Solutions*, 8, 11349–11360. doi:10.1109/access.2020.2968009

Hasan, A. R., & Shah, N. A. (2020). Cyberbullying and its impact on mental health: A review of the literature. *Cureus*, *12*(8), e9635. PMID:32923236

Iftikhar, N., Mustafa, A., Abbas, N., Khan, M., Raza, S., & Bashir, S. (2020). A review of cyberbullying: A new era of bullying. *Journal of Interpersonal Violence*, *35*(7-8), 1687–1710.

Jones, A., Horsley, T., & Runnels, V. (2021). Exploring the Relationship Between Cyberbullying and Mental Health Among University Students: A Systematic Review. *Journal of Interpersonal Violence.* Advance online publication. doi:10.1177/08862605211004219

Kohn, K., Wright, M., & Tuffin, K. (2020). Cyberbullying in the workplace: A review of the literature. *Aggression and Violent Behavior, 50,* 101354.

Liao, Y., Katz, S. J., & Stylianou, A. M. (2020). A systematic review of cyberbullying prevention programs: Research methodology and intervention frameworks. *Aggression and Violent Behavior, 50,* 101358. doi:10.1016/j.avb.2019.101358

Mishra, S., & Sahoo, S. (2021). Cyberbullying in Social Media and Its Impact on Mental Health: A Systematic Review. *International Journal of Mental Health and Addiction,* 1–18. doi:10.100711469-021-00540-1

Rafique, M., Anwar, H. N., & Khalib, S. (2020). Perceived parenting styles and adolescent cyberbullying behaviors: The mediating role of moral disengagement. *Journal of Interpersonal Violence, 35*(21-22), 4771–4792.

Sahin, E. (2020). An investigation of the influence of culture on cyberbullying perpetration and victimization among adolescents. *International Journal of Adolescence and Youth, 25*(1), 102–116.

Stylianou, A., Liao, Y., & Katz, S. J. (2021). The Dark Side of Social Media: Cyberbullying and Mental Health Among Adolescents. *Journal of Youth and Adolescence, 50*(2), 308–320. doi:10.100710964-020-01329-9

Suresh Babu, C. V. (2022). *Artificial Intelligence & Expert System.* Anniyappa publications.

Suresh Babu, C. V. & Srisakthi, S. (2023). Cyber Physical Systems and Network Security: The Present Scenarios and Its Applications. In R. Thanigaivelan, S. Kaliappan, & C. Jegadheesan (Eds.), Cyber-Physical Systems and Supporting Technologies for Industrial Automation (pp. 104-130). IGI Global. https://doi.org/10.4018/978-1-6684-9267-3.ch006

Suresh Babu, C. V., Andrew Simon, P., & Barath Kumar, S. (2023). The Future of Cyber Security Starts Today, Not Tomorrow. In S. Shiva Darshan, M. Manoj Kumar, B. Prashanth, & Y. Vishnu Srinivasa Murthy (Eds.), Malware Analysis and Intrusion Detection in Cyber-Physical Systems (pp. 348-375). IGI Global. https://doi.org/10.4018/978-1-6684-8666-5.ch016

Suresh Babu, C. V., Suruthi, G., & Indhumathi, C. (2023). Malware Forensics: An Application of Scientific Knowledge to Cyber Attacks. In S. Shiva Darshan, M. Manoj Kumar, B. Prashanth, & Y. Vishnu Srinivasa Murthy (Eds.), Malware Analysis and Intrusion Detection in Cyber-Physical Systems (pp. 285-312). IGI Global. https://doi.org/10.4018/978-1-6684-8666-5.ch013

Thomas, R., Horton, R., Lianos, A., & Adams, C. (2020). Cyberbullying among college students: The role of online anonymity and social media use. *Journal of Interpersonal Violence, 35*(3-4), 619–643. doi:10.1177/0886260517696874

Wright, M. F., Jones, L. M., & Tuffin, K. (2020). Online harassment: A review of the literature and its relationship to cyberbullying. *Aggression and Violent Behavior, 50,* 101358. doi:10.1016/j.avb.2019.101358

Wu, X., Xie, H., & Huang, Y. (2020). Self-disclosure and cyberbullying victimization among adolescents. *Journal of Youth Studies, 23*(7), 921–937.

Yılmaz, Ş., & Kürşün, E. (2020). The effects of social norms and personal beliefs on cyberbullying behavior among adolescents. *Children and Youth Services Review, 113*, 104956.

Zareen, S., Boutaba, R., & Ahmad, A. (2020). Predicting Cyberbullying in Social Media: An Ensemble Learning Approach. *IEEE Transactions on Computational Social Systems, 7*(2), 373–384. doi:10.1109/ TCSS.2019.2938796

Chapter 6
Cognitive Warfare:
A Psychological Strategy to Manipulate Public Opinion

Szde Yu
Wichita State University, USA

ABSTRACT

Information warfare is one crucial aspect of cyber security. Unlike physical targets, such as network systems or electronic devices, information warfare is aimed at manipulating what people believe to be true and thereby swaying public perceptions. A more organized and advanced form of information warfare is called cognitive warfare. It is a psychological strategy intended to gradually influence the targeted public's belief, opinion, and perception about a subject, such as an event, a politician, a government, or an ideology in general. This chapter discusses the tactics commonly used in cognitive warfare. Using the China-Taiwan relationship as an example, this chapter illustrates how such warfare is carried out.

INTRODUCTION

Global political conflicts are intensifying, both internationally and domestically. Many entities have resorted to cyber operations as a weapon. Even in a traditional war featuring guns and bombs, cyber operations are playing a more and more important role, not to mention in most conflicts where political struggle usually takes place in a more clandestine manner. Aside from the attempts to disrupt the enemy's cyber operations or steal valuable data, information warfare has become one popular strategy to manipulate public opinion. For example, Russia has been accused of interfering with political elections in other countries in an attempt to help certain politicians be elected (Vilmer & Conley, 2018; Keating & Schmitt; 2021). Japan is also known for paying Chinese journalists, scholars, and Internet influencers to tell a different version of history regarding what Japan did in China during World War II in an attempt to justify invasion and deny massacres (Honda, Gibney, & Sandness, 2015; Li, 2017; Song, 2021). It seems whoever controls how information is dissemi-

DOI: 10.4018/978-1-6684-8846-1.ch006

nated and what message is being conveyed in such information could ultimately sway the intended audience to form a belief in favor of the controller's political agenda. However, this is easier said than done, especially in modern days when information is overabundant and seemingly everyone has a way to become a source to spread and produce information. Thus, to prevail in information warfare, it takes more than generating fake news. News, fake or not, needs to catch attention from the intended audience, and more importantly, such news needs to be convincing enough to either strengthen current belief or change people's mind. This calls for cognitive influence. Hence, a higher level of information warfare emerges in the name of cognitive warfare. It is usually more elaborate and more organized than usual information warfare. It takes time but if successful it could effect some fundamental changes in one's belief system.

This chapter discusses cognitive warfare and its common tactics. A good example of cognitive warfare can be derived from the complicated China-Taiwan relation. This chapter discusses China's "Three Warfares" strategy as an example of cognitive warfare and also how Taiwan's cognitive warfare is aimed at the Taiwanese people as a counterforce to China's political influence.

WHAT IS COGNITIVE WARFARE?

Cognitive warfare can be defined as "an unconventional form of warfare that uses cyber tools to alter enemy cognitive processes, exploit mental biases or reflexive thinking, and provoke thought distortions, influence decision-making and hinder actions, with negative effects, both at the individual and collective levels (Claverie & du Cluzel, 2022). Alternatively, it can also be defined as "the weaponization of public opinion by an external entity for the purpose of influencing public and governmental policy and destabilizing public institutions (Bernal et al., 2020). Cognitive warfare is now an important aspect of many government's cyber operations. It is usually seen as a form of military operation (Chiriac, 2022), but cognitive warfare can be carried out by any civilians as well.

The abovementioned definitions tend to assume cognitive warfare is aimed at foreign enemies. Although this is largely true, it is not always the case. Cognitive warfare can also be directed at any audiences that the enforcer intends to control or gain support from. This implies a government can engage in cognitive warfare on its own people in order to strengthen support or suppress domestic dissidents. As most countries now seem to face internal struggle no less than external threats, cognitive warfare can be seen as an approach to stabilizing a government's political power or to help an opposite party attain ruling power. The most notable example is probably regarding the former president of USA, Donald Trump. His MAGA campaign, both officially and unofficially, has alleged the mainstream media in USA as fake news generators. Essentially, he is accusing his political enemies within the country of using mainstream media as a tool to wage cognitive warfare on him to lessen his political influence.

Therefore, a more comprehensive definition proposed in this chapter is, "cognitive warfare is an organized cyber operation that is aimed at manipulating an intended audience's opinion and belief by shaping their perceptions through deliberately designed information which may or may not contain truth."

TACTICS

Choose the Medium

To start a cognitive war, it is imperative to first recognize what medium is to be used for information dissemination. In this era of information technology, finding a medium to convey messages is not hard, but selecting the most proper platform can facilitate cognitive warfare in a more cost-efficient manner. In light of this notion, social media are often a popular choice, since social media are designed to attract people to be connected. Social networks formed on social media allow information to be passed on within the network quickly, and because people tend to know one another within the social network, such acquaintance could make a message perceived as more believable. Social media with Web 2.0 or even Web 3.0 concepts also enable people to frequently interact with people outside their social networks, which helps spread information further into different social groups.

After choosing the media platform, the next step is to study how to utilize such platforms to organize information to increase cognitive impact. The effort to design and organize information with the purpose to change cognitive belief is called information weaponization. As aforementioned, the difference between cognitive warfare and some ransom information warfare is the fact that weaponized information used for cognitive warfare is much more elaborate and organized. Different social media platforms have different features, functions, restrictions, and user cultures. A full understanding on a platform's characteristics can help decide how information should be weaponized to capture attention and generate momentum. For example, some platforms are more text-based (e.g. Twitter) while others could be more photo-based (e.g. Instagram). Moreover, information shared on some platforms could be more politically oriented while on other platforms users could be more indifferent to political topics. Censorship is another factor to consider. It is important to note that although cognitive warfare is generally serving a political purpose, it does not mean the information used in such warfare must be political in nature. In fact, popular cultures, such as sports, movies, video games, and short videos (e.g. TikTok) could become very influential in cognitive warfare as they could be easier to be received and appreciated regardless of preexisting political biases. After taking into account all these factors, social media can more effectively serve as the medium for information dissemination, and in turn a cognitive war is more likely to see desirable results.

In sum, at the beginning of cognitive warfare, choosing a suitable platform to send messages is crucial. Messages need to be tailor-made for the platform for them to become weaponized. Without drawing enough attention, it is unlikely for the weaponized information to result in the kind of effect expected. On the other hand, knowing what medium is being used by the enemy is also important. Naturally, people tend to rely on what appears to be more friendly, but what is friendly to your enemy might not be friendly to you and vice versa. For example, Donald Trump probably would not consider Twitter and Facebook to be friendly platforms, and therefore he created his own platform (Forman-Katz & Stocking, 2022). However, to win a battle in cognitive warfare sometimes it requires engagement on unfriendly grounds. As mentioned, cognitive warfare is more than just sending messages you created. It also involves countering the messages sent by your enemy. If your enemy is spreading fake news on their platforms, for example, then you probably need to debunk the lies on their platforms rather than simply telling your version of truth on your platforms. Hence, a common mistake in cognitive warfare is to stay inside one's comfort zone and find support from the people who are already friendly. This rarely could change anything because these people who are already friendly is not the ones who need to be convinced by a cognitive war.

Take Initiative

To prevent a platform from becoming too unfriendly, taking initiative is important. Being sensitive to new development in information technology is very helpful in identify new battlegrounds in cognitive warfare. If one can gain footings on a platform before the enemy does, it provides some advantages. First, you get to tell your story first and create a strong first impression. Second, you have more time to be familiar with this platform's characteristics, such as its unique functions, rules, restrictions, and user cultures. Third, you have more time to cultivate an audience base and create social networks, which will later help you spread your messages.

Taking initiative also means being the first to sense a useable topic for weaponizing information. Cognitive warfare often relies on news events because they are what most people tend to pay attention to. Not all news events are worth weaponizing but some can be very inflammatory with intentional provocation or hyping. Some events might not even appear on the news at first, but they could be hyped up to become trendy news. Nowadays, a lot of journalism involves finding something newsworthy on the Internet (Fortunati et al. 2009; Burgess & Hurcombe, 2019). If one is preceptive enough to take initiative before others notice such newsworthy events, one has a better chance to control the direction of discussion once they become a hot topic, which would benefit cognitive warfare in terms of how the information is shaped to generate cognitive impact.

Create a Good Story

A good story is a critical component in cognitive warfare. A good story first is able to catch attention and then is able to generate topics for discussion. To accomplish this, it is often accompanied with a few catchy phrases. These phrases can be controversial but as long as they successfully catch attention, being controversial is not necessarily a bad thing as it usually means more people will be talking about it. For example, Donald Trump's campaign slogan "Make America Great Again" was able to generate abundant discussion and his followers seem to embrace this slogan wholeheartedly. As for what exactly was going to be great again and how "great" will be measured, it became less important. The same can be observed in the anti-China sentiment popular in recent years. The US government and its allies have been repeatedly claiming China is a threat and all things made in China cannot be trusted (Yee & Storey, 2013; Kim & Park, 2023; Tang, 2020). They banned Huawei, for instance, in the name of national security by alleging Huawei's 5G equipment and devices could be stealing data on behalf of the Chinese government. Nonetheless, they never presented any proof to back up that allegation. In fact, the UK's spy chief admitted there is no threat posed in Huawei's technologies (Reuters Staff, 2020), and they banned Huawei only because the US told them to (Fox, 2022). Whether or not Huawei's technologies are truly capable of doing what they are accused of doing remains debatable, but it does not matter too much in a cognitive war. As long as the concept "China is a threat" has been established and well-received by the public in some countries, their politicians and governments now can develop full political agenda based on it. To establish a well-received concept is not easy. It needs a good story to begin with and several stories to follow before an impression is made on enough people to form desirable public opinion.

Similarly, since the 911 attacks in 2001, the US government has successfully changed the public perception of terrorism from a criminal justice issue to a military issue, and thereby justified not only military actions on foreign soil but also policies that used to be considered unethical or even unconstitutional. For instance, suspects labelled as terrorists can be detained indefinitely without a charge or a trial (Lee, 2021; Miller, 2021) and the USA Patriot Act has permitted searches without due process (Alshrari, 2019; McBride, 2020). The tragic events of 911 attacks unfortunately became an impressive story to initiate this change. These policies probably would not have been deemed acceptable in a country emphasizing human rights so much, but once the cognitive perception has changed, public opinion changes accordingly and such policies are thus more likely to be considered necessary in the name of national security. It does not mean they do not care about human rights anymore. Rather, the concern for human rights becomes selective and double standards ensue. It does not apply to everyone anymore. After all, in the story there are bad people who do not seem to deserve equal rights. When cognitive warfare is successful, double standards can be observed everywhere. That is why nations like Iran are not allowed to develop nuclear weapons while USA can have as many as they want, because cognitively most people in the world accept the notion that Iran is evil and evil people should not possess such powerful weapons. Likewise, USA can invade Iraq in 2003 without the United Nations' approval and received no sanctions, while Russia's invasion of Ukraine in 2022 induced international sanctions. The cognitive belief of who is bad definitely requires several stories to strengthen over time. A simple Google search can reveal how the mainstream media portray countries like Russia, Iran and China historically. Hence, it cannot be stressed enough that cognitive warfare is more than just speaking ill of someone occasionally. Its success takes time and whoever is capable of consistently telling a good story usually earns the upper hand.

Control Volume

Having a good story is a start but there needs to be a momentum to further the discussion so as to form a narrative. This narrative in turn shapes perception, and perception ultimately determines belief. For this momentum to sustain, cognitive warfare needs to be able to turn up the volume. Cognitive warfare inevitably will entail argument, and in any argument there will be more than one side of voice. Ideally, for course, one would prefer the friendly side is the louder one, because the louder voice not only gets more attention but also is more likely to be perceived as the righteous one (Green, 2020). When you get more attention and appear to be righteous, you have a better chance to convince more people to join your side even if these people probably did not care about what the issue is in the first place. Psychologically, this is called the bandwagon effect (Schmitt-Beck; 2015). A louder voice also overshadows the enemy's voice and makes it hard for them to present their side of argument, and therefore your political rhetoric will appear to be preferable over your enemy's. When you control the volume, you might even mute your enemy. This is usually done by controlling the media that most people rely on to receive news on a daily basis. A century-old issue can suddenly become a hot topic again when the volume is intentionally turned up through the emergence of a good story. Some headline news could suddenly become invisible when someone decides to turn down the volume. Whoever controls the volume certainly owns the vantage point in cognitive warfare.

Find Allies

To increase volume on favorable rhetoric, finding allies is one imperative tactic in cognitive warfare. Allies could include those who share the same political agenda or those who have the same enemy despite some differences in political views. Some allies might simply help you for money regardless of your political stance. Allies can amplify your voice by retelling your story and echoing your rhetoric to make a stronger impression on the public. Allies also provide a sense of verification, which could enhance credibility, because now it would appear multiple sources are confirming the same story. The more allies you have, the more it will seem like everyone agrees you are the righteous one. Allies thus help you build a public image that can convince those who did not have a strong opinion on the issue in the first place. They might not become an active participant in your cognitive warfare but they could become sympathizers. Sympathizers are silent supporters (Oegema & Klandermans, 1994; Thomas & Louis, 2014). Although typically they do not participant in the movement or campaign, their silent support can still make a huge difference because their silence may mitigate resistance or at least they are less likely to make the enemy's voice louder. Hence, in cognitive warfare, both salient and covert allies are important in determining success. The more people are on your side, the more people can potentially help you convince others.

On a flip side, it can also be argued that in cognitive warfare one should avoid antagonizing potential allies and sympathizers. For example, some people perhaps agree with your cause but they may not appreciate your methods, such as using violence to protest social injustice. When the method or rhetoric is considered too extreme or obnoxious, you might lose their support even if they share the same political ideology. At times, having allies could actually backfire if some of the allies are overzealous and become repulsive to other allies. This could create discord within. Some allies might have their own agenda in addition to yours and this might be troublesome if in the long run their agenda are actually at odds with yours. For example, a white supremacy group and some minority groups might have the same short term goal to help one candidate win an election, but after this short term goal is met, they will have to face the reality that they probably want different policies.

All in all, it is easy to understand why allies are important in a cognitive war and it is usually not hard to find some allies in a political conflict since everyone wants a helping hand in a war. However, choosing your allies wisely and keeping all allies in harmony is certainly challenging. Any infights among allies or allies turning into enemies can be seriously detrimental to the legitimacy of the kind of cognitive belief you are trying to cultivate through cognitive warfare. Despite the risk, however, finding allies remains one crucial step in cognitive warfare. Without enough allies helping spread messages and control volume, it will be difficult to weaponize information adequately.

Lie With Partial Truth

Having allies to help you tell your story does not automatically guarantee success. A good story needs to be convincing. A story used for cognitive warfare is unlikely to be 100% truthful. Misinformation and disinformation are very common in cognitive warfare (Ecker, 2017; Guadagno & Guttieri, 2021). This is because the purpose of cognitive warfare is never about the truth. Instead, it is mainly about what you want people to believe to be true. You want the public to believe something that benefits you, and the truth oftentimes could be more harmful than beneficial as far as personal interests are concerned. Moreover, not everything can be clearly defined as true or false. For instance, is it true that illegal immigrants are a threat to social security? There are different ways to look at this issue and different standpoints may bring about different perspectives. It means even if we look at the same facts we could still come to different conclusions. Therefore, it is hard to say what the true answer is when it comes to politics. As a result, cognitive warfare typically is only concerned about how to convince the audience rather than get the facts straight.

A convincing story may not be a true story, and a true story may not be deemed believable. Accordingly, lying is a common tactic in cognitive warfare. However, to make lies more believable they need to be mixed with some truth (Garsten & Jay, 2011). A complete lie can rarely withstand examination, but with some partial truth mixed in, the story will be more verifiable. To avoid the lying part being scrutinized first, a common tactic is to offer the partial truth part for verification voluntarily before being questioned. This is tied to the tactic of taking initiative as discussed in a previous section. Once some parts of the story have been verified, an impression can be made that suggests the story is credible. Even if some lies about the story are exposed later, the first impression might be strong enough to withhold the skepticism. For example, if a politician is to claim an election is rigged, he or she may point to the fact that some voters were found to use fake identification for voting. As long as this part is true, the claim of unfair election itself is likely to become more convincing, regardless of how much such illegal voting really had an impact on the election results.

Shift Attention

If unfortunately the lies in the story are being exposed, the next tactic to considered is shifting public attention to what is more desirable by diverting public attention. If there is some truth in the story, that is something to focus on rather than the whole story. If the entire story is being discredited, then a new story might be needed to shift attention. This tactic has long been used to deal with scandals (Fine, 1997; Rieger, Kuhlgatz, & Anders, 2016; Elkayam Shalem, & Ben-Nun Bloom, 2022). It is equally useful in cognitive warfare. The availability of allies plays a crucial role in this tactic. Your allies, especially those ones without an obvious tie, may create a timely new story to help avoid the spotlight if something ugly is about to be revealed. Also, when you and your allies can successfully control volume as discussed previously, you have a greater chance to control where the audience will pay attention. It basically means you have greater power to define an issue in the say you prefer and to design narratives in a context suitable for your agenda. For example, in the COVID-19 pandemic, some political entities were able to somewhat successfully discussed it like a political debate rather than a public health crisis, and therefore oddly but naturally, people's perception of how much this virus should be concerned somehow is determined by their political stance (Kerr, Panagopoulos, & van der Linden, 2021; Jiang et al., 2020). It is odd because the virus probably does not care about one's political view before infection, but it is also natural because the pandemic since its onset has been discussed in a political context for the most part. Once it is politicized, this story then can be used to challenge the authorities, to discredit science, and even to justify discrimination under various political pretenses. It will work to some extent, because now the attention has been shifted to how much we hate each other rather than how much we need to solve the problem.

CONTROL INFORMATION

Controlling how an issue is defined and in what context it is discussed provides tremendous advantage in cognitive warfare. However, more or less the enemy will still have a voice and sometimes their voice could actually be fairly loud. It means the enemy is also telling the story from their point of view and in their preferred context. This is when the ability to control information becomes particularly important. Controlling information not only means sending your side of information out, but also follows stopping your enemy's information from being spreading. Some social media platforms are very keen on imposing censorship according to their own self-righteous standards. If a message is deemed inappropriate by the administrator, it is likely to be removed without notification. Some platforms might suspend a user account or demonetize a content creator's channel as a way to keep unwanted voices quiet. One may argue the enhanced sense of political correctness nowadays is a product of cognitive warfare facilitated by these social media platforms as well as other traditional media outlets trying to force their value onto everyone, or conversely one may claim the standards being upheld by these media participants are simply a result of the heightened awareness of political correctness in today's civil society (Herzogenrath-Amelung, 2016; Maass, Suitner, & Merkel, 2013; Felaco et al. 2023). Either way, there is no denying that the ability to control what part of information can be loudly disseminated while some information is blatantly labelled as unappreciated or even unacceptable has a great effect on how the audience will receive information and such filtered information will inevitably make a cognitive impact either gradually or strikingly.

Penetrate the Enemy

In cognitive warfare, it is very likely for one to pretend to be someone else and thus gain access to the enemy's camp. This tactic is fairly easy to implement since cognitive warfare mostly takes place on the Internet and anyone can easily create fake identities online. Moreover, one can even create multiple fake identities and engage in role playing. By doing this, even if allies are lacking, one may still create a false presence of allies through these fake identities. Fake identities can be used to pretend to be one's own allies and of course they can be used to pretend to be the enemy's allies as well. Becoming a fake ally or supporter on the enemy's side has many advantages. The most notable one is with regard to accessing insider information, such as the enemy's tactics, real allies, operation networks, resources, real-life identities, and other sensitive information. Another advantage is that one can spread weaponized information from the enemy's inner circle, which if convincing enough could result in more damage than doing do so on the outside. For example, if the purpose is to make the public see a group as radical and extreme, one may pretend to be a member of this group and intentionally issue controversial remarks on behalf of the group to shift public attention from the group's true cause to controversies so that most people would cognitively become reluctant to support this group because most people are not comfortable with extremism (Peay & Camarillo, 2021; Teixeira, Leach, & Spears, 2022). This could successfully reduce the enemy's outspoken supporters as well as silent sympathizers, which in turn reduces the volume of their voice. To win a cognitive war, oftentimes it is not about recruiting people to join your side as it can be as effective if you can make those who disagree with you unwilling to join the enemy's side.

Divide the Enemy

Another tactic related to penetrating the enemy's camp is to divide the enemy by causing internal conflicts. This would be also more effective if one can create friction on the inside. Even like-minded people inevitably have differences from time to time, not to mention allies engaging in cognitive warfare often have different self-interests and different long-term goals. We can see that in the Russia-Ukraine conflict the members of the North Atlantic Treaty Organization (NATO) do not necessarily agree on everything regarding sanctions, even though they all subscribe to the narrative that Russia is the bad guy in the story. There is no doubt they are allies, but when it comes to each nation's individual best interests, there is always disagreement to say the least. Such disagreement tends to be amplified if someone on the inside is intentionally trying to emphasize it. Once a group appears to be divided, this public image could discourage others from joining them and the perceived disharmony could reduce the legitimacy of the story being told in cognitive warfare.

Even without an insider, dividing the enemy may still be achieved by the old tactic, "divide and conquer." With enough incentives, some enemy's allies might change positions or at least take a step back to be less aggressive. Incentives may include potential harm and potential gain. Naturally people tend to avoid harm and pursue gains. Since the enemy can be made up of a variety of parties, some parties' gain could mean others' harm. If the reward of winning a cognitive war is limited and is not enough to be shared among all allies, then it would be wise to point it out for the enemies to see clearly so that they would irresistibly start realizing their true enemy might not be whom they think it is. Once allies start to calculate individually instead of collectively, the alliance tends to become weakened if not broken. Although providing incentives might succeed in creating some division among enemies, the most difficult hurdle to overcome in a cognitive war is usually ideology. When people are bound by ideology, they usually become less practical, which means even if they are aware of the undesirable effect ahead, they might still insist on staying on the course (Purvis & Hunt, 1993; Feuer, 2017). Trying to divide the enemy by changing their ideological view is hard. This is not to say ideology cannot change, but any ideological change happens gradually rather than abruptly. In fact, the main purpose of cognitive warfare is exactly to result in ideological changes, but the change is unlikely to be caused by one thing or one tactic employed at one time. This is why cognitive warfare, as stressed, typically takes time to play the long game rather than shoot for a quick win. That said, it would be wrong to assume allies in a cognitive war must share the same ideology. There could be ideological differences among allies, as long as for the time being, they believe they are facing the same enemy. It does not even matter if the enemy is real. They just need to cognitively believe there is such an enemy. In other words, cognitive warfare is not always about fighting against someone as it could be reversely used to create an alliance or to reinforce solidarity within a population, e.g. nationalism.

CHINA-TAIWAN EXAMPLE

Brief History

It is well-known that there is a complicated relationship between China and Taiwan. China claims Taiwan is part of China while Taiwan asserts its independence. This relationship stems from the aftermath of a civil war on mainland China in the 1940s. The Chinese Communist Party eventually claimed victory and chased out the original Chinese government led by the Nationalist Party of China (aka Kuomintang). Kuomintang fled to Taiwan and intended to regroup there waiting for an opportunity to retake mainland China. This never happened and as a result there were two governments both claiming they represented "China". The People's Republic China (PRC) was gradually accepted by the international community as the bona fide Chinese regime after it replaced the Republic of China (ROC) led by Kuomingtang to become a member in the United Nations in 1971 and later established official diplomatic relationship with USA in 1979. After PRC was recognized as the real China, the Chinese Communist Party started to promote the "One China" policy in hopes to delegitimize the status of ROC as a nation. According to PRC, ROC is no longer existent as it has been replaced by PRC. This stance obviously is problematic to the people in ROC since the ROC government has not stopped operating. It has its own laws, land, currency, and military forces. Its passport is recognized by most countries around the world. For the people in ROC, there is no reason for them to see their own country as dead. Therefore, for decades, ROC positioned itself as the democratic China as opposed to the autocratic PRC. So far, most people in ROC still considered themselves Chinese.

This started to change in the 1990s when the Democratic Progressive Party (DPP) grew stronger in Taiwan. DPP is a Taiwanese nationalist party calling for Taiwan independence in the sense that the Taiwanese people are not Chinese. This is fundamentally different from Kuomingtang's position although they both refuse the idea that Taiwan belongs to PRC. DPP initially intended to get rid of the name Republic of China and instead use Taiwan as the official name of the nation. Although this is probably still what they hope to see, they adopted a more practical stance after DPP became the ruling party in Taiwan by claiming there is no need for Taiwan to seek independence because Taiwan is already an independent country. DPP is willing to continue using ROC as the official name but whenever possible they still prefer to use "Taiwan" as the name of the nation. This compromise seems to be found acceptable by the majority of Taiwanese people. The reluctance to change its name officially is mainly due to the threat of China's willingness to take military action against Taiwan independence. For now, at least, PRC does not seem to have a legitimate reason to invade Taiwan as long as Taiwan keeps its name of ROC. Ironically, PRC does not admit the existence of ROC but the existence of ROC is now the only official link that suggests Taiwan is part of China. If Taiwan changes its name, by which ROC will officially be dead, it would indicate the complete severance of Taiwan's tie to China.

China's Three Warfares

Contrary to popular belief, China (PRC) does not prefer to use military action to resolve the China-Taiwan problem. To China, the best case scenario is to have Taiwan accept "one country, two systems", similar to what is implemented in Hong Kong (So, 2011; Hung & Kuo, 2010). Not surprisingly, it is not well supported in Taiwan. Even Kuomingtang, who is believed to be more friendly to China shows strong rejection to this idea. Kuomingtang's attitude toward China has changed noticeably ever since they lost the regime to DPP first between 2000 to 2008 and then again in 2016 (to present). Kuomingtang has been intentionally keeping distance from PRC and sometimes is even eager to follow DPP's rhetoric regarding Taiwanese is not Chinese. This change reflects the general public's attitude in Taiwan currently as fewer and fewer Taiwanese people would consider themselves Chinese. The Chinese root of Taiwanese culture is also being downplayed or denied in order to accentuate Taiwan's independence from China.

Conceivably, Taiwan's ever-weakening relation to Chinese nationalism worries the Chinese government. Since military action is the last resort, China has developed a strategy called, "Three Warfares" including psychological warfare, public opinion warfare, and legal warfare (Lee, 2014). Essentially, it is a cognitive warfare strategy aiming at changing Taiwanese people's perception of China from negative to positive. The rationale is that once Taiwanese people view China favorably, they will be more inclined to maintain a stronger relation with China. When there are enough voters calling for stronger ties with China, Taiwanese politicians will have to adjust their positions and reconsider the "one country, two systems" offer. This strategy was inspired by studying the US operations in the first Gulf War and in Kosovo. The Chinese government came to realize modern warfare involves more than just guns and bombs. Non-military tactics play a significant role as well. Hence, in addition to military and economic leverages, China decided to incorporate cognitive warfare into their foreign policy. Taiwan might not be the only target of such a strategy, but it certainly is the most important one (Hung & Hung, 2022).

In terms of legal warfare, China does not have too much clout. While USA can create long-arm jurisdiction and force foreign countries to cooperate with American best interests, China does not have that kind of power. China mostly can only repeatedly emphasize the One-China policy and ask other countries not to consider Taiwan an independent country. In this regard, China is not much successful as most countries still practically treat Taiwan as an independent entity despite the lack of official diplomatic relationship. As to public opinion warfare, China looks for avenues to spread information that sets a positive image of China, such as emphasizing how fast China has developed over the past twenty years and propagating China's achievements in infrastructure building, aerospace exploration, military upgrades, and economic transformation in impoverished areas. There are quite a few videos produced in line with this goal on various social media platforms. It wants to change public opinion by showing China's strength. At the same time, China seeks both official and unofficial opportunities to refute accusations against China. For example, when NASA accused China of not willing to share information about their aerospace exploration in 2022, China used every opportunity to remind the world that USA is the one enacting a law in 2011 to ban any cooperation with China in the field of aerospace (Kohler, 2014). Likewise, after the former speaker of the United States House of Representatives, Nancy Pelosi, visited Taiwan in 2022, China engaged in a series of military drills around Taiwan to express its discontent, which was expected, but it also convinced more than 170 countries to reiterate the support for the One-China policy in the aftermath. This is more than just a regular diplomatic rebuttal. It is an attempt to reshape China's image by claiming USA was the provocative one and Chine had a legitimate reason to respond. Establishing legitimacy is something China has failed in the past decades and therefore it can be easily portrayed as the villain in the stories told by the western media. Now, China is more serious about using cognitive warfare to win over support, although this certainly does not mean they will give up using military and economic leverages. The "Three Warfares" strategy also creates a psychological impression that the more Taiwan alienates China the more likely a war will result between China and Taiwan. On the other hand, China gives Taiwanese businesses and students some privileges, which are generally called "favoring Taiwan policies." Such psychological warfare serves as a reminder for Taiwanese people if Taiwan and China become closer, it is good for Taiwan.

All in all, China wants to gain a position to tell the story about China. They believe they have a good story now because there is no denying that China in the past 20 years has seen some impressive growth (Zenglein & Holzmann, 2019; Lin 2011). They intend to turn up the volume so that more people can hear their version of story. This is not easy to do because when the Chinese government customarily controls information, they not only suppress unfriendly voices but also tend to shut down friendly ones as collateral damage. The restricted freedom of speech makes the voice of the Chinese people largely isolated from the world's mainstream media. This probably is changing, albeit slowly. More organized campaigns coupled with voluntary participants now can be observed on various platforms. In other words, China is gaining allies. In terms of Taiwan, China has always had allies inside. Kuomingtang used to be considered one, and there are smaller parties or groups considered "pro-China" in Taiwan. These allies may not accept China's "one country, two systems" offer, but at least they can help contain DPP, the biggest anti-Chinese force in Taiwan. If DPP loses its appeal to the people due to scandals or incompetence, the society's resentment for DPP can successfully shift attention from the anti-Chinese sentiment to more practical issues, such as economy and unwanted wars. This is something China prefers to see.

Although the effectiveness of the "Three Warfares" strategy remains arguable, some effects may be observed in Taiwan's 2022 elections. In these regional elections, DPP suffered a huge defeat, which implies DPP's usual anti-Chinese tactics are losing appeal. It does not mean Taiwanese people like China more now, but it could mean voters might be getting tired of the same rhetoric that blames everything on China. The Taiwanese government certainly believes China's cognitive warfare has had some success. After the election setback, DPP believes voters were affected by fake news spread by China and it also accuses some Taiwanese citizens of helping China with propaganda. From DPP's perspective, it is imperative to counter China's cognitive warfare with Taiwan's own cognitive warfare.

Taiwan's Cognitive Warfare

Although DPP certainly wants to turn Chinese people to hate the Chinese Communist Party, their primary concern is within Taiwan. DPP's primal fear is that Taiwanese people like China too much. Hence, DPP's cognitive warfare is a domestic one for the most part. Just like China likes to promote Chinese nationalism, DPP wants to strengthen Taiwanese nationalism.

It is a known fact that DPP is good at orchestrating cyber armies to launch attacks on political enemies. Many participants have openly admitted to it. These groups create memes for easy dissemination of information and attempt to sway public opinions by urging their members to leave online comments in bulk (Wang, 2022). DPP also lets their allies, such as scholars, journalists, or online influencers go on TV shows to defend their policies or to attack enemies. DPP wants the textbooks and teaching materials used in schools designed in the way that they emphasize Taiwan's independence more than Taiwan's relations with China (Tong, 2021). DPP has banned some China-based media and products in the name of national security. Basically, DPP's cognitive warfare is aimed at equating supporting DPP to supporting Taiwan, making Taiwanese people believe whoever speaks for China is betraying Taiwan, and most importantly Taiwanese is not Chinese. To be fair, all political parties in Taiwan have cyber armies made up of different online groups. However, DPP as the current ruling party has more resources to support such operations. Besides, since DPP is the ruling party, other parties' cyber armies are more concerned about creating an anti-DPP sentiment while DPP is busy fostering the anti-Chinese sentiment.

DPP's cognitive warfare within Taiwan has been successful overall. Otherwise, they would not have earned the ruling power through elections. It took time for their rhetoric to gain popularity, and the long cultivation worked. In Taiwan, DPP supporters firmly believe DPP loves Taiwan no matter what they do actually. On the other hand, Kuomingtang can say they love Taiwan, too, but it is usually deemed doubtful because of its historical root in Chinese nationalism. A DPP politician can do business in China without much criticism whereas a Kuomingtang politician doing business in China can easily be labelled as a traitor. DPP has lost some elections for sure. Usually it was because the people disapproved of their policies combined with some scandals. In 2018 they suffered a loss in regional elections similar to the one in 2022. However, they were able to recover quickly and won the presidential election in 2020, largely thanks to the anti-Chinese sentiment working again. Therefore, there is no reason for DPP to believe they need to abandon this strategy. It is not only ideological but also practical. In Taiwan, DPP has no problem telling a story in the way they want and controlling information dissemination. They certainly have many allies both inside and outside Taiwan. The biggest challenge in DPP's cognitive warfare is how to consistently keep the people's attention on the anti-Chinese rhetoric, especially when the enemy tries to shift attention.

POLICY IMPLICATIONS

Cognitive warfare is an ongoing issue. Unlike other military operations, it does not usually have a clearly defined onset and cessation. It can be carried out by different types of entities. It is mainly a cybersecurity issue because modern day cognitive warfare mostly takes place in cyberspace. However, there is no firewalls or anti-virus programs to prevent cognitive warfare. There is a fine line between freedom of speech and cognitive warfare, and hence policymaking is tough, especially for a democratic country. Despite being known for its strict control over public information, even China cannot completely stop unfriendly information from surfacing on China-based platforms. For democratic countries that like to preach freedom of speech, it is a dilemma as to how far they are willing to go to suppress undesirable information without appearing to violate people's freedom. Currently, all nations have a tendency to define all negative remarks about the government as the enemy's cognitive warfare. For instance, the Taiwanese government likes to accuse any Taiwanese citizens who praise China of acting as China's agent in cognitive warfare. Some might even be officially investigated in terms of national security threats. Likewise, China tends to define any anti-Chinese remarks as a deliberate attempt to denigrate China with false information. The same can be observed in USA, Europe, and perhaps any other countries.

In response to the threat of cognitive warfare, national security has become a popular excuse for controlling information and suppressing dissidents domestically. While national security is indeed important and there are authentic threats, policies cannot become a tool for the ruler to abuse power and persecute those who dare to disagree. Even if the dissidents really have an ulterior motive and want to weaponize information, the most important thing to judge is whether such information is based on facts. Policies need to emphasize the difference between fact and opinion, instead of focusing on political agenda as if you must be penalized for being politically incorrect. People have rights to express opinions, but any opinions need to be based on facts rather than ignorance, biases, or falsehood. Policies should allow truth to be told even if it is not pleasurable, and take into consideration that truth can be multifaced, meaning a different perspective may see a different side of the truth. If disinformation is detected, policies should have the effect on holding the spreader accountable. It is noteworthy that there is a difference between disinformation and misinformation. The former refers to inaccurate information that is intentionally misleading and deceptive, while the latter means the information is inaccurate largely due to ignorance or misunderstanding (Stahi, 2006; Carmi et al., 2020). Policies can note the difference and design punishment accordingly to avoid overreaction to honest mistakes.

CONCLUSION

Cognitive warfare is an important aspect of cybersecurity. Unlike other types of cyberattacks, cognitive warfare tactics typically do not require advanced technical skills, which makes it easy to recruit participants. Actually, many people could be unwittingly participating in it when they engage in spreading information on the Internet on a daily basis. The goal of cognitive warfare is usually about manipulating public opinion on someone or something through changing their perception and eventually their belief. Although similar psychological warfare is nothing new, modern day cognitive warfare is more complicated in the sense that now there are more digital platforms that can be orchestrated to weaponize information without relying on traditional media. No one can gain full control over information dissemination anymore. It is harder for the authorities to lie to the public and conceal information, but at the same time it is also easier for any random entity to spread false information at a very quick pace, which lessens anyone's ability to clarify facts and do damage control at a timely manner. When there is so much conflicting information floating around the Internet, people have started to choose only what they prefer to believe as truth and simply define anything undesirable as fake news. This tendency has been further facilitated by most social media's AI algorithms which learns to present personalized information that each user prefers to see in order to keep users stay longer on the platform. Consequently, different versions of reality are being formed and everyone thinks what they perceive is the true reality (Wohn & Bowe, 2014; Couldry & Hepp, 2018). This phenomenon does not necessarily make cognitive warfare more successful, because cognitive changes require the willingness to accept new information. However, it certainly makes the world more divided, which provides more motivation to engage in cognitive warfare as a psychological strategy to either win public support or dismantle the enemy's solidarity. A vicious circle thus perpetuates.

REFERENCES

Alshrari, A. (2019). Patriot Act, Section 206: Its Impact on Muslim Populations in the US (With Special Reference to Roving Wiretap Policy). *Public Policy and Administration*, *7*(1), 15–21.

Bernal, A., Carter, C., Singh, I., Cao, K., & Madreperla, O. (2020). *Cognitive warfare: An attack on truth and thought*. NATO / John Hopkins University. https://www.innovationhub-act.org/sites/default/files/2021-03/Cognitive%20Warfare.pdf

Burgess, J., & Hurcombe, E. (2019). Digital journalism as symptom, response, and agent of change in the platformed media environment. *Digital Journalism (Abingdon, England)*, *7*(3), 359–367. doi:10.1080/21670811.2018.1556313

Carmi, E., Yates, S. J., Lockley, E., & Pawluczuk, A. (2020). Data citizenship: Rethinking data literacy in the age of disinformation, misinformation, and malinformation. *Internet Policy Review*, *9*(2), 1–22. doi:10.14763/2020.2.1481

Chiriac, O. (2022). Military applications of cognitive sciences: Cognitive warfare, a matter of perception and misperception. *International Scientific Conference" STRATEGIESXXI"*, *18*(1), 474-484. 10.53477/2971-8813-22-55

Claverie, B., & du Cluzel, F. (2022). The Cognitive Warfare Concept. *Innovation Hub Sponsored by NATO Allied Command Transformation*, 2022-02.

Couldry, N., & Hepp, A. (2018). *The mediated construction of reality*. John Wiley & Sons.

Ecker, U. K. (2017). Why rebuttals may not work: The psychology of misinformation. *Media Asia, 44*(2), 79–87. doi:10.1080/01296612.2017.1384145

Elkayam Shalem, H., & Ben-Nun Bloom, P. (2022). Don't scratch the moral itch: Restoring political image following a scandal. *Acta Politica*, 1–21.

Felaco, C., Nocerino, J., Parola, J., & Tofani, R. (2023). I Correct or Canceling You: Political Correctness and Cancel Culture on Social Media–The Case of Twitter Communication in Italy. In Research Anthology on Social Media's Influence on Government, Politics, and Social Movements (pp. 495-512). IGI Global.

Feuer, L. S. (2017). *Ideology and the Ideologists*. Routledge. doi:10.4324/9780203789193

Fine, G. A. (1997). Scandal, social conditions, and the creation of public attention: Fatty Arbuckle and the "problem of Hollywood". *Social Problems, 44*(3), 297–323. doi:10.2307/3097179

Forman-Katz, N., & Stocking, G. (2022, November 18). *Key facts about Truth Social*. Pew Research Center. https://www.pewresearch.org/fact-tank/2022/11/18/key-facts-about-truth-social-as-donald-trump-runs-for-u-s-president-again/

Fortunati, L., Sarrica, M., O'Sullivan, J., Balcytiene, A., Harro-Loit, H., Macgregor, P., Roussou, N., Salaverría, R., & De Luca, F. (2009). The influence of the Internet on European journalism. *Journal of Computer-Mediated Communication, 14*(4), 928–963. doi:10.1111/j.1083-6101.2009.01476.x

Fox, B. (2022, January 10). *UK banned Huawei because US told us to: Former minister*. EURACTIV. https://www.euractiv.com/section/politics/short_news/uk-banned-huawei-because-us-told-us-to-former-minister/

Garsten, B., & Jay, M. (2011). The Virtues of Mendacity: On Lying in Politics. *Modern Intellectual History, 8*(3), 697. doi:10.1017/S1479244311000424

Green, N. L. (2020). Recognizing rhetoric in science policy arguments. *Argument & Computation, 11*(3), 257–268. doi:10.3233/AAC-200504

Guadagno, R. E., & Guttieri, K. (2021). Fake news and information warfare: An examination of the political and psychological processes from the digital sphere to the real world. In Research Anthology on Fake News, Political Warfare, and Combatting the Spread of Misinformation (pp. 218-242). IGI Global.

Herzogenrath-Amelung, H. (2016). The new instantaneity: How social media are helping us privilege the (politically) correct over the true. *Media Culture & Society, 38*(7), 1080–1089. doi:10.1177/0163443716664855

Honda, K., Gibney, F., & Sandness, K. (2015). *The Nanjing Massacre: A Japanese Journalist Confronts Japan's National Shame: A Japanese Journalist Confronts Japan's National Shame*. Routledge. doi:10.4324/9781315699370

Hung, H. F., & Kuo, H. Y. (2010). "One country, two systems" and its antagonists in Tibet and Taiwan. *China Information, 24*(3), 317–337. doi:10.1177/0920203X10382710

Hung, T. C., & Hung, T. W. (2022). How China's Cognitive Warfare Works: A Frontline Perspective of Taiwan's Anti-Disinformation Wars. *Journal of Global Security Studies, 7*(4), ogac016. doi:10.1093/jogss/ogac016

Jiang, J., Chen, E., Yan, S., Lerman, K., & Ferrara, E. (2020). Political polarization drives online conversations about COVID-19 in the United States. *Human Behavior and Emerging Technologies, 2*(3), 200–211. doi:10.1002/hbe2.202 PMID:32838229

Keating, V. C., & Schmitt, O. (2021). Ideology and influence in the debate over Russian election interference. *International Politics, 58*(5), 757–771. doi:10.105741311-020-00270-4

Kerr, J., Panagopoulos, C., & van der Linden, S. (2021). Political polarization on COVID-19 pandemic response in the United States. *Personality and Individual Differences, 179*, 110892. doi:10.1016/j.paid.2021.110892 PMID:34866723

Kim, J. H., & Park, J. (2023). Perceived China threat, conspiracy belief, and public support for restrictive immigration control during the COVID-19 pandemic. *Race and Justice, 13*(1), 130–152. doi:10.1177/21533687221125818

Kohler, H. (2014). The Eagle and the Hare: US-Chinese Relations, the Wolf Amendment, and the Future of International Cooperation in Space. *Geological Journal, 103*, 1135.

Lee, A. (2021). Defense Attorneys at a Dead End: Representing Stateless Terrorist Clients Detained Indefinitely. *The Georgetown Journal of Legal Ethics, 34*, 1113.

Lee, S. (2014). China's 'Three Warfares': Origins, Applications, and Organizations. *The Journal of Strategic Studies, 37*(2), 198–221. doi:10.1080/01402390.2013.870071

Li, P. (Ed.). (2017). *Japanese war crimes*. Routledge. doi:10.4324/9780203788059

Lin, J. Y. (2011). China and the global economy. *China Economic Journal, 4*(1), 1–14. doi:10.1080/17538963.2011.609612

Maass, A., Suitner, C., & Merkel, E. M. (2013). Does political correctness make (social) sense? In *Social cognition and communication* (pp. 345–360). Psychology Press.

McBride, D. (2020). USA Patriot Act Boosts Government Powers While Cutting Back on Traditional Checks and Balances. In *Bioterrorism: The History of a Crisis in American Society* (pp. 307–310). Routledge. doi:10.4324/9781003123644-34

Miller, S. (2021). Preventive detention of terrorists. In *Counter-Terrorism* (pp. 92–104). Edward Elgar Publishing. doi:10.4337/9781800373075.00014

Oegema, D., & Klandermans, B. (1994). Why social movement sympathizers don't participate: Erosion and nonconversion of support. *American Sociological Review, 59*(5), 703–722. doi:10.2307/2096444

Peay, P. C., & Camarillo, T. (2021). No justice! Black protests? No peace: The racial nature of threat evaluations of nonviolent# BlackLivesMatter protests. *Social Science Quarterly, 102*(1), 198–208. doi:10.1111squ.12902

Purvis, T., & Hunt, A. (1993). Discourse, ideology, discourse, ideology, discourse, ideology.... *The British Journal of Sociology, 44*(3), 473–499. doi:10.2307/591813

Reuters Staff. (2020, June 4). *UK spy chief says no threat to Five Eyes alliance over Huawei.* Reuters. https://www.reuters.com/article/us-britain-huawei-tech-five-eyes/uk-spy-chief-says-no-threat-to-five-eyes-alliance-over-huawei-idUSKBN23B2T3

Rieger, J., Kuhlgatz, C., & Anders, S. (2016). Food scandals, media attention and habit persistence among desensitised meat consumers. *Food Policy, 64*, 82–92. doi:10.1016/j.foodpol.2016.09.005

Schmitt-Beck, R. (2015). Bandwagon effect. *The international encyclopedia of political communication*, 1-5.

So, A. Y. (2011). "One country, two systems" and Hong Kong-China national integration: A crisis-transformation perspective. *Journal of Contemporary Asia, 41*(1), 99–116. doi:10.1080/00472336.2011.530039

Song, S. (2021). Denial of Japan's Military Sexual Slavery and Responsibility for Epistemic Amends. *Social Epistemology, 35*(2), 160–172. doi:10.1080/02691728.2020.1839811

Stahl, B. C. (2006). On the difference or equality of information, misinformation, and disinformation: A critical research perspective. *Informing Science, 9*, 83. doi:10.28945/473

Tang, M. (2020). Huawei versus the United States? The geopolitics of exterritorial internet infrastructure. *International Journal of Communication, 14*, 22.

Teixeira, C. P., Leach, C. W., & Spears, R. (2022). White Americans' belief in systemic racial injustice and in-group identification affect reactions to (peaceful vs. destructive)" Black Lives Matter" protest. *Psychology of Violence, 12*(4), 280–292. doi:10.1037/vio0000425

Thomas, E. F., & Louis, W. R. (2014). When will collective action be effective? Violent and non-violent protests differentially influence perceptions of legitimacy and efficacy among sympathizers. *Personality and Social Psychology Bulletin, 40*(2), 263–276. doi:10.1177/0146167213510525 PMID:24311435

Tong, C. (2021, October 25). *De-sinicization again in Taiwan's teaching materials.* Yazhou Zhoukan. https://theintellectual.net/zh/referrals/asia-weekly/3621-202147m.html

Vilmer, J. B. J., & Conley, H. A. (2018). *Successfully Countering Russian Electoral Interference.* Center for Strategic & International Studies.

Wang, G. (2022, November 29). *DPP finally admits their own cyber armies.* Chinatimes. https://www.chinatimes.com/newspapers/20221129000473-260109?chdtv

Wohn, D. Y., & Bowe, B. J. (2014, February). Crystallization: How social media facilitates social construction of reality. In *Proceedings of the companion publication of the 17th ACM conference on Computer supported cooperative work & social computing* (pp. 261-264). ACM.

Yee, H., & Storey, I. (2013). *China threat: Perceptions myths.* Routledge. doi:10.4324/9780203060414

Zenglein, M. J., & Holzmann, A. (2019). Evolving made in China 2025. *MERICS Papers on China, 8*, 78.

KEY TERMS AND DEFINITIONS

Cognitive Warfare: An organized cyber operation that is aimed at manipulating an intended audience's opinion and belief by shaping their perceptions through deliberately designed information which may or may not contain truth.

Disinformation: Inaccurate information that is intentionally misleading and deceptive.

DPP: Democratic Progressive Party is a Taiwanese nationalist political party, which is best known for its anti-Chinese stance.

Misinformation: Inaccurate information that is likely due to ignorance or misunderstanding rather than intentional deception.

Public Opinion: People's collective view on a specific topic in a society.

Three Warfares: A political strategy developed by the People's Republic of China with the intention to incorporate non-military operations to engage in cognitive warfare, including psychological warfare, public opinion warfare, and legal warfare.

Weaponized Information: Messages that are designed to affect the recipient's perception so much that it can bring about a change in belief or attitude toward someone or something.

Chapter 7
The Fifth Space of Military Action and Confrontation

Nika Chitadze
International Black Sea University, Georgia

ABSTRACT

The concept of fifth dimension operations is conceptually based on adding the five-dimensional, holistic approach to warfare that uses the three dimensions of land, sea, and aerospace but also incorporates the temporal and cyber dimensions of warfare. In more recent times, the concept of fifth dimensional operations, as a concept under military operations, has taken a wider scope than its original information operations background, focusing on the advanced space-time manipulating capabilities cyberspace offers. This development was begun as early as 1996 in regards to advanced battlespace and cybermaneuver concepts.

INTRODUCTION: TECHNOLOGY DEVELOPMENT AND THE ISSUE OF USING TERMS IN THE INFORMATION (CYBER) SPACE

In the information age, one of the main factors in the development of the socio-political system has become the production and use of information. It plays a decisive role not only in public and state institutions but also in the life of each person and is the only reality of communication with the world. Computers and digital information and telecommunication systems are used in everyday life, in all spheres of human, society, and state activity - ensuring national security and state governance as a whole (health care, education, housing and communal services, air and railway communications, trade, etc.).

Comprehensive internet technologies have changed the political, economic, and social reality. Along with the emergence of the World Wide Web, the state gradually loses certain functions, its role and influence on human relations decreases, and the state border changes its original purpose. For example, cyber terrorists can "invade" another state, conduct criminal operations and cause great damage to the country. The nature of war and the standards of its understanding have also changed.

Thus, from the second half of the 20th century, the classic forms of military armed wars and conflicts are gradually being replaced by new forms of conflict, among them cyberterrorism, and cyberwar. The

DOI: 10.4018/978-1-6684-8846-1.ch007

area of military action and conflict has become cyberspace - a complex interconnection of information and telecommunication technological infrastructure, which includes the global Internet network, computer systems, telecommunication networks, and processors. Cyberspace does not exist in any physical form, it is a complex virtual environment that is created as a result of the interaction between people, software, Internet services, technological devices, networks, and network connections.

The fifth form of war, cyber war (besides land, sea, air, and space dimensions), attempts to gain informational-technological superiority in the information age have given rise to new dangers, where no one obeys the imposed restrictions and prohibitions.

The urgency of the problem of cyberspace protection is due to the unprecedented development of information communication and cyber technologies, the irreversible processes of cyber-attacks of an indefinite scale, which present to the whole world the need to strengthen security measures.

The Growing Danger and the Expansion of the Scientific-Research Area

Back in the industrial era, the technical term "security" (computer, information, cyber) is used to protect the computer from threats arising after the emergence of computer viruses, which refers to the protection of computer and information-telecommunications components (networks, computers, programs, data, devices) from cyber-attacks (Digital attacks, damage, unauthorized access, etc.) A set of technical protection technologies, methods, and processes.

Since the end of the last century, viruses have become not only a narrow target of computers but also an unpredictably damaging weapon and have become a huge problem with catastrophic consequences for the world. For the creators of viruses, on the battlefield of cyberspace, the computer becomes not a goal, but a means, and a multi-step combined target - national security mechanisms, and state and defense military infrastructures.

Both, states and the provision of national security of individual countries, moreover, humanity as a whole, faced danger. It is a fact that in the information age, following the unprecedented development of digital technologies that damage computer components, extremely diverse and unpredictable threats arising from computer viruses have gone beyond the narrow scope of the computer and have created a threat to all spheres of state and public life, threatening the fundamental values of national security: personal safety, social security, and state security, national security assurance system.

Coping with the emerging danger in itself required serious socio-political decisions at the national and international levels (as well as academic research, development of new political theories, new normative requirements, regulation systems, social norms, etc.).

To solve the problem, if technical measures taken by informatics specialists were sufficient before, today it is necessary to take political, legal, economic, military-defense, and social measures.

Dr. Robert Dewar, a Swiss specialist in cyber security and cyber defense, notes that there is an increasing focus on cyberspace from politicians and the military, as cyber security is already a legal, military, and economic challenge. No state can cope with this global problem alone, only with its forces and resources (Dewar, 2022).

It is welcome that in the last decade, a whole plethora of researchers working on cyber security problems who develop this point of view have appeared in Western scientific circles (Collier, 2018). For example, Professor Miriam Dan Cavelty of the Zurich Center for Security Research and Professor Andreas Wenger, a recognized researcher on the "threat politics" of cyberspace, points out that "as these technical systems become more closely connected and integrate more aspects of society and the economy, the problems related to cyber security will inevitably spread in more and more areas of politics, both nationally and internationally" (Cavelty, 2022). "These developments will create new demands for technical and organizational research that should be better integrated with social and political science approaches" (Cavelty, 2022). The authors emphasize that "political and social aspects are becoming increasingly visible, which will influence patterns of cooperation and conflict in politics and society at the national and international levels" (Cavelty, 2022).

The problem has gone beyond the narrow field of the creation of antiviruses for the technical protection of computers by specialists in the field of informatics. The global danger has brought politicians and the military, as well as researchers working in various fields of science, to the battlefield to solve the problem, and the scope and area of academic scientific research have significantly expanded. Created reality is:

First, the issues of technical protection of computers were and are mainly researched only by informatics specialists:

Second, specialists from social, humanitarian, legal, military, and other fields have been widely involved in the research of cyber security problems. The new reality made clear the need to clarify the issue of using terms in cyberspace by researchers in the scientific field of many countries.

It is known that in cyberspace the term "security" is used when it refers to the technical protection of components (networks, computers, programs, data, devices) included in the computer and information-telecommunications sphere from cyber-attacks (digital attacks, damage, unauthorized access, etc.). Talking, that is, ensuring cyber security, in this case, is more a matter of "technique", protection from "technical" threats. For example, it is associated with the more well-known "protection of labor security" and not with setting socio-political goals, e. i. Appropriate organizational and technical measures should be taken to ensure cyber security at the given facility: determine the person responsible for the security of operation of the computer and information-telecommunications field (networks, computers, devices, programs, databases) and introduce the appropriate technical infrastructure and security system (Kuprashvili, 2022).

Based on the created reality, in the background of these cardinal and large-scale changes, when we are dealing with an essentially new process, that is, there is a transition from considering cyber security as a technical problem to its solution as a political task (cyber security), the purely technical conceptual term "computer (information, cyber) security" can no longer fully reflect and convey the essence of the changes that have occurred. Therefore, using the same term to describe two different processes leads to confusion.

The conversation refers not only to technical activities, but also to socio-political processes, when the state policy of defensive response to cyber threats is developed by the relevant services and institutions of the country's government - national security, and the national security strategy of cyber threats is formed to protect national interests, which is established in cyberspace (information space) and the systematic understanding of solving cyber threats, analyzing the possibilities of perfect use of information and communication technologies for a response, etc.

Thus, based on the comprehensive scope of the dangers, to achieve the technical support of cyber security, the government should establish socio-political measures: the development and adoption of laws, and legal acts, including - the protection of national interests, the perfection of the management process, the division of functions and duties between state agencies Separation, improvement of coordination, cooperation and information exchange mechanisms, determination of the list of critical infrastructure, etc.

Finally, it will be ensured that the result corresponding to the requirements of the political goal of cyber security will be achieved when the components included in the computer and information-telecommunication sphere will be technically protected from cyber attacks.

In the new reality, the need to use the appropriate term has arisen, when a decisive role is played in the process of technical protection of computers, and in the research, specialists from various scientific fields are involved.

As for the term security, it is clear that the term "security" should be used in cyberspace if the avoidance (harmlessness) of the expected threat (threats) requires socio-political activity, planning, and implementation of measures of a socio-political nature (policy development, concept, planning, etc.), that is, it is related to the socio-political activity of a person, society and the state.

Thus, since the 80s of the 20th century, viruses have become not only a narrow target of computers but also an unpredictably damaging weapon and a problem with catastrophic consequences for the world. For the creators of viruses, on the battlefield of cyberspace, the computer becomes not a goal, but a means, and a multi-step combination target for national security mechanisms, and state infrastructures.

Dealing with the emerging danger in itself required serious socio-political decisions at the national and international levels. The problem has already touched not only technical activities, but also socio-political processes, when the country's government develops a state policy of defensive response to cyber threats, and a national security strategy to protect national interests from cyber threats is formed. It is necessary to: develop and adopt laws, and administrative acts, perfect the management process, separate functions and duties between state agencies, improve coordination, cooperation, and information exchange mechanisms, establish a list of critical infrastructure, etc.

To solve the problem, if technical measures taken by informatics specialists were sufficient before, today it is necessary to take political, legal, economic, military-defense, and social measures.

The problem has gone beyond the narrow field of creating antiviruses for the technical protection of computers by specialists in the field of informatics. The global danger has brought politicians and the military, as well as researchers working in various fields of science, to the battlefield to solve the problem, and the scope and area of academic scientific research have significantly expanded. A new reality has been created: 1. Until now, the issues of technical protection of computers were mainly researched and researched only by informatics specialists; 2. This time, specialists from social, humanitarian, legal, military, and other fields were widely involved in the research of cyberspace problems.

CURRENT SUBSYSTEMS OF THE NATIONAL SECURITY SYSTEM (TYPES, COMPONENTS)

Information Security

Dialectic of Information Security (Information Age, Information-Technological Revolution, Information Society)

Morphology of Information

Understanding the role of information in a new way in the 21st century, as well as the utilization and management of information as a strategic resource and driving factor for the further development of civilization, is a particularly important and urgent problem. It is not only of general scientific importance but also determines the future fate of modern civilization.

There is no doubt that in our reality, the problem of the development of information technologies, modern information, and communication tools, as well as the development of informatics as a field of science, requires special attention, because:

- Information is the main source of development and vitality of any sphere of society and the state, and the informational factor is an integral part of any internal political and external political process;
- Information is the basis of the formation of each member of the society as a person, the relationship between the members of the society, the civil society, and its institutional structures;
- Information between the civil society and the state government, between various administrative-territorial and autonomous formations, and between all branches and structures of the central and local government is the most important condition for political modernization, sustainable development of the state, maintaining its unity and integrity;
- Information is the initial resource for the development of state policy and the implementation of state governance in any field. The information provision of the state government and its timely provision of reliable information is the most important prerequisite for the effective functioning of the state mechanism, and the realization of all stages of the governance process.

It is known that the Latin word information (informatio – introduction, transfer, notice, message) as a scientific term entered the scientific literature together with the development of cybernetics in the second half of the 20th century. It is from this period that researchers pay special attention to information. It soon received the status of a general scientific category and was used not only in cybernetics but also in natural, social, and humanitarian sciences.

Nevertheless, information remains a fundamental concept of science, which is not completely clear yet, characterized by the diversity of its content. The search for general properties and regularities of the concept of information attempts to explain its meaning and essence continues to this day.

It is not surprising that the information is not easily explained. It is known that the universe is a certain system, that is, a system of interconnected elements. In turn, this system includes billions (up to trillions) of galaxies.

Among these billions of galaxies is the small, Milky Way galaxy (up to 400 billion stars), which includes the solar system, Earth, and humans.

It is clear (it is impossible to even imagine the scale) that a person, as an unimaginably small part of the system, can receive information about the system and study it only from the inside of the system, that is, only to the edge where the hand (mind) can reach. Therefore, people can obtain information and understand only some parts of the properties of the world. At whatever level science should be developed, it will be accessible to man only from the inside and he/she will be able to obtain only small (also subjective) information about the world, that is, he/she will have data about only a part of the infinite set. For the same reason, it is clear that absolute information is unattainable for humans, and can be achieved only by an absolute observer (creator of the universe).

Also, it is difficult to talk about having absolute knowledge because only the absolute observer has it. In the existing reality, simply along with the development of science, there is an expansion of the limits available to human experimental knowledge. Any matter (object, body) - starting from a subatomic particle, ending with the metaverse as a whole - is a system of interconnected subsystems.

As a result of continuous movement (displacement in space, interaction, and development in time), the state of matter changes. The set of states of the matter system (all its subsystems) represents by itself information about the system. Due to the indeterminacy and infinity of the property or structure, the amount of information in itself is infinite in any material body.

Therefore, in front of and around a person - there is an infinity of an unknowable world and absolute information inaccessibility... Therefore, in a broad sense, information, as a common property of matter, exists in the world independently of human will and consciousness.

It is the self (primary, real, objective, initial) information, as a property of transforming matter, its different forms (structure, morphology) into a variety of material bodies, which is transmitted through interaction and imprinted in their structure and arrangement.

Perhaps this information was meant by Norbert Wiener, the greatest scientist of the 20th century when he said that true information cannot be measured (Kuprashvili, 2022).

Information in the narrow sense, information related to human consciousness, i.e. the content of information about the objects and processes of the material world, which is formed by the subjective consciousness of a person, differs from self-information (Kuprashvili, 2022).

From the point of view of the perception of the real environment, it is a fact that the mental and physical capabilities of a person are limited and he perceives (reflects) reality subjectively, that is, within the limits of the limited capabilities provided by nature.

The organ of vision can be used as an illustration, which is not perfect and perceives only a certain, limited part of the color spectrum. At this time, specialists believe that more than 90% of all information about the outside world is received by a person through this limited vision, which, in turn, depends on the presence of sunlight (or artificial) light (Kuprashvili, 2022).

This time, the subject of interest is precisely this secondary, in a narrow sense, "human" information, which is related to human logical thinking (the highest category of reflection of reality on Earth) and is used in society (in the highest form of development, on Earth), that is, information about the outside world and About the processes taking place in it, which is perceived by a person or a special device connected to it. Further in the text, the term "information" will be used only in this context.

Researchers have formed completely different and sometimes contradictory views and ideas about the nature of information, its essence, and its definition, which is reflected in the scientific literature dedicated to the study of this important problem.

One thing is clear, the approach to the definition of the concept of information still has an intuitive nature, and therefore, as mentioned, it receives different meanings from different fields of human activity:

- Normally, information is any data, information, or knowledge that interests someone. For example, a message about an event or someone's activity, etc.;
- In technology, information is a message that is transmitted in the form of signs or signals (in this case there is a communication channel, message source, and message receiver);
- Information in cybernetics is part of knowledge that is used for management, orientation, and active action, that is, for system maintenance, improvement, development, etc. (Kuprashvili, 2022).

In a simple and general definition, information is a form of reflection of matter (subject) and process, i.e. information about the world and its existing objects and current processes, a message perceived by a person or a special device related to it.

As mentioned above, in this case, the focus is mainly on the information that refers, first of all, to people's relationships, their interactions, needs, interests, etc., that is, information used by society. Information circulates in society, which represents both social and natural knowledge, information to the extent that society will use it, that is, to the extent that it is included in the orbit of public life. This information bears a deep trace of social and public relations, it is an imprint of the needs, interests, and mental qualities of the society, the relationships that the information reflects, and that benefit from the information.

Therefore, the public's attitude towards different types of information is not uniform. For example, technical and natural scientific information does not contain direct political motives. Political direction may be revealed here indirectly, depending on the purpose for which this information is used.

In this context, the starting point for information study and research can be, for example, information:

- as a set of necessary data for the optimization of the management system;
- as a set of highly specialized data produced in large quantities in all spheres of society's activity;
- as a necessary reserve and resource for the socio-economic development of society, like other resources: labor, energy, material, etc.;
- as an intellectual resource in the system of ensuring the vitality of the society, the most important part of the intellectual property of the society, the share of which is increasing more and more in the modern world, etc.

The following main types of information can be found in public relations:

- political;
- economic;
- social;
- technical;
- natural sciences;
- scientific;
- aesthetic;
- ideological and others (Dewar, 2018).

From a practical point of view, the information is presented in the form of a monthly notification. An information message is related to a source of information, a receiver of information, and a channel of transmission. The message is transmitted from the source to the receiver in a material-energy form (in the *form of sound, light, electronic and other signals*).

A person perceives a message through sense organs. In technology, the receiver of information receives the message with the help of various measuring and recording equipment.

The special feature of information is that, regardless of its continuously growing consumption, its accumulation is constantly increasing in raising the volume.

When characterizing information, attention is drawn to its following features:

- The scale of circulation - from minimal (directly from personal relationships) to maximal (global);
- Circulation time - at least - one time, according to duration - uncertain;
- Direction of movement - either horizontal (between individuals or structures of one social level), or vertical (between individuals or structures of different social levels. Direct - directive-normative, reverse - control-reporting;
- Emotional coloring - imperative during top-down movement, and agreeable during bottom-up and horizontal movement;
- The manner of creation - can be personified (information coming from an individual, related or not related to his social role) or impersonal (information coming from a group, structure, as well as - an individual, but without reference to it);
- Purpose of creation - impact (consent, incitement, etc.).

So, according to the classification, the following types of information are mainly distinguished:

- Information about the past;
- Information about the present;
- Information about the future (forecast - indicative, normative, warning);
- Planning information (Gomez, 2019).

Information is also distinguished according to the addressee: internal information and external information.

Information performs the following functions:

- Communication (providing connection between people);
- Governance;
- Scientific-cognitive;
- Educational;
- Agitation-propaganda and others.

Also, based on different criteria, information is divided into types:

1. According to perception:
   ◦ Visual - sensed by the organ of sight;
   ◦ Auditory – sensed by the hearing organ;
   ◦ Tactile - felt by tactile receptors;
   ◦ Gustatory - will be felt by the taste receptors;
   ◦ Fragrant - will be felt by the smell receptors (Hitchens, Gallagher, 2019).
2. According to the submission form:
   ◦ Written - text, numbers, special characters, and other forms;
   ◦ Graphic - in the form of images, tables, photography, and other forms;
   ◦ In the form of sound signals - transmitted orally or through a recording;
   ◦ In the form of light;
   ◦ In the form of radio waves;
   ◦ In the form of electrical and nerve impulses;

- ◦   In the form of magnetic records;
- ◦   In the form of gestures and mimicry;
- ◦   Oral, in verbal form (speech);
- ◦   In the form of smell and taste sensations;
- ◦   In the form of chromosomes (through which the characteristics of the organism are inherited) and others (Hitchens, Gallagher, 2019).

3.   According to the public purpose:
- ◦   Mass - every day, public-political, aesthetic;
- ◦   Special - scientific, technical, management (managerial), production;
- ◦   Personal - knowledge, ability, intuition.

The following main features of information deserve special attention:

- •   Objectivity - does not depend on someone's opinion;
- •   Relevance – corresponds to the user's needs (demands);
- •   Timeliness – meets the user's needs at the right moment;
- •   Infallibility – the absence of hidden errors. Infallible information may become outdated over time and may no longer reflect the true state of affairs;
- •   Reliability – reflects the real situation;
- •   Completeness – it is exhaustive (given to the user), sufficient for understanding and decision-making;
- •   Relevance - it is essential, to respond to today's situation;
- •   Availability – the possibility of receiving it for a given user;
- •   Security - the impossibility of unauthorized changes and use of information;
- •   Value (usefulness, importance) - provides a solution to the task.. Needed to make the right decision;
- •   Certainty (clarity, clearness) – expressed in a language that everyone can understand (Kello, 2013).

In addition, information has other properties:

- •   Attributability (belonging) – discrete (information consists of individual parts, signs), continuity (possibility of accumulating information);
- •   Practicality – information volume and density;
- •   Dynamism (related to changes in information over time) - copying (multiplication of information), transfer from source to user, translation from one language to another, transfer to another carrier, obsolescence (carrier - physically, value - morally) (Kello, 2017).

An information carrier is an environment or a physical body for the transmission, storage, and recovery of information (electrical, light, heat, sound, radio signals, magnetic and laser discs, printed matter, photography, etc.).

Certain operations are performed within informational operations, that is, information can be: created, received, transmitted, stored, processed, searched, perceived, divided, multiplied, combined, decomposed, and measured (Lewis, 2018).

Information measurement parameters are also of interest - the amount of information and the volume of data. Accordingly, the parameters of information quality are representativeness, meaningfulness, sufficiency, accessibility, relevance, accuracy, reliability, and sustainability.

It is a fact that the system of public relations determines the information processes in society. Information impact of social groups, individuals, and different spheres of social life - is a very important specific form of social interaction. The progress of production, science, culture, and society as a whole depends a lot on how efficiently and rationally this form is organized. On the other hand, the degree of effectiveness and fluency of informational interaction is a significant indicator of public progress.

Information is knowledge to a certain extent, but not everything that humanity possesses, only that part that is used for orientation, active action, and management, i.e. perfection and development of the system, and protection of its qualitative specificity.

Information connection, information communication, that is, the truth about events and processes is a constant exchange of information. The continuity of the information flow ensures the continuity of the management process.

Since management is a process of continuous implementation of appropriate actions on the system, it is based on continuously received information that the subject of management can influence the management system. Each cycle of management begins with the collection and processing of information and ends with receiving information, which, in turn, is the starting point for a new cycle of management. From this point of view, the importance of information is immeasurable, because it has become the dominant factor that creates the system.

Information and Management

Management is related to the development and implementation of targeted governance impacts on the system, which, in turn, includes the collection, transmission, and processing of necessary information, and making and implementing appropriate decisions (Finnemore, 2016).

Management and managed systems cannot exist without information, which has a kind of signaling character, which gives impulses about deviations from the goal and signals for order and correction of errors. Perceives what they are, the system reacts and adjusts its actions and behavior accordingly.

Thanks to information flows, feedback is also provided, which reflects the changes in the system under the influence of governance. Information also provides forward reflection, which allows the governance system to "get ahead" of events. In management activities, information is a set of data about the state of the manager and the systems under management.

Without information, both forecasting and planning are inconceivable, as forecasts and plans are born based on them. Without information, it is difficult to prepare a decision. Information is also collected at the control stage, which allows reasoning about actual changes in the control object.

Information is the initial resource for the development of state policy and the implementation of state governance in any field. Information provision of the state government, its timely provision with reliable information - is the most important prerequisite for the effective functioning of the state mechanism, and the realization of all stages of the governance process. Information provision plays a crucial role in the management process. Information is a "necessary food" to create a general prerequisite for the management process, during which the connection between the subject and the object of management is carried out to make an optimal management decision.

Information-Technological Revolution, Information Society, Knowledge Management Infrastructure

The post-industrial or information era is the presence of unlimited human capabilities in the modern stage of receiving and transmitting information, with the fastest access to sources of knowledge acquired by humanity, which was unimaginable in previous eras of human development.

The founders of the concept of the information age are: American scientist, mathematician and philosopher, the founder of the theory of cybernetics and artificial intelligence, Norbert Wiener (1894-1964); American engineer and mathematician, founder of information theory Claude Elwood Shannon (1916-2001); American sociologist and publicist Daniel Bell (1919-2011), the founder of the theory of post-industrial (informational) society; American sociologist and futurologist, one of the authors of the post-industrial society concept Alvin Toffler (1928); American scientist of Austrian origin, 20th century management theorist, author of the concept of "information worker" Peter Ferdinand Drucker (1909-2005); Manuel Castells, an American sociologist of Spanish origin, the greatest specialist in the theory of information society (1942); Canadian philosopher, philologist, theoretician in the sphere of influence of means of communication on people and society, Marshall McLuhan (1911-1980) and others (Kuprashvili, 2022).

The information revolution affected:

- The development of information technology - the creation of the first computing machines, and computers, the invention of transistors, their miniaturization, the birth of global networks, etc.
- The creation of the most complex technical systems was made possible by the achievements in the development of technologies, which, in turn, made it possible to quickly process incredibly large volumes of information compared to previous years.
- Development of the scientific base for the management and effective operation of these systems.

The imperfection of the mechanistic explanation of development processes led to the emergence of a new systematic approach in the research methodology.

- In the middle of the 20th century, Norbert Wiener created a new science - cybernetics - about communication and system management.
- The information theory developed by Claude Shannon changed the approach to information. It has become a certain quantity that can be measured and transmitted over long distances without a loss (Fischerkeller, 2018).

In the context of the information revolution, the quality and need for information are increasing; The main thing has become not the production of goods, but the provision of services, that is, there is a tendency to move to a service economy.

At the same time, the following were created and developed: 1. Social networks (Facebook, Twitter...) and Internet media - long distance gradually lost their content. 2. Mass culture. Several subcultures are created - with their language, advantages, values, etc (Georgieva, 2020).

The trilogy of Manuel Castells played a special role in the birth of the new theory. He investigated the processes of the emergence of a new society, culture, and economy from the point of view of the informational-technological revolution that began in the 70s in the USA, the revolution that started the fundamental transformation of society from the 80s of the last century.

In the twentieth century, three great revolutions took place in science:

1. Quantum;
2. Biomolecular;
3. Computer.

These revolutions gave the world three great discoveries:

1. Atom;
2. Gene;
3. Computer (Egloff, 2019).

Therefore, in terms of development, humanity has made a huge leap. These discoveries did not take a "purely academic" look, they did not remain only in the field of abstraction and theory, on the contrary, they had a significant impact on the daily life of the rest of the world.

It is enough to turn a scientific discovery into a technology and use it in everyday life for it to acquire a huge socio-political meaning. Also happened the revolution in the field of thought and information. The information revolution has created the digital world, which has brought people to modern information technology, and new technologies have created incredible opportunities for communication so that science fiction and reality are almost synonymous.

An information-technological revolution is a historical event as big as the industrial revolution of the 18th century, which caused a revolution in the foundations of society, economy, and culture. The history of technological revolutions shows that they were characterized by an all-encompassing influence, penetrating all spheres of human life and activity, and becoming its vital fabric (Gheciu, 2019).

According to Manuel Castells, unlike all other technological revolutions, the core of the transformations the world is experiencing today is related to information and communication technologies. Information technology based on electronics has an incomparable capacity for memory and an unprecedented speed of combining and transmitting information bits. Anyone who works with a word processor knows that electronic text is characterized by great and essential flexibility of text feedback, interaction, and processing, which completely changes the process of communication itself.

Information technology determines the information revolution, and explains - what new sources of energy were included in the industrial revolution. As Manuel Castells points out, today's technological revolution is characterized: not by the prioritization of information and knowledge, which was highlighted in the previous first and second industrial revolutions, but by the use of this knowledge and information to generate such knowledge and devices that process information and implement communications innovations and innovations in the cumulative space of feedback between directions of use (Kuprashvili, 2022). Users not only learn technologies but also create them, enrich and transform networks, finding new fields themselves. The feedback loop between introducing new technologies, using them, and advancing them in new areas is a very fast process within the new technological paradigm. As a result, we find that the diffusion of technology infinitely expands its power to the extent that these technologies are appropriated and redefined by users. Thus, new information technologies are not just tools to be used, but processes that need to be developed. In such a case, the user and the inventor (creator) can be united in one person, that is, the user can take control of the technology, as happened in the case of the Internet.

The biggest sign that characterizes the new informational-technological revolution is the immediate use of the technologies created by it for self-development, thus connecting the world into a single whole. Based on the information-technological revolution, the rapid development of information technologies gave an impetus to the formation of such social relations, the formation of such a society, the power of development of which was not the production of material products, but the production of informational products. Material products contain more and more information and theoretical knowledge, which means an increase in the share of innovation, design, and marketing in its values.

From the point of view of cultural and social changes, the information revolution affects all areas of human life - health and education, politics, etc. One thing is clear, the world has become faster today, because there is the internet, mobile phones, etc., and the economy has been electrified - it has also become digital. The global financial economy is completely dependent on information technologies. A computer is run like clockwork in a globally integrated financial market. Millions of dollars worth of transactions can be transacted electronically in seconds.

The information revolution is changing both the workplace and the content of work itself. These changes, according to the researchers, are manifested in the following:

- a computer system program already "takes decisions";
- Work and labor become more abstract. If in the industrial society the worker had more contact with his product, now, in the post-industrial-information age, abstract words and symbols through a sophisticated computer program solve this;
- Integration at the workplace is limited, the information revolution has tied people to the computer, which means that they have to present themselves to the computer and, accordingly, have less contact with each other;
- Through the computer, the supervisor can constantly monitor the working personnel. The computer program determines the social order, and establishes a hierarchical dependence between the employer and the hired personnel;
- Various social movements, which are formed through social networks (Facebook, Twitter, etc.), influence politics through the same networks, which is the so-called digital (electronic) democracy;
- Digital relations, etc., have gained a large scale (Maness, 2016).

Cyberspace, virtual reality, i.e. digital world, where communication, politics, religion, and other aspects of social life are intertwined. It is clear that there are certain risks associated with information technology, but it is still difficult to identify the negative consequences of the digital world. Some of the changes brought about by it are of a much deeper social nature. A "post-human society" is gradually being formed. A person goes beyond his/her humanity. New forms of life are created (new forms of feeling time), and the classical rhythm of life is destroyed.

At the same time, Cyberspace has created many other problems:

- Since the main thing is to connect to the network, the computer network, in turn, will finally take such a mass means of communication as television (that is, centralized broadcasting for a homogeneous audience), because through it communications become individual and interactive;

- The Internet contributes to the fragmentation of society. Even today's cable and satellite television is tailored to the target audience, it separates the viewers with pre-selected information. The medium itself becomes a message. different markets of the audience are provided with customized and diversified programs and channels;
- the domestic way of life, which is focused on recreation and entertainment, grows and develops;
- The Internet (of interactions and individualization) promotes the creation of electronic communities that will connect people rather than separate them. "virtual communities" are being created in the network;
- "Real virtuality" is formed, which includes an alloy of text, audio, video, and visual forms, i.e. multimedia. When a person is intense networked relationships and therefore enters into relationships with others, he experiences the only reality - the reality of the media (McCarthy, 2018).

Castells was not wrong when he pointed out that this system is completely covered and immersed in a virtual world, a fictional world, in which external reflections not only inform us about some experience but also become an experience (Weber, 2018).

In the 21st century, the main driving force of progress is knowledge and information generation, exchange, distribution, and consumption technologies, the so-called became intelligent technologies. The new world is cyberspace, the world of computers, the Internet and mobile phones, the world of networks, on the scale and efficiency of which the well-being of peoples and states directly depends.

Today, the one who focuses on the production of information and knowledge wins. Unlike the old times, knowledge, obtaining, and exchanging new information is no longer the privilege of the chosen ones. The strength and wealth of the state are determined not by the amount of knowledge that lies as "dead weight" somewhere in the foundation of fundamental sciences, but by the ability to acquire this knowledge and information as widely as possible and, therefore, by the speed of their spread; In other words, by using cyberspace, by using communication networks. The higher the rates of information (knowledge) production, distribution, and dissemination, the faster they are transformed into new technologies, and useful inventions, and the higher the growth rates of economic and social integration of the country.

As a result of the information revolution, not only production but also the way of life of people, the value system has changed, and the importance of cultural, post-materialist values has increased compared to material values. On its basis, a new social system was formed - an information society, where the priority is not the production and service of goods, but the production and consumption of knowledge and intelligence, which leads to the expansion of the share of mental labor; An information society was created, which requires creativity from people and where the demand for knowledge is increasing.

The term "information society" was introduced by Fritz Machlup (1902-1983) and Umesao Tadao (1920-2010) in the early 60s of the 20th century. The theory of transformation of the industrial society into an information society, predicted by Daniel Bailey, was developed by the Japanese Yoneji Masuda (1905-1995) and others. According to Masuda, computerization changes human nature and transforms it from Homo Sapiens to Nomo Intelligens (Kuprashvili, 2022).

Most importantly, new means of communication systems and connections are reducing the distance between people and other artificially created barriers. Moreover, they do not recognize the boundaries between countries and peoples. New information, new knowledge produced by one intelligence, instantly becomes available to all and accessible to all. The world has never been the same. It resembles a "global village" where everyone knows everything about everyone else. A global information society is being formed, the unity of which is ensured by modern intelligent technologies. Informative is the stage of development of society, at which information and scientific knowledge become the determining factor of public life and productivity of production:

There is also an exponential increase in the amount of knowledge, and a rapid reduction in the time of doubling knowledge; (Since the beginning of our era, it took 1750 years to double knowledge, the second doubling occurred in 1900, and the third in 1950) (Stevens, 2016).

Knowledge management infrastructure. The amount of information doubles every year (tomorrow this time will be incredibly reduced), this is the "information explosion", but the main thing is not only the quantitative increase of information, the main thing is the new intelligent technologies that revolutionize themselves every year and information and knowledge through the acquisition of "knowledge by knowledge" They turn it into one of the main social values that unite the society and turns it into the main product of production, a commodity.

According to the analysts of the famous American company Arthur Andersen LLP, the amount of knowledge at the disposal of mankind doubles every five years. In the 30s of the 21st century, human knowledge will double every 72 days. The future generation, from the informational point of view, will live in a completely different difficult environment. This company has developed another interesting formula: knowledge is a person plus information, taken as the quality of the means of disseminating this information (Sabbah, 2018).

If we analyze the development of information technologies over the last 20 years, there is a clear trend of movement from data processing technology to tools for working with information, to systems that help users to effectively analyze, understand information and make decisions based on it. But information analysis tools are still behind the times. As Reuters research showed, most of the interviewed specialists in the field of information technologies identified information overload as a problem with the efficiency of internal communication (including the Internet network).

The wide implementation of information technologies has created a problem for organizations to accumulate knowledge, and experience and use accumulated theoretical or practical knowledge. Therefore, the importance of effective use of knowledge, and knowledge management in the information society is increasing day by day.

Currently, there is no universally recognized methodology for evaluating the economic effect obtained by introducing information systems. It is even more difficult to evaluate the creation and implementation of a knowledge management system. However, this does not mean that individual assessments cannot be made in individual-specific cases. We are talking about a universal, universally useful method. We will consider the approaches available today that allow us to estimate the effectiveness of decision-making at least approximately (Shires, 2018).

Concepts of knowledge management. Among the existing concepts, the approach that is focused on the technological platform or the employees of the organization is the main one.

Concepts of knowledge management identify four business tasks, the solution of which improves the organization's activities through knowledge management: innovation, perception ability (speed of reaction), labor productivity, and competence (Mueller, 2010).

Innovation - finding and developing new ideas, bringing people together in a virtual team, creating forums for "brainstorming" and employees - are the main conditions for gaining an advantage over competitors.

Ability to perceive (quickness of reaction) - providing employees with the necessary information, at the right time, for the most efficient and quick adaptation to changes.

Productivity of work – efficiency of repeated use of knowledge arrays.

That is why special efforts in knowledge management are directed at documenting, cataloging, and distributing corporate information resources (Shires, 2020).

Competence – development of organizational knowledge. The concept that views knowledge as an organization's capital suggests that it consists of the following assets: market, human, infrastructural and intellectual property.

Market assets are intangible assets related to market operations.

Human assets mean the set of knowledge of the organization's employees, their creative abilities, ability to solve problems, leadership characteristics, and entrepreneurial and management habits (Slayton, 2017).

Infrastructure assets – technologies, methods, and processes that ensure the operation of the organization.

Intellectual property includes patents, copyrights, trademarks of goods and services, innovations, commercial secrets, etc.

The constant increase in the importance of intellectual capital reflects the organization's even greater dependence on intangible assets, and, accordingly, the importance of this concept and its relevance. Moreover, new types of organizations are emerging that own only intangible assets and produce only intangible products. These are mass media, consulting, and other organizations whose main resource is knowledge.

Organization's knowledge management system. To create a knowledge management system, three types of infrastructure are necessary: organizational, social, and technological.

Organizational infrastructure – a set of regulations that ensure the formal side of information processing in the organization. For example, the introduction of a knowledge management system is often hindered by the internal competition of the organization: many people get used to it and believe that sharing knowledge with colleagues is not advantageous for them. If there is a knowledge base in the organization, then every employee risks having his know-how or idea stolen and appropriated, so these issues need to be regulated.

Social infrastructure is based on corporate culture. It is the quality of relations between the employees of the organization that is most important for the dissemination and use of knowledge. Workgroups must have the ability to share information both among themselves and within the group. Employees should have access to all kinds of information from their workplace. The organization needs to acquire new knowledge, that is, the ability to acquire knowledge without significant expenditure of time and labor.

The technological infrastructure must be supported by a searchable architecture since it is impossible to manage intellectual capital without quick and easy access to it. It's also not possible to manage knowledge just by installing and running the appropriate application – it's usually a complex hardware-software complex. If the knowledge is received, then there is a question of finding out where and how to store it. Usually, unlike databases, such storage is not based on information, but on tasks and their solutions. The knowledge base should be organized in such a way that the search presents the most relevant results that can be used immediately.

Difficulties arise during the implementation of a knowledge management system project due to mistakes made in the organization of any type of infrastructure. In particular, it can be mistakes made during the design of the technical platform, although it is much easier to correct such mistakes since hardware and software tools are relatively less connected to business processes or social structures of the organization, which cannot be said about organizational and social infrastructures.

Problems related to the tasks that are realized based on the organizational infrastructure are often caused by such factors as the untimely reaction of the responsible department regarding the necessary change of regulations.

The disconnection of the collective can be attributed to the problems caused by the social infrastructure. Ideally, a knowledge management system should perform several functions, including:

- Export – selection of knowledge from external repositories, sorted by topic, identification of analogs;
- Performance – formulating a problem or topic, searching for relevant knowledge;
- Mediation – evaluation of hidden knowledge. Given the interest of users, the system can connect people working on the same problems to exchange knowledge. The function is performed through group software, internet portals, workflow support systems, and document management;
- Cognition – use of acquired knowledge. To solve this task, artificial intelligence can be included, which allows the system to decide on its own.

The portal option for realizing solutions in knowledge management is popular in European countries. Usually, this is a resource that is integrated with various information systems and applications. It is a corporate library, which is divided into thematic sections and in which information is updated in real-time. The peculiarity of the portal is the possibility of personalization - the user can choose the attachment he needs at a given moment. According to data from the US analytical group Meta group, 81% of the organizations implementing knowledge management systems have stopped their attention on the portal option.

The software and hardware of the system must be scalable, that is, it must have the ability to develop following changes in the organization. At the same time, the systems should be as open as possible, ie. It should be possible to exchange data with other systems, so that when communicating with external partners, information can be exchanged promptly, without excessive delay.

These epochal changes in the development of humanity require proper awareness because they are fully reflected in the provision of national security.

Several Aspects Related to the Fifth Space

The urgency of the problem is due to the unprecedented development of information communication and cyber-technologies in the information age, with the irreversible processes of cyber-attacks of an indefinite scale, which puts before the whole world the need to strengthen security measures.

From the second half of the 20th century, the classical forms of military conflicts are gradually being replaced by new forms of confrontation between states, and new forms of modern wars: informational, economic, diplomatic, hybrid, psychological, etc. wars.

This time, the subject of our interest is the variety of information war, cyber war, and the area of its military action and conflict - cyberspace. To date, there is no agreed official definition of cyberspace. For example, according to the Oxford Academic Dictionary, it is considered an imaginary space without a physical location in which communication is done through computer networks. The same Oxford English Dictionary gives a different definition: cyberspace is a complex of interconnected information-technological infrastructure, which includes the global Internet network, computer systems, telecommunications networks, and processors. The Cambridge Dictionary defines it as "an electronic system that enables computer users around the world to communicate with each other and access information for any purpose". According to the dictionary of the official website of the US government "COMPUTER SECURITY RESOURCE CENTER - CSRC", cyberspace is a global area in the information environment consisting of an interdependent network of information system infrastructures, including the Internet, telecommunications networks, computer systems, embedded including processors and controllers. More than 30 definitions of cybercrime can be found in both scientific literature and official government sources; Therefore, for everyone's understanding, it can be said more simply that cyberspace is a conditional environment in which communication takes place through computer networks (Apsny, 2016).

Until now, the traditional spaces of warfare were known - land, sea, and air, and space was added later. At the beginning of the 21st century, a completely new and different field of military operations emerged - cyberspace. Traditional wars with a 14-thousand-year history are completely different from cyber wars. American political scientist, South Carolina University professor Conway W. Henderson points out: "From 3500 BC to the end of the 20th century, there were 14,500 wars that killed 3.5 billion people, mankind lived in peace for only 300 years." This means that the history of mankind has been a history of wars (Kuprashvili, 2022).

Archaeologist Lawrence H Keeley, a professor at the University of Illinois at Chicago, in his classic book "The War Before Civilization," believes that traces of the first war can be found in a 14,000-year-old Mesolithic burial ground, where 45% of the skeletons show signs of violent Mesopotamia.

Professor of Tel Aviv University, head of the national security course, and author of the book "War in Human Civilization", Azar Gat notes that approximately 5 thousand years ago, starting from the formation of states, wars covered most of the earth (Hagmann, 2019).

In any case, organized war at the societal level, when one society opposed another, must have been an event arising from the food production revolution (Neolithic Age), which was probably largely due to the desire to seize the surplus product created as a result of this revolution. According to archaeological excavations, the first traces of war (struggle for territories, property, and women) can be found in the ancient Middle East.

According to military historians, it is no coincidence that well-organized armies were formed for the first time in the history of mankind in those countries (Sumeria, Egypt) where agriculture and cattle breeding first reached a special scale. For example, the Mesopotamia city-states could field an army of about ten thousand warriors. The fighters were armed with copper (later bronze) tools, bows and arrows, spears, and axes. BC year From the middle of the 3rd millennium in Mesopotamia, as well as in Egypt, the products of high-quality, increasingly sophisticated weapons made of bronze gradually increased. At that time, the Sumerian infantry was armed with spears and spears, swords and clubs, and battle axes and clubs. A widespread weapon throughout the ancient East was the bow and arrow and the spear, with which the infantry in Mesopotamia, Egypt, and China was armed.

BC year From the beginning of the 2nd millennium, a technological innovation appeared in the military affairs of the Middle East - a horse-drawn, light chariot. The following were placed in the chariot: a spear, a sword, a staff, and a bow and arrow. Chariots were Bronze Age tanks in their efficiency. Their use reached its peak during the Battle of Kadesh (1274 BC) when up to 6,000 chariots from both sides were to take part on the battlefield. Then the advent of gunpowder and the acceleration of technical progress ushered in the wars of the Industrial Age. The 20th century is especially distinguished by destructive global wars. The First World War (1914-1918) killed up to 9 million people, and the largest and bloodiest World War II (1939-1945) - was more than 60 million (Kuprashvili, 2022).

The First World War was characterized by old-style war battles, skirmishes of armed men, the use of cavalry, and tanks and airplanes that played an insignificant role. Equipment played a decisive role in the Second World War - tanks, airplanes, and artillery. A great role was given to propaganda and ideological influence on the opponent. It should be noted that before the advent of the information age, the traditional understanding of war did not go beyond the standards established thousands of years ago about its content, soldiers, battlefield, and weapons.

Also of note are William S. Lind, Col. Keith Nightengale, Capt. John F. Schmitt, Col. Joseph W. Sutton, and Lt. Col. Gary I. Wilson. "The Changing Face of War: Into the Fourth Generation" was published in 1989 in the US Military Journal. The famous concept of four generations of war also originates from this. The summary of the four generations of war described by the authors is as follows:

The war of the first generation covers approximately the years 1648-1860. It was preceded by the conclusion of the 30-year war, which ended in 1648, with the Treaty of Westphalia, the fundamental act of the system of international relations, which meant: the fundamental right of states' sovereignty and political self-determination; The principles of (legitimate) equality between states and non-interference by one state in the domestic affairs of another (Leese, 2019).

The first-generation war was a period of transition from unorganized hand-to-hand warfare to organized, disciplined warfare. At that time, they used extended formation (soldiers moved side by side, arranged in one extended line) and marching column (arrangement of troops in a single marching column echeloned in depth), i.e., the main characteristic of the first generation war was moving on the battlefield in an organized, extended formation. During this period, military insignia, differentiation of ranks, uniforms, a form of greeting, etc. were created. Smoothbore muskets were mostly used in the wars of this generation.

Second-generation wars, or wars of the industrial age, span the period from the US Civil War through World War I. The authors associate the beginning of the war of this generation with the creation of muzzle-loading muskets and breech-loading weapons, machine guns, and artillery, which allowed for more accurate, long-range destruction of the target. As a result, the practice of moving soldiers in the direction of the enemy in an open formation became very risky and ended with great losses, so the search for new means began. Emphasis was placed on a small group of soldiers, on the maneuverable and independent use of new technologies. For example, a machine gun allowed a small group of soldiers to act independently. Centrally controlled firepower was meticulously synchronized. Detailed plans and orders were developed for all types of troops. Commanders were strictly limited and largely dependent on superiors.

The war of the third generation was not based on firepower, but was characteristic of it: speed, surprise, tactical maneuvers, blitzkrieg, etc., maneuverable and not linear deployment mainly related to the development of maneuver warfare, blitzkrieg. Third-generation warfare focused on speed and surprise, outflanking the enemy's advance forces and attacking his rear positions. In essence, it was the end of line warfare at the tactical level, where armed forces did not try to meet each other head-on and then fight, but to outflank, outmaneuver, outmaneuver, and gain similar advantages. Also, relatively decentralized management was characteristic of this generation.

During fourth-generation warfare, the lines between war and politics, soldier and civilian, peace and conflict, and battlefield and security are gradually blurring and becoming almost invisible. The front line as such does not exist. In this generation of war, there is a tendency to revert to the pre-war state of the first generation, as the state loses its monopoly on war. In the fourth generation war, the state may no longer be a party, and, worldwide, the party may be a terrorist organization, for example, Al-Qaeda, Hamas, Hezbollah, Taliban, etc.

In this article, the authors characterized four generations of war for the period of the article's publication (1989), that is, when the industrial age was fading into history and the information age was being born. Therefore, in our opinion, the essential factors that led to the beginning of a new era, that is, when the main strategic resource for the development of society is not coal and steel (for the production of armor), but information, were not properly reflected in them. Accordingly, the war was essentially transformed into an information war (information, in the modern sense, based on the concepts of Norbert Wiener and Claude Shannon), where the content of the war is determined by the possibilities of information possession and manipulation and the use of modern information and telecommunication technologies.

The information age has changed the standards of understanding of war. From this point of view, the modern classic of the art of war by Chinese Colonel Qiao Liang and Air Force Colonel Wang Xiang-sui, Unlimited War, published in China in 1999 (published in English in 2002) is interesting. They put forward the concept of "unrestricted warfare". They gave us a thorough description of 25 types of war (conventional, diplomatic, terrorist, intelligence, financial, network, legal, psychological, etc.) strategies, formed a new vision of the content and nature of war, hidden in the information age, in the age of globalization, and an interesting understanding of the ongoing changes in it. In their view, unrestricted war need not be uncontrolled and brutal; Violence is no longer the defining characteristic of war. Now wars are being fought not only on the battlefield but also in economic, financial, informational, ecological, energy, psychological, and other fields.

In short, today the level of development of information technologies has completely erased the borders between states in the information space and the form of information warfare has created unprecedented opportunities to defeat the opponent without using traditional, violent, destructive means. The destructive power of the impact of information war (informational-psychological war and cyber war) is so great in modern conditions that, according to researchers, not only the independence of the defeated state is called into question, but even the fact of the existence of its people as a national unity.

As mentioned, the transition from the industrial age to the information age has completely changed the situation. The firstborn of the new era is the information war, which is based on a completely new strategic resource for the development of humanity, expressing the content of the new era, the information era - information.

In the information age, the nature and content of war, and the manner of its production, are essentially changing. And in just a few decades, it will change so much that it will have very little to do with the traditional understanding of war. Therefore, accordingly, the determining factor of the content of the modern era - "information" is the determining factor of the content of modern wars, the basis and the starting point. Whatever the term may change, in a broad sense, depending on its main definition, it is called information war. The information age has ushered in age-matched warfare and spawned its arena of warfare—cyberspace.

In cyberspace, an adversary-initiated cyber-attack is carried out on government networks, computer systems of electric utilities, transportation or cellular telephone companies, financial institutions, and industrial control systems, even to create chaos, demoralizing the population, or even preparing the battlefield for a kinetic attack, or even to carry out cyber attacks in parallel with the kinetic attack, etc.

The tactics of conducting warfare in cyberspace, cyber-attacks, to be explained simply, are as follows: a network consisting of thousands of infected computers (the so-called botnet) starts attacking a server at the same time. The attack is carried out by sequentially sending packets of information to restart and shut down the server - a DoS attack. The most common means of infecting computers are viruses called Trojan horses. The main function of this virus is to infiltrate the system and allow the owner of the virus to control the opponent's computer.

The rapid development of information technologies in the modern world has had a great impact on the formation of a new, "virtual" dimension of political space, which plays an increasingly important role in domestic and foreign policy. It is to this virtual dimension that cyberspace belongs, which marks a special sphere of social interaction, determined by a set of processes, flows through the world's computer networks, and turns into another environment of human activity and existence.

In addition to the Internet, there are many other computer networks in cyberspace, such as transnational ones, through which data about financial flows, trades on various exchanges, and credit card transactions are transmitted. In addition, various machine and mechanism control systems operate in cyberspace, for example, transport and energy systems, control panels for generators, elevators, pumps, etc.

The most important and special part of cyberspace is the computer networks for the management of military equipment, including unmanned (drones), combat robots, and missiles of various distances. Even from this incomplete list, it can be seen that today cyberspace is a vitally important area of informational, economic, political, and military activities of individuals, corporations, states, their connections, supranational structures, and formations.

In the modern world, cyberspace without state borders has turned into an important field of political, economic, informational, and cultural competence. Essentially, cyberspace, against the background of the unprecedented development of information and telecommunication technologies, represents a new (virtual) type of political space, in which the interests of various political subjects, states, and centers of political power collide. Since its inception, cyberspace has become the fifth field (after land, sea, air, and space) of political and military forces.

The fact that cyberspace is becoming another area of NATO's influence, along with sea, air, and land, is very telling. Accordingly, it will be necessary to use the agreement on collective defense (Euronews, 2016). On July 8, 2016, the NATO summit in Warsaw recognized cyberspace as an equal area of defense. NATO Secretary General Jens Stoltenberg noted: Contemporary challenges require us to recognize that cyber-attacks and defense against them are as important as a defense on land, sea, and air (Apsny, 2016).

Today, wars between the intelligence organizations of different countries, and their military structures, as well as economic and information battles, including economic espionage and financial sabotage, are taking place in cyberspace. This circumstance determines the great importance of the processes in cyberspace for modern political analysis, theory and practice of international relations, and political sciences.

As a result of the technological revolution, information systems became a part of human life and fundamentally changed it. Accordingly, as mentioned, a new term - "Information Era" appeared. Information reaches all spheres of modern life. For the population of the earth, it has already become the only reality of communication with the world. For ordinary people to feel like the owner of the information and, therefore, all-powerful, it is necessary for this: Internet, TV, and printed mass media.

At the same time, the information space for the political party has turned into a theater of military operations, where each opposing party tries to gain superiority. The information era has also changed the way military operations are conducted in two directions - it has become possible: direct manipulation of the enemy with information (information has become a potential weapon and a public target) and information technologies. as means to successfully conduct combat operations.

Cyber warfare is the fifth form of warfare, along with land, sea, air, and space dimensions, as stated at the NATO Warsaw Summit. In the 21st century, attempts to gain technological advantage are becoming more and more fierce. There are no limits and prohibitions here. States are trying to gain a competitive advantage in the digital world (Minárik, 2018).

Internet technologies have changed the existing reality. With the advent of the World Wide Web, all-natural boundaries between "information territories" have disappeared, and "combatant armies" have gained the ability to invade other people's lands, to conduct military operations in essentially the same way as "conventional" armies do in "conventional" wars. In modern wars, cyber armies confront each other. The United States of America, China, Russia, and other states have had cyber armies for a long time.

Scientists and soldiers in the developed countries of the world are actively working to create new informational weapons for warfare in cyberspace, moreover, some countries have already established special groups in the armed forces and other power structures in this direction.

Informational weapons in cyber war are characterized by a minimal level of expenditure and high efficiency of use. It does not destroy the opponent's manpower, does not require the creation of complex structures, and at the same time, it is not necessary to cross the official state border.

Along with the influence of telecommunication means, as mentioned above, one of the main objects of influence of informational weapons remains a person and his worldview. It violates spiritual values by affecting the individual, group, and mass consciousness of the country's population. Manipulation of consciousness is the main factor in causing harm with information weapons.

The Internet plays a huge role in the globalization of information wars. With its growing popularity, some people are so involved in the virtual space that they prefer the Internet to reality, spending most of their time at the computer. This is a dizzying imaginary world, and the thinking of a person immersed in it becomes autistic, which makes the effect of manipulation even easier (Waever, 2010).

To the users of information, which includes the entire population of developed countries and the majority of the inhabitants of developing countries, politicians study their habits and desires to introduce the instructions, desires, and knowledge necessary for manipulation in the next population.

CONCLUSION

Today, many countries have taken a course on information warfare. The amount of funds allocated for this purpose proves that they consider gaining an advantage in the information field as one of the main means to achieve the national strategy of this country in the 21st century.

In today's era, it has become much more difficult to maintain security and stability. The government of some countries, various organized crime groups, and terrorist organizations, based on their interests, use new technologies. Uncontrolled cyberspace has given rise to different actors and new fields of battle space. New threats are emerging that are equivalent to armed attacks in the 21st century; A new type of struggle can be much more harmful to the country's security, such as, for example, terrorism.

Some countries have separated cyberspace in their new military doctrine. Many countries have already openly affirmed their policies of readiness to embrace cyberspace and are rapidly developing their capabilities in this direction.

In the modern realities of development, an important aspect is the provision of sovereignty, that is, the expansion of the system of command and subordination relations in the social space, which is not characterized by the sign of territoriality. We are talking about cyberspace and network spaces as a specific form of social interaction. Appropriate ways to effectively spread state sovereignty in this area should be found. The legislature, executive, and judicial authorities, when they pass acts concerning cyberspace and relations in network spaces, in fact, project state power over this area. Different terms appeared in the scientific space, for example, "virtual sovereignty", "network sovereignty" and others.

The influence of the state government on the virtual union is limited. Despite the combination of governmental powers as a whole, the state in cyberspace today is represented as a virtual actor with more developed informational resources and the ability to limit the access of other actors to cyberspace (as a whole or in its separate sector). The spread of the sovereignty of the state on the virtual union is made difficult by the cyberspace organized on the network principle. Cyberspace parameters (ephemerality, interactivity, the conditionality of parameters, anonymity of actors, formation of virtual identity, etc.) play a special role in limiting sovereignty over the virtual union.

The non-acceptance of the principles of social stratification by the virtual union, the principles that dominated the pre-industrial society, is significant. The level of knowledge of the virtual actor appears as a determining factor for stratification in cyberspace. The privileged layer is formed by actors who have wider access to information and who are better versed in information flows.

In essence, cyber wars are taking place in cyberspace, and the political and economic sovereignty of the modern state significantly depends on their results. Considering this circumstance, the task of the Georgian Air Force is not only to repel enemy attacks in cyberspace but also to prepare to create cyberspace. Otherwise, it will always be an object of manipulation by the states.

REFERENCES

Apsny. (2016). *NATO has recognized cyberspace as an equal area of defense.* Information and Analytical Portal Georgia Online. Retrieved from: https://www.apsny.ge/2016/pol/1468046923.php

Cavelty, M., & Wenger, A. (2022). *Cyber Security Politics Socio-Technological Transformations and Political Fragmentation.* Retrieved from: https://library.oapen.org/bitstream/handle/20.500.12657/52574/9781000567113.pdf?sequence=1

Collier, J. (2018). Cyber security assemblages: A framework for understanding the dynamic and contested nature of security provision. *Politics and Governance, 6*(2), 13–21. doi:10.17645/pag.v6i2.1324

Dewar, R. (2022). *Cyberspace is a Consensual Hallucination.* Available from: https://www.researchgate.net/publication/325216608_Cyberspace_is_a_Consensual_Hallucination

Dewar, R. S. (Ed.). (2018). National Cybersecurity and cyber defense policy snapshots. Zurich: Center for Security Studies (CSS), ETH Zurich,

Egloff, F. J., & Wenger, A. (2019). Public attribution of cyber incidents. In F. Merz (Ed.), *CSS analyses in security policy, 244.* Center for Security Studies.

Euronews. (2016). *NATO equates cyber attacks with military aggression.* Retrieved from: https://ru.euronews.com/2016/06/15/cyberspace-is-officially-a-war-zone-nato

Finnemore, M., & Hollis, D. B. (2016). Constructing norms for global cybersecurity. *The American Journal of International Law,* 110.

Fischerkeller, M. (2018). *Offense-defense theory, cyberspace, and the irrelevance of advantage*. Institute for Defense Analysis.

Georgieva, I. (2020). The unexpected norm-setters: Intelligence agencies in cyberspace. *Contemporary Security Policy*, *41*(1), 33–54. doi:10.1080/13523260.2019.1677389

Gheciu, A., & Wohlforth, W. (2019). Trajectories of cyber security research. In A. Gheciu & W. C. Wohlforth (Eds.), *Oxford Handbook of international security*. Oxford University Press.

Gomez, M. A. (2019). Sound the alarm! Updating beliefs and degradative cyber operations. *European Journal of International Security, 4*.

Hagmann, J., Hegemann, H., & Neal, A. W. (2019). The politicisation of security: Controversy, mobilisation. *Arena Shifting. European Review of International Studies*.

Hitchens, T., & Gallagher, N. W. (2019). Building confidence in the cyber sphere: A path to multilateral progress. *Journal of Cyber Policy Kello, L*, 2013.

Kello, L. (2017). *The virtual weapon and international order*. Yale University Press. doi:10.2307/j.ctt1trkjd1

Kuprashvili, H. (2022). *Cyberspace and terminologies: Cybersecurity*. Georgian Technical University.

Leese, M., & Hoijtink, M. (Eds.). (2019). *Technology and agency in international relations*. Routledge.

Lewis, J. A. (2018). *Rethinking cyber security: Strategy, mass effects, and states*. Center for Strategic and International Studies.

Maness, R., & Valeriano, B. (2016). The impact of cyber conflict on international interactions. *Armed Forces and Society*, *42*(2), 301–323. doi:10.1177/0095327X15572997

McCarthy, D. (Ed.). (2018). *Technology and world politics: And introduction*. Routledge.

Minárik, R., Jakschis, L., & Lindström. (Eds.). (2018). *10th international conference on cyber conflict CyCon X: Maximising effects*. Tallinn: CCDCOE.

Mueller, M. L. (2010). *Networks and states: The global politics of internet governance*. The MIT Press. doi:10.7551/mitpress/9780262014595.001.0001

Sabbah, C. (2018). *Pressing pause: A new approach for international cybersecurity norm development*. The MIT Press.

Shires, J. (2018). Enacting expertise: Ritual and risk in cybersecurity. *Politics and Governance*, *6*(2), 31–40. doi:10.17645/pag.v6i2.1329

Shires, J. (2020). Cyber-noir: Cybersecurity and popular culture. *Contemporary Security Policy*, *41*(1), 82–107. doi:10.1080/13523260.2019.1670006

Slayton, R. (2017). What is the cyber offense-defense balance? Conceptions, causes, and assessment. *International Security*, *41*(3), 41. doi:10.1162/ISEC_a_00267

Stevens, T. (2016). *Cyber security and the politics of the time*. Cambridge University Press.

Waever, O. (2010). Towards a political sociology of security studies. *Security Dialogue, 41*(6), 649–658. doi:10.1177/0967010610388213

Weber, V. (2018). Linking cyber strategy with grand strategy: The case of the United States. *Journal of Cyber Policy, 3.*

Chapter 8
Collective Cyber Defense:
Legalization of Cyberspace

Mariam Nebieridze
Universitat Regensburg, Germany

ABSTRACT

In the 21st century, activities in cyberspace rose and developed significantly. New security dynamics aftermath of the Cold War have led to a shift in the world's power structures. Non-state actors (corporations, organizations, and individuals) now can reflect strategic global power due to modern information and communication technologies. Collective defense in cyberspace might be more challenging considering the nature of the virtual dimension which accomplishes two factors. They pledge the signatories to resist a shared threat, and as a result, are designed to dissuade possible aggressors. They stand at the nexus of law and strategy, as well as the junction of war and peace because of their dual objectives. But with hybrid threats on the rise, some have begun to wonder if the mutual aid provisions established in the North Atlantic and EU treaties still apply in the context of the current security situation.

INTRODUCTION

Modern technologies have put humanity under new threats and risks. With the development of digital technologies, cyberattacks acquire complex, sophisticated forms, and cyberspace becomes increasingly vulnerable. Since cyberspace is not limited to geographical boundaries, one of the biggest challenges for mankind today is the fight against cybercrime. It is important to legalize cyberspace, to develop new norms of international law and new cyber doctrines. Following Pijpers et al (2020), defensive and offensive operations take effect in cyberspace itself. 2016 Warsaw Summit Communiqué, North Atlantic Treaty Organisation acknowledged the significance of cyberspace and positioned it among other domains including air, land, and sea (NATO, 2016). NATO is primarily focused on cyber defense, whereas individual Member States have started to take the initial steps toward developing offensive cyber capabilities. Cyberspace broadens and evens the playing field for States and non-State actors to influence individuals, groups, or other audiences, notwithstanding the many similarities between operations in all domains.

DOI: 10.4018/978-1-6684-8846-1.ch008

Emerging opportunities and dangers appear to unleash State power to alter public perception or reveal or delete material in cyberspace (Pijpers and Arnold, 2020).

The reduced obstacles to entry, anonymity, the unpredictability of the threat area, and lack of public transparency in cyberspace have given rise to threats like cyberwarfare, cybercrime, cyberterrorism, and cyber espionage from both strong and weak actors such as governments, organized crime groups, and even individuals (Yuchong and Qinghui, 2021). This renders cyber threats distinct from conventional security threats, which encompass government, cover a specific geographical area, and are transparent (Sarker, 2021). Therefore, before addressing the main topic of collective cyber defense, the question of what constitutes a cyberattack, what distinguishes it from other types of attacks, and whether or not virtually any attack that occurs in cyberspace can be regarded as an attack in the traditional and classic sense emerges. Hence, it is necessary to have an appropriate definition, for the introduction of the topic and its justification, and analysis.

FUNDAMENTAL CONCEPTS

Today information is everywhere. Communication, knowledge acquisition, intelligence gathering, and persuasion all include the use of information. In the end, it can be weaponized to sway a certain audience's perceptions and choices (Pijpers and Arnold, 2020).

Even though cyberspace is becoming more crucial for national security plans, the phrase has yet to be given a widely agreed definition. However, we can highlight a range of definitions provided by various actors, including Germany, the USA, the International Telecommunication Union (ITU), and the Tallinn Manual due to their major role and central position in information and communication technologies. Considering its significant role and strategic location within the EU, Germany provided the following definition of cyberspace as "...the virtual area of all information technology systems in the world which are or could be interconnected at data level" (Federal Ministry of the Interior, Building, and Community 2021, p.125).

According to the US National Institute of Standards and Technologies cyberspace stands for "the interdependent network of information systems infrastructures including the Internet, telecommunications networks, computer systems, and embedded processors and controllers" (NIST 2012, p. B-3).

Moreover, the International Telecommunication Union (ITU) an agency of the United Nations, mentions the following elements, specifically the software that runs on computing devices, the transferred and stored data, as well as the information produced by these devices, are all included in the cyber environment. Such factors must be taken into account while discussing cybersecurity (ITU 2008).

The Tallinn Manual on the International Law Applicable to Cyber Warfare (Tallinn Manual) provides legal aspects of how international law applies to cyber disputes, as well as supports NATO with specialized multidisciplinary expertise in the areas of cyber defense research (Georgetown Law Library 2023). According to the manual, cyberspace is made up of both physical and immaterial elements, which alter, and exchange data across computer networks (Schmitt 2013).

Characteristics of Cyberspace

More specifically about cyberspace, Pijpers et al (2020) emphasize five factors that distinguish cyberspace from other domains, namely *reaching, time and speed, versatility and reusability, asymmetric effect, and anonymity*. Due to the wide presence and connectivity of cyberspace, attackers can have an impact on the regions of the world. Additionally, in terms of timing, on one hand, compared to conventional weapons, the time between the decision to cause effects and the actual use of the cyber capability may be much longer for cyberattacks. Albeit, cyber acts in one nation can have remote, direct digital repercussions in many other nations in a matter of milliseconds, while indirect effects in the real world may follow shortly after. In terms of versatility, the possible impacts of cyber acts can be applied to a wide range of potential targets (NATO 2020). Cyber tools can be modified, allowing the adversary to deploy them against the original author or new targets. Furthermore, the asymmetric effect of cyber acts is as well as worth mentioning, which is characterized by strategic and massive impacts, while likewise permitting attackers to conceal their identity and their purpose.

Owing to these qualities, cyber operations are especially well suited for use by States or State-controlled entities in circumstances that call for intelligence gathering (Pilpers and Arnold 2020). The abovementioned definitions identify certain overlaps and contrasts. It should be noted that cyberspace is conceptualized either at a virtual or physical level which represents a significant debate. In addition, the USA and ITU have recognized the "human domain" as a third level, stating that cyberspace also contains individuals (Ebner, 2015).

Heinegg (2013) referred cyberspace to as the "fifth domain" due to its enigmatic qualities in which operations are carried out, akin to the land, sea, space, or air. Therefore, facilitates the transmission of information across borders, with increased options for anonymity and cheap costs. Pijpers and Arnold (2020) conceptually separated the information environment into three dimensions.

1. The physical network layer includes the entire world in addition to every imaginable tangible object;
2. Our individual and societal knowledge, perception, comprehension, and wisdom are all included in the cognitive dimension;
3. And the third layer of the virtual realm illustrates the digital, fictitious reflection of the other two dimensions; cyber personas, which are representations of specific individuals or groups that allow them to interact in cyberspace (i.e. on the Internet and social media).

Although this split is not rigid, the information environment can also be broken down into seven layers as shown in Figure 1. So, cyberspace can be viewed as a component of the information environment. Access to the second, logical layer is made possible by these virtual identities such as usernames, alias, or email address. The third, the physical network layer, is necessary for the logical layer to operate. Information is generated, communicated, processed, and stored in physical components of various networks, and (non-physical) data is produced in physical elements as well. The potential target objects for defense or assault in military cyber operations are included in the three layers of cyberspace.

Interestingly, the Netherlands Defense Academy (NLDA) divides the so-called hard-cyber and soft-cyber activities. Hard cyber operations include hacking and targeting virtual entities to produce impacts, usually hacking activities, or disabling software completed in cyberspace. Information sent over cyberspace is used in soft cyber operations or 'influencing', that aims to affect psychology *through* cyberspace. However, implementation of both hard and soft cyber operations is possible (Pijpers et al 2021).

Figure 1.

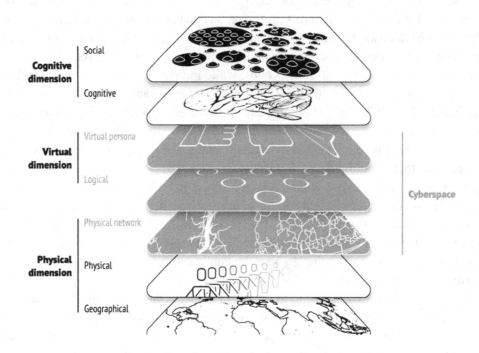

Cyber Operation vs. Kinetic Attack

It is worth mentioning that the term 'cyber-attack' does not always mean an armed attack defined by international law of self-defense. Most occurrences that are referred to as 'cyber attacks' have not involved the use of force that one might qualify as a military attack (Gill and Ducheine 2013). Likewise, the majority of prospective cyber-attacks are not expected to result in actual mortality or seriously impair a state's vital infrastructure for an extended length of time. Even though real cyber threats such as cyber espionage, cyber-sabotage, and cybercrime may be threats to the economic and national stability of the state, albeit they do not amount to violent attacks that would warrant the use of self-defense force.

Related to this Finlay and Payne (2019, p.203) highlighted two aspects of the so-called attribution problem. More precisely, the first emphasizes the technical challenge of determining the precise origin of a specific attack and the perpetrators. Whereas, the second is to illustrate the legal issue of whether and when accurate attribution makes it possible for a state to be held legally accountable for the cyber-attack. As a result, cyberattacks frequently take longer to identify and assess than conventional kinetic attacks. This study might call for the use of sensitive information and cutting-edge tools that a state would wish to keep secret. It is tough to assign blame for cyberattacks due to all of these considerations (Pijpers et al 2021).

THE NOTION OF COLLECTIVE DEFENSE

The purpose of this part is to explore the fundamentals and legal justification for self-defense.

The right of the state self-defense against an armed attack stems from the concept of statehood itself (Boddens 2017), as well as is supported by the principle of necessity and proportionality and is acknowledged in Article 51 of the UN Charter. Gill and Ducheine (2013) distinguish *legal* – action approved by the UN Security Council to maintain or restore international peace and security and *illegal* – applications of force that lack recognized legal grounds. According to Article 2(4) of the UN Charter, the use of force is prohibited, however, there are some exceptions to this rule including self-defense. The right to self-defense was and still is included in the Charter with two goals in mind: to acknowledge the preexisting right of States under customary international law and to be integrated into the Charter's system of collective security to provide a clear legal foundation for collective self-defense. The right is described as 'inherent' in Article 51 which existed at the same time the Charter came into effect.

Moreover, the founding treaty of NATO is based on the idea of collective defense. It continues to be a distinctive and enduring value that unites its member states, pledging them to defend one another and fostering a sense of unity inside the Alliance.

Thus, Article 5 is considered a cornerstone of collective self-defense of the alliance "…an armed attack against one or more of them in Europe or North America shall be considered an attack against them all" (NATO, 2022).

Article 42(7) of the European Union recalls Article 51 of the United Nations Charter which is known as the 'Mutual defense clause' and is enshrined in the Treaty on European Union (TEU) (EUEA 2022). Hence, the article ensures that Member States will stand together in the event of an armed attack on one of them. Assistance includes diplomatic or technical support, as well as logistical or medical assistance. Both the EU and NATO's mutual defense articles, which both adhere to Article 51 of the UN Charter, have a similar aim but different details. The variations concern the activation condition, the territorial scope, and the obligatory nature of the clause, as well as the implementing setup (Pijpers et al 2020). In fact, the United Nations Charter's article 51, which provides a nation's right to self-defense, is referred to in both Art. 42.7 TEU and Art. 5 NATO.

While NATO and EU members are obliged to support one another if the clause of collective defense is invoked, the difference between the EU's and NATO's actual capacities for carrying out their respective obligations is relatively wide (Perot 2019). Compared the Article 42(7) TEU, it can not apply equally to all Member States in case of neutrality, however, NATO demands such action, rather than requiring the Member States to provide assistance "by all means in their power" as article 42(7) mandates. Regarding this, Perot (2019, p.4) emphasizes the significant role of the United States, precisely what makes the framework of NATO more trustworthy is due to the actual participation of the US. Interestingly, in history for the first time, the mutual defense clause was effectively used by the U.S. following the terrorist attack carried out by Al Qaeda on September 11, 2001.

Members of the EU and NATO are permitted to retaliate using whatever means available to them, including but not limited to the use of force. Yet, while the EU contribution may not transcend political and diplomatic support, the military contribution of NATO Member States is, or can be, significant (Pejpers et al 2019).

Both EU and NATO's mutual defense provisions include a territorial scope means that both apply to the attacks on the Member States (Perot 2019). Referring to Article 6 of the North Atlantic Treaty, NATO includes transboundary military hardware but excludes foreign possessions (NATO 2019). Unlike the EU, Article 222 so-called solidarity clause covers both EU members as well as requests for assistance for military forces and embassies engaged abroad (Perot 2019).

Collective Cyber Defense

Considering the emergence of terrorism, kinetic attacks and the consequent employment of the collective defense became a complex issue. Remarkably, the 9/11 terrorist act on the Twin Towers by non-state actors that led to the first use of Article 5, as well as the 2015 terrorist attack in Paris prompted France to invoke Article 42(7) (ECFR 2015).

Although, it may be considerably more difficult to match cyberattacks using the virtual dimension with the system of collective defense and therefore, the following question is whether the collective defense mechanism is relevant to attack needs to be addressed. Even though some experts have expressed skepticism about the likelihood of cyberwar, cyber security has been one of the top concerns for both national and international security (Osawa 2017). During the presidential elections in 2017, President Trump signed an Executive Order "Strengthening the Cybersecurity of Federal Networks and Critical Infrastructure" (White House 2017). Requiring the strengthening of cyber protection as well as vital infrastructure was following the policy steps of President Trump (White House 2017). Additionally, considering the statement of a former U.S. special adviser on Cyber Security and Cyber Terrorism, Richard Clarke, cyber war is real and in reality, numerous nations are already making preparations for a cyberwar (Osawa 2017, pp.124-25).

The North Atlantic Treaty Organization (NATO) officially recognized cyber defense as a component of member states' *collective defense* commitments when it established an Expanded Cyber Defence Policy at the Wales Summit in September 2014 (NATO 2014, para.72) The new policy acknowledges that, in some circumstances, a cyber assault may result in the NATO Charter's Article 5 commitment to act—possibly including the use of military force—to assist another state facing an armed attack. On June 14, 2016, NATO Secretary General Jens Stoltenberg stated at a press conference, "Cyber defense is part of collective defense. [...] We have decided that a cyberattack can trigger Article 5, meaning that a cyberattack can trigger collective defense, because we regard cyberattacks as something that can cause a lot of damage and can be very dangerous (Stoltenberg, 2016).

Furthermore, Japan and US are collaborating closely to improve their cyber security cooperation in the context of global cyber security. The U.S – Japan Security Consultative Committee (SCC), the so-called "2+2" session normally with 2 ministers + 2 secretaries. The 2+2 summit in Tokyo in 2013, addressed a wide variety of alliance-related challenges but particularly focused on the cyber realm as one of five topics apart from fostering cyber collaboration, both governments established the U.S – Japan Cyber Defense Policy Working Group CDPWG (Osawa 2017). In a joint statement, the U.S.-Japan Cyber Defense Policy Working Group promised strong coordination in cyberspace … "if such a cyber incident occurs as a part of an armed attack against Japan, the MOD, and DOD will consult closely and take appropriate cooperative actions" (Nakatani 2015). Following this, in 2017 Prime Minister of Japan Shinzo Abe and President of the United State Donald J. Trump issued a joint statement regarding the fifth Japan – U.S Cyber Dialogue, "…which reaffirmed that the two countries will expand bilateral security cooperation in the field of cyberspace" (Office of the spokesperson 2017).

Referring to the treaty of Mutual Cooperation and Security between Japan and the United States (MOFA 1960), an armed attack against either party would be declared as a common danger. Although the international community is gradually defining what counts as an armed attack using cyber tactics, political leaders will ultimately decide when the repercussions of a cyber incident rise to the level of the use of force or an armed attack. Likewise, determining what form of cyberattack entails mutual defense duties is a political choice. NATO has reached an agreement on a general understanding of the types of cyber acts that set off its obligations to mutual defense. In general, a cyber event that causes casualties, or has the same effect as a kinetic attack, plainly demonstrates the use of force. It is crucial that such consultative procedures exist and is regularly used by Japan and the United States.

Some offensive cyber attacks such as denial of service (DoS) carried out by Russia against Estonia in 2007 can be labeled as ambiguous while the attack was clearly aggressive in nature, there was an absence of conventional use of force. Another is disruptive attacks that erase data is as well as ambiguous because they necessitate a political choice about whether their extent and severity of effect constitute a use of force sufficient to elicit mutual defense obligations (Lewis 2015).

The Concept of Swarming

Swarming relies on the power being distributed to small units and the ability to join those units together to work as a single entity. However, prior to the information revolution, this was almost unachievable. More precisely, the concept of swarming encompasses centralized planning and decentralized execution, which requires autonomous or semi-autonomous positions, as well as strong coordination and communication in order to function successfully. Hogarth (1987) emphasized the role of swarming during the Cold War. During the Cold War, swarming had also been considered by military wisdom. NATO created a swarming-based defense in reaction to the Soviet Union's development of an operational maneuver group (OMG) intended for armored deep and surprising invasion. Through the use of air power and ground forces coordinated under the swarming idea, NATO developed a reaction to eliminate the element of surprise.

In order to ensure the success of swarming, three main elements are required to be considered, convergence, focus, and agility (Tran et al 2015). Firstly, an organization or unit authorized to undertake to swarm must develop an agile attitude. The authority that specifies a goal and creates postures to achieve swarming must be the center of attention. This rule should apply to intelligence systems that provide information to the swarming defenders as well as peer unit postures that are used to detect targets. Convergence is the crucial characteristic that enables swarming units to take their actions, use force, and know when to quit using force (Hadji-Janev and Bogdanoski 2017).

In general, swarming will work best when used in a group setting, collectively. The concept of swarming defense is ideal for developing a collective defense system like NATO has set tactics and mechanisms. Using swarming increases the possibility of a successful cyber defense since NATO promised to make major efforts (established doctrine and mechanisms) to preserve peace and security by cooperating with partner countries and in line with the rule of law. Nevertheless, using swarming in cyberspace necessitates considerable adjustments to the current security postures that are typically the first line of defense against cyber threats. One must take into account the commonality of all swarm characteristics to ensure a successful operation (Haider and Schmidt 2022).

Adopting SWARM-based cyber defense requires adopting a new conceptual framework. As an example, the ability of the defender to influence the thinking of possible opponents, allies, and partners is one of the success indicators when using this approach. Simply put, this means that the defenders must be able to persuade allies, partners, as well as unbiased actors, that their activities are vital and justified. Likewise, assuring potential adversaries about their willingness to address threats in a fundamentally unique way is significant. As an outcome, defense teams construct a base that limits their opponents' options and raises the possibility of retaliation (Hadji-Janev and Bogdanoski 2017). In this situation, states should adapt their conceptualization of cyber combat by taking into account diplomatic, economic, and informational efforts to understand swarming-based cyber defense. SWARM consists of four phases. First, it identifies the cyber threat, the second step focuses on gathering intelligence from all sources, and the last phases facilitate threat modeling and emulation (Lilly et al 2021).

Role of Diplomacy

In the context of today's globalized world, diplomacy is one of the essential fundaments for effective swarming-based cyber defense. Considering that conflicting interests among the stakeholders (which might be the nation-states) may be balanced through diplomacy, it could also get them ready for coordinated action and swift threat adaptation. International organizations can be regarded as the best way diplomacy is functioned due to their established structure and channels ensuring cooperation (Hadji-Janev and Bogdanoski 2017).

As already mentioned, NATO serves as a prime example in this context. In detail, NATO recognized the importance of cyber defense from an earlier period. After the Bucharest Summit in 2008, Member States adopted 'The Declaration and Policy on Cyber Defense', in reaction to the cyberattack against Estonia in 2007. The fact that NATO was also among the first to develop a cyber defense policy is crucial considering the fact that NATO's collective security involves not only the member states but also partners, so-called aspiring countries. This was further strengthened, in the 2011 Lisbon Summit which was supported by a number of high-level meetings at the NATO Headquarters and led to the adoption of the Mutual Cyber Defense Capability Development Project signed by the five NATO members (Canada, Denmark, The Netherlands, Norway, and Romania). The project aimed of enhancing technical information sharing, and raise awareness regarding the threats (NATO 2014).

It is important to consider the role of other international organizations as well, referring to Annan (2004) the United Nations embraced a wider definition of peace and security, even though White (2015) claims that expecting the UN to resolve complicated issues in cyberspace is virtually "utopian." Therefore, as part of the overall endeavor to alter the notion of defense in cyberspace, diplomatic initiatives to reform the conceptual approach to the cyber conflict are essential prerequisites.

However, some limitations might apply to swarming in cyber warfare. The approach might be characterized by ambiguity in coalition due to the varied threat perception and willingness to act. For instance, even while collective self-defense is introduced as a common response to a cyberattack in the scope of NATO's cyber defense policy, it is unclear whether or not every NATO member agrees with the discussions over the levels that would constitute collective self-defense. Regarding this, former NATO Secretary General Rasmussen stressed cyber defense as the national responsibility of the member states (Hadji-Janev and Bogdanoski, 2016).

Referring to the U.S., the 2022 National Security Strategy acknowledges the new environment and emphasizes and emphasizes the importance of "...building collective capabilities to rapidly respond to attacks" (The White House, 2022, p.34). Based on this, the US Department of Defense (DoD) has dedicated its efforts to establishing strong partnerships with US allies and foreign partners in order to boost global cyber security (Department of Defense 2018).

Overall, diplomatic effort plays a significant role in order to ensure collective cyber defense. However, it requires a combination of economic, technical, and informational measures.

The Role of the Economy

Domestic and international economics may also suffer due to cyber activity, notably some state or non-state entities use cybercrime to indirectly damage their alleged adversaries for political or economic gains. it might equally be argued that by weakening the economy, the attacker is weakening the capacities necessary to maintain successful national security. This type of assault compromises democratic systems, economic security, healthcare, and safety (ENISA, 2012). The traditional components of deterrence should be paired with economic initiatives to alter the conceptual approach to cyber conflict in order to enhance the swarming-based cyber defense. As an instance from the 2014 Ukraine war, NATO, the EU, and the United States have all attempted to exert influence over Russia throughout the crisis. To affect an enemy, attempts should be supported by conventional economic forces, Singer (2011) offers that the rising economic cost is essential through sanctions and trade tariffs that would negatively influence opponents' cost-benefit analysis.

Hence, for collective cyber defense effective combination of both diplomatic and economic measures are essential in order to prevent the adverse effects of cyberattack.

CYBER SPACE AS COLLABORATIVE EFFORT OF THE EU, NATO, AND THE UNITED STATES

The majority of international organizations at the global level, transatlantic, and regional levels such as the UN, NATO, the EU, G8, OSCD, OECD, ASEAN, etc.) have created policy initiatives and tools to tackle the increasing cyberattacks against vital services and facilities.

Cyber security represents a strategic priority for NATO and the EU that affects both the defensive and security interests of member states and of the organizations as a whole. They both place a higher priority on the security and resiliency of their own networks, organizations, and goals, making it a national obligation to protect each member states' cyberspace. NATO focuses on the security and defense aspects of cyber security, while the EU deals with a wider, primarily non-military range of cyber concerns including Internet privacy, online rights, and information security), as well as internal security challenges (Pernik 2014).

The United States

Moreover, according to the recent U.S. national cyber security strategy, some progress is highlighted in the way of establishing the Joint Cyber Defense Collaboration (JCDC) that will strengthen planning and operations between the government, private sector, and international partners (White House 2023). The unstable and hostile behavior of the People's Republic of China (PRC)in cyberspace has traditionally been a main concern to the United States and its allies that constitutes a serious threat to the economic and strategic security of the country (The White House 2021). Hence, referring to the official statement of the White House, the United States with its allies and partners including the European Union, NATO, and the United Kingdom is taking additional steps to oppose the malicious cyber activities of China. The collective approach of the allies includes diplomatic cooperation, information sharing with both the public and the private sectors, defending against, and mitigating cyber threats aids in holding China accountable.

The importance of assisting partners in improving institutions and bolstering their capacity to mitigate cyber threats has been recognized by U.S. diplomats in light of the rise of cyberattacks around the world (Fisher 2021). To modernize their security institutions and bring them in line with the needs of their citizens, nations like Albania, Palau, Kosovo, Ecuador, Argentina, Bulgaria, and North Macedonia are among those the Global Defense Reform Program (GDRP) under the Office of Global Programs and Initiatives (GPI) of the PM Bureau. To handle cybersecurity and cyber defense concerns, design national-level policies, improve coordination, set up efficient "command and control," and hire and educate a trained cyber workforce, GDRP consultants collaborate with partner states' ministries of defense. These activities assist U.S. foreign policy goals relating to cyber defense and cybersecurity in addition to improving the efficiency and transparency of security institutions._

Ecuador - Following a string of occurrences, including data breaches and cyberattacks, the U.S. Embassy in Quito collaborated with the Ecuadorian government and its defense ministry to solve cyber defense challenges. A retired colonel from the U.S. Army named Gustavo Santiago arrived in Ecuador in January 2021 to serve as the GDRP's cyber advisor. Since then, he has provided guidance on national cyber policy, facilitated inter-ministerial agreements, and developed a 10-year plan to increase the Ministry of Defense's cyber capability. Since his arrival, Gustavo has contributed his knowledge and experience to the military ministry of Ecuador, working on the creation of planning papers that divide the development of the country's cyber capabilities into four categories, including protecting national cyberinfrastructure; increasing the coordination between the Ecuadorian defense ministry and Computer Security Incident Response Teams aims to prevent the likelihood of future cyber threats; strengthening the cyber defense skills and implementing cyber defense program in accordance with the nation's cyber position (Fisher 2021).

In the case of Argentina, a cyber advisor of a Global Defense Reform Program (GDRP) contributed to the detection of the country's cyber vulnerabilities. This action is a component of the endeavor to build ties and mutual trust between the U.S. and Argentina while also fostering partnerships in cyber cooperation (Solar 2020).

Central and Eastern European nations are receiving assistance from the Global Defense Reform Program to protect themselves from Russian influence and hostile cyber activity. The program is aiding the Bulgarian Ministry of Defense in modernizing its Cyber Defense Center to provide cutting-edge cyber support and to educate and train the workforce of government for upcoming cyber problems. To provide students with the practical and technical expertise required to direct a successful cybersecurity operations center, a new cyber program of training has been developed. The GDRP advisor has taken a step in forging connections to create the framework for cyber cooperation with Bulgaria's success (Fisher 2021).

In order for North Macedonia to be a ready and active member of NATO, the Global Defense Reform Program is collaborating with the country's defense ministry to enhance the nation's cyber policies, equipment, and capacities (Fisher 2021). The project's key objectives are to redesign cyber defense planning, create and implement a thorough cyber strategy, increase capacity and knowledge in cyberspace, and advance good governance as well as accountability. According to the office of the spokesperson (2022), by placing a higher priority on cybersecurity at the strategic level, the United States is assisting other nations in defending against harmful cyber activities and safeguarding key infrastructure.

Several alliances between the EU and the U.S. as well as between the U.S. and Germany have been established as a result of the increasing likelihood of cyber threats. As an example, the Transatlantic Cybersecurity Partnership between the United States and Germany addresses the dangers presented by virtual propaganda and cyberwarfare (Czirkl 2022).

Furthermore, referring to the 2021 Annual Threat Assessment of the US Intelligence Community (2021), cyber threats remain acute from Russia, China, Iran, and North Korea. In response to Russia's invasion of Ukraine, the cybersecurity agencies of five nations—the United States, Australia, Canada, New Zealand, and the United Kingdom—issued a joint cybersecurity guideline on April 20, 2022, alerting organizations to the possibility of an increase in illicit digital activity (CISA 2022 b). The warning emphasizes the potential for cyberattacks the Russian state-sponsored groups. By outlining these organizations and their strategies, advice attempts to assist organizations in defending against cyber threats. The alert also mentions the possibility of this increased activity having an impact on groups outside the region. As stated in the article, the extraordinary financial burdens placed on Russia as well as the material support given by the United States and its friends and partners may be the causes of Russia's cyber activities.

America's Cyber Defense Agency (CISA) as well as provides an assessment of Russia's activities in cyberspace. The following sectors and organizations including governments, electoral groups, healthcare and pharmaceuticals, energy, computer games, commercial establishments, and the COVID-19 research industry in the United States and other Western countries are being targeted by Russian state-sponsored threat actors, according to recent advisories released by CISA and other undisclosed sources (CISA, 2022). The same sources linked Russian actors to a number of notorious cyberattacks, A number of instances of malicious cyber activity connected to Russian actors are mentioned in the statement, including the 2020 SolarWinds supply chain consensus, the attack of American businesses making COVID-19 vaccines in 2018, as well as the 2017 NotPetya attack and the 2016 DNC files revelations.

European Union

Effective cyber response methods depend heavily on international cooperation, as digital borders are ill-defined and do not line up with national boundaries. Cyber crimes are no longer something that individuals should handle on their own but rather are becoming a communal and civic obligation that affects all facets of the digital society (Skopik et al 2016). The European Network and Information Security Agency (ENISA), a primary European organization, promotes information and strategy sharing to improve the integration of efforts from the various Member States. Ensuring a collective approach to threats to information and network safety is one of ENISA's responsibilities to assist the institutions and Member States of the European Union (ENISA 2023).

In light of Russia's unjustifiable military intervention against Ukraine in 2022, the EU started to reevaluate its security and defense approach, as well as its capacity to advance its goals and protects interests, particularly, in cyberspace. Cyberspace is becoming a more disputed realm alongside land, sea, and air as authoritarian regimes strive to destabilize and disrupt the rules-based international order. The EU cyber defense community operates under a different governance structure which is made up of the defense agencies of Member States and backed by EU institutions, organizations, and agencies (EUIBAs) (EC, 2022).

In place of the rather dated collective defense mechanism of the Western European Union (WEU), nowadays, the European Union possesses a clause for mutual defense akin to NATO's Article 5, specifically Article 42 (7) of the Treaty of the European Union (EUR-Lex)

NATO

The safeguarding of NATO's activities, organizations, and centers has always been the primary focus of the alliance's cyber defense strategy. Throughout the 1990s, the Alliance has been enhancing its cyber defense capabilities. The first well-known cyberattack on NATO occurred in 1999 when hacking groups from Russia and Serbia affected the organization's internal networks during NATO's

Operation "Allied Force" in Kosovo. A few decades previously, during the 2002 Prague Summit, NATO made the first political mention of cyber security, pledging to enhance the alliance's capacity to protect against cyber threats. 2007 cyber-attacks against Estonia and in 2008 in Georgia due to the Russia-Georgia war rendered its official webpages, enabling NATO to realize the significance of empowering cyberspace (Pernik 2014).

In terms of NATO's collective cyber capabilities 2012, Chicago Summit is worth mentioning which announced the adoption of "Smart Defense" to guarantee that the alliance could build and retain the capabilities necessary to accomplish its objectives (NATO, 2012). The strategic framework of 'Smart Defense" may result in a lower cost for the member states' overall burden-sharing while recruiting potential new elements and attaining cyber-innovative approaches (Efthymiopoulos, 2019). Following this, NATO Allies reaffirmed their commitments during the Wales summit in 2014, as well as confirmed the growing significance of the cyber-defense component. Likewise, the policy of resilience within the context of collective defense was highlighted during NATO's Warsaw Summit in 2016 (NATO, 2016). Cyber-defense has become a key part of NATO planning and cyber espionage in the course of Russian aggression. Considering the US and UK, are characterized by close collaboration ties in cyber espionage as well. The US National Security Agency (NSA) and the British Government Communications Headquarters (GCHQ) are the center of this collaboration (Lewis, 2015). Furthermore, an updated Cyber Defence Policy was approved in June 2011, reaffirming NATO's commitment to defending its connections and supporting member nations in the event of a cyberattack, as well as the Defense Policy and Planning Committee in Reinforced Format (DPPC(R)) was also established to handle the entire cyberspace planning process (Pernik 2014).

The cyberattacks in Estonia in 2007 remain the largest and most well-organized attack to date that gave NATO a goal or mission to establish the Center of Excellence (CCDCOE). It is believed that the Estonians' removal of a bronze statue of a Red Army soldier catalyzed an attack. As a result, it led to cyberattacks on both the public and private sectors. By 2008, Germany, Italy, Latvia, Lithuania, Spain, and Slovakia facilitated Estonia in achieving full operational capacity. In reality, the leadership of NATO was right to believe that such a center was necessary that would constantly evaluate and research potential malicious developments in technologies and cyber-security, additionally adopting resilience was required taking into account future risks and challenges (Efthymiopoulos 2019). According to the CCDCOE, its stated goal is to improve the Alliance's cooperation in collective cyber-defense by improving the capabilities to combat hybrid vulnerabilities and maintain the resilience of NATO and its members. In the context of the EU, the European Network and Information Security Agency (ENISA) of the EU provided technical evaluations of the evolving situation (Herzog 2013). Interestingly, during the 2018 Brussels meeting, the member states of NATO approved creating a cyberspace center, ensuring joint preparedness and agility.

In response to the Russian invasion of Ukraine in 2022, Klipstein and Japaridze (2022) state the need for NATO to develop an agile collective cyber defense policy under Article 5. As an example, in February 2022, Russian assaults on Viasat satellite networks affected German windmill electricity production and distribution interrupting communications with Ukraine. Moreover, in April 2022 by targeting electrical power plants and transmission networks with cyberattacks. As the aforementioned cases demonstrate, cyberattacks do not just affect online targets; their effects can also be experienced offline. Hence, NATO must thus get ready for the hybrid forms of conflict to develop and increase its actions in both kinetic and non-kinetic spheres.

In NATO's strategic planning, preparing for a significant cyber-attack is already a regular component. The most recent NATO cyber defense exercise, which simulated cyberattacks based on real-world scenarios, was held in Estonia in 2021. With this exercise, cyber professionals were put to the test and taught to improve their capacity to safeguard national and NATO networks. The practice includes a variety of difficult, realistic scenarios such as cyberattacks on gas pipelines, as well as pandemic-related cyber assaults that affected vaccination programs and stole vaccine data (Czirkl 2022).

The Reflection on the Roles of NATO and EU: Similarities and Differences

NATO and the EU emphasize that each member state is responsible for ensuring its own citizens' online safety and both strive toward the creation of thorough cybersecurity regulations and establishing minimal security requirements for shared infrastructure. There is no one agency in charge of ensuring universal cyber security in the EU, but NATO's senior political decision-making body monitors the evolution of the alliance's cyber defense capability. Prioritizing cyber security for their institutions, infrastructure, operations, and missions is a priority for both organizations.

There are numerous shared non-military activities and interests including placing a high priority on fostering collaboration between the nations that is characteristic of both organizations. However, unlike the EU, NATO is not mandated to exert jurisdiction over or provide recommendations about infrastructure in the public and private sectors, whereas the EU lacks the technical know-how and assistance to offer to its members, serving instead as a forum for information and best practices exchange. Moreover, Robinson (2013) highlights another distinction in managing networks. While NATO possesses its control, leadership, and data management, the EU depends on member state networks for Common Security and Defense Policy (CSDP) missions. Additionally, compared to the EU, NATO has been capable of building strong points in many areas that make up a systematic approach, particularly through integrating cyber defense into NATO's Defense Planning Process (NDPP) setting up instruments for aid to the member states, and intense training and exercise efforts (Pijpers et al 2022).

Regarding the capacity to handle cyber threats, collective cyber defense between NATO and the EU come into a stronger focus. State and non-state actors can operate on a nearly equal basis in cyberspace; additionally, even if they are prone to incite conflict and sometimes even use force, they do not fall under the traditional military's purview. Language variations are as well as interesting. An "armed attack," by the language of Article 51 of the UN Charter, serves as the *casus foederis* or the catalyst for using NATO's Article 5. The term "armed attack" is used in the EU's mutual help clause. Notwithstanding linguistic variations, the factual variations are insignificant. The mutual defense provisions of NATO and the EU both relate to assaults on the territory of the Member States and have a territorial reach. In the area defined by Article 6 of the North Atlantic Treaty, NATO includes extraterritorial military assets, however, it does not cover foreign territories (such as the Dutch or French Antilles) (Bumgardner, 2019). On the other hand, the EU includes the most recent. The EU might still request help for disasters affecting armed units or diplomatic missions stationed outside the EU following Article 222 TFEU because the EU solidarity provision still applies to territory, albeit to a lower level.

Article 42(7) TEU utilizes tougher wording, but because certain Member States are neutral, it cannot apply to all of them equally (Sari 2019, p.435). NATO asks for such action as the Member States feel necessary, rather than requiring the Member States to provide help and assistance "by all means in their power" as Article 42(7) mandates (EEAS 2022).

In addition to the fundamental right of self-defense, the EU solidarity clause expands the available alternatives to other, more general collective cybersecurity measures. While NATO is capable of making statements about unwanted situations within its borders, it essentially lacks the tools necessary to carry out its mandate without resorting to force. This applies differently in the context of the EU. Although the EU has certain plans on how to respond to an armed attack, the majority of its tools are unrelated to the use of force because they are consistent with the EU's status as a soft power and are gathered in the "cyber diplomacy toolbox". This toolkit illustrates the potential for a collective cyber defense mechanism against cyberattacks without resorting the force (Pijpers et al 2022).

Nevertheless, to address the question of whether the EU is more prepared than NATO to offer a mechanism of collective defense against cyberattacks several factors might be considered.

LEGALIZATION OF CYBERSPACE AND DIFFICULTIES OF COOPERATION

According to Kello (2021), modern forms of rivalry between states do not fit into the destructive criteria of war and express the current situation in terms of unpeace, which represents an intermediate form of rivalry between countries and is a much more severe type than other confrontations like, for instance, economic sanctions. Today, nations no longer need to use kinetic forms of war, rather cyberspace plays a significant role in achieving political and strategic goals. However, as the professor emphasizes the West, in short, struggles with an issue of under-proportionate reaction, and the issue is likewise recognized by the authorities (Kello, 2021). As an example, in 2017 Senator John Mccain stated the lack of strategy for Russia's disruptive cyber operations (McCain 2017). Likewise, in 2018 the US Director of National Intelligence Daniel Coats emphasized the threat posed by China and Russia that their cyber operations will work unless they confront real ramifications for their cyber actions (Coats 2019). Opponents have not, however, been punished severely enough to stop further tribulations below the threshold of war. According to Microsoft, political hacking actions by Russian and North Korean actors were targeted at American presidential campaign targets in July 2019 (Perlroth and Sanger 2019). Three months later, the business issued a warning that about 3000 US government employees, members of the presidential campaign, and journalists' email accounts had been attacked by state-sponsored Iranian hackers. Although US officials discussed attacking Iran's computer network in response, there is no proof that this ever happened. Specifically, in the "SolarWinds" incident numerous US federal departments and agencies' computer systems were allegedly compromised by Russian hackers. This revealed a persistent sore point in Western security policy to implement deterrent consequences in cyberspace (Kello 2021).

And yet, why do not nations band together to resist cyberattacks with collective forces? What hinders collaboration to dismantle cybercrime and establish a global organization that would deal with combating cyberattacks?

Given that cyberspace is a complex, unpredictable, and dynamic phenomenon, it is still not possible to fall within its legal framework. Today, there is significant leverage in the hands of the Internet state to carry out sabotage, espionage, intelligence gathering, and blackmail. Existing international norms are weak and vague. On the use of force in cyberspace, there is no international agreement, uncertainty exists regarding the threshold of war as well as the point at which military force may be used to carry out a retaliatory response. Referring to Keith Alexander, 1st commander of U.S. cyber command, the extent to which cyber operations should be utilized to employ military force is left up to individual nations. Moreover, international law does not cover cyber-espionage, which makes it very difficult to implement criminal legislation to combat this expanding crime. Recalling the UN Charter which provides the principles of the use of force under international law, allows the use of military force if aggression leads to the mass destruction of infrastructure, a large number of casualties, or the encroachment of the country's sovereignty (Kunz, 2017). So far, no cyberattack has met the criteria, since existing international law does not allow countries to act beyond these laws and norms. For instance, we can cite the case of Staxnet, which is still a matter of dispute between politicians and scientists over the likelihood of using retaliatory force (Rosenbaum 2012). The absence of international agreement on the development of a common cyberweapon is another hindering factor. An effective way to deter aggressor states is to create a joint cyber potential, cyber-weapon, by NATO and allied countries, however, as researchers and experts suggest, this cannot be done in a short time. Likewise, countries that have incurred the greatest financial costs and large resources to create cyber potentials, do not want to share all this with other countries for virtually free, without any compensation; Moreover, at the national level, intelligence services strictly maintain confidentiality about cyber weapons created. Consequently, consensus between countries is very difficult to reach. Another example is the cyber-attack carried out by Russia in 2016 to interfere in the US elections. Despite U.S. warnings that the Kremlin would have to pay a high price in the event of a cyberattack, the Obama administration has refused to respond to the operation. According to the White House, cyber-operation would be ineffective, making public America's secret cyber weapons and intelligence gathering over the years. Moreover, according to the United States, this may have been a provocative act by Russia, aimed at disclosing confidential information (Kunz 2017). These instances highlight how insufficient the West's response to cybercrime is and how there are now no established legal standards that will enable nations to act in compliance with the law. Furthermore, it is challenging to foresee the potential dangers and political repercussions that could result from the use of offensive (offensive) weapons, forcing political leaders to abdicate their responsibility for waging offensive cyber politics to prevent hostilities from escalating to the level of a state or state.

Furthermore, there is no institution at the international level today – neither in NATO, the European Union, nor the United Nations, that control and monitor the proliferation of cyber weapons in the world. Cyber expert Kelo (2021) claims that despite the several experiences of cyberattacks, the study of virtual weapons remains at a primitive level, and there is no international agreement that would directly address the international legal issues of cyber-attacks. In this context, the 2001 Convention on Cybercrime, which does not classify cyberattacks as a means of waging war, solely takes criminal law into account when discussing cyber violations.

In addition, the concept of collective cyber security includes real-time intelligence and data sharing, however, because countries do not want to exchange such sensitive information, access to confidential information from other states, which, in their view, is tantamount to giving up sovereignty. The fundamental reason for this is that current technology and inexpensive, simple access to the Internet provides cybercriminals a significant edge in carrying out harmful operations, notwithstanding the efforts of countries to preserve their sovereignty in cyberspace. Added to this is the complex attribute of identifying the traces of the offender, which further complicates the enactment of international norms. Since cybercrime does not recognize borders, successful cyber politics between countries can only be achieved through close cooperation based on mutual trust (Kelo 2021).

The collective approach to cyberbullying is also hampered by the lack of a unified vocabulary of cyber-terminology and the lack of proper conceptual understanding, and perception of terms, which is important for legal and political decision-making on the complex issue of cyber security. In the discourse of NATO and Tallinn textbook the term cyberwarfare, cyber war reinforces NATO's views as the greatest threat to the future. The term "cyber warfare" "contains the prefix "cyber" which expresses the interrelationship between the Internet and computer technology, and the term war, warfare", can explain it as an armed conflict between states. Although the term is widely used in military circles, especially in the United States, its conceptual understanding is far from consensus among politicians, experts, scientists, and researchers. At the same time, it should be emphasized that cyber-attacks cannot be considered trivial in war, it focuses on the threats that await the world in the future (NATO, 2013). For future perspectives, Cavelty claims "the stronger the link between cyberspace and a threat of strategic dimensions becomes, the more natural it seems that the keeper of the peace in cyberspace should be the military (Cavelty 2013, p. 119).

The data exchange likewise represents hindering factor for international collaboration. According to the European Network and Information Security Agency (ENISA), the information exchange network must be reliable between the parties. The reliability of information exchange is particularly crucial among countries whose native language is different - when two or more states are countries that carry different cultures and conduct information exchange through interconnected Internet networks (Vázquez et al 2012).

We can therefore infer that in the age of the technology revolution, the inadequate legislative procedures used today have not been successful, since old legal frameworks cannot ensure the sustainability of global security architecture. Adhering to national interests and values with the right response is necessary to prevent cyberattacks.

CONCLUSION

With the development of terrorism, kinetic operations and the ensuing employment of the collective defense system grew even more complicated. It can be determined that collective defense clauses intended for armed attacks are incompatible with the majority of cyberattacks because, in the first place, cyberattacks frequently fall below the threshold for employing force. Second, non-state entities frequently carry out cyberattacks. Although the inherent right to self-defense reflected in Article 51 of the UN Charter was intended to govern State behavior, it is a different principle of traditional international law (Kunz 51).

Moreover, given the gap intervals between malicious cyber-activity and the actual impact of a cyber-attack, it can be challenging to identify the author and source of cyber-attacks (whether they are carried out by State or non-State actors). That affects and hinders collective cyber defense considering the difficulty of determining whether the territory of the EU or NATO Member State is harmed by the attacks as they frequently have no visible evidence (Pijpers et al 2022). Nonetheless, a wider range of the EU's capabilities can be used to address concerns relating to cyberattacks. By concentrating on collective actions other than the use of force, such as diplomatic or economic tools, the EU can support NATO rather than subtly compete with it. Although the existing cyber diplomacy toolkit is a positive starting step, its lack of concentration prevents it from functioning as a cohesive EU collective response mechanism (Herzog 2011).

The complex and asymmetrical legal and political duties supporting Europe's collective defense system, such as Article 5 of the NATO Charter, Article 42.7 of the TEU, and Article 222 of the TFEU, produce obligations that are similar but not equal. Due to legal limitations and political realities, there is no transparent separation of duties between NATO and the EU in the area of collective defense, nor can it be assumed that collective defense throughout Europe is a consistent responsibility. Any of these collective defense provisions may not always be beneficial, and nations may decide to handle a security problem on a strictly national level (Perot 2019). Thus, detecting a threat, where it can manifest or be resisted, is the basis of collective defense. However, the answers to those queries will depend on the situation. Collective defense in the end requires juggling a variety of legal and political restraints while managing changeable and unforeseen situations.

REFERENCES

America's Cyber Defense Agency (CISA). (2022). *Russia Cyber Threat Overview and Advisories*. Retrieved from https://www.cisa.gov/russia

Annan, K. A. (2004). *A More Secure World: Our Shared Responsibility Report of the Secretary-General's High-level Panel on Threats, Challenges, and Change*. The United Nations.

Article 42(7) TEU - The EU's mutual assistance clause | EEAS Website. (n.d.). Retrieved 4 April 2023, from https://www.eeas.europa.eu/eeas/article-427-teu-eus-mutual-assistance-clause_en

Bumgardner, S. (2019). Article 4 of the North Atlantic treaty. *Emory International Law Review*, *34*, 71. https://scholarlycommons.law.emory.edu/eilr/vol34/iss0/6

Cavelty, M. D. (2013). From Cyber-Bombs to Political Fallout: Threat Representations with an Impact in the Cyber-Security Discourse. *International Studies Review*, *15*(1), 105–122. doi:10.1111/misr.12023

CISA. (2022, May 9). *Russian State-Sponsored and Criminal Cyber Threats to Critical Infrastructure*. Retrieved from https://www.cisa.gov/news-events/cybersecurity-advisories/aa22-110a

Coats, D. R. (2019, January 29). *Worldwide Threat Assessment of the US Intelligence Community*. Academic Press.

Ducheine, P., Jelle, H. v., & Harskamp, R. (2017). *Manoeuvring and Generating Effects in the Information Environment*. Amsterdam Center for International Law. doi:10.1007/978-94-6265-189-0_9

Ebner, N. (2015). *Cyber Space, Cyber Attack, and Cyber Weapons; A Contribution to the Terminology*. Institute for Peace Research and Security Policy at the University of Hamburg.

Efthymiopoulos, M. P. (2019). A cyber-security framework for development, defense, and innovation at NATO. *Journal of Innovation and Entrepreneurship*, *8*(12), 1–26. doi:10.118613731-019-0105-z

ENISA. (2012). *Deployment of Baseline Capabilities of n/g CERTs - Status Report 2012*. ENISA.

ENISA. (2023). *ENISA Single Programming Document 2023-2025*. ENISA.

EUR-Lex. (1992). https://data.europa.eu/eli/treaty/teu_2008/art_42/oj/eng

European Council on Foreign Relations (ECFR). (2015). *Article 42.7: An explainer*. Retrieved from https://ecfr.eu/article/commentary_article_427_an_explainer5019/

European Union External Action. (2022). *Article 42(7) TEU - The EU's mutual assistance clause*. Retrieved from https://www.eeas.europa.eu/eeas/article-427-teu-eus-mutual-assistance-clause_en

Federal Ministry of the Interior, Building, and Community. (2021, August). *Cyber Security Strategy for Germany 2021*. Retrieved from shorturl.at/gCDO4

Finlay, L., & Payne, C. (2019). The Attribution Problem and Cyber Armed Attacks. *AJIL Unbound, 113*, 202–206. doi:10.1017/aju.2019.35

Fisher, B. (2021, December 11). *U.S. Diplomats Build Cyber Defense and Cybersecurity Partnerships Worldwide*. Retrieved from U.S Department of State: https://www.state.gov/u-s-diplomats-build-cyber-defense-and-cybersecurity-partnerships-worldwide/

Georgetown Law Library. (2023, February 10). *International and Foreign Cyberspace Law Research Guide*. Retrieved from https://guides.ll.georgetown.edu/cyberspace/cyber-conflicts

Gill, D. T., & Ducheine, A. P. (2013). Anticipatory Self-Defense in the Cyber Context. *International Law Studies, 89*, 438–471.

Hadji-Janev, M., & Bogdanoski, M. (2016). The swarming-based cyber defense under the framework of collective security. Security Journal, 30(1), 39-59.

Haider, A., & Schmidt, A. (2022, July). *Defining the swarm—Joint air power competence center*. https://www.japcc.org/articles/defining-the-swarm/

Heinegg, W. H. (2013). Territorial Sovereignty and Neutrality in Cyberspace. *U.S. Naval War College, 89*, 123–156.

Herzog, S. (2011). Revisiting the Estonian cyber attacks: Digital threats and multinational responses. *Journal of Strategic Security, 4*(2), 49–60. doi:10.5038/1944-0472.4.2.3

High Representative of the Union for Foreign Affairs and Security Policy. (2022). *Joint Communication to the European Parliament and the Council EU Policy on Cyber Defense*. European Commission.

Hogarth, F. (1987). Dynamic Density: A Deterrent for the OMG. *RUSI Journal, 132*(2), 29–34. doi:10.1080/03071848708523163

Hosang, B. J. (2017). *Rules on the Use of Force as Linchpin for the International Law of Military Operations*. Universiteit van Amsterdam.

Huy, T. (2015). Evaluating the agility of adaptive command and control networks from a cyber complex adaptive systems perspective. *Journal of Defense Modeling and Simulation: Applications, Methodology, Technology, 12*(4), 1–18. doi:10.1177/1548512915592517

Kello, L. (2021). Cyber legalism: Why it fails and what to do about it. *Journal of Cybersecurity, 7*(1), 1–15. doi:10.1093/cybsec/tyab014

Klipstein, M., & Japaridze, T. (2022, May 16). *Collective cyber defense and attack: NATO's Article 5 after the Ukraine conflict*. Retrieved from European Leadership Network: https://www.europeanleadershipnetwork.org/commentary/collective-cyber-defence-and-attack-natos-article-5-after-the-ukraine-conflict/

Kunz, J. L. (1947). Individual and Collective Self-Defense in Article 51 of the Charter of the United Nations. *The American Journal of International Law, 41*(4), 872–879. doi:10.2307/2193095

Lewis, J. A. (2015). *The Role of Offensive Cyber Operations in NATO's Collective Defence.* Tallinn Paper No.8, 1-15.

Lewis, J. A. (2015). U.S. - Japan Cooperation in Cybersecurity. Center for Strategic & International Studies (CSIS).

Lilly, B., Moore, A. S., Hodgson, Q. E., & Weishoff, D. (2021). *Rand's scalable warning and resilience model (Swarm): Enhancing defenders' predictive power in cyberspace.* RAND Corporation. https://www.rand.org/pubs/research_reports/RRA382-1.html

McCain, J. (2017). *John McCain says the US has no strategy to deal with Russian cyber warfare.* Retrieved from The Guardian: https://www.theguardian.com/us-news/2017/jan/27/john-mccain-says-us-has-no-strategy-to-deal-with-russian-cyber-warfare

Ministry of Defense, Government of Japan. (2015). *Joint statement of the U. S.-Japan cyber defense policy working group.* Retrieved 4 April 2023, from https://nsarchive.gwu.edu/document/21938-document-07

Ministry of Foreign Affairs MOFA. (1960, January 19). *Japan-U.S. Security Treaty: Treaty of Mutual Cooperation and Security between Japan and the United States of America.* Retrieved from Ministry of Foreign Affairs of Japan: https://www.mofa.go.jp/region/n-america/us/q&a/ref/1.html

National Institute of Standards and Technology (NIST). (2012, September). *Information Security.* Retrieved from https://nvlpubs.nist.gov/nistpubs/Legacy/SP/nistspecialpublication800-30r1.pdf

NATO. (2012, July 5). *Chicago Summit Declaration.* Retrieved from https://www.nato.int/cps/en/natohq/official_texts_87593.htm?selectedLocale=en

NATO. (2013, June 4). *Press conference by NATO Secretary General Anders Fogh Rasmussen following the NATO Defence Ministers meeting on 4 June 2013.* Retrieved from https://www.nato.int/cps/en/natolive/opinions_101151.htm

NATO. (2016, July). *Warsaw Summit Communiqué.* Retrieved from https://www.nato.int/cps/en/natohq/official_texts_133169.htm

NATO. (2022, September 20). *Collective defense and Article 5.* Retrieved from https://www.nato.int/cps/en/natohq/topics_110496.htm

NATO Press conference by NATO Secretary General Jens Stoltenberg following the North Atlantic Council meeting at the level of NATO Defence Ministers. (2016, June 16). Retrieved from https://www.nato.int/cps/en/natohq/opinions_132349.htm

North Atlantic Treaty Organisation. (2016, July 8-9). *Warsaw Summit Communiqué.* Retrieved from https://www.nato.int/cps/en/natohq/official_texts_133169.htm

North Atlantic Treaty Organization. (2014, September). *Wales Summit Declaration.* Retrieved from https://www.nato.int/cps/en/natohq/official_texts_112964.htm

North Atlantic Treaty Organization. (2019, April). *The North Atlantic Treaty Washington D.C. - 4 April 1949.* Retrieved from https://www.nato.int/cps/en/natohq/official_texts_17120.htm

North Atlantic Treaty Organization. (2020, January). *Allied Joint Publication-3.20 Allied Joint Doctrine for Cyberspace Operations.* Retrieved from shorturl.at/EGNWZ

Office of the Spokesperson. (2017, July 24). *Joint Statement of the Japan-U.S. Cyber Dialogue.* Retrieved from https://2017-2021.state.gov/joint-statement-of-the-japan-u-s-cyber-dialogue/index.html

Osawa, J. (2017). The Escalation of State-Sponsored Cyberattack and National Cyber Security Affairs: Is Strategic Cyber Deterrence the Key to Solving the Problem? *Asia-Pacific Review, 24*(2). doi:10.108 0/13439006.2017.1406703

Perlroth, N., & Sanger, D. E. (2019). *Iranian hackers target Trump campaign as threats to 2020 mount.* Retrieved from The New York Times: https://www.nytimes.com/2019/10/04/technology/iranian-campaign-hackers-microsoft.html

Pernik, P. (2014). *Improving Cyber Security: NATO and the EU.* International Centre for Defence Studies.

Perot, E. (2019). The art of commitments: NATO, the EU, and the interplay between law and politics within Europe's collective defense architecture. *European Security, 28*(1), 40–65. doi:10.1080/096628 39.2019.1587746

Pijpers, B. P., & Arnold, L. K. (2020). Conquering the invisible battleground. *Atlantisch Perspectief, 44*(4), 10–14.

Pijpers, B. P., Boddens, J. H., & Ducheine, A. P. (2021). *Collective Cyber Defence – the EU and NATO perspective on cyber attacks.* Amsterdam Law School Legal Studies Research Paper No. 2021-37.

Pijpers, P. B. M. J., Hosang, B. H., & Ducheine, P. A. L. (2022). *A language of power? Cyber defense in the European Union* (Vol. 176). European Union Institute for Security Studies (EUISS). https://data.europa.eu/doi/10.2815/57567

Rosenbaum, R. (2012, April). *Richard Clarke on Who Was Behind the Stuxnet Attack.* Retrieved from https://www.smithsonianmag.com/history/richard-clarke-on-who-was-behind-the-stuxnet-attack-160630516/

Sari, A. (2019). The Mutual Assistance Clauses of the North Atlantic and EU Treaties: The Challenge of Hybrid Threats. *Harvard National Security Journal, 10*, 405–460.

Sarker, I. H. (2021). CyberLearning: Effectiveness analysis of machine learning security modeling to detect cyber-anomalies and multi-attacks. Elsevier.

Schmitt, N. M. (2013). *Tallinn Manual on the International Law Applicable to Cyber Warfare.* Cambridge Univesity Press. doi:10.1017/CBO9781139169288

Singer, P. (2011, September 20). *Deterrence in Cyberspace: Debating the Right Strategy With Ralph Langner and Dmitri Alpetrovitch.* Retrieved from https://www.brookings.edu/events/deterrence-in-cyberspace-debating-the-right-strategy-with-ralph-langner-and-dmitri-alperovitch/

Skopik, F., Settanni, G., & Fiedler, R. (2016). A problem shared is a problem halved: A survey on the dimensions of collective cyber defense through security information sharing. *Computers & Security, 60*, 154–176. doi:10.1016/j.cose.2016.04.003

Solar, C. (2020). Cybersecurity and cyber defense in emerging democracies. *Journal of Cyber Policy, 5*. https://www.tandfonline.com/doi/epdf/10.1080/23738871.2020.1820546?needAccess=true&role=button&

Telecommunication Standardization Sector of ITU. (2008, April). *SERIES X: Data networks, open systems, communication, and security.* Retrieved from International Communication Union: file:///C:/Users/595-424-424%20Windows/Downloads/T-REC-X.1205-200804-I!!PDF-E.pdf

The Department of Defense (DoD). (2018). *Summary Department of Defense Cyber Strategy.* Retrieved from https://media.defense.gov/2018/Sep/18/2002041658/-1/-1/1/CYBER_STRATEGY_SUMMARY_FINAL.PDF

The White House. (2017, May 11). *Presidential Executive Order on Strengthening the Cybersecurity of Federal Networks and Critical Infrastructure.* Retrieved from https://trumpwhitehouse.archives.gov/presidential-actions/presidential-executive-order-strengthening-cybersecurity-federal-networks-critical-infrastructure/

The White House. (2021, July 19). *The United States, Joined by Allies and Partners, Attributes Malicious Cyber Activity and Irresponsible State Behavior to the People's Republic of China.* Retrieved from https://www.whitehouse.gov/briefing-room/statements-releases/2021/07/19/the-united-states-joined-by-allies-and-partners-attributes-malicious-cyber-activity-and-irresponsible-state-behavior-to-the-peoples-republic-of-china/

The White House. (2022, October). *National Security Strategy.* Retrieved from https://www.whitehouse.gov/wp-content/uploads/2022/10/Biden-Harris-Administrations-National-Security-Strategy-10.2022.pdf

The White House. (2023, March). *National Cybersecurity Strategy.* Retrieved from https://www.whitehouse.gov/wp-content/uploads/2023/03/National-Cybersecurity-Strategy-2023.pdf

United Nations. (n.d.). *United Nations Charter (full text).* Retrieved from https://www.un.org/en/about-us/un-charter/full-text

Vázquez, D. F., Acosta, O. P., Spirito, C., Brown, S., & Reid, E. (2012). Conceptual Framework for Cyber Defense Information Sharing within Trust Relationships. *4th International Conference on Cyber Conflict,* 429-445.

White, K. (2015, September 24). *A Few Comments on the UN Broadband Commission's "Cyber Violence Against Women And Girls" Report.* Retrieved from https://www.popehat.com/2015/09/24/a-few-comments-on-the-un-broadband-commissions-cyber-violence-against-women-and-girls-report/

White House. (2017, August 18). *Statement by President Donald J. Trump on the Elevation of Cyber Command.* Retrieved from https://trumpwhitehouse.archives.gov/briefings-statements/statement-president-donald-j-trump-elevation-cyber-command/

Yuchong, L., & Qinghui, L. (2021). A comprehensive review study of cyber-attacks and cyber security; Emerging trends and recent developments. Elsevier.

Chapter 9
Cyber Security Strategies:
International Experience

Liza Partsvania
International Black Sea University, Georgia

ABSTRACT

In this chapter, the main concept of cyber security strategy and policy of several states in the field of cyber defense policy are discussed and analyzed. This factor allows the authors to make a comparative analysis of the cyber security strategies of such states and organizations as NATO, the European Union, the USA, Estonia, Lithuania, and Georgia. Particularly, there are analyzed appropriate documents in the field of cyber security and cyber defense taking into account the current realities in world politics.

INTRODUCTION

In the era of technological development, every sphere of life became more dependent on the Internet, software, artificial intelligence, and online systems than ever. Revolutionary changes during the previous decades promoted business, science, education, energy, transportation, communication, healthcare, and a variety of other sectors to adjust to reality and become more digital. In a progressively internet-centered world, the importance of protecting data, assets, and other electronic information has significantly increased. Since the contemporary world is highly interconnected cyber security breaches in a particular state affect other neighboring states and not only. According to the International Telecommunication Union, "Cybersecurity is the collection of tools, policies, security concepts, security safeguards, guidelines, risk management approaches, actions, training, best practices, assurance and technologies that can be used to protect the cyber environment and organizations' and users' assets" (ITU, 2009). Cyberattacks can also cause significant damage to businesses and individuals, including data breaches, identity theft, and reputational harm.

Furthermore, cyberspace could become the theater of warfare in the 21st century when cyberattacks are targeted against a particular state. The use of cyber operations as a means of warfare in armed conflicts poses a real risk of harm to civilians. Since Russia's illegal annexation of Crimea in 2014, there have been ongoing cyberattacks by Russia against Ukraine, which escalated right before the 2022 invasion.

DOI: 10.4018/978-1-6684-8846-1.ch009

The public, energy, media, financial, commercial, and nonprofit sectors in Ukraine have been mostly damaged during this time. Their effects have included data theft and disinformation, the use of deep fake technology, and restricting access to fundamental services. Initiatives supported by the EU, US, and NATO have been implemented to defend critical infrastructure and avoid cyber threats to strengthen Ukraine's cyber defense. The case of Ukraine proves the significance of developing a National Cyber Security Strategy to understand the enemy's tactics, techniques, and procedures and respond effectively to any cyberattack during the war.

To address the global challenge of cybersecurity that significantly influences all institutions on national and international levels, the international community has been working to collectively develop plans for defense of the cyberspace. The Enhanced Cyber Defense Policy of NATO recognized cyberspace as a vital element of NATO's collective defense in 2016. It is outlined that "a decision as to when a cyber attack would lead to the invocation of Article 5 would be taken by the North Atlantic Council on a case-by-case basis."[1] NATO, EU, and other partner states have developed the National Cyber Security Strategy - the conceptual document that encompasses the existing cyber threats and challenges and provides essential strategical information, the tools, and approaches to defend critical infrastructure and guides states to strengthen their cyber resilience. This chapter analyzes the international cyber experience in the example of the United States and the European Union. It provides a detailed discussion of national cyber security policy and the recommendations that the international community should adopt to improve cyber resilience.

The Experience of the Different Countries in the Field of Cyber Security Strategies

The main conceptual document for ensuring cyber security is the national cyber security strategy, which includes the challenges and threats facing the country, and an action plan to overcome these challenges. Every state needs to have a strong cyberspace. Cyber security is a global challenge that transcends national borders and requires increased cooperation at the international level. At the 2014 Wales Summit, NATO member states declared cyber defense a key component of collective defense and stated that a cyber attack could trigger Article 5 of NATO's collective defense (Global Affairs Press, 2022). NATO member countries have begun to develop joint defense mechanisms. NATO, EU, and US partner countries have developed cyber security strategies to collectively address global cyber challenges.

The cyber security strategy is an important document that ensures the cyber resilience of the country. This chapter presents international experience, which includes an overview of cyber security strategies of the European Union, America, Estonia, and Lithuania and a detailed, comparative analysis of cyber security strategies of Georgia. On December 16, 2020, the European Union adopted a new strategy for combating cyberattacks, which involves joint actions with EU members and partner countries to combat cybercrime. In July 2021, the European Union, for the first time in its history, imposed sanctions in response to cyber attacks on the EU (European Commission, 2022).

According to the strategy:

- EU countries should ensure the security and stability of cyberspace through joint efforts;
- to strengthen the collective capabilities of combating cyber threats, to help member countries to protect the national security of the country, to counter cyber-attacks jointly;

- Together with international partners, ensure a global, safe, stable cyberspace where human rights, rule of law, and democratic values will be protected;
- ensure the security of the Internet network and information systems through joint efforts;
- Collectively provide funding for scientific research and innovation.

Along with the development of modern technologies, cybercrime is increasing, the target of which is such sectors of the country's critical infrastructure as the economy, business, health care, transport, energy supply, and others. In the age of digital technologies of the 5th-6th generation, the risks will increase even more. To deal with the risks, the European Union formed an expert group in October 2019, which issued the 5G Internet Risk Assessment document, which lists identified cyber risk mitigation opportunities, strategic and technical measures; Relevant legislative measures, security requirements, recommendations on diversification of network component suppliers are also provided. The mentioned document will largely help Georgia, its partners, and allied countries to implement an effective cyber policy, both at the national and global levels.

Back in 2009, the United States identified cybersecurity as the most serious economic and national security challenge. According to experts' analysis, the economic progress of America, which has repeatedly become the target of Russian cyber attacks, depends on the strengthening of the country's cyber security. Russia is actively using cyberspace to disrupt critical US infrastructure and undermines the American public's trust in democratic institutions; It also actively engages in online anti-government propaganda, carries out intelligence activities, and directs cyber attacks on government and industrial sectors. One of the important players is North Korea, which carries out cyber-attacks, violates sanctions and obtains funds through cryptocurrency exchanges, which helps to strengthen armaments.

In 2018, the US Department of Defense (DoD) approved a new cyber security strategy to deal with cyber risks, which, unlike the strategy document adopted in 2015, focuses on an aggressive, offensive (Defense Forward) policy to protect cyberspace. The main goal of this concept is intelligence activity, which involves the preliminary collection of information about possible malicious actions by the adversary in cyberspace, the purpose of which is to detect the adversary's malicious activities, destroy the aggressor's cyber infrastructure and cyber capabilities in time before he can launch a cyber attack. At the 2018 Cyber Security Strategy Symposium, US Cyber Command (USCYBERCOM) addressed the synchronization of information operations and cyberspace capabilities. The future vision of the strategy includes the integration of diplomacy, information, military, and economic tools to realize national goals (Media Defense, 2018).

The cyber security strategy is based on 5 global goals:

- United States forces must be the guarantor of operations in cyberspace;
- By combining cyber capabilities, the military advantage of the united forces should be achieved;
- It is important to deter cyberattacks that threaten America's critical infrastructure, which could lead to a serious cyber incident;
- ensure the security of the US Department of Defense information system and information networks that do not belong to the Department of Defense;
- To strengthen the cyber cooperation of the Department of Defense with partners, allied countries, and private sectors.
- Implementation of these cyber strategy goals is based on 5 main aspects:

- Creation of a strong destructive cyber force;
- Deterrence and engagement during cyber-attacks;
- Expansion of cyber cooperation with partner and allied countries;
- Reform of the Department of Defense;
- Training of cyber experts.

The strategy focuses on those states that can pose a strategic threat to US national security. Particular attention should be paid to such countries as China and Russia. The strategy also mentions North Korea and Iran, which have carried out cyber attacks on various US agencies and private industries. The Department of Defense attaches great importance to the use of all levers of state power to neutralize the malicious actions of the adversary in cyberspace so that the national interests of the United States and its allied countries are protected as much as possible. The Pentagon also emphasizes the need for continued response to daily malicious cyberattacks, ensuring deterrence of cyberattacks, and strengthening the cybersecurity of Defense Department systems and networks. The strategy includes the Department of Defense (DoD) readiness to streamline information-sharing mechanisms with agencies and industry partners; Prioritize the resilience of critical infrastructure and strengthen the cyber capabilities of allied and partner nations internationally (Media Defense, 2018).

The US government also places great importance on training cyber specialists. To train specialists, the government allocated 578 million dollars for the 2020 fiscal year to implement the integrated program STEM (Science, Technology, Engineering, Mathematics including Computer science), which combines science, technology, computer engineering, mathematics, computer science (US Department of Education, 2022).

The US cyber security system is three-tiered:

1. The first level includes federal agencies:
   ◦ Ministry of Defense (DoD, Department of Defense);
   ◦ Ministry of National Security (Department of Homeland Security, DHS);
   ◦ Office of Cyber Security and Communications (Office of Cyber Security and Communications);
   ◦ United States Department of Justice.
2. The second level includes the groups/centers included in the first level structures:
   ◦ Cyber Crimes Center;
   ◦ National Cyber Security Center (National Cyber Security Division, NCSD);
   ◦ Cyber threat operational center (NSA/CSS Threat Operations Center, NTOC);
   ◦ United States Cyber Command, USCYBERCOM.
3. The third level includes regional and local structural subdivisions. They are controlled by the above-mentioned organizations (Svanadze, Gotsiridze, 2015).

In 2018, Estonia developed the 3rd version of the National Cyber Security Strategy to combat cyber challenges, which is based on the previous strategies (the first version of the strategy covered the years 2008-2013; the second version - 2014-2017) and highlights Estonia's leading role among various countries in the world as one of the priority directions. To help develop cyber defense capabilities and combat cyber threats.

The management of cyber security policy in Estonia is carried out at the national level by the Ministry of Economy and Communications, whose prerogative is the introduction and development of electronic services, the development of the country's information systems and technologies, including rapid response to cyber incidents, and constant preparedness. The Estonian Information Systems Authority RIA (Estonian Information System Authority) is subordinate to the Ministry of Economy and Communications, which provides administration and coordination of the state's information systems. The Information Systems Agency RIA is also responsible for overseeing Estonia's e-government platform, including the national electronic personal identification and data exchange infrastructure. In addition, the said agency provides internet service for local and state agencies. RIA is subordinated to the Estonian Computer Security Incident Response Team (CERT-EE), which provides:

- Monitoring the country's computer networks and responding to cyber incidents;
- Raising the awareness of users about cyber-attacks;
- Data exchange infrastructure management;
- Preparation of a report on threats and cyber incidents in the country's cyberspace, the so-called

Managing the Virtual Situation Room (VSR). This is a crisis management platform, through which it is possible to exchange information in one space. Through the Virtual Situation Room (VSR), the communications and the current situation of the agencies during the crisis are fully recorded to analyze possible situations. The platform is also used for staff training. The country's cyber defense is led at the national level by the Ministry of Defense, and the Department of Cyber Defense, which has been operating in the Ministry of Defense since 2014, is directly responsible for the planning, implementation, and development of information and communication technologies in the defense system.

The country's cyber defense security is provided by the Estonian Cyber Defense Unit, which was established in 2011 under the Estonian Defense League. It is a group of volunteers that has been part of the Defense Forces since 2013 as a legal entity under public law and represents a union of professionals. They take care of strengthening cyber defense capabilities without any compensation. In peacetime, the unit's main function is to raise public awareness of cyber threats, while in times of crisis, the unit, together with the Estonian Computer Security Incident Response Team (CERT_EE), protects the country's cyberspace. Unit members are not required to have specific technical knowledge and skills, with exceptions. Its members are representatives of various fields, whose knowledge and experience are related to cyber security.

In 2017, according to the National Defense Development Plan 2017-2026, the Estonian Cyber Command unit was established within the Estonian Defense Forces.

On August 1, 2018, the Cyber Command of the Estonian Defense Forces was established, the function of which is:

- Complete organization of operations in cyberspace;
- Management of information and communication technologies of the Ministry of Defense;
- Ensuring cyber security in the defense domain;
- support of headquarters of subdivisions in support of joint headquarters;
- formation of military and reserve units;
- Leadership and coordination of cyber defense and management capacity development;
- Strategic communications support of the defense forces;
- Organization of information operations (Cyber Security of Estonia, 2020).

Estonia's critical infrastructure is overseen by the Estonian Information Center (RIA), a non-police civilian agency. It sets safety standards as needed; is authorized to have access to the information system of critical entities; Serves to eliminate cyber incidents. All critical entities are obliged to comply with the security norms established by the Estonian Information Center and to provide it with information within 24 hours about cyber incidents that may cause significant damage to national security. In case of violation of obligations, the organization or private structure is fined 20,000 euros.

The list of critical infrastructure includes:

1. Energy and networks: electricity, oil and gas storage, transmission, and distribution systems.
2. Communication and information technologies: telecommunication, transmission and message systems, software, hardware, and networks, including Internet infrastructure.
3. Financial system: banks, investments.
4. Healthcare: hospitals, healthcare facilities, laboratories and medicines, search, rescue, and emergency services.
5. Food: safety, means of production, wholesale, and food industry.
6. Water supply: reservoirs, water pipelines, and water networks.
7. Transport system: airports, ports, intermediate means of transport, railway and mass transit networks, and traffic management systems.
8. Production, storage, and transportation of dangerous goods: chemical, biological, radiological, and other dangerous materials.
9. Government bodies: critical services, government facilities, information networks that provide national security and defense, databases and court records, and cultural assets of national importance.

Estonia has developed the field of cyber security in the shortest possible time and has become a leading country among the EU member states in this field. In 2011, the NATO-accredited cyber defense center of Excellence - NATO Cooperative Cyber Defense Center of Excellence (NATO CCDCOE) was established in Tallinn. It is a training-research analytical military organization, the purpose of which is to conduct consultations, training, and exercises in the field of cyber security; Also - cooperation and information exchange with NATO allies and partner countries.

The NATO Cyber Defense Competence Center is staffed by international cyber security and cyber security experts. It includes legal scholars, policy and strategy experts, as well as technological researchers with the military, government, and industrial experience. The NATO Cyber Defense Competence Center offers continuing education in the field of cyber security. The training is based on the latest research and materials related to recent cyber training.

Estonia is one of the leading countries in the European Union in terms of the development of digital technologies. Pass legislation that will significantly reduce cyber risks. According to the legislation, telecommunications companies are obliged to consult with the government agency when purchasing any new device, and only after this inspection obtain permission to connect the device to the network. The mentioned measures are a step forward to neutralizing cyber threats and reducing risks.

Lithuania approved the National Cyber Security Strategy on August 23, 2018 (the first strategy was developed in 2011). The main goal of the cyber security strategy is to strengthen the cyber security and cyber defense of the state, timely detection and prevention of cybercrime, improvement of cooperation between the private and state sectors, cyber resilience, deepening of international cooperation, fulfillment of international cyber obligations within the country by 2023 (Ministry of National Defense of Lithuania, 2018).

The cyber security strategy is an important document that will define specific goals and objectives for both the state sector and scientific and educational institutions for the next 5 years. The main goal of the strategy is to raise public awareness and protect the people of Lithuania from cyber incidents, and cyber-incidents threaten the national security of the country and put at risk the functioning of state and public institutions, business development, personnel databases, and protection of human rights. The main goal of the strategy is to make the Lithuanian people aware of how important the role of information and telecommunication technologies is for the timely and effective detection of cyber incidents, and the prevention and neutralization of cyber attacks.

The strategy is based on 5 main objectives:

- Strengthening the country's cyber security and developing cyber defense capabilities - the Computer Emergency Response Team in Lithuania or "CERT-LT" recorded 54,414 cyber incidents in 2017. Compared to 2016, the number of attacks increased by 10%. Espionage cyber-attacks on state information strategic facilities, private critical information infrastructure and other strategic national security facilities are at risk. The most harmful software viruses were found in the energy sector - 27%, legal and public sector - 22%, and foreign and security sector - 21%. Compared to 2016, public sector websites were down, affecting the country's cyber security.
- Ensuring prevention and detection of cyberattacks in cyberspace - Cybercriminals are taking a toll on the global economy. According to research, the losses reach hundreds of millions of dollars per year and are increasing day by day. To fight against cybercrime, it is important to increase the professionalism of law enforcement agencies so that they can quickly identify and investigate cybercrime. Lithuania has ratified the Convention adopted by the Council of Europe on November 23, 2001 (Convention on Computer Crime), which, in turn, involves the establishment of an information and analysis system for increasing the professional capacity of law enforcement authorities; implementation of the latest operational methods, procedures and technologies designed specifically for combating cybercriminals; International cooperation in the investigation of cybercrime. Also - close cooperation between law enforcement agencies, scientific, public, and private sector representatives, and society.
- Promotion of cyberculture and development of innovations - promotion of raising the cyberculture of employees by the heads of the state and private sector, which provides for regular training of employees. More than 30% of cyber-attacks were carried out by employees opening a suspicious email or a suspicious link that contained malicious code and caused the entire network to become infected. It is also important to disseminate information about the latest cyber incidents and share them with employees; Financing and promotion of innovations and scientific research projects.
- Strengthening close cooperation between private and public sectors based on mutual trust and mutual benefits. It is important to create a cyber security information network, which involves sharing experiences among network members, exchanging information, recommendations, and instructions, and exchanging information about ways to solve cyber incidents in technical ways; Encouragement of small and medium-sized businesses, which provides for the implementation of cyber security measures by companies (Ministry of National Defense of Lithuania, 2018).
- Strengthening of international cooperation and fulfillment of international obligations in terms of cyber security - to fulfill the mentioned goals, it is important to participate in the exercises and training of the European Union, NATO, the United Nations, the United Nations, the Baltic region and other international organizations; Permanent Structured Cooperation in Security and Defense Policy (PESCO) to strengthen cooperation with the advanced countries of the European Union.

The strategy emphasizes the improvement of bilateral cooperation between the United States and Lithuania in the field of cyber security at the technical and political levels; the implementation of joint cyber security projects in the cyber defense of Lithuania and to enhancement of cyber potential.

Cyber Security Strategies of Georgia: The State, Which Was the Victim of Russian Full-Scale Aggression, Including a Cyber Attack in 2008

The Russian-Georgian war of 2008 and the mass cyber attacks carried out by Russia showed us how vulnerable Georgia's cyberspace was. In parallel with the large-scale attack on the land, sea, and air space, the Russian military forces delivered a mass, so-called DDoS attack that brought down the banking sector, transportation, telecommunications companies, and government websites. As a result of the support of international organizations and partner countries, the infrastructure of the governmental, banking, and private sectors of Georgia was saved from destruction (Palitra, 2020). In March 2020, at the Security Council of the European Union, Estonia raised the issue of Georgia for the first time, which was related to the massive cyber attack carried out by Russia on Georgia in 2019. International experts assessed Russia's cyber attack as an "informational cyber war" against Georgia.

In August 2008, the large-scale cyber-attacks carried out by the Russian Federation against Georgia demonstrated that the protection of cyberspace is as important to national security as the protection of land, sea, and air spaces. Based on the hard experience gained, the Georgian government started working on a legal-normative basis in this direction, as a result of which the Cyber Security Strategy of Georgia was published in May 2013, which is part of the package of conceptual and strategic documents created within the framework of the "National Security Review" process. This strategy is based on the "Georgia Threat Assessment 2010-2013". the document" and "National Security Concept of Georgia". The National Cyber Security Strategy is the main document defining the state policy in the field of cyber security, which reflects strategic goals, and main principles, and establishes action plans and tasks (Cybersecurity Strategy of Georgia, 2017-2018).

Before the adoption of the strategy, in 2012, the "Law on Information Security" came into force. The draft law addressed public sector cyber challenges but did not cover the business sector and therefore required constant updating. There were no cyber security requirements in the energy, insurance, and medical fields in the mentioned bill. Cybersecurity was relatively protected only in the large banking sector (Law of Georgia on Information Security, 2012).

For the second time, on January 13, 2017, the government of Georgia published the 2017-2018 national cyber security strategy and approved action plan. The main directions of the cyber security policy were a set of measures for effective response to cyber threats and challenges facing the country. The main directions of the 2017-2018 cyber security strategy of Georgia are:

1. Research and analysis;
2. Development and improvement of the legal base;
3. Raising public awareness and improving the educational base;
4. International cooperation.

According to the strategy, research and analysis included the following areas:

• Studying the best practices of other countries and sharing experiences;

- Research of criteria and standards for identification of critical information infrastructure objects.
- Critical information infrastructure stability analysis;
- Studying the problems in the region in the field of cyber security;
- Development of cyber security defining standards for their further implementation;
- Periodic preparation of proposals for the detection of threats and risks facing the cyberspace of Georgia.

The creation of the legal base provided for the implementation of the following measures:

- Initiation of legislative acts on information security;
- Creating a normative base defining the critical information infrastructure and ensuring its cyber security;
- Legal provision of computer incident assistance group functioning;
- Fulfillment of obligations undertaken as a result of the ratification of the 2001 "Cybercrime" Convention of the Council of Europe;
- Identification of the body or bodies at the legislative level, whose authority will include the definition of the information security policy and the implementation of the coordinating function;
- Writing backup plans and procedures for action during crises related to cyber security.

The creation of an inter-departmental coordination mechanism included the implementation of the following measures:

- Further development of computer incident response team;
- Further development of the 24/7 international contact point for high-tech crime (cybercrime);
- Determination of expert assistance group (unit) on cybercrime cases;
- Establishing the format and mechanisms of cooperation between the state and private sectors.

Raising public awareness and improving the educational base included: training specialists, planning training, and creating of an educational base, which provided for the following measures:

- Raising public awareness and creating educational programs in the field of cyber security and cyber security;
- Training of personnel and technical personnel of critical information infrastructure entities and other interested organizations to study international and national standards of information security;
- Specialized training of cybercrime experts in the field of electronic evidence (cyber criminology);
- Promotion of scientific-research projects in the field of cyber security, and creation of a research laboratory.

International cooperation included:

- Cooperation with NATO and EU countries, sharing of experience, participation in international exercises and educational training;
- Active participation in international initiatives in the field of cyber security and regional support for these initiatives;

- Initiating bilateral and multilateral cooperation with other countries' Computer Incident Response Teams (CERT) in the field of cyber security.

According to the Resolution N482 of the Government of Georgia, on September 30, 2021, the National Cyber Security Strategy and Action Plan for 2021-2024 (3rd version) was approved. "The strategy aims to develop cyberculture and cyber education in the fields of cyber security, cyber defense, and cyber-crime. ensuring the stability of the governance system, and strengthening public-private cooperation. Creating solid human resources and strengthening the role of Georgia as a safe and secure country in the international arena" (Cybersecurity Strategy and Action Plan of Georgia for 2021-2024).

The latest version of the strategy offers a three-year vision for the country's secure development and provides information on how to effectively deal with cyber threats. The strategy and action plan were developed with the active participation of representatives of the public, private sector, business, academia, and experts from the United States, partner countries, and Great Britain. In the process of developing the strategy, the Government of Georgia took into account the advice and recommendations of the partner state, the best international practice, and experience. At the same time, it should be noted that the group of British experts, in close communication with the National Security Council, will monitor the implementation process of the strategy and action plan, both at the strategic and tactical levels.

The strategy document includes an assessment document prepared by The Global Cyber Security Capacity Center of Oxford University, which outlines the cyber security environment in Georgia, specific recommendations, and initiatives for its development (Cybersecurity Strategy and Action Plan of Georgia for 2021-2024).

Unlike the previous two strategies, the document identifies specific directions that are important to consider to neutralize cyber threats:

- Threats associated with the supply chain of digital equipment, that is, from which country the digital equipment is purchased;
- Threats originating from Russian software;
- Human errors or other factors.

The new strategy, unlike the previous two strategies, deals with cyber threats from Russia. However, it should be noted that, based on that, cyber-attacks have no borders, society has not perceived how dangerous and destructive cyber-attacks that Russia is carrying out against Georgia are. Russia has developed hybrid warfare tactics and has recently actively refined and started implementing hybrid activities. Since these attacks take place in cyberspace and are less perceptible, it is necessary to raise the awareness of the population, which does not mean technical knowledge at the expert level, but the general knowledge of public officials, the business sector, the population, and citizens about cyber security. It is important for government and business decision-makers to correctly perceive and analyze the threats and cyber risks posed by aggressor countries, particularly Russia.

The strategy emphasizes the human factor, which is the biggest risk in the digital world. As studies confirm, the largest cyber incidents in the world are explained by improper assessment of risks and threats by the user, lack of knowledge, or intentional unauthorized actions. Despite the funding allocated by the government or private sector to strengthen cyber defense mechanisms, such as anti-virus programs, network security monitors, encryption mechanisms, and others, which help to minimize cyber attacks, these measures are still not enough to neutralize cyber threats. A person is the weakest link, he easily becomes a target for hackers, and his mistakes can paralyze the entire system. It means not only the so-called Getting on the hook for phishing but also misguided programs. As the research shows, 45% of cyber attacks on organizations are so-called. It happened with phishing emails. Small and medium-sized businesses are mainly focused on profit, which often leads to overloading and exhaustion of service personnel. Research shows that technology and financial workers, who often have to respond quickly to incoming e-mails, often become victims of phishing. Therefore, a hacker can easily penetrate the system, and paralyze the system, which has a devastating effect on the organization. It is important to raise the awareness of service personnel, through frequent training; Must have information on how to avoid cyber attacks (Sosanya, 2022).

In December 2020, the US Department of Defense (DoD), Department of Homeland Security (DHS), and Infrastructure and Cyber Security Agency (CISA) were damaged as a result of a large-scale cyber attack on the American company SolarWinds. SolarWinds is an American-registered company that provides information technology (IT) services to the private and public sectors. This attack was blamed on the Russian Foreign Intelligence Service. A group of hackers infiltrated the company's secure infrastructure, secretly injecting malicious code into SolarWinds software update system, Orion. Specialists regularly made software updates (updates) in which malicious code was embedded, which created a so-called "backdoor"[1] to the client's information technology system, through which hackers installed more malicious codes. The Russian intelligence service secretly carried out cyber espionage on American government agencies for 9 months.

All this time America's critical infrastructure was vulnerable (Jibilian, Canales, 2022). The lack of knowledge and awareness explains the fact that a large number of state agencies of the country still use such programs as Kaspersky, rambler.ru, and mail.ru, even though it is clearly stated in the cyber security strategy for 2015-2018 that Russia is our active and a dangerous enemy in cyberspace. The use of these programs carries a great risk, which has been repeatedly emphasized by foreign experts.

Unlike the previous strategy, version 3 takes into account the risk of using unlicensed software, both in the private and public sectors and by individuals, which poses a major threat and remains a significant problem. According to the 2018 estimate of the Business Software Alliance, the risk rate is 81%, which makes the business sector and consumers even more vulnerable. When purchasing an information and communication technology product, it is also important to take into account the security component, which the private sector and critical infrastructure do not have on the Georgian market, which implies possible threats and risks during purchases, which are expected to endanger the integrity, availability, and confidentiality of the information system (Cybersecurity Strategy of Georgia and action plan, 2021-2024).

Since 2008, the Russian Federation has been constantly conducting cyber-attacks and cyber espionage in the cyberspace of Georgia. The cyber attacks on Georgia in 2019-2020 became the subject of discussion and debate among Western partner countries. They put the responsibility directly on the Russian intelligence services, and not on any of the Russian criminal cyber actors, which are also actively used by the Kremlin. The US, UK, Australia, New Zealand, and NATO countries said that Russian foreign intelligence was conducting cyber attacks against Georgia.

The 3rd version of the strategy envisages the strengthening of cooperation between the public and private sectors, which should be based on mutual trust. Critical infrastructure facilities are in the hands of the private sector, be it the banking sector, internet providers, and others. Therefore, it is important to strengthen the cyber security of the private sector so that they do not arbitrarily take countermeasures, which may be ineffective and lead to disastrous results for the state. There is a need for information exchange between the private and state sectors, coordinated action, and strengthening of mutual trust.

The document focuses on threats and risks. these are:

- Cyberwar, information war, cyber espionage, and cyber attacks directed by state actors.
- Cybercrime (including attacks against critical infrastructures).

Since 2008, Russia has carried out cyber attacks in 2015, 2016, 2019, and 2020. Georgia was the first country when, in 2008, Russia conducted a cyber war alongside military operations, which reached the kinetic phase.

The second type of risk is information war/information-psychological operations, which Russia actively uses against Georgia. The information war has increased compared to 2008, due to the greater use of Internet space, and today it reaches 70%, while it was only 7% during the war. The pandemic also contributed to the consumption of Internet space, when business, government activities, education, and commerce moved to the Internet space, which doubled and increased the scale of Russia's disinformation campaign (Cybersecurity Strategy of Georgia and action plan, 2021-2024).

What is the information war mainly aimed at? Georgia's strategic goal is integration into the Euro-Atlantic space, which Russia cannot adapt to, and actively spreads false information, engages in anti-Western policy, calling: "Georgia a failed state" and that "the West often interferes in Georgia's domestic affairs" (Cybersecurity Strategy of Georgia and action plan, 2021-2024).

The Kremlin's main goal is to weaken trust in the country's democratic institutions, discredit Western democracy and return Georgia to the Russian orbit. Russian disinformation propaganda can cause a psychological impact on the people, increase the pro-Russian orientation elite, which will be relied on later, cause polarization among the people and threaten the sovereignty of the country.

The strategy outlines such vulnerable areas as cyber espionage, cyber espionage. Back then, APT-28 was considered a cybercriminal group linked to Russian military intelligence. In 2019-2020, British, American, and Australian experts assessed the cyber attack on Georgia as a massive cyber attack carried out by the Russian intelligence group. An example of cyber espionage is the 2020 cyberattack on the Lugar lab when Russian cyber-knifes stole personal data. The pandemic has increased the scale of the transition to digital technology, which has created even more favorable conditions for cybercriminals. Financially motivated cybercriminals use ransomware, which occurred in 2019, 2020, 2021 (Barker, 2021).

One of the main goals of the strategy is an international cooperation with partner countries, strengthening the role of Georgia as a safe and secure country in the international arena of cyber security. The country should become a center (hub) in the Caucasus region, which will contribute to raising the prestige of Georgia in the international arena. Also - Georgia should become a reliable and reliable partner for the international community in the field of cyber security; Georgia's involvement in international initiatives of bilateral and multilateral relations, cooperation with the relevant agencies of the Caucasus, Central Asia, and the Black Sea countries, which includes sharing experience in the fight against cybercrime, prevention of cyber threats and electronic governance (Cybersecurity Strategy of Georgia and action plan, 2021-2024).

The question arises, what can Georgia do to deal with cyber threats directed from Russia? Georgia, as a non-NATO country, has been participating in NATO cyber exercises since 2014. NATO's 28 member countries have agreed that they will take countermeasures in case of a Russian cyber attack. It is important to include Georgia in the mentioned union, and it is also important to strengthen diplomatic ties with NATO member states. Georgia should develop active cyber defense and cyber attack mechanisms. In addition, it is possible to form a cyber union of non-NATO countries: Australia, New

Zealand, and Japan. The inclusion of Georgia in the mentioned union will strengthen the cyber potential of our country. The support of Estonia and Lithuania towards Georgia is also important. Under their mentorship, they included Georgia in cyber exercises. Because cyberspace has no borders, cyber challenges are transnational, and no state, including Georgia, will be able to deal with cyber threats with its resources, without collective international cooperation and collaboration. Because the data required for the investigation of cyber incidents are stored in the infrastructure under the jurisdiction of different countries, international cooperation is a necessary condition for the prevention and suppression of cyber incidents. For the smooth and safe functioning of cyberspace, it is necessary to share the experience of the EU and the Alliance countries and compatibility with cyber security standards.

The Cyber Security Policy of Georgia

The development of an effective cyber security policy became especially relevant for Georgia after the August 2008 war, when Russia launched a large-scale cyber attack on Georgia's critical infrastructure. The security environment has significantly worsened since Russia occupied the Tskhinvali region and Abkhazia, the so-called border region of Abkhazia and Tskhinvali region.

The declaration of independent republics was followed by the seizure of Georgian territories, violation of Georgian sovereignty, violation of international law, and the rights of the local population. The country met Russia's aggressive actions completely unprepared. The Kremlin's aggressive foreign policy is the main challenge to Georgia's national security. That is why the issue of how to repel such aggressive cyber attacks in the future has gained great relevance.

The cyber policy has a special place in the national security concept of Georgia, the main goal of which is to effectively protect the country's cyberspace and create a strong digital system. "The security of the information space and the security of electronic information is very important for Georgia. Along with the rapid development of information technologies, the dependence of the state's critical infrastructure on them is increasing. Considering this, great importance is attached to the fight against cybercrime and the protection of the country's cyberspace from subversive acts" (National Security Concept of Georgia, 2011).

"The massive cyber attack by Russia in 2008 clearly showed that the protection of cyberspace is as important for national security as the protection of land, sea, and air spaces" (Cybersecurity Strategy of Georgia and action plan, 2021-2024). Georgia has repeatedly been targeted by the Kremlin (a large-scale attack in 2019, a cyber attack on the database of the Richard Lugar Public Health Research Center in September 2020) (MoD, 2020). The Kremlin's hybrid war is a unified tool of psychological manipulation and information warfare on society, the main goal of which is to weaken the country psychologically, sow mistrust in society, and shake confidence in democratic institutions (White, 2018). Russia is waging a hybrid war against Georgia, regularly conducting information warfare, cyber-espionage, and cyber-attacks on our country's critical infrastructure.

The August war was assessed by international experts as an information/cyber war against Georgia. After the end of the August war, the authorities of our country realized the fact that the cyberspace of Georgia was completely vulnerable and started to create a legal-normative base to solve this problem. In 2008, a roadmap and cyber strategy framework were created with the help of Estonian experts. In 2011, a computer incident response group was formed, which was tasked with managing incidents against information security in the cyberspace of Georgia. In 2012, the "Law on Information Security" was enacted, and in 2013-2015 and 2017-2018, two cyber security strategies were developed. The Cyber

Security Bureau was established in the Ministry of Defense, the Cybercrime Bureau in the Ministry of Internal Affairs, and the Digital Governance Agency in the Ministry of Justice. "In the law on information security" the minimum standard of information was established, and the concept of "critical information system subject" appeared for the first time. "Subject of a critical information system" was defined as an organization whose continuous operation of the information system is important for the defense, economic and public security of the country (Law of Georgia on Information Security, 2012). The competence of the Digital Governance Agency (previously - Data Exchange Agency) under the Ministry of Justice of Georgia is the implementation and coordination of information security norms; The Computer Incident Response Team (CERT.GOV.GE) is subordinate to it, which manages priority cyber attacks in Georgia's cyberspace (Law of Georgia on Information Security, 2012).

In 2014, the Cyber Security Bureau of the Ministry of Defense was established, which is responsible for the implementation and protection of the minimum standard of information security in the defense structure. The Cyber Security Bureau is responsible for responding to computer incidents (Malvenishvili, 2020). Since 2012, the Ministry of Internal Affairs has had a Cybercrime Division, which is responsible for detecting, suppressing, and preventing cyberattacks throughout the country. In addition, the division is a contact point that performs functions related to international police cooperation on "cybercrime" following the Council of Europe Convention (Malvenishvili, 2020). It should also be noted that the State Security and Crisis Management Council established in 2014, which was the main coordinating body, was abolished on January 1, 2018. In its place, the Emergency Situations Management Service was established, which reports directly to the Prime Minister.

In 2019, the National Security Council was established, the main purpose of which is to prepare political decisions on issues threatening national security and state interests, to plan and coordinate national security policy at a strategic level, prepare recommendations and decisions, and inform the Prime Minister (Malvenishvili, 2020).

"The Law of Georgia on Information Security" was created in June 2012. This law was an important step forward in strengthening the country's cyber security. It was amended on June 10, 2021. At the legislative level, the powers of the State Security Service of Georgia were clearly defined in the process of ensuring the country's cyber and information security. According to the mentioned legislation, a list of critical infrastructure entities was formed, which was divided into the first, second, and third categories:

- The list of the first category includes state bodies, institutions, legal entities under public law;
- Electronic communication companies belong to the second category;
- The third category - banks and financial institutions.

The responsibility for the protection of critical information system subjects was assigned to the Operational Technical Agency of Georgia (OTA) within the sphere of governance of the State Security Service of Georgia. The computer incident response team (CERT.OTA.GOV.GE) is under his authority, through which, following his competence, he manages incidents against information security in the cyberspace of Georgia, and is also responsible for activities related to information security coordination, which serves to eliminate priority cyber security threats (Law of Georgia on Information Security, 2012). OTA will coordinate the agencies and organizations included in the first and second categories. Subjects of the third category of critical information systems remain in the field of regulation of the Digital Governance Agency, which may lead to the duplication of rights and duties between the National Bank and the Digital Governance Agency because the National Bank supervises the provision of information security of private, commercial banks.

According to a study conducted by the Institute for the Development of Freedom of Information: "By law, the State Security Operational-Technical Agency (OTA) is allowed to have direct access to the information systems of the legislative, executive or judicial authorities, as well as the telecommunications sector, and indirect access - to personal and commercial information protected in the systems. A law enforcement agency is allowed to have access to personal data to the extent that the vagueness of the norms raises the real danger of unlawful and disproportionate processing of personal data" (IDFI, 2021).

It should be noted that it is unclear on what basis the division of critical infrastructure into categories was determined. As the research showed, in 39 institutions defined as critical infrastructure entities, compliance with the cyber security policy and compliance with the requirements of the law is not a priority (Jgarkava, 2021).

If we return to the cyber security strategies of America, Estonia, and Lithuania, when determining the list of critical infrastructure, priority is given to agencies whose operation is vital for the country, such as finance, healthcare, banking, energy, medical, Internet communication technologies (ICT), insurance, agriculture, and other critically important industries. Accordingly, the list of critical objects is different in different countries and depends on which branch of security is strategically important for the country. The list of critical infrastructure of Georgia requires a review, and determination of priority of agencies, based on the national security policy of Georgia.

It should also be noted that the change in the law, which entered into force after 10 years, is undoubtedly a step forward, although there are still many gaps in the law that need to be improved. When analyzing the challenges and threats facing the country, attention should be paid not only to future threats from Russia but also to those countries that are hostile to our strategic partners and can cause great harm to Georgia as well.

Even though there are still many gaps in the country's legislation, Georgia has achieved some successes in the field of cyber security in recent years: with the help of Estonian experts, a computer incident rapid response team (CERT) was formed. In 2019, the Cyber Bureau participated in the cyber training of NATO - "Cyber Coalition" with an increased status. Georgia is the second non-NATO country to join the NATO Smart Defense Project, which is a multinational platform for exchanging information about malicious software. The mentioned project will prevent cyber incidents. This project is mutually beneficial, allowing Georgia to contribute and share valuable information about cyber incidents with NATO member and non-member countries. An agreement was reached with American and British experts on the creation and development of the Cyber Security Operational Center. The strategy of the mentioned center includes the protection of the organization from cyber incidents and the detection and prevention of incidents. Within the strategic partnership with NATO, work is underway to establish a cyber laboratory equipped with the latest technologies (Georgian Cybersecurity Forum, 2020). The representatives of the Cyber Security Bureau of the Ministry of Defense of Georgia participated in the NATO Cooperative Cyber Defense Center (CCDCOE) cyber exercise "Lock Shield 2022", which is a real-time information and communication system security training, and the purpose of which is to develop the cyber capabilities of the participating teams. Georgia has been participating in this exercise since 2015 (SHAPE, NATO, 2022).

Cyber threats from the uncontrolled occupied territories of Georgia are important. Active cooperation and increasing militarization between the de facto authorities of the occupied Abkhazia and Tskhinvali region and the Russian Federation, joint agreements, and the absence of international peacekeeping forces increase the risk of renewed military aggression. In addition to the military dangers, the current events in the occupied territories create a fertile ground for the spread of transnational organized crime. Russia's main strategic goal is to return to the status of a global player on the world stage. Moscow cannot imagine achieving its global goal without restoring exclusive influence in the neighborhood, that is why it is actively carrying out information/psychological operations, disinformation campaigns, and cyber attacks on Georgia to cause destabilization and encroachment on the country's sovereignty.

In addition to the threats and cyber risks that come from our northern neighbor, one must take into account the wide range of potential threats that Georgia may face - from regional instability to terrorism. To protect cyberspace, it is necessary to analyze, study and take effective measures.

If we summarize, we can conclude that, although Georgia has carried out important work in terms of cyber security, if we compare the cyber security strategies of the European Union, America, Estonia, and Lithuania, these measures and the current cyber policy are insufficient to respond to modern challenges. There is no strict separation of functions and duties between state agencies in the country, coordination, cooperation, and information exchange mechanisms need to be improved; A complete list of critical infrastructure has not been developed; The country suffers from a lack of qualified personnel; It is important to implement the cyber security strategy action plan, conduct cyber security measures from the private and public sector; Strengthening and deepening of cooperation with international organizations, partner countries, sharing of the best experience, which will be a prerequisite for developing effective cyber defense mechanisms, training qualified staff, harmonizing with international legal norms and standards, strengthening the country's cyber resilience.

CONCLUSION

In general, a cyber security strategy is an action plan that details how a business will protect itself from cyber threats.

An effective cybersecurity strategy provides insight into what needs to be prioritized to create a safe and secure cyber environment. Thus, a good strategy is based on cybersecurity principles and focuses on how you should allocate resources to meet the business's cybersecurity goals.

Without a strategy, much of what we do is pointless and inefficient.

This applies to any endeavor, not just cybersecurity. For example, if you want to grow your business, do you start by picking random sales-related items and hoping for the best? No, you are developing a specific business strategy with planned elements.

REFERENCES

Barker, W. C. (2021). *Cybersecurity Framework Profile for Ransomware Risk Management*. U.S. Department of Commerce. doi:10.6028/NIST.IR.8374-draft

Canmales, K., & Jibilian, I. (2022). *The US is readying sanctions against Russia over the SolarWinds cyber attack*. Retrieved from: https://www.ft.com/content/d7d67ea7-8423-4b9c-819d-761fa4a10fa0

Commission, E. U. (2020). *The EU's Cybersecurity Strategy for the Digital Decade*. Retrieved from: https://ec.europa.eu/commission/presscorner/detail/en/IP_20_2391

Department of Defence. (2018). *Cyber Strategy*. Retrieved from: https://media.defense.gov/2018/Sep/18/2002041658/-1/-1/1/CYBER_STRATEGY_SUMMARY_FINAL.PDF

Freedom Development Institute (IDFI). (2021). *Parliament adopted the draft of the law on Information Security*. Retrieved from: https://idfi.ge/ge/the_parliament_of_the_10_convocation_adopted_the_problematic_draft_law_on_information_security

Global Affairs Press. (2022). *NATO's Cyber Defense Evolution*. Author.

Insider. (2021). *What Is the SolarWinds Hack and Why Is It a Big Deal?* Retrieved from: https://www.businessinsider.com/solarwinds-hack-explained-government-agencies-cyber-security-2020-12

Jgharkawa, I. (2022). *Georgia's cyber security policy, challenges and opportunities*. GCSD Research.

Malvenishvili, M., & Balarjishvili, N. (2022). *Cyber security reform in Georgia: current challenges, international practice, and recommendations. Institute for Development of Freedom of Information*. IDFI.

Mastne. (2012). *Law of Georgia on information security*. Legislative Herald of Georgia.

Matsne. (2017). *2017-2018 National Cyber Security Strategy of Georgia. On the approval of the 2017-2018 national strategy of cyber security of Georgia and its action plan*. Legislative Herald of Georgia.

Matsne. (2021a). *2021-2024 National Cyber Security Strategy of Georgia and its Action Plan. On Approval of the National Cyber Security Strategy of Georgia for 2021-2024 and its Action Plan regarding making changes to Resolution No. 482 of the Government of Georgia*. Legislative Herald of Georgia.

Matsne. (2021b). *Georgia's Cyber Security National Strategy for 2021-2024 and its Action Plan. On the Approval of Georgia's Cyber Security National Strategy for 2021-2024 and its Action Plan on amending Resolution No. 482 of the Government of Georgia*. Legislative Herald of Georgia.

Matsne. (2021c). *Georgia's Cyber Security National Strategy for 2021-2024 and its Action Plan. On the Approval of Georgia's Cyber Security National Strategy for 2021-2024 and its Action Plan on amending Resolution No. 482 of the Government of Georgia*. Legislative Herald of Georgia.

Ministry of Foreign Affairs of Georgia. (2020a). *The concept of national security of Georgia*. Retrieved from: https://www.mfa.gov.ge/national-security-concept

Ministry of Internal Affairs of Georgia. (2020b). *Statement of the Ministry of Internal Affairs of Georgia about the cyber attack*. Retrieved from: https://police.ge/ge/saqartvelos-shinagan-saqmeta-saministros-gantskhadeba/13926

Public Television of Georgia. (2021). *Cyber Security Forum of Georgia*. Retrieved from: https://www.youtube.com/watch?v=XDKGueqfG1I&t=57s

Ria. (2020). *Cyber Security in Estonia*. Retrieved from: https://www.ria.ee/sites/default/files/cyber_aastaraamat_eng_web_2020.pdf

Sarah, W. (2018). *Understanding Cyberwarfare, Lessons from the Russia-Georgia War*. Modern War Institute. Retrieved from: https://mwi.usma.edu/wp-content/uploads/2018/03/Understanding-Cyberwarfare.pdf

SHAPE. (2022). *Exercise Locked Shields 2022 concludes*. Retrieved from: https://shape.nato.int/news-archive/2022/exercise-locked-shields-2022-concludes

Sosanya, V. (2022). *Beyond Cyber Security Tools: The Increasing Roles Of Human Factors And Cyber Insurance In The Survival of Social Media Organisations*. Research Gate. Retrieved from: https://www.researchgate.net/profile/Olutunji-Sosanya

Svanadze, V., & Gotsiridze, A. (2015). *Cyber defense. Major players in cyberspace*. Cyber Security Policy, Strategy, and Challenges. Cyber Security Bureau of the Georgian Ministry of Defense, Collection of Papers and Articles.

US Department of Education. (2022). *Science, Technology, Engineering, and Math, including Computer Science*. Retrieved from: https://www.ed.gov/stem

KEY TERMS AND DEFINITIONS

Cybersecurity Policy: A written document that contains behavioral and technical guidelines for all employees in order to ensure maximum protection from cybersecurity incidents and ransomware attacks.

Cybersecurity Strategy: A high-level plan for how your organization will secure its assets during the next three to five years. Obviously, because technology and cyber threats can both change unpredictably, you'll almost certainly have to update your strategy sooner than three years from now. A cybersecurity strategy isn't meant to be perfect; it's a strongly educated guess as to what you should do. Your strategy should evolve as your organization and the world around you evolve.

Chapter 10
War in Ukraine and US:
Russian Information Warfare – A Comparative Analysis

Irakli Kervalishvili
Georgian Technical University, Georgia

ABSTRACT

The chapter reviews the main aspects of the Russia-Ukraine war on the example of the information policy carried out within the framework of the mentioned war between the USA and Russia. In particular, the information policy of the US on the one hand, which is aimed at protecting the independence and territorial integrity of Ukraine and providing democracy enlargement, and on the other, the disinformation policy of Russia, which aims to mislead the international and primarily the Russian public, are discussed.

INTRODUCTION

Along with political and military confrontations, the conflict in Ukraine is marked by a robust information warfare operation. The United States has suffered recently. Along with allegations that Russia manipulates public opinion and foments conflict by utilizing sophisticated propaganda and misinformation techniques. Social media's emergence and growth have given nations previously unheard-of chances to sway opinions and alter facts. The U.S. and Russia intensified their counterintelligence operations during the Ukraine War of 2022, which marked a turning point in this battle. The Russian military operation in Ukraine was swiftly denounced by the United States, which also offered the Ukrainian government financial and military help. Russia has retaliated using various strategies to undermine U.S. influence, including disinformation operations, hacking, and propaganda. Both nations extensively used social media and digital platforms to communicate with the people and sway opinion. With an emphasis on their information warfare operations, this comparative research seeks to explore the methods and tactics

DOI: 10.4018/978-1-6684-8846-1.ch010

used by the U.S. and Russia during the 2022 Ukraine War. This research aims to provide insight into the changing terrain of international warfare and the function of information in forming perceptions of war by examining the parallels and variations in their techniques, as well as their objectives and efficacy.

The History of Propaganda in the USA and Russia

Generally, in both the histories of Russia and the United States, propaganda has been a crucial instrument for swaying perceptions and forming public opinion. Propaganda has been used by these two nations in a variety of ways and settings to project power, control narratives, and alter opinions both domestically and internationally (Galeotti, 2014). This part of the research explores the development, significant moments, and lasting effects of propaganda throughout the history of Russia and the United States.

Russia

In the history of Russia and the Soviet Union, propaganda has been a key instrument for organizing the populace and forming public opinion. Propaganda has been used to shape stories, advance particular ideologies, and preserve political power from the time of the Tsars to the rise and fall of the Soviet state (Dekhtyanko, 2015). The broad and changing history of propaganda in Russia and the Soviet Union is examined in this essay, including its earliest manifestations, its usage during pivotal eras like the Russian Revolution and the Stalinist era, its significance in the Cold War, and its effects on society (Clifford, 1987). We may learn a lot about the socio-political forces that molded these areas by looking at the tactics, goals, and long-term effects of propaganda. In Russia, propaganda dates back to the Tsarist era, when the country's leaders aimed to instill a sense of loyalty and national solidarity in their people. The monarchy employed various strategies to influence public perception, including elaborate ceremonies, construction initiatives, and cultural events. The Tsars cemented their status as the legitimate leaders of the Russian people by stressing the divine prerogative of the rulers and tying their power to Orthodox Christianity. The Orthodox Church, which had a close relationship with the monarchy, contributed significantly to the spread of both religious and political propaganda. The idea of an autocracy that had been established by God was promoted through sermons, religious art, and iconography. The church evolved to become a crucial tool for upholding social order and quashing criticism. The character and reach of propaganda underwent a seismic upheaval during the Russian Revolution of 1917. Vladimir Lenin led the Bolsheviks, who understood the use of publicity in furthering their revolutionary cause (Timothy, 2004). They started the Bolshevik journal Pravda, which served as a major forum for the dissemination of revolutionary ideas and mobilizing the populace against the previous government.

To spread the Bolshevik message of class struggle, worker empowerment, and the downfall of capitalism, posters, leaflets, and public speeches were crucial. Slogans, striking imagery, and appeals to the working class were all used to rally support and influence public opinion. The Bolsheviks' success in capturing power and founding the Soviet Union was greatly aided by their mastery of propaganda. Propaganda became a crucial instrument for the Communist Party to maintain its power when the Soviet Union was founded in 1922 (Wentz, 2009). All media outlets came under official control, ensuring that propaganda promoted the objectives of the in-power dictatorship. The Department of Agitation and Propaganda (Agitprop) of the Communist Party was created to produce and disseminate publications that promoted socialist principles, extolled party officials, and demonized political rivals and other deemed enemies of the state. The Soviet authorities used cutting-edge techniques in addition to conventional media outlets to spread propaganda. The party's message was disseminated to the populace via agitation steamers and mobile vehicles for propaganda. The government also made extensive use of literature, movies, and the arts to promote ideological conformity and provide a romanticized view of Soviet society. Joseph Stalin's tenure saw the Soviet Union's propaganda reach previously unheard-of heights of scope, ferocity, and brutality. Stalin consolidated his power, created a cult of personality around himself, and imposed rigorous adherence to Communist ideology through the use of propaganda. Dissenters were painted as traitors and enemies of the people during the propaganda efforts that accompanied the Great Purge in the 1930s, which was marked by widespread arrests, mock trials, and executions (Klishin, 2015).

USA

Many governments and institutions throughout the world have used propaganda throughout history as a potent technique for swaying public opinion. The use of propaganda to sway public opinion, advance national interests, and rally support for certain causes is nothing new in the United States. This essay examines the historical background, major techniques, intended outcomes, and effects of propaganda on American society and politics. When the United States was first established, propaganda was a key tool in mobilizing support for the American Revolution. Invoking ideas of independence, freedom, and self-determination, patriotic speeches, pamphlets, and newspaper articles were utilized to energize public sentiment against British control. The Committee on Public Information (CPI), led by George Creel, used a variety of propaganda strategies to shift public opinion in favor of the war effort during World War I. The CPI used lectures, movies, and posters to foster a sense of patriotism and duty in Americans and to garner support for the war. Another notable time when propaganda was vital in influencing public opinion and rallying support was during World War II (Bedritsky, 2008). Propaganda was used by the United States to uphold morale, foster a sense of national identity, and defend the nation's engagement in the conflict. To spread pro-war propaganda through many media platforms, such as radio, film, and print, the Office of War Information (OWI) was founded. The adversary was portrayed in posters and movies as vicious and cruel, whereas the American ideals of freedom, democracy, and homeland defense were emphasized. As the U.S. and the USSR engaged in a bitter ideological conflict, propaganda operations increased during the Cold War era. The U.S. government presented itself as the defender of freedom and liberty by using propaganda to advocate the superiority of democracy and capitalism over communism. The Red Scare and McCarthyism are two noteworthy examples of anti-communist propaganda efforts that were launched to identify and eliminate supposed communist supporters in the United States. As a result of the government's and the media's portrayal of communism as a danger to American ideals and national security, people who were thought to have ties to the movement were persecuted and put on a blacklist. The use of propaganda techniques has been widespread in American political campaigns. Propaganda is used by candidates and their parties to sway public opinion, delegitimize rivals, and build support. To sway voter beliefs, political debates, speeches, and ads frequently use persuasive strategies such as emotive appeals, loaded language, and selective factual presentation. The introduction of social media in recent years has increased the use of propaganda in political campaigns. Candidates and interest groups can target particular demographics with customized messaging, maximizing the impact of their disinformation campaigns by utilizing algorithms and user data. Propaganda is often used in corporate and commercial settings in addition to politics. Different strategies are used by advertisers to influence consumer behavior, foster brand loyalty, and market goods and services. Businesses employ propaganda to sway consumer desires, perceptions, and purchase decisions through carefully planned language, images, and emotional appeals. Business-sponsored P.R. efforts also function as a type of propaganda with the goals of enhancing business reputations, swaying public opinion on divisive topics, and modifying regulatory regulations to benefit corporate interests (Bedritsky, 2008).

Thus, propaganda has played a significant role in Ukraine, especially in the context of the Russia-Ukraine conflict. Both sides have used propaganda to sway public opinion, distort the truth, and advance their respective agendas. Online campaigns, social media platforms, and state-controlled media have all been used to spread propaganda and sway public opinion. Ukraine's media landscape has been significantly impacted by propaganda, with state-controlled institutions being accused of biased reporting and information manipulation for political purposes. A crucial component of Russia's hybrid warfare techniques has been the dissemination of false information, disinformation, and fake news, which has exacerbated tensions and divisions in Ukrainian society. Propaganda has also influenced historical narratives and national identities, with the Ukrainian government countering pro-Russian viewpoints while advancing a nationalistic narrative. Through propaganda, differences in language and ethnicity have been exploited, feeding prejudice and fostering hostility between them. Nevertheless, measures to fight propaganda have surfaced in its wake. Independent media sources, fact-checking agencies, and civil society organizations have sought to dispel myths, advance truthful reporting, and encourage people to think critically. Concerns regarding information manipulation, trust loss, polarization, and the repression of opposing views are raised by the use of propaganda in Ukraine. It emphasizes the value of media literacy, critical thinking, and having access to reliable information from a variety of sources. To overcome the obstacles presented by propaganda and guarantee an informed and resilient society in Ukraine, upholding democratic norms, fostering independent media, and supporting initiatives to combat misinformation is essential.

Russian Media Outlets During the War in Ukraine

"Sanctions don't work or hurt the West more than Russia, Ukrainians are followers of the Nazis and Stepan Bandera, Zelensky is a drug dealer, the West is waging war, the Ukrainian government uses its population as a shield, the West's secret Biolabs operate in Ukraine and Georgia" - this is a small list of false and manipulative narratives that Regarding the war in Ukraine, it is spreading in the sources of different countries of the world.

It will be considered one of the studies organized by the company "Myth Detector". In particular, "Myth Detector" monitored Russian, Belarusian, Ukrainian, and Georgian social media within the framework of Facebook's third-party fact-checking program from February 24 to April 24, 2023, and published the report "Russia's information war - 2 months after the intervention in Ukraine", the first part of which discusses the spread The amount, topic and typology of disinformation and manipulative content, and the second part will concern the communication channels of Russian information operations and their tactics.

According to the report, out of 160 fake and manipulative content, which was distributed mainly in Russian and Georgian sources, the largest share (49.4%) was directed against Ukraine, 28.1% - against the West, and 16.3% - to justify Russia's actions (Netgazeti, 2023).

For example, one of the most widespread campaigns in the early stages of the war was related to the blogger Mariana Podgurskaya from Mariupol, who was accused of a fake pregnancy. "Myth Detector" identified 61 posts on Facebook coordinated by various accounts on this topic. Several publications and posts devoted to the denial of Russia's role in the Buchi tragedy.

To illustrate that Ukraine fakes victims, video manipulations were used, where in one case, a fragment of the Russian rapper Husky's clip was used, in which the person playing the role of the dead person smokes a cigarette, and in another case, footage of a symbolic performance held in Austria to protest climate change, in which a protester's corpse moves. To illustrate Zelensky's addiction to drugs, 3 fake videos were released during the monitoring process.

The report states that disinformation and manipulative content linked to the Azov Battalion and Stepan Bandera were consistent with the Kremlin's message to justify Russia's invasion of Ukraine under the pretext of denazification of the country. An old video, which claimed that the Azov battalion nailed a warrior from Donbas to a cross and burned it, was widely distributed on the Georgian social network. There was also misinformation that claimed that a monument was erected in Poland in honor of the saviors of the children killed by Bandera, which depicted the tragic story of a mother killing her children.

The rally against the Conservative Movement/Altinfo, a Kremlin party in Kobuleti, Georgia, during which the party's representatives physically confronted the rally participants, was misrepresented by Russian Facebook accounts and claimed to be disrupting pro-Ukraine rallies in Georgia.

According to the report, the Kremlin used a variety of communication channels for information operations and propaganda on Facebook and Instagram. Cases were revealed when some news media, to bypass monitoring, disseminated political content materials through entertainment channels (Россия 1, Музыка 80-90-00's) or coordinatedly through individual Facebook accounts supporting the party (Georgia, Alt-info/conservative movement).

In addition to the Russian government and propaganda media (RT, Первый канал, Россия 1, Телеканал «Звезда», Царьград and others), there was a coordinated distribution of comments by English language experts (Scott Ritter, Gonzalo Lira). The Facebook accounts of the Russian diasporas and the Immortal Regiment in various countries were revealed, which were used both to influence public opinion and to mobilize local diasporas during the Ukraine-Russia war. Mobilization of communist parties abroad was done against NATO and to show support for Russia.

According to "Myth Detector", in addition to the human and media resources of the Kremlin parties, anti-vaxxers and, in some cases, religious actors were also involved in spreading disinformation about Ukraine in Georgia.

According to the report, Georgian-language sources that disseminated propaganda and disinformation materials identical to those of the Kremlin were fragmented. However, several groups were identified that were actively involved in the disinformation campaign and mobilized various actors for this purpose:

- Two Kremlin parties – "Alt-Info/Conservative Movement" and "Patriot Alliance" were aligned with the Kremlin's information agenda through their communication channels.
- Online platforms: "Georgia and the World" (Geworld. ge), Sezonitv.ge, Newsfront, as well as spnews.io, which is a publication related to Newsfront and Politician. On the other hand, "Politico" is a Facebook page related to Primakov's Russian-Georgian Center, which sponsored anti-Ukrainian and anti-Western posts on Facebook both before and after the war in Ukraine.
- Ermile Nemsadze, a former soldier and member of the far-right "Georgian March", who manages the Facebook page Azimut/Azimut and who participated in violent actions of the far-right JFUFs in the past.
- Shota Apkhaidze's Facebook account and separate individual Facebook profiles related to "Eurasia Institute" and Newsfront.

- Anti-vaxxers: Facebook accounts that were involved in anti-vaxxer information campaigns during the pandemic focused on campaigns against Ukraine and justifying Russia's actions after the Russian intervention in Ukraine, and considered the ongoing war along with the pandemic as conspiracies, including the "New World Order".
- Statements against Ukraine and justifying Russia's actions were often made by a clergyman, Archbishop of Skhalti Spiridon Abuladze, whose video appeals were coordinated by supporters of the alt-info and conservative movement, as well as profiles of religious content (Sxaltis Mtavarepiskoposi Spiridoni, God, Fatherland, Man). The main the clergy

The messages were related to the fact that Russians and Ukrainians are one nation and that the West is trying to break down the divide between them (Netgazeti, 2023).

American Media Outlets

When the battle started, the media actively engaged in tracking every development. Every newspaper had an article about Ukraine, and major talk shows often featured segments about the conflict. But as the war rages on, other problems have gradually displaced it in the media. For instance, the Russian invasion of Ukraine has been overshadowed in the United States by inflation, rising food and gas prices, and the potential for a recession. The midterm elections also caught the interest of many Americans. However, recent surveys reveal that the majority of American lawmakers, government officials, and commentators continue to strongly support Ukraine. The majority of Americans also strongly support it. Fifty-five percent of Americans polled by the Pew Research Center in May 2022 expressed serious fear about the likelihood of a Ukrainian loss. Twenty-eight percent of those polled expressed some anxiety that Russia would try to annex Ukraine. Similarly, 31% of Americans thought that America was not helping Ukraine enough, while 35% said that America was helping Ukraine just enough. However, as the war has gone on, fewer Americans have shown worry. Only 38% of Americans, or seventeen percentage points fewer Americans than in May, said they were very concerned about the chance that Ukraine would lose the conflict. In addition, 18% of respondents said they thought the U.S. wasn't helping Ukraine sufficiently, which is a thirteen-point decline from May 2022 (Chitadze, 2023). Even if the drop in American anxiety may be concerning, there is a bigger tale to be told. On three fronts in Ukraine, the Russians made progress in the early stages of the conflict. Russia was advancing on the eastern Ukrainian regions it had conquered, had taken control of the southern province of Kherson, and was beginning an attack in the north through Sumy. However, as more severe sanctions were placed on Russia and more support was given to Ukraine, the Ukrainians were able to mount a successful counter-offensive. The Ukrainians drove the Russians out of northern Ukraine during the summer. All of the northernly seized lands were returned to Ukraine, effectively ending one of Russia's combat fronts. Ukraine has since recaptured land in its eastern and southern regions. After successfully defending Kharkiv, a significant province in the east, there are reports that Ukrainian forces may shortly take back Kherson before the winter months. Americans' worries may have lessened without a lack of interest in the conflict. Instead, it might be because Americans believe Ukraine will triumph. (The Pew Center poll did not include the decline in the numbers between May and September.) To determine how society feels about Russia's invasion of Ukraine, several polls and news organizations have surveyed Americans nationwide. Even though the participants came from a variety of interests and backgrounds, the majority of Americans still passionately support this Eastern European nation. The results of the polls indicate that at whatever cost, the United States is willing to support Ukraine in its war effort. This is encouraging for Ukraine.

CONCLUSION AND RECOMMENDATIONS

The Study's findings on U.S. and Russian information operations during the 2022 Ukraine War shed light on the efficiency and influence of information operations in the conflict. The important findings concerning the research questions are discussed in the paragraphs that follow. The Study found that both nations used a variety of strategies, including propaganda, disinformation, and social media manipulation, to shape the narrative of the conflict in response to the research question on the tactics used by the U.S. and Russia in their information warfare campaigns. However, the analysis showed that Russia was more successful than the U.S. at slanting the narrative in its favor with more effective disinformation campaigns and media manipulation. The study also looked at how information warfare affected the Ukraine War. The findings showed that information warfare had a substantial impact on the battle and was used by both sides to sway public opinion, create favorable impressions, and gain a tactical advantage. According to the Study, the deployment of propaganda by the U.S. and disinformation by Russia led to an uptick in tension and a decline in mutual trust, which led to a further escalation of the conflict. Thirdly, the Study looked into how social media is used in information warfare operations. The findings revealed that both sides made considerable use of social media platforms, including Facebook, Twitter, and YouTube, to spread misinformation and disinformation and sway public opinion. The Study concluded that social media usage offered both sides a potent instrument for information warfare, with Russia being more skilled at exploiting social media to its advantage. The study also looked at how information warfare affected Ukraine's civilian population. As a result of both sides conducting information warfare to sow fear, doubt, and mistrust among the populace, the results showed that information warfare had a substantial impact on civilians. According to the Study, both sides' employment of propaganda and disinformation campaigns increased tension and eroded confidence among the civilian population, which in turn aided in the conflict's escalation. Overall, the Study offers insightful information about the use of information warfare in the Ukraine War, emphasizing the tactics used by the U.S. and Russia, the influence of information warfare on 26 the conflict, the function of social media in information warfare operations, and the effects of information warfare on civilians. The Study's findings imply that information warfare is a formidable instrument for influencing public opinion and achieving a tactical advantage and that it also can aggravate conflicts and hurt civilian populations. The results of this study have significant policy and military leadership ramifications, emphasizing the necessity for efficient approaches to thwart the use of information warfare in wars. In contemporary conflicts, the use of information warfare as a technique to sway public opinion, mold views, and achieve a strategic edge has increased. Both the U.S. and Russia used information warfare strategies to rewrite the conflict's history in the context of the Ukraine War in 2022. This conversation compares the U.S. and Russian information warfare techniques and strategies used in the 2022 Ukraine War. Propaganda was one of the main tactics employed by both the U.S. and Russia. The purposeful dissemination of information to sway public opinion and advance a specific point of view is known as propaganda. Both the U.S. and Russia employed propaganda to shape the conflict's storyline and present themselves favorably. For instance, while Russia utilized propaganda to portray itself as a victim and the defender of ethnic Russians in Ukraine, the U.S. circulated messages emphasizing its support for Ukraine and its dedication to safeguarding democracy. Disinformation was another important tactic used by both sides. The purposeful dissemination of incorrect or misleading information to sway public opinion or cause confusion is known as disinformation. Disinformation was a particularly effective tool that Russia used to slant the conflict's narrative in its favor. For instance, it spread false information about Ukrainian forces being responsible for the downing of a passenger airliner, which aided in the conflict's escalation. To sway public opinion and refute Russian assertions, the U.S. likewise deployed deception, but to a lesser extent. During the Ukraine War, social media was a crucial area for information warfare.

Facebook, Twitter, and YouTube were all used by both sides to spread propaganda and false information. However, because of its significant use of trolls and bots in spreading false information and distorting public opinion, Russia was more successful in using social media to achieve its goals. During the Ukraine War, the use of cyberattacks and hacking also contributed to information warfare. Both parties launched cyberattacks on one another, with Russia accused of breaking into the office of the U.S. government and the Ukrainian power grid. Cyber-attacks were employed to obtain a tactical edge and damage the credibility of the opposition. Both sides had difficulties in their information warfare tactics in terms of limits. It was more difficult for the U.S. to spread effective propaganda and misinformation due to its lack of cultural and language knowledge. On the other hand, Russia's access to Western media platforms was restricted, which made it more challenging for it to spread its propaganda and misinformation. The 2022 Ukraine War's use of information warfare strategies underscores the growing significance of influencing conflict narratives through the spread of propaganda, misinformation, and social media manipulation. These strategies were used by both the U.S. and Russia to sway public opinion and obtain a tactical edge. Although there were drawbacks for both sides, the success of Russia's information warfare campaign shows how important it is for Western democracies to create effective plans to fight information warfare in the future.

Summary of the Main Findings

Several crucial discoveries with significant ramifications for future conflicts are revealed by the comparative examination of the information warfare methods and tactics deployed by the U.S. and Russia during the 2022 Ukraine War. First, to influence the conflict's narrative and further their objectives, both the U.S. and Russia used propaganda and disinformation. Although propaganda has been employed in conflicts for a long time, the employment of false information and the manipulation of social media platforms are new strategies in the field of information warfare. Second, during the Ukraine War, Russia used information warfare more successfully than the U.S. did to further its goals. Russia's success was aided by its vast use of trolls and bots, its capacity to disseminate false information, and its control over social media. The success of Russia's information warfare campaign emphasizes the necessity for Western democracies to create more potent information warfare countermeasures for upcoming conflicts. Thirdly, the Study shows that both sides faced obstacles and constraints when waging information warfare. Lack of cultural and language proficiency made it more challenging for the U.S. to spread effective propaganda and misinformation. On the other hand, Russia's access to Western media platforms was restricted, which made it more challenging for it to spread its propaganda and misinformation. The Study also discusses the ethical issues and constraints associated with studying information warfare. Collecting trustworthy and accurate data might be difficult because information warfare methods are hidden. These strategies can also have detrimental effects on people and societies, which raises crucial ethical questions for researchers. These findings have important repercussions for both military strategists and policymakers. Western democracies must create effective measures to fight the use of propaganda, disinformation, and social media manipulation by opposing nations, as information warfare continues to be a common strategy in contemporary wars. Investment in linguistic and cultural know-how and cybersecurity and I.T. skills will be necessary for this. It will also necessitate a stronger emphasis on comprehending the nature of information warfare, its effects on people and society, and the ethical issues involved in researching these subjects.

Evaluation of the effectiveness and impact of the U.S. and Russian information warfare campaigns during the Ukraine conflict.

There are several methods to assess the success and impact of the U.S. and Russian information warfare campaigns during the Ukraine conflict, including their capacity to influence public opinion, create the conflict's narrative, and accomplish strategic goals. Both the U.S. and Russia were effective in advancing their own goals and framing the war in a way that favored them in terms of molding the conflict's narrative. For instance, whereas Russia framed the conflict as a fight against Western imperialism and for the protection of ethnic Russians in Ukraine, the U.S. highlighted Ukraine's right to self-determination and sovereignty. The effectiveness of information warfare tactics to sway public opinion is less evident. Although both sides used social media to spread their propaganda and misinformation, it is hard to determine how much of an impact these efforts had on public opinion. Depending on the target population and the exact messages being spread, it is likely that the impact of these campaigns differed. The efficiency of information warfare campaigns varies in terms of attaining strategic goals. Due in part to the deployment of information warfare strategies, Russia accomplished its strategic goals of annexing Crimea and causing instability in eastern Ukraine. On the other hand, neither the U.S. nor its allies could stop Russia from intervening in Ukraine. The U.S. and Russian information warfare initiatives throughout the crisis in Ukraine had a mixed record of efficacy and impact. Although both sides effectively influenced how the conflict was portrayed, it is unclear how these strategies affected public opinion. Additionally, these programs had varying degrees of success in attaining their strategic goals, with Russia outperforming the U.S. These findings have significant consequences for both military strategists and policymakers. Western democracies must create effective measures to fight the use of propaganda, disinformation, and social media manipulation by opposing nations, as information warfare continues to be a common strategy in contemporary wars. Investment in linguistic and cultural know-how, as well as cybersecurity and I.T. skills, will be necessary for this. It will also necessitate a stronger emphasis on comprehending the nature of information warfare, its effects on people and society, and the ethical issues involved in researching these subjects.

Reflections on the Ethical Considerations of the Study

Several ethical issues must be considered when researching information warfare, propaganda, and misinformation. These include concerns about confidentiality, informed consent, privacy, and potential harm to research subjects. The use of private or sensitive data is a significant ethical issue. To preserve the privacy of those participating, researchers must ensure that any data they acquire is anonymized and any identifiable information is erased. Additionally, participants must consent after being fully informed about the Study's nature and objectives and their right to withdraw at any time. This is crucial in research that involves vulnerable populations or people who have experienced trauma or violence. The possible harm that research subjects might endure is another ethical factor. Studies on information warfare and disinformation may cover sensitive subjects or subject people to propaganda or disinformation, which could negatively affect the participants' psychological well-being or reinforce damaging stereotypes or ideas. Researchers must take precautions to limit injury and ensure participants have access to services and help if needed. The wider influence of research on society is also a subject of ethical debate. Studies on disinformation and information warfare can greatly impact policy and national security. Researchers must be careful about how their findings are applied and avoid supporting false or damaging narratives. Additionally, they must ensure that their work is rigorously reviewed by peers and scrutinized while being open and honest about the methods they utilize. Given the delicate nature of the subject and the possible impact on international relations, ethical questions are particularly crucial in the specific context of the U.S. and Russian information warfare during the Ukraine conflict. Researchers must conduct their job objectively, impartially, and without escalating the disagreement or politicizing it in any way. Additionally, researchers must be open and honest about their methods and make sure that their findings are subject to rigorous peer review and examination, given the possible impact of their work on policy and national security. Finally, ethical questions are of utmost significance when investigating information warfare and misinformation. Researchers must take precautions to preserve the privacy and well-being of research participants and ensure that their work is handled objectively and impartially. Researchers must also consider how their Study will affect society and policy more broadly and ensure that their findings are subject to rigorous peer review and criticism.

REFERENCES

Bedritsky, A. (2008). *Information war: concepts and their realization in the USA*. RISI.

Chitadze, N. (2023). *Geopolitical Consequences of the Russia-Ukraine War*. IGI Global. doi:10.4018/978-1-6684-8521-7

Clifford, R. (1987). Reflexive Control. In B. D. A. P. Parker (Ed.), *Soviet Military Planning, Soviet Strategic Deception*. Lexington Books.

Dekhtyanko, A. (2015). *Russia is preparing for a big world war, the dates are determined— military expert from Russia*. Apostrophe. Retrieve from: http://apostrophe.com.ua/article/ world/ex-ussr/2015-07-26/ rossiya-gotovitsya-k-bolshoymirovoy-voyne-datyi-opredelenyi--- voennyiy-ekspert-izrf/2007

Galcotti, M. (2014). *The 'Gerasimov Doctrine' And Russian Non-Linear War*. Retrieved from: Https:// Inmoscowsshadows. Wordpress.Com/2014/07/06/The-Gerasimov-Doctrine-AndRussianNon-Linear-War/

Klishin, I. (2015). *Botovoysko: Why playing with soft power is not working out for the Kremlin*. Carnegie Moscow Center. Retrieved from: http://carnegie.ru/2015/07/21/ru60728/idgi

Krylatov, M. (2015). *Moscow launched another 'information war workshop' in Crimea*. Radio Free Europe/Radio Liberty. Retrieved from: http://ru.krymr.com/ content/article/26957545.html

NetGazeti. (2023). *Who and how the Kremlin spreads disinformation against Ukraine — research*. Retrieved from: https://netgazeti.ge/news/612725

Thomas, T. (1996). Russian Views On Information-Based Warfare. *Airpower Journal*.

Thomas, T. L. (2004). Russia's Reflexive Control Theory And The Military. *Journal Of Slavic Military Studies*. Retrieved from: https://www.rit.edu/~w-cmmc/literature/ Thomas_2004.pdf

Wentz, L. (2009). *Cyber Warfare: Protecting the Soldier*. Retrieved from: http://Ctnsp.Dodlive. Mil/ Files/2014/03/Cyberpower-I-Chap-20.Pdf

KEY TERMS AND DEFINITIONS

Disinformation: False information deliberately spread to deceive people. It should not be confused with misinformation, which is false information but is not deliberate.

Information Warfare: Any action to Deny, Exploit, Corrupt, or Destroy the enemy's information and its functions; protecting ourselves against those actions and exploiting our military information functions.

Propaganda: Communication that is primarily used to influence or persuade an audience to further an agenda, which may not be objective and may be selectively presenting facts to encourage a particular synthesis or perception, or using loaded language to produce an emotional rather than a rational response to the information that is being presented.

Chapter 11
The EU's Cyber Security Strategy:
The Question of Cyber Crime Management and Challenges in Europe

Mukesh Shankar Bharti

https://orcid.org/0000-0002-3693-7247

Jawaharlal Nehru University, India

ABSTRACT

This chapter aims to discuss the EU's cyber security strategy and how its policy is capable of restricting cybercrime in Europe. The study explains the role of EU Member States in dealing with cybercrime in this region. This research draws on qualitative comparative analysis to examine various EU initiatives to tackle cybercrime issues in Europe. Furthermore, this chapter discusses the core literature of primary and secondary resources through an empirical approach. Since globalisation reached its highest level across the world, the question of cyber security has emerged as a key area of multiple cooperation between the global actors. Cybercrime is now a complex issue among the global actors to restrict its expansion. The EU also started cooperation with Asian, American, and African countries on cybercrime issues. Finally, this chapter suggests that cybercrime is the central area of cooperation between the global actors to restrict it which is dangerous for humanity.

INTRODUCTION

The European Union (EU) is the largest political and economic platform of the regional organisation in Europe. Since 1951, it has been shaping multiple cooperation and public diplomacy in the EU and non–EU countries in Europe and have been establishing bilateral cooperation at the continental level. Through strategic partnerships, the EU is committed to working with other countries around the world

DOI: 10.4018/978-1-6684-8846-1.ch011

on cybercrime issues. It is an emerging question of how to tackle cybercrime between major economic blocks at the global level. The EU's policy is to provide security from cyber threats and strengthen trustworthy digital technologies to build resilience to cyber threats and provide a safe and secure digital world to protect their citizens and businesses. The EU faces descriptive and normative challenges in Europe and its policy is binding against internal and external security threats to limit these types of cybercrime. Thus, the EU policies are intensely working to protect of potential security issues in Europe. The EU's very keen to target the most urgent security threats, such as terrorism, organised crime, cybercrime, and cross-border issues. The EU's policies and management seem to secure its external borders and protect against civil disasters. The first EU "Cybersecurity Strategy" came into force in 2013 as a formal setting out of a new policy as security armor to protect against the possibilities of potential danger in Europe (European Commission and High Representative, 2013).

This chapter provides an extensive overview of cybercrime management and policies regarding sought out the major challenges in the EU. The chapter also aims to delve into the current state of the cybersecurity landscape in Europe. It has deeply analysed the EU's key agenda and legislative initiatives in an attempt to operate cybersecurity. Through the EU policy area, the EU seriously identifies the main challenges and conceptualizes the main areas of use of the legislation. Furthermore, the EU is focusing on and triggers to shape cybersecurity regulation between the member states. The EU's first priority and commitment are to provide security to its people in Europe and restrict any possibility of danger outside the border. In recent years, the EU's focus on pragmatic work on digital dependency always seems to unify the legal framework of constitutions. According to Ramses Wessel, cybersecurity forms "an excellent example of an area in which the different policy fields need to be combined (a requirement for horizontal consistency), and where measures need to be taken at the level of both the EU and Member States (calling for vertical consistency)" (Wessel, 2015). The EU's common understanding is that cybersecurity entails a combination of cybercrime, resilience, cyber defence, cyberspace and several concurrent concerning issues. EU diplomacy must work on these issues, which is a priority to ensure a secure Europe. The 2013 Strategy aimed to work on the abolition of prior cyber-attacks and want to achieve "to make the EU's online environment the safest in the world" (Fuster & Jasmontaite, 2020).

The EU and non-EU economies are also affected by cybercrime activities against citizens and the private sector. Cybercriminals are using increasingly sophisticated methods to interfere in the theft of critical data and information systems. They are also involved in ransoming businesses. The increase in economic espionage and state-sponsored activities in cyberspace constitutes a new category of threats for EU governments and businesses. Thus, cybercriminals cheat even the biggest entrepreneurs and sometimes the public sector is also cheated by online fraud. Although, the EU had decided to take strong action through legislation and common consensus among the member states (European Commission, 2013). The EU is also aware of the misuse of cyberspace for surveillance and control of its own citizens by governments.

Framing Cybersecurity as a Policy Area

The European Union's activities came to light in the field of cybersecurity and combating cybercrime in the 1990s. At that time, the EU adopted the first non-binding legal acts to regulate and deal with cybercrime issues in Europe. The European Union Agency for Cybersecurity (ENISA) was set up as The European Network and Information Security Agency on the 15th of March 2004 by way of Regulation (EC) No 460/2004 of the European Parliament and of the Council of the 10th of March 2004 establishing the European Network and Information Security Agency (Radoniewicz, 2022). In February 2013, the EU Cyber Security Strategy (EUCSS) came into force to cooperate and engage regarding cybercrime in Europe (Shooter, 2013). The EUCSS is accompanied by a legislative proposal from the European Commission (EC), it consists of a directive to provide solidity to the information system in the EU. The EU has five key priorities to work on cyber management to tackle the questions of cybersecurity in Europe. The EU policy area covers the complexity of issues that span across Europe and tries to make a mix of horizontal and vertical coherence between member states on the issue of cybersecurity. The EU policy to work on five key priority areas is as follows (European Commission and High Representative, 2013, pp.4-16).The Cybersecurity Strategy of the European Union (CSSEU) and the European Commission and High Representative of 2013 outlined the strategic priorities for drastically reducing cybercrime in the EU Member Countries. EU's policy is developing a cyber defence to minimise such kind of threats in Europe through industrial and technical resources. The EU representative also involves in the establishment of international EU cyberspace policy (Christou, 2018, p. 2).

EU wants to achieve 'cyber resilience" by establishing the liberal value of the minimum requirement for cooperating and coordination through responsible authorities for reliable network systems. The EU's policy to reduce cybercrime through swift transportation of EU Directives is associated with cybercrime. The EU and its other affiliated institutions also encourage ratification of the Council of Europe's Budapest Convention on Cybercrime. Thus, the EU is providing appropriate funds for the deployment of cybersecurity operational tools (Council of Europe, 2001).

The EU is regulating the concept and functionalities of the Common Security and Defence Policy (CSDP) to develop cyber defence mechanisms to project possible danger. The EU is deeply engaged in the development of various requirements to stop and minimise cyber-attacks. EU also involve in developing the cyber defence policy framework and the EU also cement the cooperation between civilian and military actors as well. At the international level, the EU is continuing to strengthen its reach to global partners and facilitating rational dialogue. It is necessary to work on industrial and technological resources to secure the cyberspace through establishment of a public-private cooperation on a common platform for National and Information Security (NIS). It will be helpful for the establishment of a strong network for modern days security standards.

The EU's core values are attracting third countries through its policy for external relations and Common Foreign and Security Policy (CFSP) is supporting capacity building with continental partners on cybersecurity. These countries are sources to provide and cooperate on resilient infrastructure building on this burning issue. More significantly, the EU is a recognized regional organisation through its credibility across the world, however, the EU could be benefitted from the third countries with exiting bilateral dialogue between third countries and the Member States. The EU aims to achieve continuous work on a high level of data protection, the EU's norms also apply to the protection of individual data transferred to third parties or countries. By and large, the EU's key priorities are to protect countries' cyberspace and people's data safety simultaneously. The 2013 Strategy also aimed to make the world's online security a priority and provide a secure environment. The EU cyber strategy is characterized by creating greater EU resilience against cyber-attacks. Furthermore, the EU reinforces it rapid detection of cyber-attacks. The EU has also established a suitable channel in Europe, Asia, Africa, Latin America and other parts of the world on cybersecurity (European Commission and High Representative of the Union for Foreign Affairs and Security Policy, 2017).

For many years, the EU has been publishing its vision on cybersecurity management to restrict cybercrime and such negative incidents which is the concern of online fraudulent in Europe. Over the last few years, the EU is very keen to document the rule of the law on cybersecurity (Falessi et al., 2012). The question of European security is a significant issue for the EU and its associated institutions for the last two decades. After the incident of 9/11 in the USA, the EU's representative raised the question of online money transfers to terrorist organisations through illegal transactions at the international platform and European countries are aware of cybercrime and want to restrict through strong law of the land. The EU Security Strategy included cyber threats as a risk to the security of the European people (Klimburg & Tirmaa-Klaar, 2011).

The EUCSS aims to ensure the Member States and private undertakings have proper channels and appropriate strategy with dealing the threats from the cyber world. There is also provision for the development of extensive mechanisms for dealing with cybersecurity threats. It has been sharing information about cybersecurity threats between the EU's Member States and private sectors and government agencies. Its objective is to provide adequate information in the context of the probable threats of cybersecurity (Vela, 2021).

The European Cybercrime Centre (ECC) was established in the Hague, the Netherlands. "As the EU's law enforcement agency, Europol has a mission to support its Member States in preventing and combating all forms of serious international and organised crime, cybercrime and terrorism" (Europol, 2023). The ECC and Europol are aiming to harmonise the cybersecurity capabilities between the EU's Member States. It is supporting the EU's fight against online fraud and cyberattacks. This is playing a leading role to secure the EU's strategy to protect its cyber world. The role of Europol is too much significant in building an adequate capacity and proper management through the help of the EU's institutions and cooperating with global partners on cybercrime. The EU's Directive on Security of Network and Information Systems came into force in 2016, which is also a kind of first specific EU cybersecurity legislation. The EU Cybersecurity Act was implemented in 2019, this act is entirely devoted to providing the EU with new legislation on the certification of cybersecurity products and services (Europa, 2019). Through the creation of Europol, the EU's response is a clear and strong message to the international community that there is a strong vision to fight organized crime, terrorism and cybercrime in Europe. Europol's Strategy frames an important cooperation for its day-to-day operations and to support the commitment of law enforcement.

The EU has also been encouraged by the provision of a €600 million fund for the creation of research and innovation to tackle the problem of cybersecurity in the period of 2014-20. EU's every Member State has cyber security centres for the development of mutual cooperation between public and private partnerships. The EU is enabling the Digital Single Market within the framework of economic and trade cooperation in Europe. Thus, the EU is committed to the establishment of concrete channels to handle the cyber security issues in the Member States (Carrapico & Barrinha, 2018). Furthermore, EU Digital Sovereignty is based on building a free and safe Europe, yet resilient cyberspace is the most extensive agenda of the EU. In 2013, the EU announced its ambitious plan to achieve "strategic autonomy" vis-à-vis the research institutions and the defense industry (Calderaro & Blumfelde, 2022). Moreover, In the Club de Berne voluntary intelligence-sharing forum, the EU almost had developed a mutual platform for sharing formal intelligence mechanisms. This forum includes the EU member states' intelligence agencies for better understanding for deeper cooperation in the field of cybersecurity and the EU Intelligence and Situation Centre of the External Action Service (Stevens & O'Brien, 2019).

The General Data Protection Regulation (GDPR) entered into force in 2016 after its adoption by the European Parliament. As of May 25, 2018, it is mandatory to follow the rule and norms of the GDPR by the responsible organisations in the EU. This new regulation of the EU is an updated version of the

1995 data protection directive. The EU wants to impose this new regulation on the data mining capacity of the private sector which is the strongest protection of privacy in its type of legislation across the world (Bradford, 2020). Over the last two decades, globalisation brought ultra-modernism across the world and the digitalization process reached a top position. It also raised several questions about cybersecurity in front of the global community. Cybersecurity become a burning question among the EU member states on how to provide a safe and secure online process to protect people's privacy. There have also been increased major challenges to data security in Europe. The security of personal data is an important issue on how to protect the privacy of ordinary people, because there is a risk of illicit use and exploitation (S. S. Bharti & Aryal, 2022). "Personal data is any information that relates to an individual who can be directly or indirectly identified. Names and email addresses are obviously personal data. Location information, ethnicity, gender, biometric data, religious beliefs, web cookies, and political opinions can also be personal data" (Wolford, n.d.).

EU's New Cybersecurity Directive

The European Commission proposed the course of action as the second Cybersecurity in 2017. It is the second Cybersecurity strategy of the EU. The EU's Cybersecurity Act 2017 was passed by the European Parliament through the Regulation (EU) 2019/881 on April 17, 2019, on ENISA (the European Union Agency for Cybercrime) and on information and communications technology cybersecurity certification and repealing Regulation (EU) No 526/2013 (Cybersecurity Act). Through this strategy, the EU institutions themselves pioneer the rational strategic rule and regulation of cybercrime. Thus, the EU as a regional organisation has been playing an important role to restrict cybercrime (European Commission, 2017). Regulation (EU) 2017/745, known as Medical Devices Regulation (MDR), this regulation marked the initial phase of the incorporation of cybersecurity requirements into the EU's safety framework (Chiara, 2022).

The EU is too thinkable to seize the opportunity to lead global communities over the next decade through the 2020 cybersecurity strategy. The 2020 EU's Cybersecurity Strategy realized that "the upcoming decade is the EU's opportunity to lead in the development of secure technologies across the whole supply chain." (Csernatoni & Mavrona, 2022). In 2020, the EU adopted a cybersecurity strategy in order to strengthen it through strong legislation. The High Representative of the Union for Foreign Affairs, the European Commission and Security Policy from the European Action Service (EEAS) presented a wide range of new EU Cybersecurity Strategies and finally adopted them (Sen, 2023). In November 2022, the European Council and the EU Parliament approved the implementation of a new policy known as the Network and Information Security Directive 2 (NIS 2.0). This new directive has superseded the EU's first wide-ranging set of cybersecurity laws of 2016. Bart Groothuis a leading member of the European Parliament stated that "We need to act to make our businesses, governments and society more resilient to hostile cyber operations, This European directive is going to help around 160,000 entities tighten their grip on security and make Europe a safe place to live and work." (Feingold & Beato, 2022). NIS 2.0 aims to strengthen the EU's cybersecurity capabilities and resilience by expanding its coverage to include various private and public sector institutions. This new security provision covers almost all Member States' requirements and tries to reinforce the basic security needs in Europe. Under the NIS 2.0 directive, the EU is trying to make cooperation with the US and other continental partners. The legislation includes a provision for a 24-hour period to become aware of any type of such incident related to cyber breaches and board attacks.

Through the new cybersecurity policy, the EU's prime motto is to achieve and wants to create deterrence power by resilience. Today's digital dependency extensively has been increasing across the world. The EU's policy is to provide safeguards to the communication and data in multiple fields, including stock markets, political institutions, trade and economic sectors, healthcare and other institutions which are related to financial sectors as well. These sectors have deeply involved in the digital world and their dependency has been growing day-by-day. Since 2020, the European Commission and EEAS and EU member states started working together on the implementation of a joint response to malicious cyber activities and it is also called the 'cyber diplomacy toolbox'. Today's young generation is deeply suffering from cyber fraud and breach of trust on online platforms. There are lots of hijackers from across the world always trying to the stolen of passwords of emails, websites, online data and other confidential as well which are related to digital platforms. Cybersecurity is more significant from the perspective of human security (Gao & Chen, 2022).

The French government is curious to cooperate at the global level on cybersecurity, cyberspace and cross-border threats. Thus, during the French Presidency, the EU initiated a bilateral partnership beyond the EU border and established successful cooperation in the Indo-Pacific Region (IPR). Where India is the biggest supporter of the EU's Cybersecurity legislation and cooperating with EU Member States in Asia and Europe, respectively (M. S. Bharti & Singh, 2023).

EU and Cybersecurity Challenge

In 2007, Estonia suffered a large-scale cyberattack and Lithuania in 2008 also suffered a massive cyberattack in the EU. This incidence of attack was against information systems which is raising since then in the EU Member States. "The botnet 'Conficker' … has since November 2008 spread to affect millions of computers worldwide, including, in the EU, France, the UK and Germany. Every individual and business using the Internet is potentially vulnerable to cybercrimes" (Christou, 2019). Since then, according to the European Commission Cybercrime remain a top priority for the European Community and other EU institutions to tackle the recurrent problem of cybercrime (European Commission, 2012). The commitment of the European Commission is to know how to eradicate the prevalent precedence of cybercrime which is a major challenge to limiting future incidents. The EC is strengthening its communication system to raise awareness among the masses of any possibility of cybercrime in the region. It is also working on a broader digital agenda initiative to deepen coordination (European Commission, 2010).

The EU is facing various such kinds of cybersecurity threats, on the other hand, the EU policy is clear that cyberspace and the cyber-criminal are not in a position to be limited by national boundaries. The EU and affiliated public institutions are continuing to present themselves as an efficient and logical way to solution to its Member States' vulnerable challenges. Thus, to address these challenges, EU Member States continue to stay in touch with the appropriate channels on how best to counter cybersecurity threats in Europe (Council of the European Union, 2005). The European Cyber Security Challenge (ECSC) is accepting challenges and working at the pan-European level. "The European Cyber Security Challenge is an initiative by the European Union Agency for Cybersecurity (ENISA) and supported by the European Commission"(European Union Agency for Cybersecurity, 2022). The EU found itself confronted with increasingly various sets of cybersecurity challenges. The main challenges are sophisticated cyber-attacks to underscore geopolitical aspirations. The EU embraces the concept of a global, interconnected Internet and rejects national firewalls protecting their societies from everything outside (Scholz, 2023). The main challenges of the EU to the establishment of the most secure digital environment in the world. Therefore, the EU institutions and its policy continue to work towards achieving the ultimate goal of providing a safer digital world (European Commission, 2019).

In the era of the cyber world, there aren't any countries across the world that are untouchable from cybersecurity threats. It is impossible to say that in the cyber age people are scared of stealing their digital data and credentials. EU as a democratic regional organisation is spreading its ideas on cybersecurity threats with other partners from all continents. The issue of protecting human rights with privacy and national security tends to become digital surveillance states (Kapsokoli, 2021). The people's dependency has been increased on Information and communications technology (ICT), that is why these types of incidents cannot be ignored and governments must govern to stop cyber fraud from ordinary people or state agencies. Similarly, cyberspace has raised a bunch of security challenges for the states. There is a need to implement to face cybersecurity challenges: the policy framework, funding and spending, building cyber-resilience and effective mechanism to handle cyber incidents.

The single market concept is crucial for the EU to be able to conduct this important policy without any kind of real disruption. The WannaCry and NotPetya incidents that happened in 2017 damaged numerous actors notably through the disruption of global logistics. Cyber incidents breach the trust in the single market system which is the EU's prime trade and economic policy to run the European economy. It has been hampering the unique concept of a single market scheme. At the same time, an established and well-functioning single market would be a great opportunity for the growth and competitiveness of the EU e-industry. The EU seeks to resolve and address these recurring challenges through cyber-resistant policy measures that build on its strong mandate to act in the single market. EU's policy to handle cyber-incidents is a proactive stance to save the single market which is worth important to the establishment of cooperation in such fields, for example, energy security, finance, transport and energy. There is a need for reliable interconnectedness between various policies to create a support system to withstand cyberattacks (Timmers, 2018).

In the 21st century, according to the 2009 Cyber Policy Review, which stated that cybercrime and related bad events are dangerous to economic and national security around the world. Cyberattackers also trap innocent tourists and small businessmen during their visits abroad. Thus, cybercrime breaks the cooperation between nations by hijacking online systems and trying to disturb one of the main partners to create a binary between them (Anagnostakis, 2021). National security takes priority over cybersecurity and internet freedoms and the EU wants to incorporate open societies to fill the void in establishing a barrier-free society. On the other hand, the position of the EU on a secure digital single market is to privilege the areas to be established on European territory rather than questions of national security. The EU can play an important role in preventing the balkanization of the Internet and should continue to coordinate joint action between EU Member States (Schaake & Vermeulen, 2016). Since 2010, digital platforms have become a vulnerable field to reach out quickly anywhere and there is no need for a transport system to contact. But those who are involved in cybercrime sitting in their room easily connect with overseas people to deceive them through online business propositions and other means as well (Braune & Dana, 2022; Cutolo & Kenney, 2021).

In modern days business and commerce activities are getting support from the online digital platform and advertisement is one of the key aspects to regulate e-commerce. Digital technology infrastructures (DTIs) create huge creative activities between entrepreneurs to accelerate extensive multiple cooperation. Thus, digital platforms are easing e-commerce activities but on the other hand, the opponent countries' policy is working to disturb the enemy countries' online websites by hijack and involved creating havoc in the opponent block (Song, 2019). Serious cyberattacks and hacks could be destroyed the digital single market and related other businesses. This scholarship is somehow disturbing but a deepening security system might be able to stop all such cybercrime. Transparency is necessary to govern the system of checks and balances between the responsible institutions (Sussan & Acs, 2017). It is necessary to establish healthy transparency mechanisms for the protection of data privacy. Transparency in digital platforms is necessary for the establishment of trust among common people and entrepreneurs. There are so many uncertainties related to cybersecurity establishment in European countries. In fact, the EU member countries need to support the cybersecurity policy to protect their territory from any such incidents.

RESULTS AND DISCUSSION

In healthy democratic countries, it is essential to support ordinary people to have adequate access to digital technology and ICTs. The EU and Member States must have clear rules and laws that protect digital users and developers of digital technologies against online fraud. EU laws are sufficient to protect the territory of member states from cybercrime. People's awareness and support is necessary to succeed in cybercrime (Wibisono, 2023). The EU has always failed to convince its member states to work intensively for more security powers. The European Commission President often stated that the EU to become a major security player which could handle the bad situations in Europe and outside as well. It is a narrative-building process by the EU official that the EU is grabbing more powers to provide security to the world communities (Cachia & DeBattista, 2022).

There is a common assessment of the EU's cyber-security strategy that needs to strengthen in the sense of clarifying what is common agenda to work through its strategy. It is prepared with well-equipped methods to deal with cybersecurity issues in EU member states and cybersecurity strategy requires more than just coordination of national actions. There needs to be a super-natural understanding between the peoples of the EU Member States to develop the capacity to tackle the challenges and threats ahead and the feasible tools to deal with them (Sliwinski, 2014). If there will be a common understanding of online fraud and those who are involved to manipulate innocent common people on the digital platform then we would get success to stop it through overall awareness among the masses. The EU's vigorous stance on personal digital privacy is attached to the decision of the Scherms. It has been supporting robust information systems and sharing information to fight terrorism and transnational crime. Thus, the EU laws and ethos support a strong digital platform which will be helpful for everyone to access it. The EU has also extended its support beyond EU borders with overseas partners (Hall, 2018). The question of the Privacy Shield is a burning issue in France where common people and civil society groups have strong demand to provide safe digital technologies for privacy concerns. La Quadrature de Net, a French advocacy group that promotes digital rights; the French Data Network, a non-profit Internet service provider; and Fédération FDN, an association of operators (Gladicheva, 2016).

Since the enactment of the EU's cybersecurity strategy in 2013, somehow EU's policy on stopping cybercrime in its territories got a success. It has made significant progress by passing relevant legislation and empowering existing public and private institutions and creating rational approaches to fight against cybercrime. Wherever it was necessary to pragmatically put in place the fight against cybercrime, EU officials also provided instruments and technical assistance to third countries. The EU's regional approach to defense and deterrence highlighted important positions in the 2017 Joint Communication. The 2017 EU directive took important steps in eradicating cyber threats in EU member states (Benincasa, 2021). Thus, the EU's diplomacy is visionary through the analysis of regular legislation have been passed by the European Parliament. This book chapter highlighted that the EU is only one regional organisation working with full strength to save its people's privacy through the implementation of the GDPR. In spite of these initiatives, the EU is also involved in Asia, Africa, Latin America and Australia to provide and support people's privacy and digital rights.

There are many non-EU countries are sharing similarities and interests regarding cybersecurity threats and want to adopt the EU types of laws in their countries. There are also interconnected infrastructures and economies that leave them vulnerable to similar threat actors. Thus, it is possible to face the same type of situation that EU Member States have had to face with cybersecurity threats for a long time (Healey, 2016; Nicholas, 2018). By and large, this chapter suggests that digital sovereignty is still uncertain and that cybersecurity is even looming in Europe, it is creating a digital threat across the world. As a whole, the EU is too much sincere about any cybercrime looming inside the EU's border and it is in a position to retaliate against security threats. Digital sovereignty is not only a buzzword or hype, as the EU is aware of its past history what is the reality behind it, wherever people need digital sovereignty. As such, the EU and the US have deeper cooperation to tackle the problems of cybersecurity. Even Australia had established the partnership in the field of space cooperation, terrorism and digital technology. The EU and India also working on those issues which are related to cybersecurity, maritime, and cybersecurity through the strategic partnership in the Indo-Pacific Region (IPR) (Bellanova et al., 2022).

The EU seems to cooperate on digital technologies in a post-traditional approach to sovereignty. This reshapes European security integration by building on the traditional notion of the modern art of the state (Bellamy, 2016). It is to evoke a new socio-technical imaginary in the era of digital technology where many nation-states struggling with cybersecurity issues in the context of online processing and other digital platforms (Jasanoff & Kim, 2015). The chapter describes the digitization of EU borders: expansion, interoperability and deterritorialization and reflects on their relationship to digital/sovereignty.

CONCLUSION

The chapter highlights the EU's new cybersecurity strategy which aims to ensure a global and open Internet with strong safeguards. There is the possibility of risk to security and the fundamental rights of people in the EU Member States and non-EU European countries (European Commission, 2022). EU created successful resilience, leadership and technological sovereignty. The EU also established strong resistance capabilities to prevent cybercrime, and deter and rapidly respond against this kind of element that wants to destabilize the EU's stability in Europe. At the global level, the EU also successfully installed cooperation mechanisms with its overseas partners. EU policy to building creative partnerships at the global level through strategic partnerships and emphasis on open cyberspace. The EU and its sister organisations are committed to supporting people's privacy in the context of cybercrime and online fraud. EU's also investing in the digital transition and supporting institutions in the connection of cyber management plans for upcoming years. The EU's commitment to work on new technological and industrial policies is the agenda of the recovery plan. The new EU cybersecurity strategy has accelerated extensive programs to make the digital decade a key part of Shaping Europe's digital future. The European Commission set the agenda for 2020-2025 and supported the recovery plan to strengthen the Security Union Strategy.

On March 22, 2021, the Council adopted an outcome document on the EU cybersecurity strategy. The new cybersecurity strategy for the digital decade was jointly presented by the Commission and the High Representative for Foreign Affairs and Security Policy in December 2020 (Wahl, 2021). This book chapter analyses in depth the EU's policy of being transparent to provide a safe and secure Europe. There is a lot of negativities against the EU's efforts to protect against cybercrime in member states. On the other hand, the EU's diplomacy has been extensively worked across the world for cyber management cooperation with its overseas counterparts. Finally, this chapter reached the conclusion that the EU is too much aware of cybersecurity issues rather than any other regional organisation in the world. The second important thing is that the EU successfully cooperates with the US, Australia, African countries and India in the area of cyberspace. By and large, the EU's first priority is to provide security to each and every people who are living in Europe or elsewhere in the world. To date, the EU's directives have been achieving major success to restrict such kinds of cybercrime in the EU Member States as well as in non-EU countries.

EU policy ensures the security of the 5G network and paves the way for its success in Europe in the context of the EU's Cybersecurity Strategy. The EU's General Data Protection Regulation also provides safeguards to the common people. All companies are responsible and binding with the EU GDPR for the security and digital sovereignty of people. The EU pursues the twin objectives of establishing a robust cybersecurity architecture across the bloc and harnessing the benefits of artificial intelligence (AI) for societal and economic (cyber) security and defence purposes more widely. Furthermore, as AI-powered cyberattacks are increasingly on the rise, the EU and its Member States, in partnership with the private sector, must be ready to respond to the growing range of risks and threats. AI-related cybersecurity issues, as well as possessing the capabilities and expertise to mitigate these challenges. Thus, the EU Cybersecurity Strategy is always aware of the insecurity in this region and, through effective policies and several mechanisms, mitigates the danger. This chapter analytically discusses the positivity and criticism of the EU's cybersecurity policy. But, after the Balkan crisis, there are no such incidents happened in Europe because of the EU's trustful and resilient management of digital technologies. Furthermore, the EU also provides digital technologies to its inter-continental partners as well. Nowadays, developing countries are being supported by the EU's successful cooperation in digital fields.

The EU's Cybersecurity Strategy have had accepted the challenges of the digital world's difficulties and its policies continue to work on these burning issues. There are also separate research and training programs designed by the EU's institutions to spreading awareness and consciousness among people to stop cybercrime. The strategy also seeks to harness cutting-edge technologies, for example, 5G, AI, and quantum technologies. Many strategic plans are based on a common understanding of digital technologies and their plans are based on their establishment. The EU plans to build a wider communication-based network of several security operations centres on its territory which has been supported by AI to constitute and establishment of the European "cybersecurity shield". These centers would detect signs of possible cyberattacks and notify the responsible authorities in order to avoid possible damage and casualties in the region. This research recommends that a study on EU cybersecurity policy is still necessary for rational work on cybercrime.

REFERENCES

Anagnostakis, D. (2021). The European Union-United States cybersecurity relationship: A transatlantic functional cooperation. *Journal of Cyber Policy*, *6*(2), 243–261. doi:10.1080/23738871.2021.1916975

Bellamy, R. (2016). A European Republic of Sovereign States: Sovereignty, republicanism and the European Union. *European Journal of Political Theory*, *16*(2), 188–209. doi:10.1177/1474885116654389

Bellanova, R., Carrapico, H., & Duez, D. (2022). Digital/sovereignty and European security integration: An introduction. *European Security*, *31*(3), 337–355. doi:10.1080/09662839.2022.2101887

Benincasa, E. (2021). The Case for Cyber 'Disarmament' in the European Union. *The International Spectator*, *56*(1), 39–54. doi:10.1080/03932729.2021.1872200

Bharti, M. S., & Singh, A. (2023). India and France bilateral partnership for advancing strategic autonomy in the Indo-Pacific region: Special reference to the Indo-French strategic partnership. *Cogent Social Sciences*, *9*(1), 2215561. doi:10.1080/23311886.2023.2215561

Bharti, S. S., & Aryal, S. K. (2022). The right to privacy and an implication of the EU General Data Protection Regulation (GDPR) in Europe: Challenges to the companies. *Journal of Contemporary European Studies*, 1–12. doi:10.1080/14782804.2022.2130193

Bradford, A. (2020). *The Brussels effect: how the European Union rules the world.* Oxford University Press. doi:10.1093/oso/9780190088583.001.0001

Braune, E., & Dana, L. P. (2022). Digital entrepreneurship: Some features of new social interactions. *Canadian Journal of Administrative Sciences / Revue Canadienne Des Sciences de l'Administration*, *39*(3), 237–243. doi:10.1002/cjas.1653

Cachia, J. C., & DeBattista, A. P. (2022). Political narrative, collective EU security and the State of the Union. *European Politics and Society*, 1–17. doi:10.1080/23745118.2022.2082035

Calderaro, A., & Blumfelde, S. (2022). Artificial intelligence and EU security: The false promise of digital sovereignty. *European Security*, *31*(3), 415–434. doi:10.1080/09662839.2022.2101885

Carrapico, H., & Barrinha, A. (2018). European Union cyber security as an emerging research and policy field. *European Political Science*, *19*(3), 299–303. doi:10.1080/23745118.2018.1430712

Chiara, P. G. (2022). The IoT and the new EU cybersecurity regulatory landscape. *International Review of Law Computers & Technology*, *36*(2), 118–137. doi:10.1080/13600869.2022.2060468

Christou, G. (2018). The challenges of cybercrime governance in the European Union. *European Political Science*, *19*(3), 355–375. doi:10.1080/23745118.2018.1430722

Christou, G. (2019). The collective securitisation of cyberspace in the European Union. *West European Politics*, *42*(2), 278–301. doi:10.1080/01402382.2018.1510195

Council of Europe. (2001). *Convention on cybercrime.* ETS No.185. Retrieved from https://www.coe.int/en/web/conventions/full-list/-/conventions/treaty/185

Council of the European Union. (2005, May 16). Council Framework Decision on Attacks against Information Systems. *Official Journal of the European Union, L,* *69*(67).

Csernatoni, R., & Mavrona, K. (2022, September 15). *The Artificial Intelligence and Cybersecurity Nexus: Taking Stock of the European Union's Approach.* Carnegie Europe. Retrieved from https://carnegieeurope.eu/2022/09/15/artificial-intelligence-and-cybersecurity-nexus-taking-stock-of-european-union-s-approach-pub-87886

Cutolo, D., & Kenney, M. (2021). Platform-Dependent Entrepreneurs: Power Asymmetries, Risks, and Strategies in the Platform Economy. *The Academy of Management Perspectives, 35*(4), 584–605. doi:10.5465/amp.2019.0103

Europa. (2019, April 17). *Regulation (EU) 2019/881 of The European Parliament and of The Council.* Retrieved from https://eur-lex.europa.eu/legal-content/EN/TXT/PDF/?uri=CELEX%3A32019R0881&from=EN

European Commission. (2010). A Digital Agenda for Europe, Communication from the Commission to the European Parliament, the Council, the European Economic and Social Committee and the Committee of the Regions. COM (2010) 245 Final/2, Brussels (26.8.10).

European Commission. (2012). Communication from the Commission to the Council and the European Parliament. Tackling Crime in our Digital Age: Establishing a European Cybercrime Centre. COM (2012) 140 Final, Brussels (7.2.13).

European Commission. (2013, February 7). *Cybersecurity Strategy of the European Union: An Open, Safe and Secure Cyberspace.* Retrieved from https://data.consilium.europa.eu/doc/document/ST%20 6225%202013%20INIT/EN/pdf

European Commission. (2017, September 13). *Joint Communication to the European Parliament and the Council Resilience, Deterrence and Defence: Building Strong Cybersecurity for the EU.* Retrieved from https://eur-lex.europa.eu/legal-content/EN/TXT/PDF/?uri=CELEX:52017JC0450

European Commission. (2019, March). *Challenges to effective EU cybersecurity policy.* Retrieved from https://www.eca.europa.eu/Lists/ECADocuments/BRP_CYBERSECURITY/BRP_CYBERSE-CURITY_EN.pdf

European Commission. (2022, June 7). *The Cybersecurity Strategy.* Retrieved from https://digital-strategy. ec.europa.eu/en/node/9690/printable/pdf

European Commission and High Representative. (2013). *Cybersecurity strategy of the European Union: an open, safe and secure cyberspace.* European Data Protection Supervisor. Retrieved from https://edps. europa.eu/sites/default/files/publication/13-06-14_cyber_security_en.pdf

European Commission and High Representative of the Union for Foreign Affairs and Security Policy. (2017, September 13). *Resilience, deterrence and defence: building strong cybersecurity for the EU.* European Commission. Retrieved from https://eur-lex.europa.eu/legal-content/EN/TXT/ PDF/?uri=CELEX:52017JC0450

European Union Agency for Cybersecurity. (2022, September 16). *European Cybersecurity Challenge 2022.* ENISA. Retrieved from https://www.enisa.europa.eu/events/european-cybersecurity-challenge-2022

Europol. (2023, January 4). *Our Thinking: A strategy for security.* Retrieved from https://www.europol.eu-ropa.eu/about-europol/our-thinking#:~:text=As%20the%20EU's%20law%20enforcement,organised%20 crime%2C%20cybercrime%20and%20terrorism

Falessi, N., Gavrila, R., Klejnstrup, M. R., & Moulinos, K. (2012, December). *National Cyber Security Strategies. Practical Guide on Development and Execution.* The European Network and Information Security Agency. Retrieved from https://www.enisa.europa.eu/publications/national-cyber-security-strategies-an-implementation-guide

Feingold, S., & Beato, F. (2022, December 2). *From stricter reporting rules to a new cyber threat hub, the EU is upgrading its cybersecurity law*. World Economic Forum. Retrieved from https://www.weforum.org/agenda/2022/12/cybersecurity-european-union-nis/

Fuster, G. G., & Jasmontaite, L. (2020). Cybersecurity Regulation in the European Union: The Digital, the Critical and Fundamental Rights. In M. Christen, B. Gordijn, & M. Loi (Eds.), *The Ethics of Cybersecurity* (pp. 97–115). Springer International Publishing. doi:10.1007/978-3-030-29053-5_5

Gao, X., & Chen, X. (2022). Role enactment and the contestation of global cybersecurity governance. *Defence Studies*, 22(4), 689–708. doi:10.1080/14702436.2022.2110485

Gladicheva, V. (2016, November 9). *Privacy Shield Lawsuits in EU Court Face*. Admissibility Hurdle, MLEX. Retrieved from https://mlexmarketinsight.com/editors-picks/privacy-shield-lawsuits-eu-court-face-admissibility-hurdle/

Hall, H. K. (2018). Restoring Dignity and Harmony to United States-European Union Data Protection Regulation. *Communication Law and Policy*, 23(2), 125–157. doi:10.1080/10811680.2018.1429773

Healey, J. (2016). The U.S. Government and Zero-Day Vulnerabilities: From Pre-Heartbleed to Shadow Brokers. *Journal of International Affairs*. Retrieved from https://jia.sipa.columbia.edu/ online-articles/ healey_vulnerability_equities_process

Jasanoff, S., & Kim, S.-H. (2015). Dreamscapes of modernity. Sociotechnical imaginaries and the fabrication of power. In *Dreamscapes of Modernity*. University of Chicago Press. doi:10.7208/chicago/9780226276663.001.0001

KapsokoliE. (2021, February 1). *The security challenges that the EU is facing in cyberspace*. Hellenic Association of Political Scientists (HAPSc). doi:10.2139/ssrn.3784083

Klimburg, A., & Tirmaa-Klaar, H. (2011, April). *Cyber Security and Cyber Power: Concepts, Conditions and Capabilities for Cooperation for Action within EU*. TEPSA and the European Parliament. Retrieved from https://www.europarl.europa.eu/RegData/etudes/STUD/2011/433828/EXPO-SEDE_ET(2011)433828_EN.pdf

Nicholas, P. (2018, March 5). *The Role that Regions Can and Should Play in Critical Infrastructure Protection*. Microsoft. Retrieved from https://www.microsoft.com/security/blog/2018/03/05/the-role-that-regions-can-and-should-play-in-critical-infrastructure-protection/

Radoniewicz, F. (2022). Cybersecurity in the European Union Law. In K. Chałubińska-Jentkiewicz, F. Radoniewicz, & T. Zieliński (Eds.), *Cybersecurity in Poland: Legal Aspects* (pp. 73–92). Springer International Publishing. doi:10.1007/978-3-030-78551-2_6

Schaake, M., & Vermeulen, M. (2016). Towards a values-based European foreign policy to cybersecurity. *Journal of Cyber Policy*, 1(1), 75–84. doi:10.1080/23738871.2016.1157617

Scholz, T. (2023, March 3). *Leveraging the EU-India Cybersecurity Partnership*. Observer Research Foundation. Retrieved from https://www.orfonline.org/expert-speak/leveraging-the-eu-india-cybersecurity-partnership/

Sen, K. (2023, March 2). *List of Cybersecurity Regulations in the European Union*. Retrieved from https://www.upguard.com/blog/cybersecurity-regulations-in-the-european-union

Shooter, S. (2013). *Cyber Security and the EU: regulating for network security*. Bird & Bird. Retrieved from https://www.twobirds.com/-/media/PDFs/News/CybersecurityandtheEU06201300125701.pdf

Sliwinski, K. F. (2014). Moving beyond the European Union's Weakness as a Cyber-Security Agent. *Contemporary Security Policy, 35*(3), 468–486. doi:10.1080/13523260.2014.959261

Song, A. K. (2019). The Digital Entrepreneurial Ecosystem—A critique and reconfiguration. *Small Business Economics, 53*(3), 569–590. doi:10.100711187-019-00232-y

Stevens, T., & O'Brien, K. (2019). Brexit and Cyber Security. *RUSI Journal, 164*(3), 22–30. doi:10.10 80/03071847.2019.1643256

Sussan, F., & Acs, Z. J. (2017). The digital entrepreneurial ecosystem. *Small Business Economics, 49*(1), 55–73. doi:10.100711187-017-9867-5

Timmers, P. (2018). The European Union's cybersecurity industrial policy. *Journal of Cyber Policy, 3*(3), 363–384. doi:10.1080/23738871.2018.1562560

Vela, J. (2021, August 2). *The Development of the EU Cyber Security Strategy and its Importance*. FINABEL: European Army Interoperability Centre.

Wahl, T. (2021, April 9). *Council Conclusions on Cybersecurity Strategy*. Eucrim. Retrieved from https://eucrim.eu/news/council-conclusions-on-cybersecurity-strategy/

Wessel, R. A. (2015). Towards EU cybersecurity law: regulating a new policy field. In N. Tsagourias & R. Buchan (Eds.), *Research handbook on international law and cyberspace*. Edward Elgar Publishing. doi:10.4337/9781782547396.00032

Wibisono, E. (2023). The digital entrepreneurial ecosystem in the European Union: Evidence from the digital platform economy index. *European Planning Studies, 31*(6), 1–23. doi:10.1080/09654313.202 3.2202683

Wolford, B. (n.d.). *What is GDPR, the EU's new data protection law?* GDPR.EU. Retrieved May 19, 2023, from Retrieved from https://gdpr.eu/what-is-gdpr/?cn-reloaded=1

Chapter 12
EU's Cyber Security Strategy Before and During the War in Ukraine

Tamari Bitsadze
International Black Sea University, Georgia

ABSTRACT

This chapter first examines the European Union's cyber security strategy and then analyzes the common principles of the member states in this regard. The authors discuss the European Union's role in the advancement of cyber security. In addition, the chapter reviews the EU Convention on Cybercrime. Most importantly, they discuss the impact of the most important and relevant issue, the Russia-Ukraine war, on the EU's cyber security strategy and investigate what changes and challenges the ongoing conflict in Ukraine has brought to the EU's cyber security strategy.

INTRODUCTION

In the modern world, informational war has become a bigger weapon than the physical one, since the beginning, the victory of the informational war in many cases meant the victory of physical war as well, a clear example of this is World War II, where, although the concentration camps were created by the Soviet Union before Germany, it did not trust the Jews either, that to this day, when we mention the concentration camp, it is associated with Germany, because it correctly calculated the methods and ways of spreading information.

The twenty-first century is the century of information technology; technologies have advanced to the point that any interested person can obtain real-time information from any location on the planet. As a result, information manipulation plays a critical role in the shaping of public opinion, and hence in the execution of effective policies.

Due to accessibility, so-called social media has become popular. Spread of fake news disinformation, various services, groups, and organizations purposefully spread disinformation against opponents, social

DOI: 10.4018/978-1-6684-8846-1.ch012

media has become an alternative arena of war, where weapons are words and materials, it can potentially lead to real war, and not only that, industrialization and the rapid spread of information have increased people's feelings of nationalism, and thus the materials spread here can cause a feeling of protest that will bring the community together and take it to the streets (Barry M., Vinton G., David D., Robert E., Kleinrock L. 1997).

If until now TV, radio, and written media were used for information warfare, now information technologies, cyber-attacks, and especially social media are the main sources. Cyber-attacks are used for various purposes, such as obtaining secret information, as well as creating an information vacuum, hindering the obtaining of information, suppressing, damaging the opponent's networks, etc. Social media and social networks such as Facebook, Instagram, and Twitter are used as a means of information warfare on a larger scale.

Information warfare can include (Reisman & Antoniou, 1994): Obtaining tactical information; Distributing propaganda and disinformation to misrepresent and manipulate the opponent; Confirming the accuracy of information; Preventing the opponent from gathering information; Distorting and mis-representing the opponent's information. It follows from the name of information war that the war takes place through information, and the main source of information dissemination is information technology, this is where cyber security is involved, which should provide defense against various constituent parts of information war.

The European Union is the leading entity in the world in terms of activity, developed strategies and projects in terms of cyber security, cyber security is often the main topic at various conferences and meetings of the European Union, moreover, cyber-attack is considered the most urgent problem in the European Union. This topic is overseen by special agencies: "European Union Network and Informa-tion Security Agency" - ENISA, European Cybercrime Center - EUROPOL/EC3, European Defense Agency - EDA. There are also non-profit (Non-profit) self-financing organizations in the field of cyber security. The fact that so much attention is paid to the topic of cyber security makes it clear how seri-ously the European Union takes this issue.

Apart from various terrorist organizations, the biggest threat to the European Union is the Russian Federation, especially in cyberspace, where Russian propaganda is particularly active. Fighting through propaganda is nothing new for Russia; during the Soviet Union, a separate direction called "special propaganda" was taught. However, in Putin's Russia, these approaches have become particularly active; Russia actively leverages the advancement of information technology to disseminate disinformation and propaganda.

Anti-Western propaganda is a part of Russia's information war, they present the European Union and the West in general as countries against traditions, Europe is a nest of depravity. In doing so, they pres-ent their own superiority and pretend that it is their duty to protect the conservative values of the state.

In Russia, the presence of non-governmental organizations is strictly controlled, and similar organizations financed from Europe are practically minimized. The EU is always one step behind when it comes to Russian propaganda and disinformation, not because Russia is strong or Europe is weak, but because of the difference in political views and political cultures between the two sides. In Russia, fighting with similar methods is accepted, and blocking the opponent's opinion with different methods is part of their policy. Unlike Russia, one of the main values in Europe is freedom of speech, therefore it is not possible to control disinformation. Due to Russia's active information warfare, there is no other way for the EU countries to take some steps, one of the first was the UK law, which involves putting internet trolls who are clearly harmful in a penitentiary for 6 months. Corresponding legislation is also being developed in various EU countries (Čižik T., 2017).

Current events related to Russia's illegal invasion of Ukraine and the waging of war have intensified the existing challenges related to the EU's cybersecurity. That is why the paper reviews the changes and challenges that the European Union's cyber security strategy has undergone in light of the current historical event. Here should be emphasized that for the EU to resist disinformation from Russia, it needs a creative and serious approach, by developing various 29 legislations, which in turn will not violate European values. First, let's review some general tricks and strategies for the EU before the Russia-Ukraine War.

European Union Agency for Cybersecurity: ENISA and Other Agencies

ENISA works with various groups to develop advice and recommendations on information security. ENISA is territorially located in Greece, Crete, and its headquarters are in Athens. Since its establishment in 2004, ENISA has been actively ensuring and raising awareness of network and information security in the EU. ENISA's work includes conducting cyber security lectures, implementing software, developing national cyber security strategies, and participating in the development of network and information security legislation. ENISA aims to raise awareness of cyber security for the benefit of EU citizens, consumers, and public organizations. ENISA offers all EU member states the opportunity to contact it for consultation. ENISA's strategies and strategic objectives are (The document issued by ENISA, which includes its strategies for 2016-2020):

- Politics - Help make cyber security a European priority. Assistance to relevant institutions of the European Union and European countries in the development of legislation in this regard.
- Expertise - European support and training in network and information security. Comparison, analysis, and expertise on key cyber security issues that could potentially affect the EU, taking into account the development of technology.
- Capabilities - Support European countries to increase their cyber security capabilities.
- Community - Striving to unify networks of European countries. By strengthening cooperation between European countries.
- Creating an environment - Increasing the impact of ENISA. By improving management and increasing access to interested countries both in Europe and the world.

Due to the rapid pace of technological development, the number of cyber threats is also increasing rapidly in Europe, because all economic and social activities are nowadays computerized, the growth of the technological society must necessarily be followed by the growth of informational and network protection methods to obtain a stable environment. According to ENISA 2020 data, the number of cyber threats is increasing every year, and they are evolving, becoming more dangerous, cyber-attacks are becoming more effective, and cyber security methods cannot keep up with the pace of development, therefore stability cannot be maintained (Højsgaard T., 2015).

In the competition between hackers and defenders, hackers are always one step ahead, but there are some changes:

- Defenders learned that defense is only one side of the coin and began to use offensive methods for defense.
- Defenders have found a method of deanonymization, as a result of which they can identify the hacker even on the dark net.

- Defenders have developed their capabilities by targeting cyber threats to their servers and studying them.
- Hackers made virus codes available to the general public to develop capabilities.
- Hackers put a lot of work and investment into developing their profitable products.

The creation of ENISA was caused by the non-uniform policies of the EU countries in terms of cyber security, all of them are aware of the need in this area, but there was no mutually agreed action, its purpose is to act as a mediator between them to adopt common standards, as well as to provide assistance and advice to all of them individually. ENISA is financed from the EU budget, and the targeting of funds is monitored by an appointed board. ENISA uses the media as its main means of communication since the EU covers many countries, and they must consult each of them when it comes to new findings, research, or advice, it trusts the media as a rapid spreader of information. The agency employs 60 full-time high-level specialists from 27 different European countries and several temporary hired specialists. Among ENISA's threats, there are 2 specific viruses cited as examples of special cyber threats, which we will discuss in more detail due to international interest: In 2017, the number of cyber incidents increased, and two incidents called Wannacry and Notpetya attracted special attention. ENISA actively cooperates with EU countries and provides consultations to prevent similar situations. The European Cybercrime Center was established in 2013 by Europol to strengthen the law enforcement framework against cybercrime to protect citizens, governments, and organizations from cybercrime. Every year, the European Cybercrime Center publishes the report: "Assessment of organized crime threats on the Internet", which is a major strategic report on the main findings of the development of cyberattacks and the alarming threats.

The agency has 2 strategic groups:

1. Outreach and support that establishes collaborations and coordinates prevention and awareness raising.
2. Strategy and development, which includes: strategic analysis; policy formulation; Development of standardized training.

The European Cybercrime Center focuses on the following issues:

- Cyber-addicted criminal
- Financial fraud
- Online sexual exploitation of Children

The management of the agency determines the policy of the agency, determines how to achieve the goal, and cooperates with different agencies. The European Defense Agency - EDA, in addition to other issues, is actively working in the field of cyber security. The agency assists EU countries in military cyber defense. In addition, it works to raise awareness in terms of cyber security. Cyber security is a topical issue in both the military and public spheres, therefore the agency focused on the military sphere works in the public sphere as well (European Strategy, 2012).

State Cyber Security Strategies of EU Countries

At the meetings of the European Commission, the issue of cyber security is discussed quite often, in many cases it is noted as a strategic problem of state importance, which affects all layers of society and all sectors of the state. The state cyber security strategy is a means to solve this problem within the country, the strategy is the tool that is the first step towards concrete actions. ENISA advises EU member states on their national cyber security strategy, as well as the development of common policies for the EU as a whole. EU countries, as well as individual legislation, have different strategies for different issues, in terms of cyber security, these differences are more obvious because this field is still unformed and everyone is trying to cope with it in their way, ENISA role in this regard is currently only at the consultation level.

The first state cyber security strategy belongs to the United States of America, it was here that cyber threats were first perceived as a real problem. For the first time in the European Union, Germany started to develop a cyber security plan, which was followed by the same actions from other European countries, although the first cyber security state strategy in Europe was published by Estonia in 2008. A brief overview of all national cyber strategies published by EU countries up to and including December 2020 (Press release, 2020).

Austria - The technological revolution has taken hold in all areas and all developed countries are trying to use the benefits of cyberspace for their technological, economic, social, cultural, scientific, and political development. Technological development and the Internet have completely changed all areas, making them more comfortable. ¾ of the Austrian population uses the Internet regularly, half of them daily. The Austrian Cyber Security Strategy is a comprehensive proactive concept for the protection of cyberspace and people in the virtual world. Cyber security strategies, common principles, and recommendations of the EU member states. The aim is also to raise the awareness of Austrian citizens in this regard.

Austria's strategic goals in terms of cyber security are: To ensure cyber security, Austria undertakes to protect against cyber threats and cooperate with the private sector; Availability, reliability, and confidentiality of information exchange are possible only in the conditions of a secure, reliable, and stable cyberspace. However, cyberspace must be prepared for change and reorganized accordingly to maintain the main stated objectives; Against the backdrop of cyber security talk and partnerships with various organizations, new initiatives in this regard are supported and actively discussed. Therefore, Austria is considered a reliable place for business; Internet governance in Austria is protected and continuously evolving. Both in the capital and in the provinces, internet security will develop over time; A legal asset in the form of "cyber security" is protected by the Austrian authorities in partnership with nongovernmental organizations; All

Austrian enterprises ensure the security of their virtual space, as well as the identity and security of their employees; Austria is creating a "Cyber Security Culture" through awareness-raising.

Belgium has developed special legislation against cybercrimes. The legislation addressed online communication, online signatures and certification, information society, privacy, and personal data protection. A cyber incident detection and resolution structure is officially in place in Belgium. There is a separate online Child Protection Institute. There is also a separate website for reporting child pornography online.

Bulgaria has divided its cyber security strategy into 9 points: 1. Establishing a sustainable state cyber security system, raising awareness, and coordinated prevention. 2. Network and information security as a foundation of cyber resilience. 3. Improving the security of infrastructure dependent on information technology. 4. Better cooperation between the state, the economy, and the population. 5. Legal and Regulatory Agreement. 6. Fight against cybercrimes. 7. Cyberdefense. (meaning both virtual and physical) 8. Awareness, education, and innovation. 9. International cooperation: EU, NATO, OSCE, UN, ITU, ICANN, and regional neighbors.

Croatia has an extensive document on this topic, although we will highlight separate strategies. 1. Systemic approach and development of national legislation. 2. Carrying out special measures for the development of stability, reliability, and security in cyberspace. 3. Development of more reliable information-sharing mechanisms. 4. Raising security awareness. 5. Promotion of the development of training programs. 6. Promotion of the development of online services. 7. Promotion of research and development. 8. Systematic approach to international cooperation.

Czech Republic • Effectiveness and expansion of all types of structures, processes, and cooperation in terms of cyber security • Active international cooperation • Protection of state critical information infrastructure and important information systems. • Cooperation with the private sector. • Research and development/consumer confidence • Learning, raising awareness, and developing the information society. • Assistance of the Czech police in the fight against cybercrime. • Development of cyber security legislation and participation in the development of

EU Regulations

The Republic of Cyprus strictly considers the general guidelines and advice of the European Union for the development of its cyber security system. Their strategy involves the development and promotion of an e-business platform, the development of an information society, gaining trust among citizens and online businesses, the establishment of a secure electronic system, effective response to cyber threats, development of security of critical infrastructures.

As in the whole world, information technologies are actively and rapidly developed in Denmark, therefore more and more areas are connected to the Internet, and society and businesses are becoming dependent on the Internet's capabilities. Denmark is one of the most technological countries in the world, the development of information technology is the key to the development of the public sector and increasing the competitiveness of businesses. Citizens establish contact with both government services and businesses via the Internet in a secure way that respects personal information. Trust is completely based on the security of cyberspace, both from internal and external cyber-attacks. In 2020, Denmark invested 1.5 billion in cyber security and information security. During these years, Denmark presents 25 initiatives aimed at developing the most critical areas in the cyber sector. Cyber threats cannot be eliminated, but the Danish government takes responsibility to ensure that its citizens are safe online.

Estonia Cyber security principles:

- Cyber security is a part of state security. It provides the functionality of society, state, economy, and innovation.
- Cyber security is guaranteed to citizens with fundamental rights, individual freedom, and protection of personal information.
- Cyber security is ensured based on proportionality, taking into account cyber threats.
- Cyber security is ensured through cooperation with the private and public sectors.
- Cyber security starts with individual responsibility.
- Of particular importance are those types of cyber threats that can spread in the real world in any way.
- Cyber security is supported by international studies.
- Cyber security is ensured by international cooperation. Estonia also contributes to the development of global cyber security.

Finland - As a small, united, and active country, Finland has great chances to be in the vanguard of cyber security. They have a wide base of knowledge and strong expertise, a long tradition of close cooperation with the public sector, based on trust, as well as intra-sectoral cooperation. Finland's vision for cyber security is as follows: ● Finland can ensure the protection of vital functions against cyber threats in any situation. ● Citizens, governments, and the business sector can work effectively on the Internet by following security rules.

France has been allocated 5 strategic tasks:

1. Protection and security of state information systems and critical infrastructure.
2. Electronic trust, privacy and protection of personal information, cyber security.
3. Awareness raising, training, and education development.
4. Promotion of e-business, and control of Internet crimes.
5. Cooperation with Europe, the autonomy of cyber strategy, and stability of cyberspace.

The strategy of the German Federation is based on current threats and a plan to protect critical infrastructure. Germany focuses on 10 points:

1. Protection of critical information structures.
2. Protection of information technology systems.
3. Strengthening of information technology security in the public administration sector.
4. State Cyber Response Center.
5. State Cyber Security Council.
6. Effective control of crime in cyberspace.
7. Effective coordinated action to ensure cyber security in Europe and the world.
8. Use of reliable and trustworthy information technology.
9. Development of personnel in federal government bodies.
10. Tools against cyber attacks.

Greece:

1. Developing and establishing a safe and stable cyberspace, taking into account national, EU, and international laws, practices, and standards, so that the fundamental rights of citizens and the business sector are protected.
2. Continued development of capabilities to combat cyber threats, prioritizing critical infrastructures.
3. Institutional protection of the national cyber security framework to minimize cyber attacks and cyber threats.
4. Development of public and private sector safety culture.

The security of Hungarian cyberspace is in the Hungarian state's interest. as well as the operation of free, democratic, and secure cyberspace, subject to the laws. The security and freedom of Hungary's cyberspace are ensured in cooperation with the private, public, and business sectors, all of which are responsible.

Ireland's Cyber Security Strategy aims to:

- Develop the resilience and resilience of critical information infrastructure and key economic sectors, particularly in the public sector.
- Continue to engage with international partners and organizations to ensure cyberspace security, freedom, and business sector prosperity.
- Raising awareness of the responsibility of businesses and private individuals for the security of personal networks, devices, and information, facilitating and training them in these matters.
- Development of appropriate legislation against cyber threats.
- Ensuring a regulatory agreement for holders of personal or other information that is robust, proportionate, and fair.
- Increasing the capacity of public administration and the private sector in terms of managing cyber incidents.

Italy - The State Cyber Security Strategy Agreement and the corresponding State Plan, both provided for in the Decree of the Prime Minister of January 24, 2013, include strategic guidelines for ensuring cyber security. The goal is to make the state ready for current and future challenges in cyberspace. Considering that the development of technologies is followed by new threats and is not effective as of now.

The goal of Latvia's cyber security policy is to provide reliable cyberspace for safe, reliable services that are important for the state and society. The fight against cyber threats is possible if there is a systematic development of the cyber security system and improvement of skills. Effective fight against cyber-threats requires domestic and international cooperation of the state. Cyber threats can be reduced if all sectors, government, private and public, participate. Cybersecurity policies should be developed in such a way that the fundamental rights and freedoms of individuals are taken into account.

Lithuania:

1. Ensuring the security of state information resources.
2. Ensuring the effective operation of critical information structures.
3. Ensuring cyber security for citizens of Lithuania and people staying in Lithuania.

Luxembourg:

1. Strengthening the internal cooperation of the state.
2. Strengthening international cooperation.
3. Increasing the reliability of electrical infrastructure.
4. Fight against cybercrime.
5. Information, training, and awareness raising.
6. Development of standards, norms, and certificates for critical information infrastructures.
7. Strengthening cooperation with the academic and research field.

Malta:

1. Fighting cybercrime.
2. Strengthening of state cyber security.

3. Protection of cyberspace.
4. Cyber security awareness and education.
5. Development of a state contract in terms of cyber security.
6. State and international cooperation.
7. Protection of state information infrastructure from cyber threats.
8. Ensuring the security of users' cyberspace.

The Netherlands is resistant to cyber-attacks and protects its vital interests in the information field.

-   The Netherlands is fighting cybercrime.
-   The Netherlands is introducing cybersecurity services and products to protect privacy.
-   The Netherlands forms coalitions for cyber freedom, security, and peace.
-   The Netherlands has enough knowledge in cyber security to innovate in this regard.

Poland's main goal is to ensure a high level of security for private, and public sectors and individuals when using important information services. Poland will take specifically targeted steps to prevent cyber incidents. It will significantly strengthen the means of combating cyber threats. The state will increase its potential in terms of cyber security and make a name for itself in the development of cyber security at the international level.

The Portuguese Cyber Security Scheme consists of 6 points:

1. Cyberspace Security Structure.
2. Fighting cybercrime.
3. Protection of cyberspace and state infrastructure.
4. Learning, awareness, and prevention.
5. Research and development.
6. Cooperation.

Romania's goal is to ensure normal and reduced risks in cyberspace by improving knowledge, capabilities, and mechanisms.

1. Creation of conceptual, effective, and organized legislation to ensure cyber security.
2. Development of state risk management and taking effective steps in cyber security.
3. Development and promotion of security culture in the cyber sphere.
4. Development of international cooperation in cyber security.

Slovakia:

1. Protection of state cyberspace.
2. Raising awareness of cyber security.
3. Internal state cooperation.
4. International cooperation.
5. Taking into account the fundamental rights of people when ensuring cyber security.

Slovenia:

1. Strengthening of systemic regulations in cyber security.
2. Protection of citizens in cyberspace.
3. Cyber security in the economy.
4. Ensuring the stability of critical infrastructure.
5. Ensuring public safety and combating cybercrime.
6. Development of defensive cyber capabilities.
7. Ensuring secure online operations and stable operation of critical infrastructures.
8. Strengthening cyber security with the help of international cooperation.

Spain:

1. Ensuring the security of telecommunications systems used by government agencies.
2. Ensuring the security of the business sector and critical infrastructure telecommunication facilities.
3. Development of detection, prevention, action, analysis, recovery, and research of cyber terrorism activities.
4. Raising awareness about future threats from cyberspace.
5. Obtaining information and skills about cyber security tasks.

Sweden - The government's goal is to create a strong platform that will work in the long term to ensure cyber security. The goal of the government is to set separate tasks for all parts of this area and solve all of them. Special commissions and services will be created to solve the tasks. Since security challenges cannot be solved once and for all, because digital technologies are constantly evolving, the strategy must be flexible and responsive to changes in cyberspace. The Swedish government plans to establish the first such practice in 2018.

Noteworthy, is that there is no international agreement on the definition of cyber security (H. Luiijf, K. Besseling, M Spoelstra, P. de Graaf, 2011). Definitions of cyber security, cyberspace, cybercrime, and related key terms can vary dramatically from country to country. Each country's approach to creating a cyber security strategy also differs. Even though all countries recognize the importance of international cooperation, there is still a lack of common main terms and a single e. year The lack of "language" makes cooperation at the international level very difficult.

However, it is noticeable that the cyber security strategies of each EU country still have common principles, which can be formulated as follows (EU,2023):

- Identifying an appropriate mechanism based on public partnerships that allow private and public sector stakeholders to discuss and approve policies related to cybersecurity issues;
- Cooperation at the international level on the exchange of information about cybercrime and the existence of the necessary legal framework for this. This enables cooperation at the international level. For example, the Netherlands (Dutch Forge, 2022) and France (ANSSI, 2022) are strengthening their legal frameworks for cybercrime, investigation, and prosecution;
- Development of a state model and policy aimed at ensuring cyber security;
- Planning and defining necessary policies and regulations, clear separation of roles, rights, and responsibilities for the private and public sectors;

- Determination of critical information infrastructure (CII – Critical Information Infrastructure Protection). including the development of core assets, services, and relationships;
- Development of a systematic and integrated approach to state risk management;
- International cooperation not only between EU member states but also with countries that are not part of the EU;
- Determining and marking the goals of informational programs aimed at offering the user new models of behavior and work;
- Conducting complex research and working on developing programs aimed at solving cyberspace security problems. Development of intellectual resources;

In an environment where cyber threats are constantly evolving, emerging, and evolving, EU Member States, which are constantly facing new challenges and global threats in cyberspace, will greatly benefit from having a flexible and operational cyber security strategy. The cross-border nature of cybercrime forces member states to cooperate closely with each other and at the international level in general. Such cooperation is necessary not only for effective preparation for cyber-attacks but also for timely response to them. Therefore, the state strategy approach to cyber security should be complex.

Despite the common principles and similarities, their non-uniformity is still clearly visible among the state cyber security strategies of the EU countries, the main moments of some of them coincide, although there are still big differences, both in the points of the strategy and in the size of the document, documents are starting from 1 page and over 40 pages. Moreover, they are based on different values. Some documents are so small it shows their frivolity, and for example, the Latvian Cyber Security Strategy document is written in a different format and then converted to Pdf format by an unlicensed program. All this clearly shows how unformed the field of cyber security is, it is not said that everyone should have a common strategy, however, since they are members of one union that is connected not only by region but also by values, their strategies need to be based on one basic strategy, as laws are based on the constitution.

Situation Before the Russia-Ukraine War: EU Cyber Security Strategy and Reform Plan

The EU has an official document, which is not so much a strategy but more a vision of the EU Cyber Security Strategy, and there is also a reform plan. Over the past two decades, the development of the Internet, and specifically cyberspace, has had a tremendous impact on all parts of society. Daily life, fundamental rights, and the economy, in general, all areas have become dependent on information and communication systems (EU Cybersecurity Strategy, 2020).

Open cyberspace has sparked political and social engagement around the world. The Internet has erased the boundaries between countries, communities, and citizens. The Internet has become a source of freedom, where everyone has freedom of expression, it has become a kind of pillar of democracy. For cyberspace to continue its role as a means of open and free information exchange, it is necessary to spread European values and laws in the Internet space as well. While ensuring cyber security and protecting people's rights is fundamental, it is challenging in cyberspace as it is difficult to draw the line between protection of rights and censorship. However, as far as cyber-attacks and viruses are concerned, this is a crime and can be eliminated, for this, states need to work and maintain cyberspace. However, there is another obstacle, which is that the private sector has a dominant position in cyberspace, and it is difficult to implement policies that do not harm anyone.

Cyberspace has become the backbone of economic growth, all kinds of financial transactions, and financial sectors depend on the Internet. By making full use of Internet services, the EU could theoretically increase its gross domestic product by 500 billion per year, but unfortunately, according to 2013 research, one in three people in Europe does not trust the Internet for financial purposes. At least one out of 10 people in the European Union has been a victim of online fraud. In recent years, despite the growing Internet services, convenience, and many positive things that the Internet brings, many threats have appeared, and it is not decreasing, but on the contrary, they are increasing at a great speed, whether it is intentional or accidental.

Threats can have different origins: criminal, political, terrorist, and state-sponsored, as well as in the form of natural events or accidents. The EU economy is already affected by cybercrimes against individuals and the private sector. The methods are different, infiltrating the system, stealing information, or extorting money through Ransom viruses, the method we have already discussed. Some countries outside the European Union misuse the Internet to control citizens, impose censorship, control content, etc. According to the decision of the European Union, the Internet should be democratic and freedom of speech and expression should be given priority.

Based on all of this, cyber security has become relevant, which is why different countries around the world are establishing state cyber security strategies. We have already learned about the European part of which, but this time we will learn specifically about the cyber security strategy of the European Union. EU cyber security is based on fundamental EU security laws, a democratic approach should also be in cyberspace. The Internet is considered a human right, everyone should be able to access the Internet and be safe there. Cyberspace is not controlled by any particular structure, there are stakeholders, most of whom are from the private sector, who set the rules.

The European Union recognizes the need for the dominance of the private sector on the Internet for democratic purposes and intends to promote them. The European Union believes that the responsibility for cyberspace security should be shared between all sectors and private individuals (Højsgaard T. 2015).

The EU must ensure freedom and security on the Internet for the benefit of all. The European Union allocates 5 strategic priorities:

- Ensuring cyber resilience.
- Development of industrial and technological resources for cyber security.
- Radical changes in terms of cyber-crimes.
- Establishing a coherent international cyberspace policy for the EU and promoting EU values.
- Development of cyber defense policies and capabilities, based on standard security and defense policies.

Awareness raising: On the basis that cyber security should be a shared responsibility, it is necessary to raise awareness in this regard, all users should be aware of cyber threats and therefore be responsible for all their actions. ENISA was tasked with raising awareness, producing publications, organizing expert workshops, and strengthening public-private sector cooperation. Europol, Eurojust and the State Data Protection Authority are also actively working in this regard.

In the European Union, three agencies work actively in terms of cyber security, namely: European Union Information and Network Security Agency - ENISA, European Cybercrime Center - EUROPOL/

EC3, and European Defense Agency - EDA. These agencies have management boards with representatives from different countries. This Cyber Security Strategy is the EU's vision of how threats in cyberspace can be tackled, with the key message being that cooperation between all sectors will lead to effective cyber security.

Achieving cyber resilience: First, concerted action by EU public authorities and the private sector, as a result of which they will be able to jointly effectively fight against cyber threats. Sharing experiences and creating a common policy is essential in this matter, otherwise, Europe will become an easy target for cybercrime. It is for these purposes that the "European Network and Information Security Agency" (ENISA) was created in 2004 to play an intermediary role.

Cyber security reform: The EU aims to strengthen cyber security rules to counter growing cyber threats and take the initiative. On October 19-20, 2017, the European Consul raised the issue of adopting common approaches to EU cyber security. This reform was proposed by the European Commission in September. The goals are Rapid implementation of network and information security directives; To create a stronger cyber security agency; Introducing an EU-wide cyber security certification scheme (Cybersecurity Strategy of the EU, 2022).

Europe's leaders consider cyber security reform to be one of their top goals. The reform became necessary due to the rapid growth of threats, tens of billions of devices worldwide are connected to the network, and threats in the form of software bugs, viruses, and cyber-attacks are increasing. As for awareness raising, 51% of Europeans believe that they are not sufficiently informed in this matter, and 69% of companies do not have basic knowledge of cyber threats (Consilium, 2020).

One of the presented reforms is also the cyber security certification scheme, which represents certain rules at both the software and technical level. The European Commission does not consider ENISA to be effective enough, and wants to create a much stronger agency to fight cyber threats more effectively (EC, 2013).

In 2021, the European Commission issued a document for "Joint Communication to the European Parliament, the Council, the European Economic and Social Committee, the Committee of the Regions and the European Investment Bank", where mentioned that: "The EU toolbox for the cybersecurity of 5G networks will guide investments in digital infrastructure. These will also be linked with standards and protocols that support network security and resilience, interoperability, and open, plural, and secure internet. The EU will also promote access to the Open Internet, given its role as a key driver of innovation, socio-political, economic, and cultural development.

The EU will offer digital economy packages that combine infrastructure investments with country-level assistance in ensuring the protection of personal data, cybersecurity and the right to privacy, trustworthy AI, as well as fair and open digital markets. For instance, the EU will build on the global trend towards convergence with the General Data Protection Regulation (GDPR) to inspire other countries to promote secure data flows. Global Gateways will promote the EU regulatory model of open and competitive markets for communications networks and services" (JOIN, 2021).

Over the next seven years, the EU is committed to supporting this goal with unprecedented investment in the EU's digital transition. This would double prior investment levels. It reflects the EU's commitment to its new industrial and technology policies, as well as the recovery plan.

The EU's new Cybersecurity Strategy for the Digital Decade is an important component of Shaping Europe's Digital Future, the Commission's European Recovery Plan, and the Security Union Strategy 2020-2025 (EC, 2020-25).

WHAT IS HAPPENING TODAY? CURRENT CHALLENGES OF CYBER SECURITY IN THE EU: EURO-CYBER SECURITY IN PRACTICE DURING THE WAR IN UKRAINE

Russia's recent aggressiveness against Ukraine has reignited the discussion about 'hybrid warfare' (The New York Times 2022. The Economist 2022; The Wall Street Journal 2022;). When academics or practitioners use the phrase "hybrid model of warfare," they may not always mean the same thing. However, the concept of "hybrid warfare" is as controversial as it is popular. Furthermore, the conceptions of 'hybrid warfare' embraced by Western states and organizations varied significantly. As a result, the term 'hybrid warfare' ultimately obscures rather than clarifies.

It is worth noting the fact that the establishment of the European Union was initially related to the economic union, the main purpose of which was to create a single market and deepen trade relations between European countries. For several decades, it was not thought of as a global actor in the political arena, however, from the 90s to the present day, we see that its role, along with the economic one, has grown significantly politically, and it plays an important role as an international actor.

Today's example of Ukraine showed us even more clearly the role of the European Union as a powerful political actor. In the current Russia-Ukraine war, the European Union has used several rigid mechanisms against Russia, and the economic and political sanctions imposed by it have had a drastic impact on Russia's current situation (a clear drop in financial markets and the Russian ruble).

Moreover, for the first time in history, the European Union purchased military equipment for a non-member state - Ukraine - for the improvement of military operations and defense. It should be noted that the European Union allocated unprecedentedly large sums of money to Ukraine for the purchase of combat equipment, about 500 million euros, including cyber security. In addition, Russia's illegal invasion of the territory of Ukraine significantly united the EU member states, with a common position and concerted action to take effective steps to support Ukraine, unlike other cases, such was at the time of the US invasion of Iran, the EU member states did not have common positions and therefore could not reach a consensus. As well as they could not agree on the issue of recognition of Kosovo. However, in the case of Ukraine, they unanimously supported all the sanctions that would significantly weaken Russia in this war, about 40 countries have introduced sanctions against Putin's war, which deals the biggest blow to the Russian economy, which concerns: trade, market access, membership in international financial institutions, crypto assets, luxury goods exports, and the metallurgy and energy sectors (Politico-EU, 2022).

The strengthened role and support of the European Union in terms of cyber security is also noteworthy, where Russia takes an advanced role in the direction of cyber attacks. Putin, traditionally, uses to his advantage the dependence of European countries on Russian natural resources, which leads to the start of hostilities on his part, mainly in the winter period (Crimea - February 20, Ukraine - February 24). Moscow creates a syndrome of fear and thus tries to indirectly influence the will of political actors (Politico-EU, 2022).

Russia began using active measures, including cyber-attacks, espionage, and disinformation, before military attacks. Putin aimed to disrupt the proper functioning of state institutions, to dismantle the national security system of Ukraine; In addition, access to vital services and reliable information was restricted for Ukrainians. All this would contribute to the loss of trust in the state, the conduct of military operations, and, ultimately, the conquest of Ukraine. The use of non-military means was 4 times higher than the number of military means. Before the siege of Mariupol, telephone messages were sent to the population with the content - your government has abandoned you. By fighting against Ukrainian "disinformation", Russia justified the attack on the TV tower in Kyiv. Several times there was black-mail with the use of radioactive substances and nuclear weapons (EEAS public conference on 'Beyond Disinformation, 2023)

Russia has now begun to use military force on a larger scale in various directions of hybrid warfare, such as Destruction of the facility - by hacking the power grid, physical infrastructure, and civil systems; Interruption of access to the system - by spreading denial of services about cyber-attacks and the so-called "fishing" and password retrieval operations; Dissemination of panic-inducing misinformation - text messages about service outages, death of loved ones; bomb threats; Propaganda - fake accounts and posts on social networks, government-commissioned articles (The Wall Street Journal, 2022).

In 2022, Ukraine has significantly changed the tactics of combating Russia's hybrid attacks: 1) Ukrainian President Volodymyr Zelensky explained in his speeches that the victory of Russia will be the defeat not only of Ukraine but of the entire Western world. The activation of this rhetoric brought Ukraine international trust and support. 2) Ukraine has used a variety of social media methods to combat Russian propaganda, it has confronted Russia in all dimensions of the war. It is also worth noting the daily active communication of the President of Ukraine with his society and the whole world, the active distribution of photo-video materials contributed to the perception of Russian brutality among the people and turned the tragedy of Ukraine into a world tragedy. This is where the footage depicting the events that took place in Abkhazia in the 1990s of Georgia appeared, which could not be disseminated at the time and was always discussed in terms of a national tragedy, and this comparison once again made clear the importance of conducting an information campaign for a country in a state of war. 3) The West has provided extensive support to Ukraine through the transfer of software, IT equipment, and training. Along with private sector assistance, real-time cyber intervention by European and US cyber agencies was critical. Since Russia did not expect this length of the war, Ukraine was not perceived as a serious advance, initially, its cyber-attacks against Ukraine were weak and poorly prepared. Western economic sanctions played a big role, and the flow of Russian IT experts hurt Russia's hybrid war. 4) These actions of Ukraine made it clear that the border between the West and Russia passed through it. The defeat of Ukraine in a war with Russia would be a great danger for the Baltic countries and Poland because Russia will not stop its military expansion. These threats are also evidenced by the fact that Sweden and Finland applied for NATO membership (EEAS public conference on 'Beyond Disinformation, 2023).

At a disinformation conference in Brussels on February 7, the EU's high representative for foreign policy and security, Joseph Borrell, announced the development of a new platform to combat the transmission of false information. In 2022, with the help of the European Parliament, they started the "EuvsDisinfo" campaign, where they mainly discuss the manipulative news spread from Russia and China, including in the Georgian language.

The idea of the new platform is that it will be a decentralized "space" where cyber security agencies, non-governmental organizations of different countries, and representatives of other sectors will be able to exchange information. Local delegations of the European Union will unite experts who will work on this topic. Additionally, this information must be available in all languages. On this platform, any interested person will be able to thoroughly study specific fake news and analyze the reason and purpose of spreading fake information. This will simplify the recognition of disinformation and will be a new "mechanism" in the fight against it.

The first report on Foreign Information Manipulation and Interference Threats was published in 2023. According to the report, the "disturbing" cooperation between China and Russia includes manipulation of the European Union and blaming the consequences of the war on the West (Josías D., Guerrero V., 2022).

Important and noteworthy messages from the conference were recorded: The Russian government is trying to make people believe that they did not attack Ukraine and are only trying to protect their own country; The degree of freedom of expression and media in Russia is reduced, and this is especially important during the war, because Russian citizens know virtually nothing about the war and victims of Russia in Ukraine; During the years the Russian government has been actively funding disinformation, thousands of people are using this system as a weapon, and it's really like a real weapon, disinformation hurts and kills, it robs people of the ability to analyze what's really going on; One of the last independent media to survive the Russian regime was declared an "undesirable organization", anyone who tries to tell the truth is a "foreign agent"; The Kremlin regime not only controls information at the internal level, but also constantly tries to discredit international organizations and foreign partners (European Union, 2023)

CONCLUSION

Russia today is not noticeably different from Russia in 2014, which cannot be said for Ukraine. The takeover of Crimea proved to be a painful lesson in fighting a Russian hybrid war. Ukraine began to respond to all forms of attacks in 2022, employing non-military tactics as weapons of war. He demonstrated to us, through his efforts and the help of the West, that it is possible to fight Russia's hybrid war effectively. Volodymyr Zelensky underlined in his statement to the US Congress that Ukraine is still alive and fighting; he called this the first joint win and proclaimed Russia a loser in the battle of international opinion (GFSIS, 2022).

For this purpose, the European Union gives general recommendations to its member states, namely: for the short-term period - to design, evaluate and support the state cyber security strategy. as well as the measures that are necessary to be carried out within the framework of the strategy;

- They should make sure that the proposals and regulations made by the state body responsible for cyber security will be considered and accepted;
- The scope of action, the goals of the strategy, and the very term "cyber security" should be clearly defined; - To ensure coordinated and coordinated cyber security cooperation, member states should cooperate, and they should have a close relationship with the European Union Commission; - The strategy should take into account the scientific community, industrial and economic representatives and civil interests; - It is necessary to recognize the fact that cyberspace and cyber security are constantly evolving, and therefore the strategy constantly needs to be edited and revised to adapt it to new challenges.

It is necessary to take into account the fact that constantly existing risks and new threats allow the development and improvement of information systems for the public, private, and civil sectors; To support the EU Commission in the work, implementation, and creation of the Internet Security Strategy. It is necessary to avoid duplication of measures and focus on new problems and challenges and the strategy be used accordingly and act on raising the level of national and European security; For the long-term period: To achieve and formulate common goals for the EU as a whole in the future, it is necessary to develop and agree on a common definition of "cyber security" and related terminology (Luiijf, H, Besseling, K. 2011).

It is necessary to take into account the fact that the cyber security strategies of the European Union and its member states should not contradict the goals of the international community and human rights, however, at the same time, they should support the fight against cyber security problems at the global level. For the implementation of the cyber security strategy, close cooperation between the private and public sectors is necessary, which at the state and general EU level should be carried out through the means of information exchange, sharing of advanced technologies and practical knowledge, as well as the closeness of scientific circles and joint work on the problem.

As mentioned above, ENISA will develop a special guide (Good Practices Guide) for the EU Commission and Member States to create a strategy. This guide provides recommendations and best practices for designing, supporting, and implementing a national cybersecurity strategy. It is a useful tool and practical advice for those who are responsible for or involved in strategy design. The guide is being developed with the participation and support of stakeholders from the private and public sectors across Europe. The international experts who conduct an interim analysis of ENISA's recommendations also participate in the development of the manual.

Unfortunately, the war between Russia and Ukraine continues, therefore all of the concerns mentioned above are still active. The variety of hybrid warfare methods and the ability to change them raises the possibility of cyber-attacks. The shift in Russia's use of military and non-military measures - focused on conventional warfare - emphasizes the necessity to arm Ukraine with contemporary combat weapons. Russia is also likely to broaden its destructive capabilities and "retaliate" against anyone who assists Ukraine. The Western response to these threats is still vital (GFSIS, 2022).

REFERENCES

Barry, M., Vinton, G., David, D., Robert, E., Kleinrock, L., & Daniel, C. (1997). *Brief History of the Internet.* Cybersecurity Strategy of the European Union: An Open, Safe and Secure Cyberspace. Retrieve from: https://eeas.europa.eu/archives/docs/policies/eu-ybersecurity/cybsec_comm_en.pdf

Čižik, T. (2017). *Information Warfare - New Security Challenge for Europe.* Retrieved from: https://www.researchgate.net/publication/322695565_Information_Warfare_-_New_Security_Challenge_for_Europe

EU. (2023). *Information Manipulation.* Retrieved from. https://audiovisual.ec.europa.eu/en/video/I-236532

European Commission. (2023). *2020 - Press release - New EU Cybersecurity Strategy and new rules to make physical and digital critical entities more resilient, Brussels EEAS public conference on 'Beyond Disinformation.* EU Responses to the Threat of Foreign.

European Council. (2022). *Cybersecurity: How the EU tackles cyber threats.* Author.

European Strategy. (2012). *Proposal on a European Strategy for Internet Strategy.* Retrieve from: http://ec.europa.eu/governance/impact/planned_ia/docs/2012_infso_003_european_internet_security_strategy_en. pdf

GFSIS. (2022). *EU's role in Russia-Ukraine War.* Retrieve from: https://gfsis.org.ge//events/live/view/1396

Højsgaard, T. (2015). *Cyber-security in the European Region: Anticipatory Governance and Practices.* Academic Press.

Josías, D., & Guerrero, V. (2022). *Ukraine Conflict: Hybrid Warfare and Conventional Military intervention.* Retrieved from: https://ceeep.mil.pe/2022/07/07/ukraine-conflict-hybrid-warfare-and-conventional-military-intervention/?lang=en

Luiijf, H., & Besseling, K. (2011). Ten National Cyber Security Strategies: compassion. *CRITIS 2001 – 6th International Conference on Critical Information Infrastructures Security.*

Michael, W., & Antoniou, T. (1994). *The Laws of War: A Comprehensive Collection of Primary Documents on International Laws Governing Armed Conflict.* Academic Press.

Politico. (2022). *War in Ukraine: a watershed moment for European defense policy and transatlantic security?* https://www.politico.eu/event/war-in-ukraine/

The New York Times. (2022). *Russia's recent aggressiveness against Ukraine has reignited the discussion about 'hybrid warfare'.* Author.

KEY TERMS AND DEFINITIONS

European Union: A supranational political and economic union of 27 member states that are located primarily in Europe. The union has a total area of 4,233,255 km2 (1,634,469 sq mi) and an estimated total population of nearly 447 million. The EU has often been described as a *sui generis* political entity (without precedent or comparison) combining the characteristics of both a federation and a confederation.

European Union Cyber Security Strategy: A key component of Shaping Europe's Digital Future, the Recovery Plan for Europe and the EU Security Union Strategy, the Strategy will bolster Europe's collective resilience against cyber threats and help to ensure that all citizens and businesses can fully benefit from trustworthy and reliable services and digital tools. Whether it is the connected devices, the electricity grid, or the banks, planes, public administrations, and hospitals Europeans use or frequent, they deserve to do so with the assurance that they will be shielded from cyber threats.

Chapter 13
Understanding US Cyber Security Policies During the Donald J. Trump and Biden–Harris Administrations

Tamar Karazanishvili
International Black Sea University, Georgia

ABSTRACT

Cybersecurity threats are one of the main national security, public safety, and economic challenges every nation faces in the 21st century. The Russia-Ukraine War becomes a defining feature of the US national cyber security strategy too. The purpose of this chapter is to analyze the increasing role of cybersecurity in US politics. It is evident that US cybersecurity strategies at a national level seems to be increasing across multiple sectors too. The chapter analyses Trump's and Biden's national cyber security strategies and challenges. It deals with different initiatives of both presidential administrations and the implications on national security of the country. The chapter focuses on the measures taken by US politicians in strengthening cybersecurity at a national level and combating both state or non-state-sponsored cyber threats.

INTRODUCTION

Cyber security became one of the top national security issues of the 21st century. The Russia-Ukraine war became another threat globally for states to think about cyber security strategies and it is the defining feature of the US national cyber security strategy too.

Due to enduring uncertainties and differences of authority and accountability on different levels, managing cyber insecurities continues to be the most challenging governance issue in contemporary politics. Cavelty M. and Wenger A. define in their book (2022) that the cyber security is "transboundary in nature, occur[s] at multiple levels across sectors, between institutions, and will impact all actors, both public and private, in complex, interconnected, and often highly politicized ways". As it evolves at

DOI: 10.4018/978-1-6684-8846-1.ch013

the intersection between fast-paced technological development, the political and strategic use of these tools by state and non-state actors, and the various attempts by the state and its bureaucracies, society, and the private sector to define appropriate responsibilities, legal boundaries, and acceptable rules of behavior for this space (Cavelty M., Wegner A. 2022).

Cavelty M. (2022) states that cyberspace is a complex system that is influenced by both human and technical factors. "The security of cyberspace is not just a technical problem. It is also a social and political problem. There is still much research to be done on how to secure cyberspace". Besides, cyberspace is not independent from other systems. This makes it vulnerable to cyberattacks that can have a cascading effect on other systems. Cyber security is a key national security issue because it is also a social and political problem. As Cavelty mentions in his book, the cyber-incidents during the US elections in 2016 highlighted the importance of cyber security for democratic processes; during the US elections in 2016 - attributed to the Russian government as well as semi-state actors - started a new chapter in the cyber security debate. "The hack and leak operations highlighted the issue of strategic manipulation – also called influence operations – as a threat to democratic processes". Current technological environment affords different actors with new opportunities (Cavelty M., Wegner A. 2022).

In addition, the cyber security discourse has changed considerably over the last 20 years: "Cyber security is moving upward in the political agenda and expanding sideways as a problem area to a multitude of additional policy domains with advancing digitization" (Cavelty D. 2019).

Beyond the technical realm, cyber security has become a type of security that refers to offensive and defensive activities of state and non-state actors in cyberspace, serving the pursuit of wider security political goals through the exploitation of various related opportunities. The role of the state in cyber security matters remains politically contested because cyber security is not only about national security; as the question is whether who should have the role, and what kind of role, they should have in different governance arrangements that aim to enhance national and international security. Obviously, states alone cannot ensure an increase of cyber security, not least because many crucial networks are in private hands. Hence, cyber security politics are defined by national and international negotiation processes about the boundaries of responsibilities of state, economic, and societal actors and the agreement or disagreement over the means these actors use (Cavelty M., Wegner A. 2022).

Consequently, analyzing current cybersecurity challenges as well as the US role, as a global actor in world politics, on cyber security priorities, strategies and policies is crucial as it is mentioned above it includes the social, technical as well as political fragmentations. The given chapter aims to analyze Donald J. Trump's and Biden-Harris' Administrations' cybersecurity policies.

Cyber Security in World Politics

Despite different approaches taken by various countries in terms of cybersecurity, politics and the approaching cyberwar, it's obvious that cybersecurity has solidified as one of the top national security challenges of the 21st century.

Certainly, different communities interpret "security" in cybersecurity differently. On a fundamental level, digital technology security is based on risk management techniques created by computer professionals to help make computers and computer networks more reliable. Yet, recent major cybersecurity incidents, including the attacks on healthcare institutions, show that cybersecurity is also very much about protecting people and their interests, not just information security. Cybersecurity keeps evolving as a politically relevant issue and it does that at the junction of rapid advances in technology, political and strategic use of these instruments by state and non-state actors, and various state and private sector efforts to describe appropriate responsibilities, legal perimeters, and proper norms of conduct. (Kjaersgaard, 2022)

With the actual war that's going on between Russia and Ukraine it's clear that a world cyberwar is, on many levels, obvious. One of the most serious risks nations face today is state-sponsored cyber warfare, which is developing against the sharp increase in geopolitical and geoeconomic tensions. State and non-state actors now have greater technical expertise, motives, and economic ability than ever before to disrupt a country's essential infrastructure. An attack on key infrastructure in one part of a country can cause major problems in other areas. Clearly, the United States' recent moves have strengthened its position as a key player in the future cyberwar. (Kjaersgaard, 2022)

According to Fick N. et al. (2022), in the weeks before the Russian invasion of Ukraine, malware that can erase hard drives was found in Ukrainian government networks; hackers conducted spear-phishing campaigns against Ukraine's defense partners; threat actors pre-positioned themselves in supply chains for future attacks on Ukraine and the North Atlantic Treaty Organization (NATO); and distributed denial of service attacks briefly rendered the websites of banks and government organizations inaccessible. Russian hackers disrupted ViaSat, a provider of broadband satellite internet services, in the early hours of the invasion, and the effects spread from Ukraine to Germany and other parts of Europe. In early April, Ukrainian defenders prevented a destructive attack on Ukraine's power grid. According to research from Microsoft, six groups linked to the Russian government conducted hundreds of operations designed to degrade Ukrainian institutions and disrupt access to information and critical services. In some instances, Russia's cyberattacks were "strongly correlated and sometimes directly timed with its kinetic military operations." Cybercrime on its own has become a threat to national security (Fick N., 2022).

US Cyber Security Challenges and Capabilities

Cybersecurity is becoming increasingly important in world politics. As Cavelty (2022) mentions, it is a major national security, public safety, and economic challenge. Cyberspace is a defining feature of modern life, and individuals and communities worldwide connect, socialize, and organize themselves through it. The need for cybersecurity is growing, and it can be used to gain national interests, achieve state goals, or influence adversaries.

Cyberspace is a defining feature of modern life. Individuals and communities worldwide connect, socialize, and organize themselves in and through cyberspace. The need for cybersecurity is growing ranging from particular cases to national and international - becoming the main problem of diplomacy and world politics, as the instrument to gain national interests, to achieve state's national interest, or as the tool to influence the adversaries' perception (Cavelty M., Wegner A. 2022).

Since 2020, the Covid-19 pandemic has re-shaped the life of people. In February 2022, another context came forth to drive change, in the cyber security market - the Russia-Ukraine war that is clearly driving the growth of the cybersecurity market. According to Fortune Business Insights, the global cyber security market size was USD 139.77 billion in 2021 and is projected to grow from USD 155.83 billion in 2022 to USD 376.32 billion by 2029, exhibiting a CAGR of 13.4% during the 2022-2029 period. (Fortune Business Insights, 2023)

The overall investment in cybersecurity is increasing. Additional security procedures at the state, municipal, and private levels are appropriately promoted by governments in the US and EU. Because of the present security scenario, organizations are beginning to invest more resources and reassess their cybersecurity strategy. (Kjaersgaard, 2022)

The North America cyber security market was valued at USD 62.41 billion in 2020 and is expected to grow due to the rise in high-profile security breaches in the region. Besides, Cloud application security solutions are becoming increasingly popular as businesses look for ways to better protect themselves. (Globe News Wire, 2023) North America is likely to dominate the cyber security market share during the forecast period according to Fortune Business Insights. Number of online e-commerce platforms increases the market growth in US and Canada, and the government implements advanced network security protocols for enhanced security measures to enterprises. (Fortune Business Insights, 2023)

Figure 1. North America cyber security market size, 2019-2030
Source: Market Research Report (Fortune Business Insights, 2023)

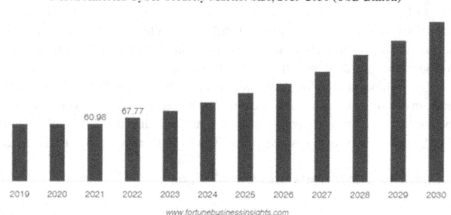

The demand on healthcare, manufacturing, and government cyber security services grew during the pandemic, according to the Report of Fortune Business Insights (2023). Furthermore, the growing investments by end-users and the high demand for enterprise security solutions boost the adoption of security solutions. (Fortune Business Insights, 2023)

US Cyber Security Strategies: Donald J. Trump's and Biden-Harris' Administrations

In 2023, Biden-Harris Administration released the US National Cybersecurity Strategy to secure the full benefits of a safe and secure digital ecosystem for all Americans. In this decisive decade, it is stated that the United States will reimagine cyberspace as a tool to achieve its goals in a way that reflects Americans' values: economic security and prosperity; respect for human rights and fundamental freedoms; trust in our democracy and democratic institutions; and an equitable and diverse society. To realize the vision, fundamental shifts are given in how the United States allocates roles, responsibilities, and resources in cyberspace:

Figure 2. U.S. cyber security market share, by industry, 2022
Source: Market Research Report (Fortune Business Insights, 2023)

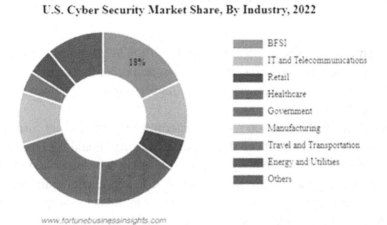

- "We must rebalance the responsibility to defend cyberspace by shifting the burden for cybersecurity away from individuals, small businesses, and local governments, and onto the organizations that are most capable and best-positioned to reduce risks for all of us".
- "We must realign incentives to favor long-term investments by striking a careful balance between defending ourselves against urgent threats today and simultaneously strategically planning for and investing in a resilient future" (The White House, 2023).

The Strategy recognizes that the government must use all tools of national power in a coordinated manner to protect national security, public safety, and economic prosperity. (The White House, 2023)

The cybersecurity strategies that the US adopts at a national level seem to be increasing across multiple sectors. The US Department of State has recently launched the Bureau of Cyberspace and Digital Policy (CDP) in an attempt to address cybersecurity issues. Their main objective will be to handle "the national security challenges, economic opportunities, and implications for US values associated with cyberspace, digital technologies, and digital policy", as well as to "advance policies that protect the integrity and security of the infrastructure of the Internet, serve US interests, promote competitiveness, and uphold democratic values". (The White House, 2023)

Infrastructure (electricity, energy, water supply, manufacturing, transportation, healthcare), an essential domain in the case of cyber - and real, for that matter - war, is also being reinforced. The Operational Technology Cybersecurity Coalition is a new industry group that strives to coordinate efforts to strengthen industrial control system security in order to boost key infrastructure components' resilience. Other initiatives too, such as the United States' Industrial Control Systems Cybersecurity Initiative, show how the US government is pressing for a greater focus on critical infrastructure security (The White House, 2023).

In addition, as it is stated, President Biden has given the National Security Agency (NSA) greater authority to strengthen the cybersecurity of US federal government computer networks that are relevant to national security. The White House has also proposed, among other initiatives:

- New requirements for reporting ransomware payments,
- A revamp of federal government software procurement standards, and
- Plans to create a roadmap for quickly patching recognized, exploited vulnerabilities in federal systems.

As it is stated, the measures taken by US are all solid, and will help to strengthen their cybersecurity at a national level and combat both state and non-state-sponsored cyber threats more effectively. However, Russia has formidable cyber skills, in the context of a (cyber)war with the Bear, thus the US shouldn't stop here. (The White House, 2023)

On March 3, the Biden administration released Interim National Security Strategic Guidance. Regarding cybersecurity, the document stated that the cybersecurity should be a top priority, strengthening capability, readiness, and resilience in cyberspace. Elevating cybersecurity as an imperative across the government, working together to manage and share risk, and encouraging collaboration between the private sector and the government "at all levels in order to build a safe and secure online environment for all Americans". Oriented on investments in the infrastructure and defending the nation against malicious cyber activity. Renewing commitment to international engagement on cyber issues, working together with allies and partners to uphold existing and shape new global norms in cyberspace. "And we will hold actors accountable for destructive, disruptive, or otherwise destabilizing malicious cyber activity, and respond swiftly and proportionately to cyberattacks by imposing substantial costs through cyber and non cyber means" (Biden Jr., 2021).

From George W. Bush administration to the end of Donald Trump's presidency, the United States promoted the idea that the internet should be free from government regulation and censorship. This agenda was both economic and political. Economically, the US government supported a laissez-faire approach to internet regulation, believing that the market should be allowed to operate freely. Politically, the US government promoted the idea that the internet should be a space for free speech, similar to the First Amendment to the US Constitution. In 2006, the Bush administration established the Global Internet Freedom Task Force to promote the free flow of data and funded grants for circumventing censorship. While, Barack Obama administration also had its own NetFreedom Task Force and spent over $100 million on encryption and anti-censorship technologies. (Nathaniel Fick, 2022) According to Fick N. et al (2022) from the earliest days of the ARPANET through the 1990s, the United States shaped the development of the internet to conform with both its national interests and its unique global image. For the last two decades, the United States continued to promote its vision of a single, open, interoperable, secure, and reliable global network, even as much of the world began to push back against this ideal (Fick N., 2022).

In April 2022, the Biden administration along with sixty-one countries issued a Declaration for the Future of the Internet. The signatories committed themselves to supporting "a future for the Internet that is an [sic] open, free, global, interoperable, reliable, and secure," as well as to protecting human rights online, securing individuals' privacy, and maintaining secure and reliable connectivity. The declaration reaffirms a positive vision of a "single interconnected communications system for all of humanity" that fosters innovation and economic growth, promotes creativity, reinforces democratic governance, and provides unfettered access to knowledge. As the author states, "the United States needs to mobilize partners around a proactive vision of what it desires to accomplish in cyberspace... the United States needs to develop a path forward based on the reality of the internet today" (Fick N., 2022).

Fick also emphasizes that since the Bill Clinton administration, policymakers and legislators have attempted to improve information sharing between the public and private sectors, define authorities and build cyber capacity in the federal government, and raise security standards in critical infrastructure networks. Besides, the Cyberspace Solarium Commission, established by the 2019 National Defense Authorization Act (NDAA), offered more than eighty recommendations as part of a strategy of "layered cyber deterrence." Twenty-five of the commission's recommendations have been codified into law, including the establishment of a Senate-confirmed national cyber director within the Executive Office of the President. In March 2022, President Joe Biden signed legislation mandating critical infrastructure owners to report within seventy-two hours if they were hacked or within twenty-four hours if they made a ransomware payment.

Even as the free and open internet loses ground, the United States and Europe remain divided over the legitimate role of privacy, antitrust, industry promotion, and data localization regulations. Despite a shared assessment of the threat of Chinese and Russian cyber operations and a commitment to the protection of human rights online, these unresolved issues have made it difficult to present a common front. Moreover, a number of democracies and more open societies have pursued new rules for technology companies on content, data, and competition, which has often resulted in limits of free expression and greater access to private data by government agencies (Fick N., 2022).

President Biden has made cybersecurity a top priority for his administration at all levels of government. To support this commitment, and to reflect that enhancing the nation's cybersecurity resilience is a top priority for the Department of Homeland Security (DHS), Secretary Mayorkas issued a call to action dedicated to cybersecurity in his first month in office. This call to action focused on addressing the immediate threat of ransomware and on building a more robust and diverse workforce (Homeland Security, 2021). It should be noted that the United States Department of Homeland Security is charged to create a national cybersecurity strategy policy. Finally, as Buresh states (2021) the US Federal government needs to take an active role in "ensuring that the cyberspace is both secure and resilient" as America experiences cyber threats daily (Buresh, 2021).

We should also focus on U.S. Cyber Command, released in 2018, as a strategic vision, announcing the concept of persistent engagement. Cyber Command would maintain "the initiative in cyberspace by continuously engaging and contesting adversaries and causing them uncertainty wherever they maneuver". Or, as General Paul Nakasone, commander of CYBERCOM, stated about the implementation of the strategy "to protect our most critical public and private institutions from threats that continue to evolve in cyberspace, we cannot operate episodically. While we cannot ignore vital cyber defense missions, we must take this fight to the enemy, just as we do in other aspects of conflict" (U.S. Cyber Command, 2018). To enable this strategy, the Trump administration relaxed restrictions on offensive cyber actions. As Fick mentions, National Security Presidential Memorandum 13 reportedly allowed Cyber Command to undertake actions that fall below the use of force or that would not cause death, destruction, or significant economic upheaval without a lengthy approval process. Provisions in the John McCain Act (2019 NDAA) preauthorize CYBERCOM to take "appropriate and proportional" action in foreign cyberspace to "disrupt, defeat, and deter" an "active, systematic, and ongoing" campaign of attacks on government or private networks. The Trump administration also reportedly issued a presidential finding allowing the CIA more freedom to conduct offensive cyber operations (Fick N., 2022).

Since the announcement of the strategy, Cyber Command, working with the NSA, actively protected the 2018 election, disrupting the Internet Research Agency and other actors. CYBERCOM has also deployed personnel to launch "hunt forward" missions in sixteen countries, including Estonia, Lithuania, Montenegro, and North Macedonia, as well as countries in Asia and the Middle East, to monitor adversary activities. Trump administration officials have argued that CYBERCOM successfully disrupted Russian information operations during the 2018 elections. These successes appear to be tactical, slowing adversaries for a time. (U.S. Cyber Command, 2018) The SolarWinds and Microsoft Exchange Server attacks suggest that the United States continues to fail to impose significant costs on adversaries for cyber espionage operations. The United States' high degree of digital dependency enforces restraint, preventing it from retaliating powerfully against harmful operations in cyberspace (Fick N., 2022).

While the United States has searched for more effective ways to impose costs on attackers, it has also worked to define the rules for responsible state behavior in cyberspace. These efforts have included multilateral and bilateral negotiations as well as public attribution of attacks, indictments, and sanctions. The United States has pursued norms - expectations about behavior that make it possible to hold other states accountable - because arms control agreements, like those used to control conventional or nuclear weapons, will not prove viable in cyberspace. Nuclear arms agreements counted, monitored, and limited the range and number of air-, sea-, land-, and space-based weapons. In contrast, cyber exploits reflect vulnerabilities in computer code and lack transparency. The certainty of verification does not exist, and as a result, the composition of a stable system of arms control in cyberspace becomes a practical impossibility. The United States has enjoyed some success gaining consensus on norms through the UN Group of Governmental Experts on Advancing Responsible State Behavior in Cyberspace in the Context of International Security (GGE) (U.S. Cyber Command, 2018). First established in 2004, the GGE now consists of experts representing twenty-five countries, including the United States, Australia, China, Russia, and the United Kingdom. In 2015, it issued a consensus report on a set of norms that largely reflected the U.S. delegation's position on the application of international law in cyberspace. Eleven norms were formally adopted by the UN General Assembly, including those of state responsibility and the duty to assist, as well as a prohibition of intentionally damaging or impairing others' critical infrastructures or targeting another state's computer emergency response teams during peacetime (Fick N., 2022). While follow-on meetings in 2017 the group was divided over how to apply international law. In 2018 US and Russia submitted proposals for parallel processes, where the United States pushed for the continuation of the GGE; while Russia advocated for an Open-Ended Working Group (OEWG) intended to run through 2025 in which all UN member states could participate. Despite fears of two diverse groups, the OEWG issued a report reaffirming the 2015 GGE consensus. A joint resolution proposed by the United States and Russia endorsed both reports, but meetings in the wake of the Russian war on Ukraine have been contentious, with the United States and its allies calling out Russia for violating the norms against interfering with critical infrastructure (Fick N., 2022).

According to the report of Council on Foreign Relations (2022) growing part of China's ambitious Belt and Road Initiative (BRI) is focused on digital infrastructure. Beijing has identified 5G technology, smart cities, utilization of the Beidou satellite system, communication infrastructure, network connectivity, and telecommunications services as central areas of focus. The United States and its partners also need to address global demands for technology infrastructure. During the Trump administration, U.S. officials warned of the cybersecurity risks of relying on Chinese tech infrastructure, stressing the potential threats of data collection and disruption. As the report underlines, Washington was less successful in providing alternatives to countries attracted by the cheaper prices and reliability of Chinese technology or developing a cybersecurity roadmap for those likely to adopt a mix of U.S. and Chinese hardware, software, and services. The United States and its coalition partners need to create funding mechanisms for the development of digital infrastructure. Congress should consolidate the State Department's foreign assistance funding and add a new line for cyber capacity building in the State, Foreign Operations, and Related Programs appropriations legislation (Fick N., 2022).

According to the report of Council on Foreign Relations (2022), the era of the global internet is over. Washington has worked closely over the last three decades with the private sector and allies to promote a vision of a global, open, secure, and interoperable internet, but the reality of cyberspace is now starkly different. The internet is more fragmented, less free, and more dangerous (Nathaniel Fick, 2022).

As the report of Council on Foreign Relations (2022) underlines, the early advantages the United States and its allies held in cyberspace have largely disappeared. The United States is vulnerable because of high levels of digitalization. Adversaries have adapted more rapidly and have a clear vision of their goals in cyberspace, developing and implementing strategies in pursuit of their interests, and have made it more difficult for the United States to operate unchallenged in this domain. Besides, states are forcing the localization of data, as well as blocking and moderating content. The United States' early lead in internet technologies motivated many countries to promote data residency and other regulations to protect national companies. China has long blocked access to foreign websites, created trade barriers to U.S. technology companies, and given preference to domestic incumbents, which now operate across the globe. European policymakers are increasingly focused on the need for presumptive digital self-sufficiency and data privacy. Beijing and Moscow, in particular, have used the United Nations and other international organizations to promulgate a vision of cyber sovereignty centered on state control over the internet (Nathaniel Fick, 2022).

According to Buresh (2021), for Donald Trump protecting American national security and the prosperity of American economy was important where as President Biden announced that cybersecurity is a top priority for the administration, strengthening the nation's capability, readiness and resilience is imperative. As Buresh emphasizes, President Trump suggested that the federal government work with the private sector to manage critical infrastructure, while President Biden declared that the federal government would collaborate with the private sector to manage and share risks, thereby securing a safe online environment. According to Lin (2021), under President Trump the federal government was asked to update 'National critical infrastructure and resilience research and development plan, emphasizing new cybersecurity approaches to emerging technologies such as the next generation of telecommunications and information communications infrastructure. Trump preferred to improve international cooperation in investigating malicious cyber activities. While President Biden-Harris Administration desired to defend country effectively by delivering opportunities to Americans of diverse circumstances, and preferred the US to reengage with its allies and partners in cyber-issues (Lin, 2021).

According to Buresh and Lin (2021), Biden stressed the significance of diversity in the national cyber talent pool, while he wanted the federal government to invest in cybersecurity. As for Trump, his administration desired the federal government to assist the private sector investment in cybersecurity (Buresh, 2021; Lin, 2021). As Buresh (2021) mentions, the SolarWinds breach that involved nine federal agencies was the reason why the Biden Administration wanted the federal government to take more significant role in national cybersecurity.

According to Mitchell (2020), Cyber threats are changing every year from big four Russia, China, North Korea and Iran, as well as from criminal enterprises, political hacktivists, and even terrorists. And, cyberspace was becoming complex during the Trump administration. Russia's cyber activities from the 2016 election put necessary thought in crafting a true national cyber strategy. The lines between the nation state cyber actors and the "criminals of the dark web" were blurring as all gained access to the same super-advanced cyber weapons. Foreign powers were using the "privateers" or cyber mercenaries to raid America's computer infrastructure. Speaking in the summer of 2018, Phatak said that "1.4% of global GDP was going to cyber criminals and the number was rising". Besides, in 2017, Trump's first year in power, the hacks and viruses in the cyber headlines included consumer credit-rating agency "Equifax, Wannacry, and the devastating NotPetya that used a stolen National Security Agency tool and struck first in Ukraine before taking down transportation and other systems across the globe: Yahoo!, Uber, and the Wikileaks revelations of "CIA Vault 7" and "CIA Vault 8", putting some of the most advanced hacking tools out into the public realm." Besides, crypto-mining operations and other ways to attack US businesses were under the threat in the coming months and years. These were issues and challenges of cybersecurity. As Mitchell states in his book thirty thousand websites were being infected every day, fully 80% of breaches were to pure password security, and 80% of Americans reused their credentials across multiple sites and services. Besides, 90% of email passwords could be cracked in less than 6 hours and Darren Guccione said, CEO of the Chicago-based Keeper Security firm. "Meanwhile, cyber as a policy area was immune". As NSS's Phatak stated Trump's approach to cyber was transactional and not grounded in any principle while Larry Clinton of the industry-based Internet Security Alliance, while steering the political turmoil of the times said, "the Trump administration is going in the right direction on many aspects of cybersecurity" (Mitchell, 2020).

CONCLUSION

According to Lin H. (2021) Biden's document is different from the Trump National Cyber Strategy in two ways (more details are discussed in the above section). First, the Biden document emphasizes the importance of diversity in the national talent base for cyber, whereas the Trump document is silent on the same issue. Second, the Biden document strongly implies government investment in cybersecurity, whereas the Trump document seeks to minimize the notion of government investment in cybersecurity and emphasizes a government role in facilitating private-sector investment in cybersecurity. While at the same time, both documents suggest strong continuity in cyber policy and strategy that suggests more continuity than change between administrations on cyber policy over the past decade and more.

As mentioned above, Donald Trump protected American national security and the prosperity of the American economy while President Biden announced that cybersecurity is a top priority for the administration, strengthening the nation's capability, readiness and resilience is imperative. As Buresh emphasizes, President Trump suggested that the federal government work with the private sector to manage critical infrastructure, while President Biden declared that the federal government would collaborate with the private sector to manage and share risks, thereby securing a safe online environment (Buresh, 2021). Trump preferred to improve international cooperation in investigating malicious cyber activities. While President Biden-Harris Administration desired to defend the country effectively by delivering opportunities to Americans of diverse circumstances, and preferred the US to re-engage with its allies and partners in cyber-issues (Lin, 2021).

To confront the realities of the modern internet and adapt to today's cyber realm, the Task Force recommends an approach resting on three pillars. The first calls for the United States to bring together a coalition of allies and partners around a vision of the internet that preserves a trusted, protected international communication platform. The second pillar calls for the United States to employ more targeted diplomatic and economic pressure on adversaries that choose to attack critical infrastructure. Finally, as is a trend across almost all walks of U.S. policy these days, the United States should put its own prover-bial house in order, blending digital competition policy with national security strategy. The Task Force concludes that the United States cannot afford to wait to reconsider its cyber policy and must instead act urgently to confront the new realities of cyberspace and develop strategies to ameliorate the pressing threat that exists (Fick N., 2022).

Moreover, U.S. strategic, economic, political, and foreign policy interests were served by the global, open internet. Washington long believed that its vision of the internet would ultimately prevail and that other countries would be forced to adjust to or miss out on the benefits of a global and open internet. The United States now confronts a starkly different reality. The utopian vision of an open, reliable, and secure global network has not been achieved and is unlikely ever to be realized. Today, the internet is less free, more fragmented, and less secure (Fick N., 2022).

Furthermore, as Segal (2022) discusses, the war in Ukraine has sparked a debate among analysts about the uses and efficacy of cyber operations during the conflict. Some have argued that cyberattacks have under-delivered; others that attacks, especially the attack against ViaSat, a provider of broadband satel-lite internet services, have in fact been disruptive and effective. Microsoft has released two reports not only detailing Russian cyber espionage efforts, but also stating that cyberattacks are strongly correlated and sometimes directly timed with its kinetic military operations. Still others have argued that the most effective cyberattacks have been those mobilized by Ukraine's IT Army, though the use of hacktivists and proxy actors raises serious questions about the development of norms of responsible state behavior in cyberspace (Segal, 2022).

According to CFR's new Task Force Report on U.S. cyber policy (2022) Cybercrime is a national security risk, and ransomware attacks on hospitals, schools, businesses, and local governments should be seen as such. The members of the Task Force argue that the conflict in Ukraine demonstrates how closely intertwined cyber and information operations are. This has long been central to Russian and Chinese cyber operations; the United States has traditionally separated the two, though this may be gradually changing. Remarking on the conflict, Lieutenant General Charles Moore, Cyber Command deputy commander, noted, "Without a doubt, what we have learned is that cyber-effects operations in conjunction - in more of a combined arms approach - with what we call traditionally information opera-tions, is an extremely powerful tool" (Segal, 2022).

In addition, the Ukraine-Russia war has reinforced another of the task force's major findings: norms of state behavior in cyberspace are more useful in binding friends together than in constraining adversar-ies. The United States and its allies have had some success in defining norms of behavior through the United Nations and other multilateral forum.

While measuring how the U.S. policy should develop in the wake of the Ukraine-Russia war the task force embraces the "defend forward" position developed by Cyber Command under the Trump admin-istration along with targeted diplomatic pressure and self-imposed restraints on some U.S. offensive operations. In particular, the United States should develop a broad effort to erode adversarial capabilities, making them less effective by taking out infrastructure; exposing tools; and creating political, diplomatic, and economic pressure on finances, authorities, and leadership.

Moreover, to address the problem of states that actively harbor cybercriminals or ignore third parties using their digital infrastructure in offensive and criminal campaigns, the United States and its coalition partners could set a policy similar to the response to international terrorism that they will hold account-able any states that provide safe havens or do not cooperate in the takedown of criminal infrastructure or in law enforcement investigations, arrests, and extradition. Washington should exert diplomatic and economic pressure, but under certain circumstances could also reserve the right to take action against infrastructure used by these groups if the countries hosting it will not do so (Segal, 2022).

Policy recommendations provided in the Report of Council on Foreign Relations (2022) are evolutionary. Although a modified strategy assumes that the United States will more proactively use cyber and non-cyber tools to disrupt cyberattacks and that norms are more useful in binding friends and allies together than in constraining adversaries, the strategy also takes into account that the major cyber powers share some interests in preventing certain types of destructive and disruptive attacks. As with the Task Force's recommendations around digital policy, this strategy is more limited, more realistic, and more likely to succeed in achieving finite goals.

REFERENCES

Biden Jr. (2021). *Interim National Security Strategic Guidance*. White House. Retrieved on 2023 from https://www.whitehouse.gov/wp-content/uploads/2021/03/NSC-1v2.pdf

Buresh, D. L. (2021). Comparison of National Security and the Cybersecurity Approaches of the United States under Presidents Trump and Biden versus the National Security and Cybersecurity Approach of Canada. *Journal of Business Management and Economics*, 1-9.

Cavelty, M. D. (2019). The Politics of Cybersecurity: Balancing Different Roles of the State. *St. Antony's International Review*, *15*(1), 37–57. doi:10.1080/13523260.2019.1678855

Cavelty, M. D., & Wagner, A. (2022). *Cyber Security Politics, Socio-Technological Transformations and Political Fragmentation*. Routledge. doi:10.4324/9781003110224

Fortune Business Insights. (2023, March 2). *Globenewswire*. Retrieved from https://www.globenewswire.com/en/news-release/2023/03/02/2619064/0/en/Cyber-Security-Market-Exhibits-13-4-CAGR-to-Hit-USD-376-32-Billion-by-2029.html

Fortune Business Insights. (2023, April 2). *Market Research Report*. Retrieved from https://www.fortunebusinessinsights.com/industry-reports/cyber-security-market-101165

Globe News Wire. (2023, March 2). *Cyber Security Market Exhibits 13.4% CAGR to Hit USD 376.32 Billion by 2029*. Retrieved from https://www.globenewswire.com/en/news-release/2023/03/02/2619064/0/en/Cyber-Security-Market-Exhibits-13-4-CAGR-to-Hit-USD-376-32-Billion-by-2029.html

Homeland Security. (2021, March 31). *Confronting Realities: A Vision for Cybersecurity Resilience*. Retrieved 2023, from https://www.dhs.gov/medialibrary/assets/videos/24094

Kjaersgaard, M. (2022, June 16). *Heimdal Security CEO*. Retrieved from https://heimdalsecurity.com/blog/the-role-of-cybersecurity-in-world-politics/

Lin, H. (2021). Comparing the Biden administration's Interim National Security Strategic Guidance with Trump's National Cyber Strategy. Academic Press.

Mitchell, C. (2020). *In the Age of Trump the Unraveling of America's National Security Policy*. Rowman&Littlefield.

Nathaniel Fick, J. M. (2022). *Confronting Reality in Cyberspace*. Council on Foreign Relations.

Segal, A. (2022). *How Should U.S. Cybersecurity Policy Develop?* Council on Foreign Relations.

The White House. (2023, March 1). *US National Cybersecurity Strategy*. Author.

U.S. Cyber Command. (2018). *Achieve and Maintain Cyberspace Superiority*. Retrieved 2023, from Cyber Command: https://www.cybercom.mil/Portals/56/Documents/USCYBERCOM%20Vision%20April%202018.pdf?ver=2018-06-14-152556-010

Chapter 14
Russian Aggressive Cyber–Policy During Russia–Ukraine War

Ilona Chukhua
International Black Sea University, Georgia

ABSTRACT

The most important details in this text are that Russia could make a military impact through cyber operations, but this was not exposed due to limitations created for Russia, the protection system of Ukraine, and support from partners. Russian cyber strategies and objectives regarding Ukraine have been addressed in the same direction as Ukraine space, and the method of collection of intelligence was the main objective for Moscow in the process of the Russia-Ukraine war, but it also had minimal benefits for the aggressor. Additionally, Russia appears to rely on non-cyber sources of target intelligence, despite previous thoughts which said that Russia used malware against the Ukrainian positions. In general, cyber-policy has both positive and negative sides, but it has a very negative impact in the case of Russia's war against Ukraine.

INTRODUCTION

Since the beginning of the war, Ukraine has struggled with an increase in cyberattacks, with Russia carrying out at least 10 attacks per day (Independent, 2023). More concretely, more than 4,500 cyberattacks have been recorded since the invasion (Independent, 2023).

The goals of cyberattacks are different: government resources, critical infrastructure facilities, etc.

The Security Service of Ukraine (SSU) declared that this institute recorded 800 cyber-attacks in 2020, about 2,000 in 2021, and more than 4,500 since the invasion. As a result, SSU opened more than 64,000 criminal cases against Russian forces, almost half of which are war crimes cases (Forbes, 2023).

Furthermore, the SBU has uncovered or detained 360 enemy agents since the invasion began last February.

In general, Russian hackers have infiltrated the Ukrainian military, energy, and other critical computer networks. Western cybersecurity experts predicted that if hostilities broke out, Ukraine would experience devastating cyberattacks.

DOI: 10.4018/978-1-6684-8846-1.ch014

In early November 2022, the German government allocated €1 billion from its 2023 budget to support Ukraine. This money will be used to protect against Russian cyber-attacks and collect evidence of war crimes.

Ukraine is documenting Russian hacking as part of a plan to prosecute Moscow in an international court.

For more than 1 year of all-out war, Russian hackers have not achieved strategic goals. in 2022, the Security Service neutralized hundreds of Russian cyber-attacks and cyber incidents on Ukrainian energy facilities, of which almost 30 could become supercritical. since October, 2022, systemic cyber-attacks of the Russian Federation have been carried out on the energy infrastructure of Ukraine (Forbes, 2022).

Russia's Wartime Cyber Operations in Ukraine

Military Impacts, Influences, and Implications

Firstly, it can be evaluated how Russia had possibility to make military impact by cyber operations, which almost was not exposed. There are many reasons of it, such as limitations created for Russia, the protection system of Ukraine and support from the partners addressed to Ukraine in many directions which has been aimed to make strong protective shell, the specific characteristics of this Ukraine-Russia war, its structural elements of cyber-policy circumstances and warfare in general. The cyber policy of Russia, like a cyberattacks effected in favor of Moscow which was objected for Moscow's military aspirations and military operations in Ukraine. It can be said that cyber fires and cyber war are equivalent of military attacks or is sometimes it is the strong catalysator or more than directly visible actions on the combat arena. In many cases, Russian cyber strategies and objectives regarding the Ukraine has been addressed the same directions of Ukraine space, battle try via kinetic capabilities which implies weapons, for example transportation infrastructure, electricity and communications with other sources as well. This everything is very dangerous and it can ensure a lot of harm. In generally everything has positive and negative sides, cyber-policy is between them, but it has very negative impact in case of Russia's war against of Ukraine. The military approaches of Russia rapidly denied any kind of goals which would reduce damages. Cyberattacks of Moscow did not achieve systematic implications and mostly they became less productive, in some situations with limitations of capabilities than it would be in the system of kinetic fires.

Instead of cyber fires, method of collection of intelligence most probably was the main objective for Moscow in the process of Russia-Ukraine war, but it also had very minimal benefits for aggressor. Although intelligence processes are more difficult for outsiders to observe and evaluate, Moscow artillery appears to rely on non-cyber sources of target intelligence, despite previous thoughts which said that Russia used malware to against the Ukrainian positions (Bateman, 2022). From the outside, it seems that maybe Russian missile powers have gained cyber-derived intelligence, however this one did not have something valuable for the main decisions and action of Moscow. Also, it's so interesting here that even influence actions, which are part of Moscow's cyber doctrine, have received only minimal support from Russian hackers and more generally, Russia's comprehensive approach to war, which implies each step from planning its campaign to occupying territory, assumes that major military decisions are not guided by a rigorous intelligence process (Bateman, 2022). Despite of the limitations created for the Russia's cyber policy productiveness, probably the most significant are not adequate Moscow cyber capacity, also weak sides in Russia's non-cyber spaces and special protective powers of Ukraine and its supporter countries. To have a significant impact on a war of this magnitude, cyber operations would need to proceed at a pace that Russia seems capable of only a few weeks at most. Somehow it is obvious that Russian President Vladimir Putin and his military appear unwilling or maybe unable to plan and conduct the war on the very intelligence-driven approach which is optimal for cyber operations (Huntley, 2023). Ukraine, from its side, has had benefits from a resilient digital ecosystem, years of cybersecurity investment, and an unprecedented cyber support from a variety of the world's most capable companies, governments and countries (Bateman, 2022). If we imagine that with many factors involved, even if a few circumstances had changed, it is possible that the overall military utility of Russian cyber operations would not have improved. The fact is that the war continues, while Russian intelligence gathering is truly the biggest cyber threat to Ukraine. It is logical to think that Russian hackers may have even greater influence, especially if they are able to collect high-value intelligence, which Moscow in turn uses effectively.

It is possible to assume that hackers will be able to obtain geographic, geolocation data at a reasonable and convenient time for them, which will allow the assassination of President Volodymyr Zelensky or the timely and accurate targeting of Ukrainian forces, they can conduct hacking and leak operations that lead to the release of sensitive military information to the Ukrainian and Western public, such as Ukraine's combat losses, internal strife or military maneuvers, or receive valuable information about Ukraine's perceptions and intentions, which could help Moscow in future negotiations, among other scenarios (Dougherty, 2022). Russian cyber fires are actually a less serious threat, however, such attacks could become more frequent if Moscow turns its full cyber capabilities toward Ukraine, of course, because of other benefits or if it gets better at using cybercriminals. Russia's war in Ukraine is clearly a lesson for the whole world in scope of military cyber operations, but it must be applied in national contexts and considered alongside a range of relevant case studies and research. Cyber intelligence collection seems to have much more potential than cyber fires in order to support different wartime military objectives and enhance the likelihood of their execution, although this likely depends on competent analysis and decision-making processes. Militaries with high capabilities, professionalism and readiness in both cyber and kinetic disciplines such as the United States and Israel have previously used high targets for cyber operations. Although even top-level militaries seem to have their greatest cyber successes only in tightly circumscribed contexts, based on this, there are opinions that cyberspace, as one of the areas of war that is equivalent to land. If there is a likelihood that cyber operations are unlikely to expand dramatically and recover quickly, it may not aspire to conduct wartime fires in major conflicts. However, it can prioritize more selective fires in peacetime, gray area or pre-war circumstances, or non-fire activities such as cyber defense and intelligence collection. In general, it is desirable that states' investments in cyber intelligence collection be matched with equal efforts in intelligence analysis, military planning, and strategic decision-making (Bateman, 2022). With the diversity of cyber capabilities, nations can acquire and collect more information than they could, accurately interpret, and effectively use in war. At such times, it is possible to carry out extensive institutional reforms, such as the renewal of analytical trading, the introduction of professionals or the fight against corruption, often this will be more important than further technical improvements in cyber collection. States that cannot afford these reforms may find that sophisticated military cyber intelligence capabilities are not worth the effort. At the same time, cyber units must be fully integrated into all intelligence processes, which will focus them on information needs that cannot be met by other means. For cyber defenders, the war in Ukraine is a reference point that can be used to revise and refine previous assumptions about those particular wars. Their main task is to review the possible capabilities of potential adversaries in times of conflict, leveraging cyber operations, taking into account Russia's humble experience.

Researchers and analysts are still relying on reports from the Ukrainian government, allied governments, cybersecurity companies and journalists to understand Russia's cyber operations and their implications for Ukraine, but this is half of the topic, cause the whole process is more difficult and complicated than anybody can imagine.

About the War Processes in Ukraine

On February 24, 2022, Russia invaded Ukraine, after which most Western analysts downplayed the role of offensive cyber operations in Moscow's larger war effort. They viewed Russian cyber operations as infrequent, as well as crude, unplanned, poorly integrated with activities in other areas defended by Ukraine and its foreign partners, and ultimately ineffective compared to the large-scale death and destruction caused by physical weapons. There is speculation as to how and why Russian cyber operations in Ukraine failed, but most agree that the key point here is a military one, implying that the cyber operations did not significantly contribute to Moscow's campaign objectives. James Lewis, for example, found that "cyber operations provided little benefit" to Russia and "failed to achieve Russian objectives" in the war (Bateman, 2022). Here we can mention that similarly to the abovementioned thought, Nadia Kostiuk and Aaron Brantley wrote that Russia's cyberattacks had "no strategic impact on Ukraine's combat capabilities" and "does not appear to have affected the course of the war" (Bateman, 2022). The Cyber Peace Institute, which maintains a public database of Russian cyber operations against Ukraine, declared it was not "a major role . . . tactical achievements" (Huntley, 2023). Even Microsoft, which describes Russia's cyber use during the conflict as extensive, skillful, militarily innovative, and very important to history, only had "limited exposure" to the Ukrainian target, yet attacks have failed strategically to disable Ukraine's defenses" (Bateman, 2022). The company concluded that, on a larger scale, the attacks so still have been strategically unsuccessful in disabling Ukraine's defense system. However, it must be said here that not everyone shares these visions. Some believe that cyber efforts against Ukraine during Russia's invasion of Ukraine are wrong. Dissenting researchers describe Russia's cyber operations as large-scale, tactically effective at key moments, and consistent with Moscow's military goals of creating confusion and offense against the Ukrainian government, armed forces, and civilians. Here, for the sake of visibility, we would like to give an example of specific researchers and their thinking, for example, David Cutler and Daniel Black, two NATO intelligence officials, claimed that Russia's greatest military success in cyber operations was in the Ukraine war. Also, the director of the UK General Staff for Communications, Jeremy Fleming, said that the idea that cyber was not a significant factor in the war in Ukraine is wrong (University, 2022). In his view, what is happening between Ukraine and Russia is a hot cyber war in Ukraine, which is being led and carried out by the Russians. This controversy stems to some extent from the partial, conflicting, and evolving information circulating about Russia's wartime cyber operations.

One example of this was the disruption of the Viasat satellite communications network by Russian military intelligence on February 24, a cyber event of war. Viktor Zhora, Ukraine's top cyber leader, initially said this led to a large loss of communications in the first period of the war. There was no information that the hacker disrupted communications in the Ukrainian army (Reporter, 2023). Dimitri Alperovich told him that it was arguably the most strategically impactful cyber operation, to which James Lewis said that over all it could not be said to have given Russia a military advantage. So, this is the question regarding the Russian cyber policy during the Russia-Ukraine war, is it fail or success? On the one hand, there are cyber skeptics who almost always focus on the inability of Russian hackers to disable Ukrainian decision-making and block critical infrastructure through "shock and awe" tactics

(Hambling, 2022). On the other side are the cyber advocates, who underline any sign of coordination between Russia's kinetic and cyber operations, however inconsistent the manifestations and outcomes.

According to most of the evaluations, it can be interpreted that Russian cyber strategy and appropriate actions have been oriented toward cyber fires. Because of their real-world similarities to kinetic strikes, disruptive or destructive cyberattacks are often thought of as a way to aid cyber forces' military campaigns. But the military must do much more than conduct these attacks and conduct cyber operations in wartime. Identifying, studying, and analyzing the cyber operations of Russia in the Ukraine war is truly a very complicated process. There are many factors, such as the Ukrainian government, partner states, cybersecurity companies, and so on. There is very little information and data on what effect Russia's aggressive cyber campaigns have had on morale in Ukraine, helping to undermine it or increasing the pushback against the invasion. Moreover, the results of a cyber operation do not always reveal the true intentions of the perpetrator. For example, it is a fact that Russian cyber jamming of the telecommunications network occurred, although this may have been a deliberate attempt to degrade Ukrainian command and control before the war. Or it may be planned differently, and it may be linked to broader efforts to isolate and degrade the Ukrainian population. Also, it could just be a random result due to a botched intelligence-gathering operation. The next challenge is that political or commercial visions inevitably shape when and how information about Russian cyber operations is shared. For example, it is worth noting that the Ukrainian government has a strategic calculation to offer a relatively optimistic view of the war so that the Western partners can continue to support it and the Ukrainian people can maintain their morale. Consequently, Kyiv refrained from fully disseminating information about casualties and other combat losses to the public (Bateman, 2022). The same can be said about cyber incidents. There were times when Ukrainian officials boasted of such cyber success that it was almost unbelievable. With all this, there is indeed a market incentive for Western tech companies to present and help support their cyber security in Ukraine, which is highly successful and aimed at strategically important goals. They may also lack military expertise to back up their conclusions. For example, Microsoft has been accused of exaggerating the threat of some Russian cyber operations, as well as overstating the importance of those operations in military history. At the same time, on the contrary, those affected by Russia may want to know the real situation. Cyber-attacks from Russia against Ukraine can be carried out in different ways, such as directly against military assets, communications networks, other computer networks, and military forces, against Industrial Control Systems Cyber and kinetic fire coordination, and Integrated Cyber-Kinetic Fires' efficacy. One of Moscow's methods in Ukraine is to suppress the power of the other side, but we have no known cases of Russian cyber actors directly disrupting military equipment in this space. During the war, Ukraine received and purchased a large number of modern, foreign-made weapons and necessary equipment. Ukraine has been using these military resources against Russia since the Russian invasion, making sense of America's earlier fears that its military and cyber leverage would be at too great a risk in conflicts emanating from Russia or others. Despite everything, there are no real arguments to prove that Russia has successfully carried out cyber-attacks to destroy Ukraine's military space.

Kyiv and its partners have sought to destroy evidence of any cyber-jamming attempts on military equipment. However, likely, Ukraine will have difficulty concealing a large number of cases in this battle arena. One example of this is electronic warfare. Russia has sometimes used a blocking method against Ukraine, even reducing Ukraine's drone capabilities. At the same time, the sources cannot prove the destructive or destructive effect of Russian cyber-attacks against Ukrainian military equipment. Despite all the circumstances under which Ukrainian military equipment has not been directly affected by any known Russian cyber operations, communications systems used by the Ukrainian military, government, and civilian population have suffered cyber disruptions. One of the most notable episodes occurred an hour before the Russian invasion of Ukraine when hackers working in the Main Directorate of the General Staff of the Russian Armed Forces conducted a hacking operation called Viasat (O'Neill Archive, 2022).

Viasat is an American company that owns communications satellites, one of which is KA-SAT. Viasat said Russian hackers caused a partial cyber outage of specific networks. The incident had a huge impact and caused internet disruptions for millions of users in Ukraine, according to Viasat. Even though the bulk of Viasat's disruptions took place outside of Ukraine, Russia's main goal was indeed to block Ukraine's communications as and when Moscow's troops crossed the border and missiles began hitting targets across the country. Mr. Zhora initially expressed the opinion that the Viasat hack caused a huge loss of communications, which many likened to military communications. However, at the same time, the representative of the Zhora agency said that they do not have information that would confirm that the hacking attack has worsened the level of communication in the Ukrainian military (Zetter, 2022).

After that Zhora later clarified that Viasat was only providing a backup connection to the military and that the primary ground networks remained online during the invasion, so the hack had no military impact. But in contrast, sources on the ground presented a different picture regarding the state of military communications at that time. Many Ukrainian ground leaders who participated in the initial defense of Kyiv reported that Russian cyberattacks at the start of the war completely shut down Ukrainian communications and satellite networks.

This facilitated the creation and strengthening of Ukrainian drones, cutting off conventional intelligence channels and leaving officers without connections to the battlefield.

Therefore, it can be said that the blocking method from the Russian side was effective during the attack on Kyiv. From Moscow's side, the combination of two elements, traditional electronic warfare and the Viasat hack, gave Russian forces the upper hand in the early stages of the war. In addition to the high-profile fact of the Viasat hack, another case was thought of, in the framework of which the main Ukrainian Internet service Triolan was the victim of a cyber-attack. After that, Triolan was hacked again by the attackers. Later, a hostile cyber-attack by Russia took place on the country's largest landline telecommunications provider, Ukrtelecom, which is owned by the state. Ukrtelecom said it temporarily suspended services for private customers and business customers. The cyber-attack and remedial measures resulted in an 85 percent loss of connectivity, but service was mostly restored the next day. Kyiv made a statement that all this would not affect military operations (Huntley, 2023). Ukrainians have indeed experienced the destruction or disruption of dozens of important Internet services due to physical attacks on telecommunications equipment and power supplies. However, in general, Ukrainian telecommunication networks - despite all this - are still quite resilient. Beyond communications networks, Russian cyber fires have targeted a wide swath of Ukraine's other government and commercial networks. A clear incident in this regard has been devastating cyber-attacks that wipe out data and render systems inoperable. Moscow carried out such attacks in very large numbers, especially at the beginning of the war. And in June, Microsoft discovered eight different malware targeting various Ukrainian agencies and enterprises. Russia has launched an unprecedented number of devastating cyber-attacks against Ukraine, arguably the largest series ever launched. The staggering scale of Russian cyber fires in Ukraine is well illustrated by the sheer volume of Russian malware. At the beginning of the war, Russia used eight to ten types of destructive malware. Moscow has invested a great deal of effort and resources in conducting wartime cyber-attacks on the Ukrainian government, information technology, energy sector, and financial institutions. The main position from Ukraine was that Russia's cyber-attacks were not effective and they don't have implications for the military space of Ukraine. In contrast, Microsoft disclosed that Russia ultimately destroyed files on hundreds of systems at thousands of organizations in Ukraine. However, Microsoft noted that the impact on victims was only of a limited operational impact nature. Moscow's destructive cyber-attacks in Ukraine had specific characteristics, namely that at the beginning of the war, the attacks were massively concentrated, and then there was a sharp decline. Based on available sources, twenty-two organizations were hit by destructive Russian cyber-attacks in the first days of the war (BURGESS, 2022). However, in the following weeks, only three hits are detected on average. Later, this indicator decreased significantly and reached one.

Cyber Policy Actions and Implications

It is challenging to assess the military effect of each of Russia's destructive cyber-fires without victim-level information. It is conceivable that the initial salvo helped in some way to alleviate some of the initial shock and confusion that Ukraine experienced right after the incursion based solely on the number of attacks and Microsoft's high-level descriptions of their outcomes. However, within a few weeks at most, Russian destructive cyber fires most likely faded into the backdrop of the conflict. Under peacetime or gray zone conditions, even one state-sponsored data deletion attack per week would be noteworthy. But in the context of a significant conflict, it still seems insignificant. Russian forces have occasionally fired hundreds of missiles and tens of thousands of rounds of artillery per week, severely damaging Ukraine's military, civilian populace, and infrastructure. It is unlikely that the trickle of destructive cyberattacks manifests on this magnitude. The majority of Russian cyberattacks have focused on digital networks, but some have also tried to manipulate or harm real-world infrastructure that is controlled by I/C systems (Huntley, 2023). However, there is currently no proof that such initiatives have been successful.

On April 8, the infamous GRU Unit 74455 attempted to cut off the power supply to an unnamed Ukrainian region by inserting malware into a vulnerable utility network. The intrusion into the network, which started in February or probably earlier, came to a head with this. The payload was a more advanced version of ransomware that Unit 74455 had previously used to disrupt electricity in a portion of Ukraine in 2016 (Huntley, 2023). The new malware was created to make it challenging to reinstate service after it had been installed. The hackers "planned to disconnect 1.5 to 2 million Ukrainians from their power supply," according to Zhora (Duffy, 2022). However, this time the national Computer Emergency Response Team of Ukraine and the Slovakia-based cyber security company ESET were able to identify and halt the attack as it was happening. Initially, a document circulated by Ukraine claimed that the hackers had been able to briefly shut down nine substations, but Zhora subsequently referred to this as false preliminary information and claimed that no power disruption took place. Moscow launched its most numerous and destructive cyberattacks, including the Viasat hack and a huge salvo of destructive operations, in the twenty-four hours before its invasion (Manson, 2023). To align with the ground and air onslaught, these attacks would have needed intensive planning and operational coordination. On July 1, a more convincing case surfaced, with Russian kinetic and cyber fires allegedly aiming at the same target (Huntley, 2023). A Ukrainian power company by the name of DTEK reported that day that Russia had tried to hack the business in an unsuccessful effort to "destabilize the technological processes at power generating and distribution companies." The Russian hacker collective XakNet, which asserts tenuous links to Moscow, admitted guilt. Russian forces attacked the DTEK Kryvorizka thermal power plant in Kryvyi Rih, Dnipropetrovsk Oblast, at the same moment with artillery and missiles (Huntley, 2023). Both DTEK and Victor Zhora highlighted this relationship, with the latter specifically referring to it as an instance of cyber-kinetic cooperation. That is one possibility, but more context raises the possibility that other interpretations are similarly strong, if not stronger. One of the eight thermal power plants that DTEK runs throughout different regions of Ukraine is the Kryvorizka plant. DTEK also operates a large number of additional energy generation, distribution, and associated facilities across the nation. Even though Kryvorizka was obviously under fire from Russian forces, the cyberattack has not been identified as being specifically directed at the DTEK facility, it may have been directed at any number of DTEK facilities. Additionally, it has been claimed that Russia repeatedly bombarded Kryvorizka in the days, weeks, and months preceding and following the cyberattack (Huntley, 2023). Russia was conducting missile, artillery, and air attacks at Kryvorizka, as well as in Dnipropetrovsk and three adjacent oblasts, at the time of the cyberattack. The conflict has frequently featured Russian kinetic attacks on Ukrainian power infrastructure. Due to "the firm and proactive stance taken by the company's shareholder Rinat Akhmetov regarding Russia's barbaric war against Ukraine and the massive assistance provided to the Ukrainian army and support to Ukrainians," Russia established a "special focus" on it (Huntley, 2023). If true, this political motivation for the cyberattack would refute the idea that XakNet's primary goal was to back the tactical objectives of Russian soldiers in the field. Meanwhile, Microsoft reported on a destructive cyberattack carried out by alleged Russian actors "on March 1 against a major broadcasting company, the same day the Russian military announced its intention to destroy "disinformation" targets in Ukraine and directed a missile strike against a TV tower in Kyiv" (Unit, 2022). Even though such instances might signify "active coordination," Microsoft correctly noted that they could also indicate that "computer network operators and physical forces are just independently pursuing a common set of priorities'' (Huntley, 2023).

With some cyber and kinetic attacks, Russia has undoubtedly managed to unite its efforts, primarily through loose alignment and less frequently through close coordination. We can investigate plausible best-case scenarios for Russia without proof of the effects of the cyberattack. If the cyberattack was successful in erasing data, it may have increased the level of anxiety among municipal officials or residents. However, the psychological effects would likely have been much greater due to the physical devastation and death brought on by the missile attacks. It is possible that the government agency that was the target of the cyberattack, has prevented local authorities from responding to the missiles if the agency in question was connected to the targets of the assault or worked in emergency services, public relations, or a similar capacity. The severity of such a cyberattack would rely on its sophistication as well as the agency being attacked's operational and digital resilience. Although significant, Russia's capacity to organize kinetic and cyber-attacks is not always decisive. Even when they are poorly or loosely coordinated across weapon systems and domains, fires can have military impacts. For instance, despite significant, ongoing issues with conventional combined arms integration, Moscow has taken and held a sizable portion of Ukrainian territory. Regarding the implications, the Russian approach to warfare is quite nebulous. In Ukraine, Russian forces have usually sought to upend and demoralize Ukraine's government, society, and armed forces. Their more primitive and evasive tactics have included rape as a weapon of war, random attacks on civilians in Russia-controlled areas, and terrorist missile strikes on civilian areas of towns far from the front lines. As the conflict has dragged on, Russian tactics have only become more indiscriminate. This does not, however, imply that they have had no strategic impact. In addition, despite their poor coordination with kinetic operations, Russia's extensive cyber fires should be evaluated for their potential cumulative effect in Ukraine.

To sum up this part, it can be said that overall, cyberattacks have not significantly increased Russia's kinetic weaponry or carried out any unique tasks that kinetic weapons could not. Instead of playing a specialized role, many Russian cyberattacks have gone after the same Ukrainian systems that are also the targets of kinetic attacks, like the infrastructure supporting communications, power, and transportation. Kinetic fires appear to have inflicted damage that was multiple orders of magnitude greater for almost all of these target groups. Although cyber fires may occasionally provide special advantages, these advantages have not been seen in Russia's conflict with Ukraine. Military planners in Moscow swiftly abandoned any plans to lessen direct harm to Ukrainian citizens or incidental damage, and their use of cyberspace hasn't given them much in the way of geographic reach or plausible deniability. The same is true for Russian cyber fires, which haven't had any systemic impacts and may have been less efficient financially or at least more capacity-constrainedly than kinetic fires.

Overview Regarding the Effects of Russia's Cyber-Policy Implications and Possibilities of These Development Processes

Russian cyber operations could be used to monitor and scout prospective high-value targets for planned, precise strikes. Throughout the conflict, Moscow has fired tens of thousands of missiles, airstrikes, and precision artillery rounds. Russian stocks were substantial but limited, raising the possibility that intelligence could be useful in validating the significance of priority targets and pinpointing precise aim points to inflict the greatest possible long-term harm. The Yavoriv military base, which was destroyed by a 30-missile salvo, and heavy weapon manufacturing facilities are examples of strategic Ukrainian assets that Russian forces have attacked with greater effect despite frequently employing precision weapons against less significant targets (Manson, 2023). Russian attacks also frequently target residential and commercial areas, as well as infrastructure related to ports, trains, air, and energy. It is difficult to determine whether and how Russian cyber intelligence operations are guiding intentional attacks from the outset. Microsoft has nonetheless highlighted two instances in which a Russian network intrusion was followed a few days later by a Russian missile assault on an apparent companion target. Russian cyber actors may simultaneously attempt to geolocate groups of Ukrainian troops in real-time to support tactical fires like artillery, in addition to providing information for the deliberate targeting process for strategic missiles and airstrikes. For much of the conflict, Moscow has relied heavily on the sheer firepower of the Russian artillery, "offsetting" the "generally mediocre performance of Russia's ground forces" (Huntley, 2023). Some people think that Russia showed off such a cyber capability before the Donbas War in 2022. According to CrowdStrike, GRU cyber actors deceived Ukrainian troops into downloading a malicious version of an artillery targeting app between 2014 and 2016. Pro-Russian forces may have been able to "identify the general location of Ukrainian artillery forces and engage them" thanks to the infected app's ability to gather the victims' "gross locational data'' (Unit, 2022). Users could not be geolocated accurately enough by the malware to facilitate counterbattery fire. Instead, it was claimed that the data collection revealed a general area for later exploration by pro-Russian UAVs, who would then finish the targeting process using aerial photography.

The Russian attribution, the presence of the compromise, and the alleged battlefield effects were all contested by the Ukrainian government, the app creator, and some Western cyber analysts. Despite the Ukrainian forces' even more widespread and successful use of apps for artillery targeting and other purposes, no comparable reports have surfaced yet since the 2022 invasion. There could be several ways for Russian cyber actors to attempt and geolocate Ukrainian units, such as by hacking into cell networks. But there is no proof that Russian artillery fire is being prompted by cyber-enabled geolocation, according to fieldwork and conversations conducted in Ukraine. If Ukrainian troops have been accidentally geolocated by Russian cyber actors, the resulting information must still be verified or improved using aerial imagery, much like CrowdStrike had anticipated. Russian cyber actors might attempt to locate Ukrainian military equipment by directly hacking it, as opposed to hacking cell phones to obtain real-time geolocation. However, there haven't been any dependable, concrete accounts of this. According to Watling and Reynolds, Russia uses EW direction finding of ground operators or signal jamming to counter Ukrainian UAVs, there have been no accounts of Ukrainian UAVs or their control software being hacked (CLARK, 2022). The majority of Ukraine's other combat systems are pre-digital and from the Soviet period. Although in principle Western-provided systems might be more susceptible to cyberattacks, Russian claims of successful penetrations seem to be empty rhetoric. Ukrainian sources claimed that Russia had fired cruise missiles at wooden dummies and if this is the case, the decoys would further demonstrate Russia's dependence on overhead imagery for targeting in the field as opposed to cyber-enabled geolocation.

Even after a piece of territory has been taken, gathering cyber intelligence can be helpful militarily. Local opposition must be put down where Russia has occupied territory in Ukraine. Theoretically, savvy occupiers would also work to restore essential services and manage the area in a manner that could eventually win local political support and generate economic value. Moscow has prioritized repression over governance and reconstruction. United Nations officials received a warning from Washington shortly before the invasion that "Russian forces are creating lists of identified Ukrainians to be killed or sent to camps following a military operation" (Hambling, 2022). The most well-known individuals hostile to Russian interests, including lawmakers, journalists, and intellectuals, could be found through open sources. The presence of human agents from Russia in Ukraine could then contribute to a more nuanced grasp of the political landscape and perhaps even the identification of less visible potential opponents. These conventional information sources could be supplemented by cyber activities in several ways. First, large-scale data gathering could be used to find common Ukrainian citizens connected to partisan activity, individuals without a history of activism, and unknown to Russian spies. Russian attempts to breach Ukraine's telecommunications firms have been made repeatedly in a cyber activity that may have been done for this reason. The political intelligence Moscow gets from its HUMINT sources may also be verified with the help of targeted cyber espionage (Huntley, 2023). For Russian intelligence services both before and during the conflict, the veracity of these sources has been an ongoing problem. Third, the tracking, capture, and/or assassination of targets may be made easier by stolen public datasets. For instance, just before the invasion, Russian cyber actors broke into the Ukrainian Ministry of Internal Affairs and obtained, among other pertinent information, a national auto insurance database. Of course, similar data could be immediately accessible to Russian occupiers through Ukrainian computer networks and individuals under their direct control. However, Ukrainians occasionally deleted crucial data before Russian territorial advances, giving higher importance to any information that Russian hackers had already obtained from a distance. Even though Russian occupiers may benefit from cyber intelligence gathering in a variety of ways, Moscow has generally seemed to prefer harsher, more direct methods in its spheres of influence. Instead of gathering a careful intelligence picture of local citizens to facilitate a process of selective suppression of basic resistance, Russian forces more often used brutal and sometimes indiscriminate large-scale violence, resorting to physical intimidation. It should be noted that the Russian brutality in the suburbs of Kyiv, especially in Bucha, is an extreme case and manifestation of the terrible facts observed throughout the country: arbitrary killings, rapes, robberies, and countless other crimes committed by the Russian army (Huntley, 2023).

Along with this, Russian forces in Mariupol destroyed the city before finally taking it, causing about three-quarters of the population to flee. It took a week to restore services such as electricity, communications, and medical care, internet, telephone. Services, of course, were of very limited intensity thereafter. Even months later, most citizens lacked electricity or running water. And in Donbas, Kyiv announced that Moscow had deported more than a million Ukrainian citizens. For example, within weeks of taking over Kherson, Russian occupiers ordered local Ukrainian officials to move Internet and mobile networks through Russia's national infrastructure, allowing Moscow to use its Internet regulations to closely monitor Kherson.

Citizens could only buy SIM cards. They needed Russian phone numbers and had to show their passports for that. Russian authorities have blocked access to Ukrainian and independent news media, as well as Facebook, Instagram, and Twitter, but not Telegram. Kherson may have received particular attention because it was "the only provincial Ukrainian capital captured intact by Russian forces" and other cities were too badly destroyed to warrant the effort (Pietromarchi, 2022). Other factors might have included Kherson's geographical setting, economic importance as a port city, and political situation. Kherson demonstrated that Russian occupation forces place a high value on cyber surveillance when the conditions are appropriate. At the same time, it seemed to suggest that physical authority over telecommunications networks gives occupiers access to the most comprehensive arsenal of cyber-collection tools; in comparison, remote hacking would be a more limited capability. The scope of Russia's propaganda, disinformation, and wartime influence operations in Ukraine is extensive and outside the purview of this study. However, there are at least two ways that cyber operations can directly support Russian influence efforts with operational support or information. First, Russian cyber actors are capable of conducting what are known as hack-and-leak operations the digital theft and publishing of private information intended to defame, divert attention from, or demoralize targets. Microsoft reported in March that two distinct cyber actors, one connected to the GRU and the other a "suspected Russian threat actor" compromised "a Ukrainian institution that has previously been mentioned in false Russian weapons conspiracies'' (Unit, 2022). Only five hacking and leak incidents involving Ukraine have been reported by the CyberPeace Institute, three of which were carried out by the self-described Russian hacktivist organization XakNet (Huntley, 2023). Second, Russian cyber players may use hacked networks or systems as distribution hubs for propaganda. A deep fake video of Zelenskyy pleading with Ukrainians to submit was posted to social media in March. The fake news was then spread by 146 hackers who had obtained access to Ukraine. On the channel's website, they posted a still from the video, and they changed the chyron text that scrolls beneath the live TV broadcast to represent the deep fake story. Despite these attempts, the video was easily refuted and was not convincing (Bateman, 2022).

According to available information, Russian cyber actors do not appear to have taken any significant steps to assist influence operations in Ukraine. However, hidden or unreported activities might paint a different image. Strategic information about the top leadership of Ukraine at that time, including its perceptions, intentions, plans, stances, debates, and schisms, would be very helpful to Moscow. Even now, when negotiations are not imminent, information about Zelenskyy's inner circle may aid Putin and his military leaders in planning military actions to increase their political clout. The Ukrainian government has tried to hack the phones of Ukrainian officials many times, mostly through malware, but none of these attempts have been successful. For some uses, top executives have access to secure networks and devices. Zelenskyy received a "secure satellite phone" from Washington to speak with the American government, and it appears that his office has secure landlines for internal communication with national security agencies (Hambling, 2022). The numerous failed assassination attempts on Zelenskyy serve as evidence that, in general, Ukrainian counterintelligence and operational security efforts have done better than any reasonable expectation.

It can be concluded for this part, Russia's wartime cyber activities in Ukraine have likely been primarily focused on intelligence gathering rather than fighting fires, but even this has not provided much military advantage. Numerous Moscow military information requirements can more easily be met by non-cyber sources. Fundamentally, Russia's haphazard general strategy for the conflict, from its planning of the campaign to its occupation of captured territory, indicates that important military choices are not supported by a thorough all-source intelligence process.

Moscow may still make strides in cyber intelligence as the conflict goes on despite its institutional constraints. Real-time geolocation information could theoretically be obtained by Russian hackers, allowing for Zelenskyy's murder or the prompt and precise targeting of Ukrainian troops, especially those using expensive Western weaponry. They may also conduct hack-and-leak operations that reveal sensitive information about the war to the Ukrainian and Western public, such as Ukraine's combat losses, internal divisions, or military suspicions, or gather information about Kyiv's perceptions and intentions that could help Moscow in future negotiations. along with several other likely scenarios. Therefore, Russian intelligence gathering poses the biggest ongoing cyber danger to Ukraine.

From the outset, the whole world, small countries, big countries, companies, institutions, and everybody is trying to make something for Ukraine to express support, help, solidarity, and kind willingness and this everything in total influences the hope of the people and Ukraine. One of the huge help and support which was addressed to Ukraine was cyber assets and strategies, such as Cyber Defense Assistance Collaborative (Huntley, 2023). To assist in the detection, mitigation, and defense against cyberattacks, the Cyber Defense Assistance Collaborative offers services such as compromise assessments, incident response, shared cyber threat data, and security transformation. To raise awareness among the security community and high-risk users and maintain the quality of the information, we also keep putting protections in place for users and monitor and disrupt cyber threats.

This includes a noticeable shift in the focus of different groups towards Ukraine, a sharp rise in the use of destructive attacks on the Ukrainian government, military, and civilian infrastructure, a surge in spear-phishing activity targeting NATO countries, and an increase in cyber operations intended to further various Russian objectives. For instance, we've seen threat actors hack and disclose private data to support a particular argument.

Moscow has used the entire range of IO, from overt state-backed media to covert platforms and accounts, to influence how the public views the conflict. Three objectives underpin these actions: undermine the leadership of Ukraine, erode worldwide solidarity with Ukraine, and keep up internal war support in Russia. The invasion has caused a significant shift in the ecology of Eastern European cybercriminals that is likely to have long-term effects on both the coordination between criminal organizations and the scope of cybercrime globally. cyber will continue to play a crucial role in armed conflict in the future, complementing conventional forms of warfare.

CONCLUSION

The Russian Federation's destructive cyber action against Ukraine, which targeted Viasat's satellite KA-SAT network, is strongly denounced by the European Union, its Member States, and their foreign allies. The cyberattack, which took place on February 24, 2022, an hour before Russia's unilateral and illegal invasion of Ukraine, supported military aggression. This hack had a significant effect on numerous Ukrainian government agencies, companies, and people as well as several EU Member States, leading to widespread communication breakdowns and disruptions. This heinous hack is just one example of Russia's continued pattern of careless online behavior, which was also a factor in its illegitimate and illegal conquest of Ukraine. Such behavior goes against what all UN Members, including the Russian Federation, anticipate from responsible State behavior and cyberspace objectives. Cyberattacks on Ukraine, including those on its critical infrastructure, could spread to other countries and have systemic repercussions, endangering the security of European residents. The European Union is considering new initiatives to stop, discourage, deter, and re-act to such hostile activity in cyberspace while cooperating closely with its allies. The European Union will continue to provide Ukraine with concerted political, monetary, and material support to improve its cyber resilience. Russia needs to put an end to this war as soon as possible to stop the horrific human suffering. Furthermore, we now have a much clearer picture of the adversary, which is possibly the most important impact of the cyberwar so far. We can identify Russia's dangers while also assessing Moscow's limitations. With enough information and resources, cyber security is attainable, just as mines and missiles are used to neutralize maritime threats. The majority of the nation has continued to have access to basic utility services despite Ukraine being the target of daily unmatched cyberattacks for more than a quarter of a year. Even more obvious is the reality that there hasn't been much of a disruption to internet connections or mobile phone service. Many Ukrainians have been able to access the internet while being attacked by Russian forces. Everyone must be responsible for their computer security, as we've learned over the past few months. Both individuals and organizations should take note of this. By ignoring cyber security risks, bigger systems are exposed to flaws that could have serious consequences for a large number of people. Similarly to this, businesses should not depend on the government to provide cyber security and should be prepared to make reasonable investments in security measures. This is now regarded as a required feature. Effective internet security also requires international cooperation. While offering its expertise, Ukraine has also gotten crucial support from several partner countries. The most effective cyber security activities are also multinational because the internet disregards national boundaries. It can be said that The Russian invasion of Ukraine has demonstrated how the modern battlefield has infiltrated almost every aspect of daily living. The development of the internet and the widespread use of digital technology have made it possible and inevitable to weaponize almost everything, from the water supply to banking services. For years, the Kremlin has been developing the tools necessary to execute such attacks. The international community is now desperately try-ing to catch up after being slow to recognize the true significance of this strategy. The conflict in Ukraine has highlighted the military functions carried out by hackers as well as the significance of cyberattacks in contemporary combat. Therefore, limiting Russian access to cutting-edge technology ought to be regarded as a top concern in terms of global security. Although the Russo-Ukrainian War was the first major cyberwar ever, and internet will play a significant role in every conflict. To live, maintaining a powerful traditional military will be just as important as maintaining cyber security. These are and will be very significant items in the process in the international arena and they need persistent, permanent, and very cautious observation as well the action.

REFERENCES

Bateman, J. (2022). Russia's Wartime Cyber Operations in Ukraine: Military Impacts, Influences, and Implications. *Carnegie Endowment for International Peace*. Retrieved from https://carnegieendowment.org/2022/12/16/russia-s-wartime-cyber-operations-in-ukraine-military-impacts-influences-and-implications-pub-88657

Burgess, M. (2022). A Mysterious Satellite Hack Has Victims Far Beyond Ukraine. *Wired*. Retrieved from https://www.wired.co.uk/article/viasat-internet-hack-ukraine-russia

Clark, B. (2022). The Fall and Rise of Russian Electronic Warfare. *IEEE Spectrum*. Retrieved from https://spectrum.ieee.org/the-fall-and-rise-of-russian-electronic-warfare#toggle-gdpr

Dougherty, C. (2022). Strange debacle: misadventures in assessing Russian military power. *Warontherocks*. Retrieved from https://warontherocks.com/2022/06/strange-debacle-misadventures-in-assessing-russian-military-power/

Duffy, R. (2022). WaPo: US Has Privately Attributed Hack of Viasat KA-SAT Ground Infrastructure to GRU. *Payload*. Retrieved from https://payloadspace.com/wapo-us-has-privately-attributed-hack-of-viasat-ka-sat-ground-infrastructure-to-gru/

Forbes. (2023). *The EU is discussing the creation of a special prosecutor's office to investigate war crimes in the Russian Federation*. Retrieved from: https://forbes.ua/ru/news/v-es-obgovoryuyut-stvorennya-spetsprokuraturi-dlya-rozsliduvannya-voennikh-zlochiniv-rf-bloomberg-27012023-11357

Hambling, D. (2022). Inventor Of 'Shock & Awe' Explains How It Might Work In Ukraine. *Forbes*. Retrieved from https://www.forbes.com/sites/davidhambling/2022/02/02/inventor-of-shock--awe-explains-how-it-might-work-in-ukraine/?sh=51bb6a3013b7

Huntley, S. (2023). Fog of war: how the Ukraine conflict transformed the cyber threat landscape. *Threat Analysis Group (TAG)*. Retrieved from https://blog.google/threat-analysis-group/fog-of-war-how-the-ukraine-conflict-transformed-the-cyber-threat-landscape

Independent. (2023). *From war crimes to spies and cyberattacks: Ukraine's domestic spy chief on fighting Russia across all fronts*. Retrieved from: https://www.independent.co.uk/news/world/europe/ukraine-russia-war-crimes-putin-b2290489.html

Manson, K. (2023). WaPo: US Has Privately Attributed Hack of Viasat KA-SAT Ground Infrastructure to GRU. *Bloomberg*. Retrieved from https://payloadspace.com/wapo-us-has-privately-attributed-hack-of-viasat-ka-sat-ground-infrastructure-to-gru/

O'Neill Archive. (2022). Russia hacked an American satellite company one hour before the Ukraine invasion. *MIT Technology Review*. Retrieved from https://www.technologyreview.com/2022/05/10/1051973/russia-hack-viasat-satellite-ukraine-invasion/

Pietromarchi, V. (2022). Russian-controlled Kherson region suffers power cuts. *Aljazeera*. Retrieved from https://www.aljazeera.com/news/liveblog/2022/11/6/live-news-us-reportedly-urging-ukraine-to-talk-to-russia

Reporter, C. (2023). Ukraine Conflict Transformed the Cyber Threat Landscape, Says Google. *CircleID's*. Retrieved from https://circleid.com/posts/20230216-ukraine-conflict-transformed-the-cyber-threat-landscape-says-google

Unit, M. D. (2022). *An overview of Russia's cyberattack activity in Ukraine.* Microsoft. Retrieved from https://query.prod.cms.rt.microsoft.com/cms/api/am/binary/RE4Vwwd

University, A. N. (2022). Director GCHQ's speech on global security amid war in Ukraine. *GCHQ*. Retrieved from https://www.gchq.gov.uk/speech/director-gchq-global-security-amid-russia-invasion-of-ukraine

Zetter, K. (2022). Viasat Hack "Did Not" Have Huge Impact on Ukrainian Military Communications, Official Says. *Zero Day*. Retrieved from https://zetter.substack.com/p/viasat-hack-did-not-have-huge-impact

Chapter 15
China's Cyber Security Policy and the Democratic World

Irakli Kervalishvili
Georgian Technical University, Georgia

ABSTRACT

In the modern world, transferring data into digital format, electronic commerce, social media, and receiving public services through online platforms are very relevant. The more states become dependent on cyberspace, the more reasons and means hostile actors have for cyberattacks, stealing and distorting information, and paralyzing systems. We must keep in mind that cyber security is not only about computer programming and information technology. Cyber security is a vital part of national security, as cyber-attacks target people, public opinion, and public and business sectors. China is indeed quite an aggressive cyber actor, but there is another, non-democratic state that has much greater economic-technological resources, ambition, and aspiration for cyber expansionism.

INTRODUCTION. THE NATIONAL CYBER SECURITY STRATEGY AND THE EMERGENCE OF HARD DIGITAL FRONTIERS

The development of the Internet, and the innovation that is associated with it, have been facilitated by an environment that has been relatively free from control. Unfortunately, however, as a result of deep integration into the social framework, the Internet has become a potential tool for influencing geopolitical conflicts, including interference in the internal affairs of other states, undermining national security, destabilizing financial infrastructure, and attacking critical infrastructure. While states derive social and economic benefits from the Internet, they fear the threat it poses to national security. In response to these threats, countries are beginning to tighten their Internet borders and develop their cyber weapons not only as a tool for deterrence but also to apply pressure during conflicts. The potential downside of such state-by-state regulation is slowing down the innovation process that the Internet has traditionally spurred and limiting the freedom of speech that has contributed to social inclusion in society. On the other hand, innovation and freedom cannot flourish in a chaotic environment with rampant crime and a

DOI: 10.4018/978-1-6684-8846-1.ch015

lack of rules, norms, and ethics. With this in mind, national policymakers face the challenge of finding a balance between regulation and the potential chaos of the Internet, while at the same time promoting the development of freedoms. In trying to strike such a balance in the national interest, cyberspace boundaries play an important role alongside international efforts to build confidence in cyberspace and slow down Internet fragmentation.

The sophistication and effectiveness of cyberattacks have steadily increased since the first Morris worm cyberattack in 1988 and have recently become a key part of the national defense strategies of several countries. Cyberspace is now considered a separate domain of conflict along with land, sea, air, and space, clearly defined in the military doctrines of the world's most powerful states, including China. Each country is strengthening its defenses while at the same time working furiously to develop cyber weapons and testing the cyber defenses of other countries. Cyber attacks have already been used to supplement military interventions in response to the policies and actions of other countries and to interfere in the elections of other countries. The ferocious cyber arms race shows no signs of abating. States now face a dilemma: whether to work together to de-escalate the cyber arms race and allow the Internet to thrive unhindered or to build boundaries on the Internet and threaten its growth and evolution.

Several attempts have been made to work out a treaty to curb the growth of cyber weapons; however, the lack of attribution, the increase in vulnerabilities, and the escalation of economic rivalry between states make reaching a consensus on these treaties very difficult. Although the attribution of cyber incidents is constantly improving due to improved analytic technologies, the activities of states in the development of cyber weapons are still undercover. From a game theory perspective, the situation suggests that each state is trying to maximize its cyber arsenal in the belief that other countries are also maximizing their efforts to develop cyber arsenals. The earliest use of cyber weapons took place in conflicts between Russia and the former Soviet republics of Georgia and Estonia. In these cases, the attacks were used for media propaganda, website corruption, and so on. Over time, however, cyberattacks have become more sophisticated, targeted, and dangerous. Likewise, more nation-states are turning to cyberattacks and starting to use cyberattacks to achieve their geopolitical goals.

Expanding the Vulnerability Landscape

The top three innovations of this decade are the smart grid, connected vehicles, and human implantable devices. All three of these innovations will radically change society in many ways, some of which are currently hard to even imagine. The discussions related to cyber-physical systems are very timely, as their impact on the future of society will be enormous.

We create networks of three classes: monolithic networks of devices and sensors in the power system; millions of ad hawk networks in the transport network; and a huge personal network of wearable devices. Each of these networks has many calls. Much of the discussion here is related to the static networks of cyber-physical systems such as industrial control, electricity, and gas distribution. The ever-changing systems of connected vehicles and wearable devices have not yet been considered. Let's take a closer look at the evolution of the Internet of Things (IoT).

Gartner estimates that 21 billion IoT devices will be in use in the next few years. Cisco estimates that there will be more than 50 billion such devices, and Intel goes even further, predicting the use of 200 billion IoT devices (Eddy, 2015). Indeed, we are just beginning to understand the potential and possibilities of the Internet of Things. The list of possible benefits expands as they come in - efficiency gains, process optimization, and cost reductions are the most important ones that will take place for any kind of business venture. The first revolution began with the creation of a mechanical loom (1784). The second industrial revolution began with the advent of the assembly line (1870) and the third industrial revolution came with the introduction of the PLC (1969). The fourth revolution is happening now, and the driving force is sensors, Artificial Intelligence (AI), and robotics.

Imagine for a moment smart farming and the increased productivity and predictive accuracy that can be realized when sensors can provide finely tuned information about temperature and moisture, soil pH, and nutrient content to inform farming and increase yields. Or the remarkable potential in medicine and biomedical informatics of insulin pumps, which can monitor blood sugar levels and adjust insulin levels in real-time, or the IBM Medical Sieve system, which uses intelligent algorithms and advanced AI to sort the entire medical history of a patient in search of clues. for compiling image analysis; learn everything there is to know about a patient in seconds for a smarter diagnosis and an infinitely more personalized treatment plan (Khan, 2012).

Imagine being able to use the time you now spend fighting vehicles on your daily commute to read or even daydream in your autonomous vehicle. The University of Albany is working on a project where road signs can communicate with each other, adjusting to increase traffic flow. Imagine a sensor system that can predict earthquakes before they happen; and the improvements that can be made as a result of greater real-time monitoring of energy consumption and environmental parameters. IW has transformed the world of production and transformation of electrical energy. Today, we are building a power system architecture that will integrate many separate power systems and make them more resilient. By overlaying a communication network on the grid and creating an information system that can link sensors across the grid to make it more resilient, an integrated electricity market will be created where everyone can buy and sell electricity.

Now 54% of the world's people live in cities, and by 2050 this share is expected to reach 66% (Chitadze, 2022). Combined with an overall increase in population, urbanization will add another 2.5 billion people to the urban population over the next thirty years (Chitadze, 2022). Rapid urbanization creates great environmental stress. Environmental, social, and economic resilience must evolve in tandem with rapid expansion, which further strains the resources of our cities. The purpose of smart cities is to promote sustainable development to solve the problems of urbanization. Efficient use of infrastructure data and self-requirement data of urban communities can improve energy distribution, optimize waste collection, reduce traffic congestion, and even improve air quality with IoT.

How can we protect ourselves from hacks, cyberattacks, and data theft? In cities where many participants exchange information, how can we be sure that the participant is what he says about himself? And how can we know that the data they share is true and accurate? Along with limitless opportunities comes great risk in terms of security and privacy damage, hacking, and system disruption. When critical infrastructure—power plants, water supplies, airports, and hospitals—are managed by IoT systems, the potential for loss of life—from disruption to cybercriminal activity—increases exponentially (Tianlong Yu, 2015).

IW risks are not speculation, they are already here. According to a study by Hewlett Packard, 80% of IoT devices tested (they tested widely used home alarm systems and thermostats, automatic garage door locks, etc.) raised privacy concerns, with an average of 25% security gaps per device (HP News, 2014). In 2016, a DDoS attack - the largest in history - was initiated against a service provider using an IoT bot with malware called Mirai, which led to the shutdown of large parts of the Internet - including Twitter, Netflix, and Reddit. Once Mirai penetrates the system, it forces computers to constantly search the Internet for vulnerable IoT devices and, using usernames and passwords by default, register, infecting them with the Mirai program as well.

The security of our future - the era of IoT - will be as secure as each of the billions of small connected devices that compromise our systems are secure. We've all had our computer crash and we've lost a document or spreadsheet, but imagine a pacemaker or a digitalized insulin pump failing, which can be hacked, resulting in death, or Volkswagen hacking into the computer system of their cars to bypass environmental control restrictions. Imagine how hackers get access to bank data and empty accounts. Unauthorized personnel can gain access to smart devices that store sensitive financial account information, passwords, or other information by exploiting vulnerabilities for identity theft or fraud. A US Federal Trade Commission report estimates that 10,000 households can generate up to 150 million data records daily, providing a significant number of entry points for hackers (Federal Trade Commission, 2015).

Nation-states are aware of these vulnerabilities and will try to use them against other countries to assert their sovereignty on the Internet. The concept of digital borders and Internet sovereignty has evolved from concept to reality, and several countries are already working to control the flow of information across their borders, as well as to actively monitor and censor information within their borders, which we will explore in the next paragraph.

Balkanization of the Internet

The Internet has operated with free access and international sovereignty for many years, allowing it to grow into a universal communication platform that now acts as a social glue for society and a platform for commerce and commerce. One of the arguments against Internet restrictions is that information is an international human right. A more practical and economically strong argument is that international trade depends on Internet access and cross-border data flow. Open and free access to the Internet is what makes the Internet very successful - but this access has also become the biggest challenge.

The enormous influence of the Internet on public opinion and the development of trade makes it an object of militarization. As the US Secretary of Defense Panetta noted, "The Internet is open. It is easily accessible, as it should be. But this turns it into a new area of warfare. This is the battlefield of the future" (Meltzer, 2013). It is used to influence public opinion and support regime change, attack the information infrastructure of nation-states, recruit new members of terrorist organizations, and compromise and disrupt critical infrastructure. What is unique about cyberspace (compared to other physical media like Earth, air, and space) is that although it is global, the cost of entry is very low.

Propaganda and dissent have long been active forces in countries, but the sheer scale and reach of the Internet have made it a powerful weapon. Whether it's YouTube videos of protests or police brutality, or powerful new online campaigning tools, the Internet plays an important role in political organization. Actors - even individual actors - can exercise a powerful influence in cyberspace that is orders of magnitude stronger than a small group of states that operate in the land, air, sea, and space operational domains can exercise.

The Internet is a domain that plays the role of a necessary (if not necessary) factor for all other operational domains. Given the enormous power of the Internet, and in response to its use for political and military purposes, the concept of international Internet sovereignty is rapidly shifting towards the concept of sovereign Internet borders. This transformation is accelerating as a result of the tightening of the Internet's boundaries in recent years. States from China to Iran to Burma are increasingly filtering and blocking access to media and blogs that promote political views that conflict with those of the government.

The original and essentially libertarian nature of the Internet is increasingly being challenged by states claiming jurisdiction over the Internet, or by the development of rules that limit the ability of individuals and companies to access the Internet and move data across national borders. The tools available to restrict Internet access and cross-border data flow are becoming more accessible, sophisticated, and widely adaptable. These include blocking the main protocol or access points in the country and filtering domain names, Internet protocols, or URLs. Governments can also restrict access to the Internet in indirect ways that restrict the work of search engines, such as by placing conditions on licenses to operate or by not sending specific materials and imposing harsh penalties for non-compliance with restrictions. Information control – for countries that have taken this path – includes restricting access to foreign information sources, blocking foreign Internet tools such as Google search, Facebook, Twitter, and certain mobile applications, and requiring foreign companies to adapt to domestic regulations (Meltzer, 2015). However, by including more and more control tools, we are choking the Internet and it is getting slower. The legitimacy of the creation of national boundaries on the Internet by states derives from rules supposedly designed to protect citizens from harmful outside influences.

Let's take a look at the increasing balkanization of the Internet as some countries work to establish national boundaries while others fight for the original free-access internationalism of the Internet. We then explore this dichotomy in more detail in the context of the growing militarization of the Internet and the accelerated development of cyber warfare tools. Is it a fake dilemma when some states - like the United States - promote the Internet without borders, while they develop cyber warfare and cyber defense? Let's first look at the picture of the Internet boundaries - who does what on this issue.

The Evolution of Means for Conducting Cyber Warfare in the Example of China

One of the examples of cyber warfare that can be considered Operation Aurora, initiated by China in 2006, is a targeted malware cyberattack against at least 30 large companies – including Google and Adobe – that exploited the zero-day flaw in the Internet Explorer browser. The flaw allowed the malware to download onto users' computers. It looks like hackers had access to the source code of many software products. Five members of Chinese Liberation Army Unit 61398 were "assigned" to conduct a massive spear-phishing campaign to allegedly hack into the systems of leading US companies. The attack included hacking into the computer systems of 141 companies from 20 major industries from 2006 to 2014. The hackers were looking for American trade secrets: from Westinghouse, for example, they took plans for a certain type of nuclear power plant. This is the first time that the term "advanced persistent threat" has been used (Dalha, 2018).

Tightening Internet Borders to Ensure National Security on the Example of China

The advent of the Internet in China has transformed Chinese media from a closed and centralized system to an open and decentralized system. In China, the new generation is actively turning on the Internet. By the end of 2017, there were 722 million online consumers in China, accounting for 55.8%, and this is the largest online population in the world. China has greatly expanded the technological capacity and human capital to control Internet content, including hiring an estimated 500,000 to 2,000,000 Internet propagandists (better known as the 50-cent army) who write online comments in defense of prestige. and the integrity of the Chinese Communist Party (Tenzin Dalha, 2018).

China, Saudi Arabia, Iran, and others have similar ambitions for the Internet: they think the state should decide what information crosses its borders, not companies and NGOs. A 2018 report by Freedom House examined the situation in 65 countries and found that internet freedom had declined in 26 of them since the previous year, with half of the decline attributed to elections (Shahbaz, 2018).

China, as the architect of "cyber sovereignty", has begun to export its Internet censorship regime to other countries, changing the Internet from the bottom up. According to the Freedom House report, at least 36 states, including Egypt, Saudi Arabia, and Vietnam, have received closed-door training on "new media and information management (Wenfang Tang, 2018). Over the past few years, China has hosted media representatives from a dozen states for two- and three-week seminars to learn about its monitoring and censorship system and has supplied telecommunications equipment, advanced facial recognition technology, and data analysis tools to various states with human rights concerns. There is evidence that some countries, such as Uganda, are using Chinese software to monitor the local Internet under the guise of fighting crime (Tenzin Dalha, 2018).

It can be said that the main challenge for the United States and its allies in cyberspace is China. China, like Russia, regularly carries out cyber attacks against the US and the EU. The purpose of such attacks is to disrupt economic activity, harm the security and defense sector, and shape or change public opinion. In addition, the "Digital Silk Road" and the "Space Information Corridor" not only promote Chinese cyber espionage but also aim to completely transform the Internet space by authoritarian standards and dominate China's cyberspace.

China's Activities in Cyberspace

For the first time, the American media was interested in cyber threats coming from China. Since 2011, much has been written about Chinese cyber-espionage and phishing cyber-attacks to steal intellectual property from American companies (Perlroth, 2021). It should be taken into account that according to the research of the Intelligence Committee of the US House of Representatives, every year only American companies suffer losses of 540 billion dollars due to the theft of intellectual property. Of these, 400 billion in losses come from stolen ideas in cyberspace. 73% of attacks are linked to Chinese cyber espionage (Hosenball 2020). China has been repeatedly accused of stealing intellectual property. Today, this topic is on the agenda like never before. Beijing has developed the national plan "Made in China 2025", which aims to transform China from a producer of low-cost products into a high-tech producer (Insikt Group 2021, 2). Preventing cyber-attacks, as well as predicting the damage caused, is very difficult. Even more so considering that the Chinese government and related hacking groups today are using far more advanced technology and tactics than ever before to access government and business sector databases. Hackers spend months trying to study the weaknesses of programs and servers, gain valuable information, and, most importantly, remain undetected in the process. It turned out well. Hackers from China's Ministry of State Security were in the Marriott Group's system for 4 years and during that time they stole the personal information of more than 500 million customers (Venard 2019). China carries out cyber attacks mainly with the help of the 3rd Department of the People's Liberation Army, domestic hacking groups, and technology companies such as Huawei. China stole a model of the

American military aircraft F-35 and then produced a similar Shenyang FC-31 (Venard, 2019). It can be said that the second cold war is going on, currently in cyberspace. China's cyberattacks and intellectual property theft were best assessed by former FBI director Robert Mueller. According to him, there are two types of American companies: "those who have already been victims of hacking attacks, and those who will be in the future" (Mueller 2012). The Chinese government is also using cyberspace to spy on European politicians and diplomats. In 2018, hackers linked to the People's Liberation Army breached the EU's diplomatic communications network and obtained sensitive information (Sanger, 2018). Many speculated that China would try to blackmail senior officials with the extracted material and force them to support China's strategic and geopolitical goals. Moreover, it should be taken into account that, unlike the United States, the European Union perceives China as less of a threat and rarely openly criticizes it. China is trying to make Huawei an important place in the European communication system. It is very risky for the security of the European Union because the company is close to the Communist Party and cooperates with Chinese intelligence. The more European market share Huawei has, the less EU cyber security will be protected. The same can be said about Georgia. 75% of the country's communications network is made by Huawei, which is detrimental to national security and cyber security (Chachanidze, 2021). In addition to espionage, the Chinese government actively uses cyberspace to spread disinformation. In this regard, they have been noticeably active since the beginning of the pandemic. The Chinese media, especially the "Xinhua News Agency" of the Communist Party, initially spread conspiracy theories about the origin of the virus. This was followed by the promotion of Chinese medical aid, while at the same time blaming the US and the EU for ineffective management of the pandemic. The latest wave of "fake news" has been directed at Western vaccines. Russian and Chinese narratives in cyberspace are very similar. The goal of both is to discredit the democratic world and show their superiority in any field.

China's Cyber Expansionism and Future Threats From the "Digital Silk Road"

The Chinese government is constantly trying to exploit new markets. The interest of the Communist Party, on the one hand, is to increase the area of economic benefits and political influence. On the other hand, China is engaging in "cyber expansionism" through technological exports, which implies the establishment of a Chinese management style in cyberspace, the dependence of developing countries on Chinese technology, and the emergence of more opportunities for Chinese intelligence. 2 years after the start of work on the "One Belt, One Road" initiative, President Xi Jinping laid the foundation for the "Digital Silk Road". Officially, the goal of the project is to improve Internet infrastructure, communications, cyber security, and e-commerce. As part of the Digital Silk Road, China exports intelligence equipment (network cameras, location services, sensors). This is another effective mechanism that opens up new markets for giants close to the party - Huawei, Alibaba, and Tencent (Ghiasy, 2021). Thanks to the project, China will export millions of intelligence and household equipment. It is worth noting that every Chinese electronic device, server, and program has access to Chinese intelligence. They can track people's movements, banking transactions, and daily activities. The dependence of developing countries on Chinese goods, services, and technology allows the Chinese government to influence local political elites. According to the International Telecommunication Union, 55% of the world's population has Internet access today. This indicator reaches 87% in developed countries, 47% in developing countries, and only 19% in the least developed countries (ITU 2019). Chinese products are mainly intended for developing and underdeveloped countries. Such states are inexperienced in cyberspace and cannot keep up with countries like China in terms of technological progress. Therefore, the Chinese government will be able to easily access weak countries' government files, valuable information, personal data, etc. Based on the above, we are talking about "cyber colonialism", that is, using the digital silk road "for economic, social and political domination in the territory of another country" (Insikt Group, 2021).

Fast internet and the latest technologies will indeed bring new opportunities, jobs, better education, and healthcare to developing countries, but not without Chinese intelligence. There is also a risk of new democracies adopting Chinese norms. China uses technology for mass intelligence of the population. It protects the interests of the Communist Party, persecutes protesting and pro-democracy groups, restricts the media, stifles protests, and systematically oppresses religious and ethnic minorities. According to the Freedom House report, 18 countries acquired Chinese intelligence technology in 2018. Today, the number of similar countries has risen to 80, including the largest part of Asian, South American, and African states (Shahbaz 2018). According to a report by American cyber security company Recorded Future, countries sometimes provide the People's Liberation Army with classified data in exchange for receiving Chinese technology at low cost, and even allow it to test facial recognition mass surveillance cameras. The above is especially relevant for African countries. China is trying to develop surveillance, and smart cameras and add the function of skin color and race detection (Insikt Group, 2021). We have already mentioned above that the Communist Party effectively controls social networks within the borders of the country. Citizens are not allowed to use Western social platforms as the party blocks sites such as Facebook, Instagram, Google, Yahoo, and others. The Chinese government explains this by promoting local applications and encouraging Chinese businesses, but the reality is the same - the government does not want the population to watch Western media, break with the party narrative, freely express their opinion, and easily find like-minded people without the control and fear of the party. The Communist Party fights for free speech on the Internet. A clear example of this was revealed at the beginning of 2020. In particular, the Chinese government persecuted all those people who spread information about the new virus on social networks to warn their relatives. Among them was Dr. Li Wenlian, who was later charged with disinformation and publicly signed a document claiming that Wenlian was spreading rumors instead of facts and that there was no deadly virus. Unfortunately, the doctor later succumbed to the coronavirus (Hegarty 2020). The case of Zhen Zhiqian, who disappeared on March 14, 2020, after blaming the government for the spread of the coronavirus in his blog, and calling Xi Jinping a "crazy clown" is also interesting. It was later revealed that Zhen Zhiqian was arrested, charged with participating in corrupt deals, and sentenced to 18 years (Mcdonell, S. 2020).

"Internet Protocol Blueprint" and 5G

In 2019, Huawei engineers presented a new "Internet Protocol Blueprint" to delegates from 40 partner countries. According to them, the current cyberspace is very limited and outdated. Huawei has developed a new design that will allow governments to more easily and effectively control digital property, population, and order in cyberspace (Murgia, 2020). The so-called People's Republic of China Supports the principle of "cyber sovereignty", according to which the government has unlimited power in cyberspace. It controls any cyber operations, infrastructure, and devices within the country. In developing, non-democratic countries, China's Internet management style and intelligence networks will give authoritarian governments the ability to not only limit free speech on social media but also to repress opposition-minded people. Huawei and the Chinese government have sided with dictators before. According to an investigative article in the Wall Street Journal, in 2018 Ugandan President Yoweri Museveni hacked opposition leader Bobby Wine's WhatsApp with the help of Huawei engineers. Museveni started to collect compromises with his opponent. Vine was first blackmailed and then arrested along with hundreds of supporters for treason (Parkinson, 2019). In addition to the representatives of authoritarian regimes of foreign countries, Huawei provides information obtained in cyberspace to the Chinese authorities. Although the management of Huawei categorically denies this, we must take into account that according to the legislative act adopted in 2017, any Chinese private company is obliged to cooperate with Chinese intelligence (Chachanidze, 2021). Even before the law was passed, in 2012, the US House Intelligence Committee designated Huawei as a national threat. Huawei was also accused of stealing intellectual property and misusing databases (Schmidt, 2012). Even as the United States warns its allies about future cyber threats from Huawei, the company is not giving up its global lead in 5G sales. It should be noted that the USA, Australia, and Great Britain also announced a boycott of Chinese 5G technology. However, in 2020, Britain lifted the restriction and allowed China to roll out a 5G network in the country (Reichert 2020). The Chinese 5G network was also adopted by the European Union but stated that in addition to Huawei's system, there will be other 5G providers in the market, in order not to become dependent on only one provider and to ensure competition and diversity (Nietsche, 2020). China's 5G system is also being used by Brazil, which initially signed a memorandum with the United States to deepen cooperation in the fields of 5G, telecommunications, and energy. With this memorandum, Brazil joined the "Clean Network Initiative" (Clean Network Initiative), which meant the purchase of equipment necessary for the security of the 5G network, the privacy of citizens' personal information, protection from unauthorized access to the telecommunications infrastructure, and provision of national security (U.S. Embassy and Consulates in Brazil 2020). However, President Jair Bolsonaro scrapped the agreement and allowed Huawei to install a nationwide 5G network. Bolsonaro's decision was largely due to the availability of Huawei's service. It should be said here that the company entered the Brazilian market 22 years ago and the vast majority of the communication network is laid by it (Chu, Daye, 2021). On January 14, 2021, Georgia joined the "Clean Network Initiative" (U.S. Embassy in Georgia, 2021). 2 years ago, it was planned to install 5G optical fiber cables in the country as part of the "Digital Silk Road". Officials have often talked about Chinese investment and making Georgia a 5G network hub. After the 100% package of shares of "Kavkasus Online" passed into the hands of "Nexon Holding", it was decided to install the cables on the territory of Azerbaijan (Chachanidze, 2021). A large number of Georgian experts consider this case as a missed opportunity, however, as we mentioned above, Chinese technologies are accompanied by Chinese intelligence. In addition, for the main strategic partner of Georgia - the United States of America - cooperation with Chinese companies on 5G Internet is a political message and indicates the eastern orientation of the country. Therefore, from the point of view of national security and international relations, the failed plan is beneficial.

Social Credit System

Along with the development of technology, the Chinese Communist Party has already started to use the social credit system, which involves the moral evaluation of a person. The system, according to the South China Morning Post, was developed by the National Development and Reform Commission, the People's Bank of China, and the Chinese judiciary. The system monitors individuals and companies in cyberspace and real life daily. Banks track what people buy, network cameras record anyone's movements and behavior, and social media has further restricted the flow of information and free speech (Lee, 2020). The social credit score increases or decreases according to the behavior of a particular person. The exact methodology is kept secret, but spreading "fake news", buying too much alcohol, smoking in places where it is not allowed, noise, traffic violations, and other similar activities lower the social score. Regarding low score results, China has already started punishing people by restricting flights, business class train travel, and luxury hotel rooms (Ma, 2021). According to Foreign Policy, social credits are affected by late payment of taxes, late repayment of credits, etc. People with low social credit are already restricted in their access to higher education (Minstreanu, 2018). Although this system reminds us of an episode of Black Mirror or some science fiction scenario, we must remember that everything is real. And as improbable as it may seem, there is a risk that the social credit system will spread beyond China's borders. The Chinese government is making society more compliant through social credits to make the regime easier to maintain. It is not excluded that other authoritarian, non-democratic states also use modern technologies for the same purpose. In developing countries, the introduction of a social credit system with Chinese technology, in addition to restricting human rights and freedom, will provide the Chinese intelligence service with information about the events, trends, and behaviors of citizens in other countries. Based on these data, China will more effectively influence the information environment and people's opinions within the framework of hybrid war will strengthen anti-American and anti-Western sentiments.

CONCLUSION

We have already mentioned in the introduction that China has become the main challenge for the United States and its allies in cyberspace. Russia is indeed quite an aggressive and experienced player, but China has much greater economic and technological resources, capabilities, and ambitions. Millions of Chinese smartphones, computer hardware, software, sensors, smart cameras, and intelligence devices are sold worldwide. Chinese intelligence has access to each of them. Therefore, in cyberspace, the People's Republic of China can do the most damage to other states. Added to this is the Chinese 5G technology, as well as the plan to completely transform the Internet and cyberspace, for the completion of which several strategic steps have already been taken (Frenkel, 2021). China's goal is to establish an authoritarian style of governance in the digital world and replace it with democratic principles. Communist Party ideas may be attractive to non-democratic or hybrid regimes. Surveillance of one's citizens, persecution of opponents and free opinion, and censorship - the means and legitimacy of the Chinese "Internet Protocol Plan" will be given to the states.

REFERENCES

Chachanidze, G. (2021). *China - The main challenge of the democratic world in cyberspace*. GFSIS.

Chitadze, N. (2022). *World Politics and Challenges in International Security*. IGI Global. doi:10.4018/978-1-7998-9586-2

Chu, D. (2021). *Brazil ditches US drive to strangle Huawei*. Global Times. Retrieved from: https://www.globaltimes.cn/page/202101/1213075.html

Dalha, T. (2018). *Assertion of China's Sovereignty over the Internet, global-is-Asian*. Retrieved from: https://lkyspp.nus.edu.sg/gia/article/assertion-of-china's-sovereignty-over-the-internet

Eddy, N. (2018). Gartner: 21 Billion IoT Devices to Invade By 2020. *Information Week*. Retrieved from: www.informationweek.com/mobile/mobile-devices/gartner-21-billion-IoT-devices-to-invade-by-2020/d/d-id/1323081

Embassy, U. S. in Georgia. (2021). *United States-Georgia Memorandum of Understanding on 5G Strategy*. Retrieved from: https://ge.usembassy.gov/united-states-georgia-memorandum-ofunderstanding-on-5g-security/

Federal Trade Commission. (2015). *Internet of Things: Privacy and Security in a Connected World*. FTC Staff Report. Retrieved from: https://www.ftc.gov/system/files/documents/reports/federal-trade-commission-staff-report-november-2013-workshop-entitled-interne

Ghiasy, R., & Rajeshwari, K. (2021). *China's Digital Silk Road and the Global Digital Order*. The Diplomat. Retrieved from: https://thediplomat.com/2021/04/chinas-digital-silk-roadand-the-global-digital-order/

Girard, B. (2019). *The Real Danger of China's National Intelligence Law*. The Diplomat. Retrieved from: https://thediplomat.com/2019/02/the-real-danger-of-chinas-national-intelligence-law/

Hegarty, S. (2020). *The Chinese doctor who tried to warn others about coronavirus*. BBC. Retrieved from: https://www.bbc.com/news/world-asia-china-51364382

Hosenball, M. (2020). *Top U.S. officials to spotlight Chinese spy operations, the pursuit of American secrets*. Reuters. Retrieved from: https://www.reuters.com/article/usa-china-espionage/top-u-sofficials-to-spotlight-chinese-spy-operations-pursuit-of-american-secrets-idUSL1N28S1B3

Insikt Group. (2021). *China's Digital Colonialism: Espionage and Repression Along the Digital Silk Road*. Retrieved from: https://go.recordedfuture.com/hubfs/reports/cta-2021-0727.pdf

International Telecommunication Union. (2019). *Measuring digital development Facts and figures*. ITU Publications. Retrieved from: https://www.itu.int/en/ITU-D/Statistics/Documents/facts/FactsFigures2019.pdf

Khan, R., Khan, S. U., Zaheer, R., & Khan, S. (2012). Future Internet: The Internet of Things Architecture, Possible Applications, and Key Challenges. In *Proceedings of 2012 10th International Conference on Frontiers of Information Technology (FIT)*. Institute of Electrical and Electronics Engineers. 10.1109/FIT.2012.53

Lee, A. (2020). What is China's social credit system and why is it controversial? *South China Morning Post*. Retrieved from: https://www.scmp.com/economy/china-economy/article/3096090/what-chinas-social-credit-system-and-why-it-controversial

Ma, A., & Canales, K. (2021). China's 'social credit' system ranks citizens and punishes them with throttled internet speeds and flight bans if the Communist Party deems them untrustworthy. *Business Insider*. https://www.businessinsider.com/china-social-credit-systempunishments-and-rewards-explained-2018-4

Mcdonell, S. (2020). *Ren Zhiqiang: Outspoken ex-real estate tycoon gets 18 years in jail*. BBC. Retrieved from: https://www.bbc.com/news/world-asia-china-54245327

Meltzer, J. (2013). The Internet, Cross-Border Data Flows and International Trade. SSRN *Electronic Journal*. doi:10.2139/ssrn.2292477

Minstreanu, S. (2018). *Life Inside China's Social Credit Laboratory*. Foreign Policy. Retrieved from: https://foreignpolicy.com/2018/04/03/life-inside-chinas-social-credit-laboratory/

Mueller, R. S. (2012). *Combating Threats in the Cyber World: Outsmarting Terrorists, Hackers, and Spies*. RSA Cyber Security Conference San Francisco. The Federal Bureau of Investigation. Retrieved from: https://archives.fbi.gov/archives/news/speeches/combating-threats-in-the-cyberworld-outsmarting-terrorists-hackers-and-spies

Murgia, M., & Gross, A. (2020). Inside China's controversial mission to reinvent the Internet. *Financial Times*.

News, H. P. (2014). HP Study Reveals 70 Percent of Internet of Things Devices Vulnerable to Attack, *HP News*, Retrieved from: https://www8.hp.com/us/en/hp-news/press-release.html?id=1744676

Nietsche, C., & Rasser, M. (2020). *Washington's Anti-Huawei Tactics Need a Reboot In Europe Efforts to convince allies of the Chinese threat in 5G have floundered*. Foreign Policy. Retrieved from: https://foreignpolicy.com/2020/04/30/huawei-5g-europe-united-states-china/

Parkirson, J., Bariyo, N., & Chin, J. (2019). Huawei Technicians Helped African Governments Spy on Political Opponents. *The Wall Street Journal*.

Perlroth, N. (2021). How China transformed Into a Prime Cyber Threat to the U.S. *The New York Times*. Retrieved from: https://www.nytimes.com/2021/07/19/technology/china-hacking-us.html

Reichert, C. (2020). *Europe allows Huawei for 5G through security guidelines*. CNET. Retrieved from: https://www.cnet.com/tech/mobile/europe-allows-huawei-for-5g-through-security-guidelines/

Sanger, D. E., & Erlanger, S. (2018). Hacked European Cables Reveal a World of Anxiety About Trump, Russia, and Iran. *The New York Times*. Retrieved from: https://www.nytimes.com/2018/12/18/us/politics/european-diplomats-cables-hacked.html

Schmidt, M., Bradsher, K., & Hauser, C. (2012). U.S. Panel Calls Huawei and ZTE 'National Security Threat'. *The New York Times*.

Shahbaz, A. (2018). *Freedom on the Net 2018: The Rise of Digital Authoritarianism*. The Freedom House. https://freedomhouse.org/report/freedom-net/2018/rise-digital-authoritarianism

Tamkin, E. (2017). *10 Years After the Landmark Attack on Estonia, Is the World Better Prepared for Cyber Threats?* Foreign Policy. https://foreignpolicy.com/2017/04/27/10-years-afterthe-landmark-attack-on-estonia-is-the-world-better-prepared-for-cyber-threats/

Tang, W., & Iyengar, S. (2012). *Political Communication in China: Convergence or Divergence Between the Media and Political System?* Routledge.

Timberg, C. (2018). Net of Insecurity: A Flaw in the Design. *The Washington Post*. Retrieved from: https://www.washingtonpost.com/sf/business/2015/05/30/net-of-insecurity-part-1

U.S. Embassy and Consulates in Brazil. (2020). *United States and Brazil Sign US $1 Billion Memorandum of Understanding*. Retrieved from: https://br.usembassy.gov/united-states-and-brazil-sign-us-1-billion-memorandum-of-understanding/

Venard, B. (2019). *The Cold War 2.0 between China and the US is already a virtual reality*. The Conversation. Retrieved from: https://theconversation.com/the-cold-war-2-0-between-chinaand-the-us-is-already-a-virtual-reality-125081

Yu, T., Sekar, V., Seshan, S., Agarwal, Y., & Xu, C. (2015). Handling a Trillion Flaws on a Billion Devices: Rethinking Network Security for the Internet-of-Things. *Proceedings of the 14th ACM Workshop on Hot Topics in Networks*. 10.1145/2834050.2834095

KEY TERMS AND DEFINITIONS

Cyber Attack: An attack, via cyberspace, targeting an enterprise's use of cyberspace for the purpose of disrupting, disabling, destroying, or maliciously controlling a computing environment/infrastructure; or destroying the integrity of the data or stealing controlled information.

Cyber Security: Refers to every aspect of protecting an organization and its employees and assets against cyber threats. As cyberattacks become more common and sophisticated and corporate networks grow more complex, a variety of cyber security solutions are required to mitigate corporate cyber risk.

Cyber Warfare: Is usually defined as a cyber-attack or series of attacks that target a country. It has the potential to wreak havoc on government and civilian infrastructure and disrupt critical systems, resulting in damage to the state and even loss of life.

National Cyber Security Strategy: The Strategy defines the scope of CII as including but not limited to basic communication and broadcasting networks, energy, finance, transportation, education, scientific research, hydraulic systems, industrial manufacturing, healthcare, social welfare, public service, and important information and internet application systems for government agencies. To ensure the protection of CII, the cybersecurity review regime will continue to expand.

National Cyber Security Strategy of China: Illustrates and reaffirms China's main positions and propositions on cyberspace development and security and serves as the guide for China's cybersecurity work. The Strategy aims to build China into a cyber power while promoting orderly, secure, and open cyberspace and safeguarding national sovereignty.

Political Regime of China: Although the CCP describes China as a "socialist consultative democracy", the country is commonly referred to as an authoritarian one-party surveillance state and dictatorship. According to the Economist Intelligence Unit's Democracy Index, China consistently ranks low as an "authoritarian regime", ranking 156th out of 167 countries in 2022. It has also been described as authoritarian and corporatist, with some of the tightest restrictions in the entire world in many areas primarily against freedom of the press, freedom of assembly, the right to have children, the free formation of public organizations, freedom of religion and free access to the Internet. Its current political, ideological, and economic system has been described by its leaders as "all-process people's democracy", "people's democratic dictatorship", "socialism with Chinese characteristics" (that is, Marxism adapted to Chinese conditions), and "socialist market economy" respectively.

Political System of China: The People's Republic of China is a one-party Marxist-Leninist state ruled exclusively by the Communist Party of China (CCP), making it one of the last countries in the world to be ruled by the Communist Party. China's constitution states that the PRC "is a socialist state governed by a people's democratic dictatorship led by the working class and based on an alliance of workers and peasants" and that public institutions "should follow the principle of democratic centralism. The body of the constitution also states that "The defining feature of socialism with Chinese characteristics is the leadership of the Communist Party of China (CCP)."

Chapter 16
Analyzing Cybersecurity Strategies in Democratic and Authoritarian Regimes:
A Comparative Study of the United States and China

Mari Malvenishvili

Cyber Security Studies and Education Center, Georgia

ABSTRACT

This chapter aims to analyze the cybersecurity policies and strategies of the United States and China, representing democratic and authoritarian regimes, respectively. The study explores the key roles played by cyber security policies, legal frameworks, and international relations in these countries. By examining these aspects, the authors discern the disparities between cyber security policies in democratic and authoritarian regimes. The chapter highlights the diverse approaches employed to ensure cyber security and the challenges faced by both countries in countering cyber threats and safeguarding their national interests.

INTRODUCTION

The United States and China are economic rivals that recognize the vital role of information resources in securing the long-term survival of their respective nation-states. Both countries prioritize the secrecy, security, accessibility, and reliability of their information infrastructure to safeguard sensitive data and knowledge, thereby safeguarding their national interests (Donilon, 2014). China, boasting one of the world's fastest-growing internet economies, possesses dedicated cyber security capabilities that pose a threat not only to the United States but also to other Western nations.

The United States, through its national security adviser, has explicitly identified Chinese cyber intrusions as a significant concern for its military, highlighting the sophisticated and targeted theft of confidential business information and proprietary technologies (Donilon, 2014). Despite these cyber security

DOI: 10.4018/978-1-6684-8846-1.ch016

challenges, the relationship between the United States and China has maintained a degree of stability, largely driven by their trade relations. According to the Office of the United States Trade Representative (2022), China is the United States' largest goods trading partner, with a total goods trade of $559.2 billion in 2020. This economic interdependence and the principles of international trade, as postulated by Angell (2007), contribute to peace and stability.

However, beneath the economic ties lie stark differences in political regimes. The United States adheres to democratic governance, while China is widely perceived as maintaining an authoritarian rule. Democracy entails the broad distribution of authority among the people, granting citizens the right to sovereign power and participation in decision-making processes. In contrast, autocracy and oligarchy concentrate decision-making authority in the hands of a single individual or a select few (Duignan, 2012). Morlino (2009) identifies several characteristics that distinguish good democracies, including the rule of law, accountability (both electoral and inter-institutional), competition, participation, protection of rights and freedoms, political, social, and economic equality, responsiveness to public opinion, and engagement with civil society.

The influence of political regimes extends beyond cyber security and permeates a country's overall strategy, whether in economics, healthcare, or other domains. Scholars have engaged in extensive discussions on the concept of national strategy. Foster (1990) defines strategy as a conventional formula encompassing ends, ways, and means to project national power. However, Meiser (2017) criticizes simplifying strategy-making, arguing that it reduces it to a formulaic allocation of resources, impeding creative and adaptive thinking. While some find Meiser's perspective extreme, they acknowledge the importance of adopting a broader perspective that incorporates the interests and decisions of other actors, including allies and adversaries, to capture the essence of strategy. In terms of grand strategy, Posen (2014) and Gray (2010) emphasize the use of military force by states to pursue their interests.

In the context of cyber security, both China and the United States, as major global powers, rely on cyberspace for their economic, social, and overall well-being (Remington, 2019). They share common concerns about national security and the reliability of their information systems. Despite their divergent political regimes, they both recognize the significance of cyber security in protecting classified data, preventing theft and loss, and countering cyber-attacks and breaches that could be exploited by adversaries such as terrorists.

LITERATURE REVIEW

Cyber security has emerged as a critical concern in the modern world, posing significant challenges to countries, businesses, and individuals. This literature review aims to provide an overview of past research on cyber security, with a specific focus on democratic and authoritarian regimes in the United States and China (Edel & Brands, 2019). In a democratic regime, power is held by the people and exercised through accountable leaders elected by them, whereas an authoritarian regime concentrates power in the hands of a small group of individuals (Kendall-Taylor et al., 2020). These two types of regimes differ in their objectives and the means used to achieve them. Authoritarian regimes decide what is best for the people, imposing their values regardless of public opinion, while democratic regimes uphold free and fair elections, freedom of expression, the rule of law, and the separation of powers among the executive, legislative, and judiciary branches (Kendall-Taylor et al., 2020).

In democratic countries, cyber security strategies are predominantly characterized by collaboration between the government, private entities, and the general public (Bauman et al., 2014). Scholars emphasize the importance of legislative frameworks that balance national security concerns with individual and corporate autonomy (Weiss, 2019). The United States, as a prominent democratic nation, has implemented various cyber security policies and the cooperation between the public and private sectors has facilitated data sharing and the collective effort to combat cyber threats (Ginsburg, 2020).

In contrast, authoritarian countries approach cyber security from a perspective of control and surveillance, often prioritizing national security over individual confidentiality (Zeng, 2020). Previous studies have shown that in authoritarian regimes, the government formulates and implements cyber security strategies and policies independently. For instance, China has established detailed cyber security regulations and policies, including the Cyber Security Law. (Edel & Brands, 2019). Research indicates that democratic countries primarily prioritize civil rights and confidentiality protection while ensuring the maintenance of national security (Liu et al., 2021). However, authoritarian governments tend to emphasize information control and surveillance as means to preserve national security.

Cyber security has also become a significant area within international relations, as cyberspace serves as a shared domain where countries interact and influence each other in different ways (Grauman, 2013). The Chinese government engages in regional forums and alliances primarily based on its strategic interests, while the US government openly collaborates with its allies to share information and develop security strategies and policies (Ginsburg, 2020a). Past studies have explored cyber security in the context of US-China international relations, highlighting challenges such as cyber threats, espionage, political tensions, and intellectual property theft, which have shaped a mutual understanding between the two countries regarding cyber security (Sinkkonen, 2021). Democratic and authoritarian regimes face various challenges in international cyber security relations due to the constantly evolving landscape of global cyber governance.

In conclusion, understanding the approaches to cyber security in democratic and authoritarian regimes is essential for comprehending their strategies, policies, and international interactions. The differences in the conceptualization and implementation of cyber security measures highlight the broader implications of political regimes on national and global cyber security landscapes.

METHODOLOGY

This research paper adopts a comparative analysis design to examine the cyber security policies, legal frameworks, and international relations between the United States and China. The study employs qualitative research methods, including an extensive review of existing literature, policies, and reports. The literature review encompasses academic articles, government policies, books, and other relevant sources to develop a comprehensive understanding of cyber security in authoritarian and democratic regimes. Moreover, the research analyzes the cyber security policies, legislation, and strategies in the USA and China to identify both the similarities and differences.

To assess the national cyber security strategies of both countries, the research utilizes the National Capabilities Assessment Framework provided by the European Union Agency for Cybersecurity (ENISA, 2023). This framework consists of four key clusters: cybersecurity governance and standards, capacity-building and awareness, legal and regulatory, and cooperation. Each cluster comprises several subdirections, such as developing national contingency plans, protecting critical information infrastructure, organizing cyber security exercises, establishing incident-reporting mechanisms, addressing cybercrime, engaging in international cooperation beyond EU members, and establishing public-private partnerships (PPPs) while balancing security with privacy.

The cybersecurity governance and standards cluster evaluates a country's ability to formulate appropriate rules, guidelines, and best practices. The capacity-building and awareness cluster assesses a nation's capacity to enhance its cybersecurity capabilities and raise general knowledge and expertise in the field. The legal and regulatory cluster examines a country's ability to implement necessary legal and regulatory measures to combat cybercrime and protect vital information infrastructure. Lastly, the cooperation cluster scrutinizes cooperation and information sharing among various stakeholder groups at the national and international levels, recognizing the need for better comprehension and response to an ever-evolving threat landscape.

By incorporating the analyses of these four clusters into a unified policy, this research paper comprehensively examines the cyber security strategies of both the US and China, shedding light on the similarities and differences between the two countries.

CYBER SECURITY STRATEGY OF CHINA

China's cyber policies primarily revolve around maintaining national security, safeguarding state secrets, and promoting national growth. The ruling political power in China lies with the Chinese Communist Party (CCP), which has governed the country since 1949 (Michael, 2013). With 90 million members, the CCP is one of the largest political parties globally. Xi Jinping, the leader of the CCP, has been in power since 2013, and in 2018, the constitutional limit on presidential terms was repealed, allowing Xi Jinping to run for President indefinitely.

China's political system is firmly communist, with the CCP exerting complete control over the nation through a highly centralized, one-party system. The party monopolizes political and social life, controlling the army, police, media institutions, and the justice system. The government influences the allocation of resources, including bank loans, as most banks in China are state-owned (Sampi, 2022). Domestic media, owned by the government, consistently portrays favorable coverage of politics. While the government retains ownership of the nation's land, individuals and companies can own houses and other properties.

China heavily relies on technology but is concerned about the development of the Internet and the flow of information. The Chinese government considers uncontrolled information as a threat to the regime and aims to reap the economic benefits of the Internet while maintaining political control. The Chinese concept of the Internet revolves around real-time censorship, which is different from the Western view. The prominent example of this censorship is the Great Firewall of China (GFW), which allows authorities to deny access to various websites by monitoring Internet traffic and isolating Chinese networks from the global Internet. The GFW is an advanced internet filtering system that blocks global IP addresses, including popular social networks such as YouTube, Facebook, Twitter, Google services, Instagram, and Wikipedia. It examines internet traffic for specific keywords related to topics the Chinese government has banned or objects to, ensuring strict control over information flow (Wessing, 2018).

China has been named the world's most repressive online environment for the past eight years according to the Freedom House's annual survey on internet freedom (Isachenkov & Tong-hyung, 2023).

The Chinese government has implemented censorship measures during the pandemic, blocking content related to the lockdown experience, campaigns against sexual assault and harassment, and tightening control over online content concerning women's rights. The government has also imposed new policies to exert greater control over Chinese technology enterprises, with proposed regulations penalizing businesses that facilitate bypassing the Great Firewall (Isachenkov & Tong-hyung, 2023). However, specific requirements for data kept or requested by the government have not been explicitly stated.

China's approach to internet governance differs significantly from that of the United States and other Western countries. China advocates for "cyber sovereignty," whereby each state exercises control over all internet users within its physical borders. This perspective challenges the Western notion of a liberal Internet that respects human rights and allows information to flow freely across borders (Ning & Wu, 2022). China has promoted the concept of cyber sovereignty and the right of states to regulate the Internet based on national interests through proposals like the International Code of Conduct for Information Security in the United Nations General Assembly.

Several government institutions in China are responsible for cybersecurity management. The Ministry of Public Security (MPS) plays a crucial role in ensuring critical infrastructure security and handling cybercrime investigations. The MPS also operates the Great Firewall of China. The Ministry of State Security (MSS) conducts counterintelligence and foreign intelligence activities, including cyber espionage operations. The Ministry of Industry and Information Technology (MIIT) sets standards, conducts cybersecurity drills, and coordinates information and telecommunications security. CNCERT/CC, the National Computer Network Emergency Response Technical Team (2023), is China's national CERT (Computer Emergency Response Team) responsible for cybersecurity event handling, threat intelligence, and providing technical guidelines and standards.

China possesses robust cyber military capabilities through the Strategic Support Force (SSF), a branch of the People's Liberation Army (PLA). Established in 2015, the SSF plays a significant role in China's military strategy by supporting the three military pillars: the People's Liberation Army Army (PLA), the People's Liberation Army Navy (PLAN), and the People's Liberation Army Air Force (PLAAF).

The SSF's responsibilities encompass various domains:

- **Space operations**: The SSF is responsible for managing China's space assets, including satellite and space-based surveillance and communication systems.
- **Cyberspace operations**: The SSF conducts operations in cyberspace to protect China's interests and counteract the actions of its adversaries.
- **Electronic warfare**: China's SSF develops and operates systems for electronic warfare, including jamming and targeting capabilities.
- **Psychological operations**: The SSF engages in psychological warfare to influence the thoughts and actions of its adversaries.
- **Covert and overt missions**: The SSF's special operations section carries out missions such as sabotage, reconnaissance, and other tasks necessary for China's military objectives.

These capabilities within the SSF contribute significantly to China's overall military strategy, especially in domains such as space, cyberspace, and electronic warfare (Kimberly & Murray, 2014).

Furthermore, China has enacted several laws and regulations to enhance cyber governance and security. The Cyber Security Law, implemented in 2017, imposes legal requirements on network operators and data privacy (Mao, 2021). It grants the Chinese government the authority to monitor and control cyberspace activities.

Another crucial law is the National Intelligence Law, also enacted in 2017. This law empowers the Chinese government to compel organizations and individuals to collaborate with intelligence agencies and provide information when required for national security purposes (Kalathil, 2017).

Additionally, China has established the Regulations on Critical Infrastructure (CII) to further strengthen cybersecurity (Government of the Russian Federation, 2015). These regulations aim to safeguard critical infrastructure and enhance resilience against cyberattacks.

China's engagement in international relations on cybersecurity primarily revolves around safeguarding its national interests (Liang & Lu, 2010). While China participates in bilateral agreements for information sharing and collaboration in law enforcement, its approach differs from that of Western democracies, emphasizing information control and cyberspace dominance (Maizland & Albert, 2022). China's engagement in regional initiatives, such as the Shanghai Cooperation Organization (SCO) and the ASEAN Regional Forum (ARF), is driven by its own interests (Hoang et al., 2021).

In contrast to Western perspectives, China upholds the concept of "cyber sovereignty," advocating that each state should have control over Internet users within its borders (Beam, 2010). This viewpoint challenges the idea of a liberal Internet that respects human rights and promotes the free flow of information across borders (Zeng, 2020).

Furthermore, China has been strengthening its cooperation with Russia in the cyber domain. The two countries have increased collaboration in the military and technological spheres, including their influence within the International Telecommunication Union (Clayton et al., 2006). Together, they aim to advance a more state-controlled approach to Internet governance and gain advantages for their national businesses.

Overall, China's cyber security strategy encompasses a strong focus on national security, information control, and the development of robust cyber military capabilities. The Chinese government maintains strict control over cyberspace activities, enforces laws and regulations to enhance cybersecurity, and actively engages in international relations based on its national interests.

CYBER SECURITY STRATEGY OF THE US

The cyber security organization in the United States is composed of various agencies with different roles and responsibilities. The critical policy coordinator is the Information and Communications Infrastructure Interagency Policy Committee (ICI-IPC) of the National Security Council (NSC). This committee, chaired by the Cyber Security Coordinator of the NSC, oversees the development and implementation of national cyber security strategies and policies (Segal, 2016).

The Department of Homeland Security (DHS) plays a primary role in cyber security. Established in 2002 by the Internal Security Act, DHS is responsible for strengthening the security and resilience of critical infrastructure, assisting federal agencies in cyber security procurement, enhancing law enforcement capabilities, and responding to cyber incidents. The DHS manages the US Computer Emergency Response Team (US-CERT) to coordinate cyber incident response efforts (Shahbaz et al., 2022).

The Department of State (DoS) coordinates and communicates the President's cyber security policy internationally. The Department of Justice (DOJ) is responsible for developing the legal framework related to cyber security, investigating and prosecuting cybercrime, gathering intelligence, and providing legal and political assistance to other agencies (Department of State, 2023). The DOJ also conducts national security operations related to cyber threats within its jurisdiction.

The Department of Defense (DOD) is tasked with protecting the military's information infrastructure and the "MIL" domain from cyber attacks. The DOD operates the US Cyber Command (USCYBER-COM), which centrally manages and controls cyberspace operations (Department of Defense, 2023).

Unlike China, the United States has 16 critical infrastructure sectors, and each sector has competent authority. While DHS is responsible for ensuring cyber security in most sectors, including the government sector, other agencies may have specific roles within their respective sectors (The State Council, 2014).

To facilitate information exchange between DHS and critical infrastructure sectors, the Critical Infrastructure Information Act establishes procedures and safeguards. The Information Analysis and Infrastructure Protection Directorate within DHS receives and processes information from critical infrastructure entities (US Department of Justice, 2014). The received information is protected from unauthorized disclosure and used solely for official duties, prevention, identification, and response to cyber threats. The CIA and the Attorney General provide consent for the use of critical information related to critical infrastructure (Department of Defense, 2023a).

The Directorate has authority to access and analyze various types of information stored in critical infrastructure entities and federal agencies. However, the acquisition and use of this information are conducted in compliance with personal data security norms and federal legislation (The White House, 2021).

Critical infrastructure entities are required by federal law to implement appropriate security mechanisms and comply with DHS regulations. Failure to comply with these obligations may result in legal consequences (Department of Defense, 2023b).

The United States has been actively developing cybersecurity policies and strategies since the 2000s. The 2010 cyber security strategy emphasized concerns over state-sponsored cyber activities, such as industrial espionage, with China and Russia identified as key threats. The most recent cyber security strategy, released in March 2023, outlines five strategic objectives: defending critical infrastructure, disrupting and dismantling threat actors, shaping market forces for security and resilience, investing in a resilient future, and forging international partnerships (Cybersecurity and Infrastructure Security Agency, 2023).

The US has enacted significant laws and regulations to strengthen cyber security. The Cybersecurity Information Sharing Act (CISA), passed in 2015, enables organizations to share cyber threat information with the federal government. The Federal Information Security Modernization Act (FISMA), effective since 2014, mandates risk-based information security procedures for federal agencies. The National Institute of Standards and Technology (NIST) Cybersecurity Framework offers voluntary recommendations for enhancing cybersecurity. The Computer Fraud and Abuse Act (CFAA) covers various computer-related offenses (Cybersecurity and Infrastructure Security Agency, 2023).

The US cyber security legislation aims to foster collaboration, information sharing, and risk management within the cybersecurity ecosystem (The White House, 2023). Although there is still work to be done to address evolving cyber threats, these laws and regulations represent significant progress.

Cyberspace plays a vital role in the United States' economic, social, and political life, and the country has developed a National Cyber Strategy to secure its cyberspace and promote a vibrant digital space for American citizens. The National Cyber Strategy focuses on ensuring the confidentiality and integrity of U.S. citizens' information (Cybersecurity and Infrastructure Security Agency, 2023a).

Additionally, the Department of Homeland Security collaborates with private entities to establish cyber security frameworks and best practices. The U.S. has implemented a comprehensive legal framework to address cyber threats and protect its citizens. This framework includes policies, laws, regulations, and dedicated agencies for cyber security.

For instance, the Federal Information Security Modernization Act (FISMA) has developed strategies to safeguard federal government data, systems, and infrastructure. The U.S. also encourages public and private entities to collaborate through information sharing to ensure data security and collectively combat cyber attacks.

Moreover, the United States actively engages in international relations to share data, discuss strategies and policies, and enforce laws in the digital space. This collaboration aims to enhance global cyber security and promote a safer cyber environment.

The rise of the internet and the growth of cyberspace have coincided with the United States' emergence as a global superpower. Cyberspace has become integral to the country's wealth creation and innovation, inseparable from its economic, social, and political spheres (Robinson et al., 2013).

In the National Cyber Strategy, China is identified as engaging in economic cyber-espionage, resulting in trillions of dollars' worth of intellectual property theft from the U.S. (Lawson, 2012). The U.S. National Cyber Strategy prioritizes combating cyber threats, securing its cyberspace, and fostering a vibrant digital environment for its citizens.

By establishing a robust cyber security framework, the U.S. aims to protect the confidentiality and integrity of its citizens' information. The Department of Homeland Security works in conjunction with private entities to develop cyber security frameworks and best practices (Coats, 2019).

The United States has also implemented a comprehensive legal framework to tackle cyber threats. This framework comprises policies, laws, regulations, and specialized agencies dedicated to cyber security. For instance, the Federal Information Security Modernization Act (FISMA) ensures the protection of federal government data, systems, and infrastructure (Coats, 2019). It requires organizations to adopt risk-based information security procedures and conduct regular security assessments.

Furthermore, the U.S. actively promotes collaboration and information sharing among public and private entities to strengthen data security and collectively combat cyber attacks (Robinson et al., 2013). This approach recognizes the importance of a unified front in addressing cyber threats.

Internationally, the U.S. engages in diplomatic relations to share information, discuss strategies and policies, and enforce laws in the digital space. By fostering international cooperation, the U.S. aims to enhance global cyber security and ensure a safer cyber environment for all nations.

Overall, the United States recognizes the significance of cyberspace in its economic, social, and political domains. Through its National Cyber Strategy, comprehensive legal framework, and international collaborations, the U.S. strives to secure its cyberspace, protect its citizens, and contribute to a resilient and secure digital landscape.

CONCLUSION

Both the United States and China have established comprehensive cybersecurity rules, laws, and regulations to safeguard themselves against potential cyber threats. However, their approaches to cybersecurity differ significantly. In the United States, the primary objective is to defend critical infrastructure, such as power plants, banking systems, and government networks, from cyberattacks. The U.S. government employs offensive cybersecurity operations and collaborates with industry to develop and implement cybersecurity standards and procedures.

On the other hand, China places a high priority on cybersecurity, with a particular emphasis on internet censorship and the suppression of online opposition as essential components of social stability and national security. China's cybersecurity laws have strained its relationships with the U.S. and other countries, granting the government broad authority to track online activity and regulate data flow. Although China and the U.S. share similar goals in protecting critical infrastructure, their divergent political ideologies and institutional setups result in contrasting approaches to cybersecurity.

The differing perspectives on privacy and security between China and the United States stem from their political and cultural origins. China's greater emphasis on security and political control sometimes places individual privacy secondary to the state's demands. Policies like the Great Firewall have been implemented in China to regulate internet access and suppress online activism. In contrast, the U.S. historically placed a higher value on individual privacy, enshrining citizen's rights in law. However, security breaches and revelations, such as those from Edward Snowden, have prompted debates on the balance between security and privacy in the U.S.

The United States has accused China of engaging in industrial hacking while distinguishing between legal data collection for national security and illegal economic espionage. China, on the other hand, denies hacking claims and rejects the American stance on internet surveillance. In response, the Chinese government has banned American internet companies from entering its domestic market to safeguard its infrastructure. These developments have strained relations between the two countries.

The tension between privacy and security remains a recurring topic in both the United States and China, driven by high-profile security breaches and terrorist incidents. Finding a compromise between these two complex challenges is an ongoing endeavor.

It is important to note that cybersecurity rules and regulations differ between authoritarian and democratic nations. Authoritarian governments typically possess more power to control and monitor online behavior within their borders, resulting in cybersecurity policies focused on information control and censorship to uphold political power. For example, China's "Great Firewall" system blocks platforms like Twitter and Facebook, while monitoring internet traffic. In democratic countries, legal and moral restrictions exist on government powers to monitor internet usage for security concerns, with rules safeguarding user privacy and requiring search warrants for digital communications.

Overall, there are significant variations in the goals and priorities of authoritarian and democratic governments, which manifest in their respective cybersecurity strategies. The United States adopts a detailed approach to defend its citizens and national interests, while China prioritizes information control, cyber sovereignty, and protection of state secrets. Additionally, the U.S. emphasizes privacy protection, public-private collaboration, and information breach notifications within its legal framework, while China's laws and regulations grant the government control over its citizens' cyberspace. Furthermore, the United States actively engages in open international relations to collaborate with allies and share information, while China's participation in international relations is often driven by its national interests.

REFERENCES

Angell, N. (2007). *The Great Illusion*. Cosimo Classics.

Bauman, Z., Bigo, D., Esteves, P., Guild, E., Jabri, V., Lyon, D., & Walker, R. B. (2014). After Snowden: Rethinking the impact of surveillance. *International Political Sociology, 8*(2), 121–144. doi:10.1111/ips.12048

Beam, C. (2010). *How Communist Is China?* Retrieved from https://slate.com/news-and-politics/2010/07/how-communist-is-china-anyway.html

Clayton, R., Murdoch, S. J., & Watson, R. N. (2006). Ignoring the great firewall of China. In *Privacy Enhancing Technologies: 6th International Workshop, PET 2006, Cambridge, UK, June 28-30, 2006, Revised Selected Papers 6* (pp. 20–35). Springer Berlin Heidelberg.

Coats, D. R. (2019). *Worldwide threat assessment of the US intelligence community*. Retrieved from https://www.dni.gov/files/ODNI/documents/2019-ATA-SFR---SSCI.pdf

Cybersecurity and Infrastructure Security Agency. (2023). *Interagency Security Committee Policies, Standards, Best Practices, Guidance Documents, and White Papers*. Retrieved from https://www.cisa.gov/resources-tools/groups/interagency-security-committee-isc/policies-standards-best-practices-guidance-documents-and-white-papers

Cybersecurity and Infrastructure Security Agency. (2023a). *Protected Critical Infrastructure Information (PCII) Program*. Retrieved from https://www.cisa.gov/resources-tools/programs/protected-critical-infrastructure-information-pcii-program#:~:text=Congress%20created%20the%20Protected%20Critical,state%2Flocal%20government%20critical%20infrastructure

Department of Defense. (2023). *Department of Defense*. Retrieved from https://www.defense.gov/

Department of Homeland Security. (2023a). *Cybersecurity*. Retrieved from https://www.dhs.gov/

Department of Homeland Security. (2023b). *United States Computer Emergency Readiness Team*. Retrieved from https://www.cisa.gov/sites/default/files/publications/infosheet_US-CERT_v2.pdf

Department of State. (2023). *Cyber issues*. Retrieved from https://www.state.gov/

Donilon, T. (2014). *The United States and the Asia-Pacific in 2013*. Asia Society.

Duignan, B. (Ed.). (2012). *Forms of Government and the Rise of Democracy*. Britannica Educational Publishing.

Edel, C., & Brands, H. (2019). The real origins of the US-China Cold War. *Foreign Policy*, 2.

Ginsburg, T. (2020). Authoritarian international law? *The American Journal of International Law, 114*(2), 221–260. doi:10.1017/ajil.2020.3

Ginsburg, T. (2020a). How Authoritarians Use International Law. *Journal of Democracy, 31*(4), 44–58. doi:10.1353/jod.2020.0054

Government of the Russian Federation. (2015). *On signing the Agreement between the Government of the Russian Federation and the Government of the People's Republic of China on cooperation in ensuring international information security.* Retrieved from https://cyber-peace.org/wp-content/uploads/2013/05/RUS-

Grauman, B. (2013). *Cyber-security: The Vexed Question of Global Rules.* Retrieved from https://www.files.ethz.ch/isn/139895/SDA_Cyber_report_FINAL.pdf

Hoang, N. P., Niaki, A. A., Dalek, J., Knockel, J., Lin, P., Marczak, B., . . . Polychronakis, M. (2021). *How great is the Great Firewall? Measuring China's DNS censorship.* Retrieved from https://www.usenix.org/conference/usenixsecurity21/presentation/hoang

Isachenkov, V., & Tong-hyung, K. (2023). *Xi awarded 3rd term as China's president, extending rule.* Retrieved from https://apnews.com/article/xi-jinping-china-president-vote-5e6230d8c881dc17b11a781e-832accd1

Kalathil, S. (2017). *Beyond the great firewall: How China Became a global information power.* Center for International Media Assistance.

Kendall-Taylor, A., Frantz, E., & Wright, J. (2020). The digital dictators: How technology strengthens autocracy. *Foreign Affairs, 99,* 103.

Kimberly, H., & Murray, C. (2014). *China and International Law in Cyberspace.* Retrieved from https://www.uscc.gov/sites/default/files/Research/China%20International%20Law%20in%20Cyberspace.pdf

Lawson, S. (2012). Putting the "war" in cyberwar: Metaphor, analogy, and cybersecurity discourse in the United States. *First Monday.* Advance online publication. doi:10.5210/fm.v17i7.3848

Liang, B., & Lu, H. (2010). Internet development, censorship, and cyber crimes in China. *Journal of Contemporary Criminal Justice, 26*(1), 103–120. doi:10.1177/1043986209350437

Liu, Z., Guo, J., Zhong, W., & Gui, T. (2021). Multi-level governance, policy coordination and subnational responses to COVID-19: Comparing China and the US. *Journal of Comparative Policy Analysis, 23*(2), 204–218. doi:10.1080/13876988.2021.1873703

Maizland, L., & Albert, E. (2022). *The Chinese Communist Party.* Retrieved from https://www.cfr.org/backgrounder/chinese-communist-party

Mao, Y. (2021). Political institutions, state capacity, and crisis management: A comparison of China and South Korea. *International Political Science Review, 42*(3), 316–332. doi:10.1177/0192512121994026

Meiser, J. W. (2017). Ends+ways+means=(bad) strategy. *Jeffrey W. Meiser," Ends+ Ways+Means=(Bad) Strategy. Parameters, 46*(4), 2016–2017.

Michael, D. (2013). *Chinese Views on Cybersecurity in Foreign Relations. China Leadership Monitor.* http://carnegieendowment.org/2013/09/20/chinese-views-oncybersecurity-in-foreign-relations

Morlino, L. (2009). *Qualities of democracy: how to analyze them.* University of Aberdeen: Centre for the Study of Public Policy.

Ning, S., & Wu, H. (2022). *Cybersecurity laws and regulations in China*. Retrieved from https://iclg.com/practice-areas/cybersecurity-laws-and-regulations/china

Office of the United States Trade Representative. (2020). *US-China trade facts*. Retrieved from https://ustr.gov/countries-regions/china-mongolia-taiwan/peoples-republic-china

Remington, T. F. (2019). Institutional change in authoritarian regimes: Pension reform in Russia and China. *Problems of Post-Communism, 66*(5), 301–314. doi:10.1080/10758216.2018.1450154

Robinson, N. (2013). *Cyber-Security Threat Characterization: A Rapid Comparative Analysis*. RAND Corporation.

Sampi. (2022). *China Cybersecurity Law: 5 Things You Should Know*. Retrieved from https://sampi.co/china-cybersecurity-law/

Segal, A. (2016). *The Hacked World Order: How Nations Fight, Trade, Maneuver, and Manipulate in the Digital Age*. Retrieved from https://www.cia.gov/static/e8955c913bf94ec5764481a03cd0f7ee/hacked-world-order.pdf

Shahbaz, A., Funk, A., & Vesteinsson, K. (2022). *Countering an authoritarian overhaul of the internet*. Retrieved from https://freedomhouse.org/report/freedom-net/2022/countering-authoritarian-overhaul-internet

Sinkkonen, E. (2021). Dynamic dictators: Improving the research agenda on autocratization and authoritarian resilience. *Democratization, 28*(6), 1172–1190. doi:10.1080/13510347.2021.1903881

The National Computer Network Emergency Response Technical Team. (2023). *CNCERT/CC*. Retrieved from https://www.cert.org.cn/publish/english/index.html

The State Council. (2014). *Ministry of Industry and Information Technology*. Retrieved from http://english.www.gov.cn/state_council/2014/08/23/content_281474983035940.htm

The White House. (2021). *The United States, Joined by Allies and Partners, Attributes Malicious Cyber Activity and Irresponsible State Behavior to the People's Republic of China*. Retrieved from https://www.whitehouse.gov/briefing-room/statements-releases/2021/07/19/the-united-states-joined-by-allies-and-partners-attributes-malicious-cyber-activity-and-irresponsible-state-behavior-to-the-peoples-republic-of-china/

The White House. (2023). *Biden-Harris Administration Announces National Cybersecurity Strategy*. Retrieved from https://www.whitehouse.gov/briefing-room/statements-releases/2023/03/02/fact-sheet-biden-harris-administration-announces-national-cybersecurity-strategy/

US Department of Justice. (2014). *US Charges Five Chinese Military Hackers for Cyber Espionage against US Corporations and a Labor Organization for Commercial Advantage*. Retrieved from https://www.justice.gov/opa/pr/2014/May/14-ag528.html

Weiss, J. C. (2019). A world safe for autocracy? *Foreign Affairs, 98*(4), 92–108.

Wessing, T. (2018). *Cybersecurity in Singapore and China*. Retrieved from https://www.taylorwessing.com/synapse/article-cybersecurity-singapore-china.html

Zeng, J. (2020). Artificial intelligence and China's authoritarian governance. *International Affairs, 96*(6), 1441–1459. doi:10.1093/ia/iiaa172

Compilation of References

A Critical Review of Concepts, Benefits, and Pitfalls of Blockchain Technology Using Concept Map. (2020). *IEEE Journals & Magazine*. Https://ieeexplore.ieee.org/document/9056816

Allianz. (2016). *Cyber attacks on critical infrastructure*. Retrieved from: https://www.agcs.allianz.com/news-and-insights/expert-risk-articles/cyber-attacks-on-critical-infrastructure.html#:~:text=Cyber%2Dattacks%20against%20critical%20infrastructure%20and%20key%20manufacturing%20industries%20have,against%20ICS%20and%20corporate%20networks

Alshawi, S. H., Alrodhan, W., & Alarifi, A. (2020). Predicting Cyberbullying on Social Media Using Machine Learning Algorithms. *IEEE Access : Practical Innovations, Open Solutions, 8*, 11349–11360. doi:10.1109/access.2020.2968009

Alshrari, A. (2019). Patriot Act, Section 206: Its Impact on Muslim Populations in the US (With Special Reference to Roving Wiretap Policy). *Public Policy and Administration, 7*(1), 15–21.

Amara, M., & Siad, A. (2011). Elliptic Curve Cryptography and its applications. *International Workshop on Systems, Signal Processing and their Applications*. 10.1109/WOSSPA.2011.5931464

America's Cyber Defense Agency (CISA). (2022). *Russia Cyber Threat Overview and Advisories*. Retrieved from https://www.cisa.gov/russia

Anagnostakis, D. (2021). The European Union-United States cybersecurity relationship: A transatlantic functional co-operation. *Journal of Cyber Policy, 6*(2), 243–261. doi:10.1080/23738871.2021.1916975

Angell, N. (2007). *The Great Illusion*. Cosimo Classics.

Annan, K. A. (2004). *A More Secure World: Our Shared Responsibility Report of the Secretary-General's High-level Panel on Threats, Challenges, and Change*. The United Nations.

Apsny. (2016). *NATO has recognized cyberspace as an equal area of defense*. Information and Analytical Portal Georgia Online. Retrieved from: https://www.apsny.ge/2016/pol/1468046923.php

Article 42(7) TEU - The EU's mutual assistance clause | EEAS Website. (n.d.). Retrieved 4 April 2023, from https://www.eeas.europa.eu/eeas/article-427-teu-eus-mutual-assistance-clause_en

Aste, T., Tasca, P., & Di Matteo, T. (2017). Blockchain technologies: the foreseeable impact on society and industry. *IEEE Computer, 50*(9), 18–28. doi:10.1109/MC.2017.3571064

Asvija, B., Eswari, R., & Bijoy, M. B. (2021). Security Threat Modelling With Bayesian Networks and Sensitivity Analysis for IAAS Virtualization Stack. *Journal of Organizational and End User Computing, 33*(4), 44–69. doi:10.4018/JOEUC.20210701.oa3

Barker, W. C. (2021). *Cybersecurity Framework Profile for Ransomware Risk Management*. U.S. Department of Commerce. doi:10.6028/NIST.IR.8374-draft

Barry, M., Vinton, G., David, D., Robert, E., Kleinrock, L., & Daniel, C. (1997). *Brief History of the Internet.* Cybersecurity Strategy of the European Union: An Open, Safe and Secure Cyberspace. Retrieve from: https://eeas.europa.eu/archives/docs/policies/eu-ybersecurity/cybsec_comm_en.pdf

Bastian, A. A. (2022). *"Foreign Policy" China Is Stepping Up Its Information War on Taiwan.* https://foreignpolicy.com/2022/08/02/china-pelosi-taiwan-information/

Bateman, J. (2022). *Carnegie, Russia's Wartime Cyber Operations in Ukraine: Military Impacts, Influences, and Implications.* https://carnegieendowment.org/2022/12/16/russia-s-wartime-cyber-operations-in-ukraine-military-impacts-influences-and-implications-pub-88657

Bateman, J. (2022). Russia's Wartime Cyber Operations in Ukraine: Military Impacts, Influences, and Implications. *Carnegie Endowment for International Peace.* Retrieved from https://carnegieendowment.org/2022/12/16/russia-s-wartime-cyber-operations-in-ukraine-military-impacts-influences-and-implications-pub-88657

Bauman, Z., Bigo, D., Esteves, P., Guild, E., Jabri, V., Lyon, D., & Walker, R. B. (2014). After Snowden: Rethinking the impact of surveillance. *International Political Sociology*, 8(2), 121–144. doi:10.1111/ips.12048

Beam, C. (2010). *How Communist Is China?* Retrieved from https://slate.com/news-and-politics/2010/07/how-communist-is-china-anyway.html

Bedritsky, A. (2008). *Information war: concepts and their realization in the USA.* RISI.

Bellamy, R. (2016). A European Republic of Sovereign States: Sovereignty, republicanism and the European Union. *European Journal of Political Theory*, 16(2), 188–209. doi:10.1177/1474885116654389

Bellanova, R., Carrapico, H., & Duez, D. (2022). Digital/sovereignty and European security integration: An introduction. *European Security*, 31(3), 337–355. doi:10.1080/09662839.2022.2101887

Benincasa, E. (2021). The Case for Cyber 'Disarmament' in the European Union. *The International Spectator*, 56(1), 39–54. doi:10.1080/03932729.2021.1872200

Bernal, A., Carter, C., Singh, I., Cao, K., & Madreperla, O. (2020). *Cognitive warfare: An attack on truth and thought.* NATO/John Hopkins University. https://www.innovationhub-act.org/sites/default/files/2021-03/Cognitive%20Warfare.pdf

Bharti, M. S., & Singh, A. (2023). India and France bilateral partnership for advancing strategic autonomy in the Indo-Pacific region: Special reference to the Indo-French strategic partnership. *Cogent Social Sciences*, 9(1), 2215561. doi:10.1080/23311886.2023.2215561

Bharti, S. S., & Aryal, S. K. (2022). The right to privacy and an implication of the EU General Data Protection Regulation (GDPR) in Europe: Challenges to the companies. *Journal of Contemporary European Studies*, 1–12. doi:10.1080/14782804.2022.2130193

Biden Jr. (2021). *Interim National Security Strategic Guidance.* White House. Retrieved on 2023 from https://www.whitehouse.gov/wp-content/uploads/2021/03/NSC-1v2.pdf

Bond, J. A. (1996). *Peacetime foreign data manipulation as one aspect of offensive information warfare: Questions of legality under the united nations charter article.* doi:10.21236/ADA310926

Bradford, A. (2020). *The Brussels effect: how the European Union rules the world.* Oxford University Press. doi:10.1093/oso/9780190088583.001.0001

Braune, E., & Dana, L. P. (2022). Digital entrepreneurship: Some features of new social interactions. *Canadian Journal of Administrative Sciences / Revue Canadienne Des Sciences de l'Administration*, 39(3), 237–243. doi:10.1002/cjas.1653

Buckland, B., Schreier, F., & Winkler, T. (2010). *Democratic Governance Challenges of Cyber Security DCAF Horizon.* Working Paper Series. Retrieved from: http://genevasecurityforum.org/files/DCAF-GSF-cyber-Paper.pdf

Buenrostro, E., Rivera, A. O. G., Tosh, D. K., Acosta, J. C., & Njilla, L. (2019b). Evaluating Usability of Permissioned Blockchain for Internet-of-Battlefield Things Security. Military Communications Conference. doi:10.1109/MILCOM47813.2019.9020736

Bumgardner, S. (2019). Article 4 of the North Atlantic treaty. *Emory International Law Review*, *34*, 71. https://scholarlycommons.law.emory.edu/eilr/vol34/iss0/6

Buresh, D. L. (2021). Comparison of National Security and the Cybersecurity Approaches of the United States under Presidents Trump and Biden versus the National Security and Cybersecurity Approach of Canada. *Journal of Business Management and Economics*, 1-9.

Burgess, M. (2022). A Mysterious Satellite Hack Has Victims Far Beyond Ukraine. *Wired*. Retrieved from https://www.wired.co.uk/article/viasat-internet-hack-ukraine-russia

Burgess, J., & Hurcombe, E. (2019). Digital journalism as symptom, response, and agent of change in the platformed media environment. *Digital Journalism (Abingdon, England)*, *7*(3), 359–367. doi:10.1080/21670811.2018.1556313

Burson-Marsteller. (2010). Social Media Check-up: a Burson – Marsteller Evidence-Based Tool. Academic Press.

Business to Business. (2016). *The five generations of computers*. Retrieved from: https://btob.co.nz/business-news/five-generations-computers/

Cachia, J. C., & DeBattista, A. P. (2022). Political narrative, collective EU security and the State of the Union. *European Politics and Society*, 1–17. doi:10.1080/23745118.2022.2082035

Calderaro, A., & Blumfelde, S. (2022). Artificial intelligence and EU security: The false promise of digital sovereignty. *European Security*, *31*(3), 415–434. doi:10.1080/09662839.2022.2101885

Canmales, K., & Jibilian, I. (2022). *The US is readying sanctions against Russia over the SolarWinds cyber attack.* Retrieved from: https://www.ft.com/content/d7d67ea7-8423-4b9c-819d-761fa4a10fa0

Carmi, E., Yates, S. J., Lockley, E., & Pawluczuk, A. (2020). Data citizenship: Rethinking data literacy in the age of disinformation, misinformation, and malinformation. *Internet Policy Review*, *9*(2), 1–22. doi:10.14763/2020.2.1481

Carrapico, H., & Barrinha, A. (2018). European Union cyber security as an emerging research and policy field. *European Political Science*, *19*(3), 299–303. doi:10.1080/23745118.2018.1430712

Cavelty, M., & Wenger, A. (2022). *Cyber Security Politics Socio-Technological Transformations and Political Fragmentation*. Retrieved from: https://library.oapen.org/bitstream/handle/20.500.12657/52574/9781000567113.pdf?sequence=1

Cavelty, M. D. (2013). From Cyber-Bombs to Political Fallout: Threat Representations with an Impact in the Cyber-Security Discourse. *International Studies Review*, *15*(1), 105–122. doi:10.1111/misr.12023

Cavelty, M. D. (2019). The Politics of Cybersecurity: Balancing Different Roles of the State. *St. Antony's International Review*, *15*(1), 37–57. doi:10.1080/13523260.2019.1678855

Cavelty, M. D., & Wagner, A. (2022). *Cyber Security Politics, Socio-Technological Transformations and Political Fragmentation*. Routledge. doi:10.4324/9781003110224

CERN. (2020). *CERN Accelerating science, "A short history of the Web - Where the Web was born"*. Retrieved from: https://home.cern/science/computing/birth-web/short-history-web

Chachanidze, G. (2021). *China - The main challenge of the democratic world in cyberspace.* GFSIS.

Chedrawi, C., & Howayeck, P. (2018). The role of blockchain technology in military strategy formulation, a resource based view on capabilities. *Researchgate.* Https://www.researchgate.net/publication/330346994

Cheng, D. (2017). Cyber dragon, inside China s information warfare and cyber operations. In The Changing Face of War. Praeger.

Chiara, P. G. (2022). The IoT and the new EU cybersecurity regulatory landscape. *International Review of Law Computers & Technology, 36*(2), 118–137. doi:10.1080/13600869.2022.2060468

Chiriac, O. (2022). Military applications of cognitive sciences: Cognitive warfare, a matter of perception and misperception. *International Scientific Conference" STRATEGIESXXI", 18*(1), 474-484. 10.53477/2971-8813-22-55

Chitadze, N. (2016). *Political Science.* International Black Sea University.

Chitadze, N. (2022). *World Politics and Challenges in International Security.* IGI Global. doi:10.4018/978-1-7998-9586-2

Chitadze, N. (2023). *Geopolitical Consequences of the Russia-Ukraine War.* IGI Global. doi:10.4018/978-1-6684-8521-7

Christou, G. (2018). The challenges of cybercrime governance in the European Union. *European Political Science, 19*(3), 355–375. doi:10.1080/23745118.2018.1430722

Christou, G. (2019). The collective securitisation of cyberspace in the European Union. *West European Politics, 42*(2), 278–301. doi:10.1080/01402382.2018.1510195

Chu, D. (2021). *Brazil ditches US drive to strangle Huawei.* Global Times. Retrieved from: https://www.globaltimes.cn/page/202101/1213075.html

CISA. (2022, May 9). *Russian State-Sponsored and Criminal Cyber Threats to Critical Infrastructure.* Retrieved from https://www.cisa.gov/news-events/cybersecurity-advisories/aa22-110a

Čižik, T. (2017). *Information Warfare - New Security Challenge for Europe.* Retrieved from: https://www.researchgate.net/publication/322695565_Information_Warfare_-_New_Security_Challenge_for_Europe

Clark, B. (2022). The Fall and Rise of Russian Electronic Warfare. *IEEE Spectrum.* Retrieved from https://spectrum.ieee.org/the-fall-and-rise-of-russian-electronic-warfare#toggle-gdpr

Clarker, A. (2010). Cyber War: The Next Threat to National Security and What to do About it. Harper Collins.

Claverie, B., & du Cluzel, F. (2022). The Cognitive Warfare Concept. *Innovation Hub Sponsored by NATO Allied Command Transformation,* 2022-02.

Clayton, R., Murdoch, S. J., & Watson, R. N. (2006). Ignoring the great firewall of China. In *Privacy Enhancing Technologies: 6th International Workshop, PET 2006, Cambridge, UK, June 28-30, 2006, Revised Selected Papers 6* (pp. 20–35). Springer Berlin Heidelberg.

Clifford, R. (1987). Reflexive Control. In B. D. A. P. Parker (Ed.), *Soviet Military Planning, Soviet Strategic Deception.* Lexington Books.

CNet. (2015). *Obama asks for $14 billion to step up cybersecurity - The president urges Congress to pass legislation that would strengthen the country's hacking detection system and counterintelligence capabilities.* Retrieved from: https://www.cnet.com/news/obama-adds-14b-to-budget-for-stepped-up-cybersecurity/

Coats, D. R. (2019). *Worldwide threat assessment of the US intelligence community.* Retrieved from https://www.dni.gov/files/ODNI/documents/2019-ATA-SFR---SSCI.pdf

Coats, D. R. (2019, January 29). *Worldwide Threat Assessment of the US Intelligence Community.* Academic Press.

Collier, J. (2018). Cyber security assemblages: A framework for understanding the dynamic and contested nature of security provision. *Politics and Governance, 6*(2), 13–21. doi:10.17645/pag.v6i2.1324

Commission, E. U. (2020). *The EU's Cybersecurity Strategy for the Digital Decade.* Retrieved from: https://ec.europa.eu/commission/presscorner/detail/en/IP_20_2391

Computer History Museum. (2009). *October 29, 1969: HAPPY 40TH BIRTHDAY TO A RADICAL IDEA!* Retrieved from: https://computerhistory.org/blog/october-29-1969-happy-40th-birthday-to-a-radical-idea/

Conger, K. (2022). Ukraine Says It Thwarted a Sophisticated Russian Cyberattack on Its Power Grid. *New York Times.* https://www.nytimes.com/2022/04/12/us/politics/ukraine-russian-cyberattack.html

Couldry, N., & Hepp, A. (2018). *The mediated construction of reality.* John Wiley & Sons.

Council of Europe. (2001). *Convention on cybercrime.* ETS No.185. Retrieved from https://www.coe.int/en/web/conventions/full-list/-/conventions/treaty/185

Council of Europe. (2018). *Guide to European Data Protection Law.* Retrieved from: https://rm.coe.int

Council of the European Union. (2005, May 16). Council Framework Decision on Attacks against Information Systems. *Official Journal of the European Union, L, 69*(67).

Csernatoni, R., & Mavrona, K. (2022, September 15). *The Artificial Intelligence and Cybersecurity Nexus: Taking Stock of the European Union's Approach.* Carnegie Europe. Retrieved from https://carnegieeurope.eu/2022/09/15/artificial-intelligence-and-cybersecurity-nexus-taking-stock-of-european-union-s-approach-pub-87886

CSIS. (2023). *Significant Cyber Incidents.* https://www.csis.org/programs/strategic-technologies-program/significant-cyber-incidents

Cutolo, D., & Kenney, M. (2021). Platform-Dependent Entrepreneurs: Power Asymmetries, Risks, and Strategies in the Platform Economy. *The Academy of Management Perspectives, 35*(4), 584–605. doi:10.5465/amp.2019.0103

Cybersecurity & Infrastructure Security Agency. (2022). *China Cyber Threat Overview and Advisories.* https://www.cisa.gov/china

Cybersecurity and Infrastructure Security Agency. (2023). *Interagency Security Committee Policies, Standards, Best Practices, Guidance Documents, and White Papers.* Retrieved from https://www.cisa.gov/resources-tools/groups/interagency-security-committee-isc/policies-standards-best-practices-guidance-documents-and-white-papers

Cybersecurity and Infrastructure Security Agency. (2023a). *Protected Critical Infrastructure Information (PCII) Program.* Retrieved from https://www.cisa.gov/resources-tools/programs/protected-critical-infrastructure-information-pcii-program#:~:text=Congress%20created%20the%20Protected%20Critical,state%2Flocal%20government%20critical%20infrastructure

Dalha, T. (2018). *Assertion of China's Sovereignty over the Internet, global-is-Asian.* Retrieved from: https://lkyspp.nus.edu.sg/gia/article/assertion-of-china's-sovereignty-over-the-internet

Damjanović, D. (2017). *Types of Information Warfare and Examples of Malicious Programs of Information Warfare; Dragan Z.* https://www.researchgate.net/publication/320254033_Types_of_information_warfare_and_examples_of_malicious_programs_of_information_warfare

Dawkins, J. (2022). *What's in a Name? The Origin of Cyber.* Retrieved from: https://alpinesecurity.com/blog/what-is-the-origin-of-the-word-cyber/

Deffere, S. (2020). *1st computer virus is written, January 30, 1982*. Retrieved from: https://www.edn.com/1st-computer-virus-is-written-january-30-1982/

Dekhtyanko, A. (2015). *Russia is preparing for a big world war, the dates are determined— military expert from Russia*. Apostrophe. Retrieve from: http://apostrophe.com.ua/article/ world/ex-ussr/2015-07-26/rossiya-gotovitsya-k-bolshoymirovoy-voyne-datyi-opredelenyi--- voennyiy-ekspert-izrf/2007

Department of Defence. (2018). *Cyber Strategy*. Retrieved from: https://media.defense.gov/2018/Sep/18/2002041658/-1/-1/1/CYBER_STRATEGY_SUMMARY_FINAL.PDF

Department of Defense. (2023). *Department of Defense*. Retrieved from https://www.defense.gov/

Department of Homeland Security. (2023a). *Cybersecurity*. Retrieved from https://www.dhs.gov/

Department of Homeland Security. (2023b). *United States Computer Emergency Readiness Team*. Retrieved from https://www.cisa.gov/sites/default/files/publications/infosheet_US-CERT_v2.pdf

Department of State. (2023). *Cyber issues*. Retrieved from https://www.state.gov/

DeVries Anita, D. (1997). *Information Warfare and Its Impact on National Security*. https://irp.fas.org/eprint/snyder/infowarfare.htm

Dewar, R. (2022). *Cyberspace is a Consensual Hallucination*. Available from: https://www.researchgate.net/publication/325216608_Cyberspace_is_a_Consensual_Hallucination

Dewar, R. S. (Ed.). (2018). National Cybersecurity and cyber defense policy snapshots. Zurich: Center for Security Studies (CSS), ETH Zurich,

DiGiacomo. (2017). *Active vs Passive Cyber Attacks Explained*. Retrieved from: https://revisionlegal.com/internet-law/cyber-security/active-passive-cyber-attacks-explained/

Donilon, T. (2014). *The United States and the Asia-Pacific in 2013*. Asia Society.

Dougherty, C. (2022). Strange debacle: misadventures in assessing Russian military power. *Warontherocks*. Retrieved from https://warontherocks.com/2022/06/strange-debacle-misadventures-in-assessing-russian-military-power/

Ducheine, P., Jelle, H. v., & Harskamp, R. (2017). *Manoeuvring and Generating Effects in the Information Environment*. Amsterdam Center for International Law. doi:10.1007/978-94-6265-189-0_9

Duffy, R. (2022). WaPo: US Has Privately Attributed Hack of Viasat KA-SAT Ground Infrastructure to GRU. *Payload*. Retrieved from https://payloadspace.com/wapo-us-has-privately-attributed-hack-of-viasat-ka-sat-ground-infrastructure-to-gru/

Duignan, B. (Ed.). (2012). *Forms of Government and the Rise of Democracy*. Britannica Educational Publishing.

Ebner, N. (2015). *Cyber Space, Cyber Attack, and Cyber Weapons; A Contribution to the Terminology*. Institute for Peace Research and Security Policy at the University of Hamburg.

Ecker, U. K. (2017). Why rebuttals may not work: The psychology of misinformation. *Media Asia*, 44(2), 79–87. doi:10.1080/01296612.2017.1384145

Eddy, N. (2018). Gartner: 21 Billion IoT Devices to Invade By 2020. *Information Week*. Retrieved from: www.informationweek.com/mobile/mobile-devices/gartner-21-billion-IoT-devices-to-invade-by-2020/d/d-id/1323081

Edel, C., & Brands, H. (2019). The real origins of the US-China Cold War. *Foreign Policy*, 2.

Efthymiopoulos, M. P. (2019). A cyber-security framework for development, defense, and innovation at NATO. *Journal of Innovation and Entrepreneurship, 8*(12), 1–26. doi:10.118613731-019-0105-z

Egloff, F. J., & Wenger, A. (2019). Public attribution of cyber incidents. In F. Merz (Ed.), *CSS analyses in security policy, 244*. Center for Security Studies.

Elkayam Shalem, H., & Ben-Nun Bloom, P. (2022). Don't scratch the moral itch: Restoring political image following a scandal. *Acta Politica*, 1–21.

Embassy U. S. in Georgia. (2017). *National Security Strategy of the United States of America*. Retrieved from: https://ge.usembassy.gov/ka/2017-national-security-strategy-united-states-america-president-ka/

Embassy, U. S. in Georgia. (2021). *United States-Georgia Memorandum of Understanding on 5G Strategy*. Retrieved from: https://ge.usembassy.gov/united-states-georgia-memorandum-ofunderstanding-on-5g-security/

ENISA. (2012). *Deployment of Baseline Capabilities of n/g CERTs - Status Report 2012*. ENISA.

ENISA. (2023). *ENISA Single Programming Document 2023-2025*. ENISA.

ESET Research Jointly Presents Industroyer2 at Black Hat USA With Ukrainian Government Representative. (2022). https://www.eset.com/int/about/newsroom/press-releases/events/eset-research-jointly-presents-industroyer2-at-black-hat-usa-with-ukrainian-government-representativ/

Eswaran, P., Gray, J. N., Lorie, R. A., & Traiger, I. L. (1976). The notions of consistency and predicate locks in a database system. *Communications of the ACM, 19*(11), 624–633. doi:10.1145/360363.360369

EU. (2023). *Information Manipulation*. Retrieved from: https://audiovisual.ec.europa.eu/en/video/I-236532

EUR-Lex. (1992). https://data.europa.eu/eli/treaty/teu_2008/art_42/oj/eng

Euronews. (2016). *NATO equates cyber attacks with military aggression*. Retrieved from: https://ru.euronews.com/2016/06/15/cyberspace-is-officially-a-war-zone-nato

Europa. (2019, April 17). *Regulation (EU) 2019/881 of The European Parliament and of The Council*. Retrieved from https://eur-lex.europa.eu/legal-content/EN/TXT/PDF/?uri=CELEX%3A32019R0881&from=EN

European Commission and High Representative of the Union for Foreign Affairs and Security Policy. (2017, September 13). *Resilience, deterrence and defence: building strong cybersecurity for the EU*. European Commission. Retrieved from https://eur-lex.europa.eu/legal-content/EN/TXT/PDF/?uri=CELEX:52017JC0450

European Commission and High Representative. (2013). *Cybersecurity strategy of the European Union: an open, safe and secure cyberspace*. European Data Protection Supervisor. Retrieved from https://edps.europa.eu/sites/default/files/publication/13-06-14_cyber_security_en.pdf

European Commission. (2010). A Digital Agenda for Europe, Communication from the Commission to the European Parliament, the Council, the European Economic and Social Committee and the Committee of the Regions. COM (2010) 245 Final/2, Brussels (26.8.10).

European Commission. (2012). Communication from the Commission to the Council and the European Parliament. Tackling Crime in our Digital Age: Establishing a European Cybercrime Centre. COM (2012) 140 Final, Brussels (7.2.13).

European Commission. (2013, February 7). *Cybersecurity Strategy of the European Union: An Open, Safe and Secure Cyberspace*. Retrieved from https://data.consilium.europa.eu/doc/document/ST%206225%202013%20INIT/EN/pdf

European Commission. (2017, September 13). *Joint Communication to the European Parliament and the Council Resilience, Deterrence and Defence: Building Strong Cybersecurity for the EU*. Retrieved from https://eur-lex.europa.eu/legal-content/EN/TXT/PDF/?uri=CELEX:52017JC0450

European Commission. (2019, March). *Challenges to effective EU cybersecurity policy*. Retrieved from https://www.eca.europa.eu/Lists/ECADocuments/BRP_CYBERSECURITY/BRP_CYBERSECURITY_EN.pdf

European Commission. (2022, June 7). *The Cybersecurity Strategy*. Retrieved from https://digital-strategy.ec.europa.eu/en/node/9690/printable/pdf

European Commission. (2023). *2020 - Press release - New EU Cybersecurity Strategy and new rules to make physical and digital critical entities more resilient, Brussels EEAS public conference on 'Beyond Disinformation*. EU Responses to the Threat of Foreign.

European Council on Foreign Relations (ECFR). (2015). *Article 42.7: An explainer*. Retrieved from https://ecfr.eu/article/commentary_article_427_an_explainer5019/

European Council. (2022). *Cybersecurity: How the EU tackles cyber threats*. Author.

European Strategy. (2012). *Proposal on a European Strategy for Internet Strategy*. Retrieve from: http://ec.europa.eu/governance/impact/planned_ia/docs/2012_infso_003_european_internet_security_strategy_en. pdf

European Union Agency for Cybersecurity. (2022, September 16). *European Cybersecurity Challenge 2022*. ENISA. Retrieved from https://www.enisa.europa.eu/events/european-cybersecurity-challenge-2022

European Union External Action. (2022). *Article 42(7) TEU - The EU's mutual assistance clause*. Retrieved from https://www.eeas.europa.eu/eeas/article-427-teu-eus-mutual-assistance-clause_en

Europol. (2023, January 4). *Our Thinking: A strategy for security*. Retrieved from https://www.europol.europa.eu/about-europol/our-thinking#:~:text=As%20the%20EU's%20law%20enforcement,organised%20crime%2C%20cybercrime%20and%20terrorism

EU-Startup. (2019). *Who was Ada Lovelace? The life of the woman who envisioned the modern-day computer*. Retrieved from: https://www.eu-startups.com/2019/10/who-was-ada-lovelace-the-life-of-the-woman-who-envisaged-the-modern-day-computer/

Falessi, N., Gavrila, R., Klejnstrup, M. R., & Moulinos, K. (2012, December). *National Cyber Security Strategies. Practical Guide on Development and Execution*. The European Network and Information Security Agency. Retrieved from https://www.enisa.europa.eu/publications/national-cyber-security-strategies-an-implementation-guide

Federal Ministry of the Interior, Building, and Community. (2021, August). *Cyber Security Strategy for Germany 2021*. Retrieved from shorturl.at/gCDO4

Federal Trade Commission. (2015). *Internet of Things: Privacy and Security in a Connected World*. FTC Staff Report. Retrieved from: https://www.ftc.gov/system/files/documents/reports/federal-trade-commission-staff-report-november-2013-workshop-entitled-interne

Feingold, S., & Beato, F. (2022, December 2). *From stricter reporting rules to a new cyber threat hub, the EU is upgrading its cybersecurity law*. World Economic Forum. Retrieved from https://www.weforum.org/agenda/2022/12/cybersecurity-european-union-nis/

Felaco, C., Nocerino, J., Parola, J., & Tofani, R. (2023). I Correct or Canceling You: Political Correctness and Cancel Culture on Social Media–The Case of Twitter Communication in Italy. In Research Anthology on Social Media's Influence on Government, Politics, and Social Movements (pp. 495-512). IGI Global.

Feuer, L. S. (2017). *Ideology and the Ideologists*. Routledge. doi:10.4324/9780203789193

Fine, G. A. (1997). Scandal, social conditions, and the creation of public attention: Fatty Arbuckle and the "problem of Hollywood". *Social Problems*, *44*(3), 297–323. doi:10.2307/3097179

Finlay, L., & Payne, C. (2019). The Attribution Problem and Cyber Armed Attacks. *AJIL Unbound*, *113*, 202–206. doi:10.1017/aju.2019.35

Finnemore, M., & Hollis, D. B. (2016). Constructing norms for global cybersecurity. *The American Journal of International Law*, 110.

Fischerkeller, M. (2018). *Offense-defense theory, cyberspace, and the irrelevance of advantage*. Institute for Defense Analysis.

Fisher, B. (2021, December 11). *U.S. Diplomats Build Cyber Defense and Cybersecurity Partnerships Worldwide*. Retrieved from U.S Department of State: https://www.state.gov/u-s-diplomats-build-cyber-defense-and-cybersecurity-partnerships-worldwide/

Fleming, J. (2022). The Head of GCHQ Says Vladimir Putin Is Losing the Information War in Ukraine. *Economist*. https://www.economist.com/by-invitation/2022/08/18/the-head-of-gchq-says-vladimir-putin-is-losing-the-information-war-in-ukraine

Forbes. (2023). *The EU is discussing the creation of a special prosecutor's office to investigate war crimes in the Russian Federation*. Retrieved from: https://forbes.ua/ru/news/v-es-obgovoryuyut-stvorennya-spetsprokuraturi-dlya-rozsliduvannya-voennikh-zlochiniv-rf-bloomberg-27012023-11357

Forman-Katz, N., & Stocking, G. (2022, November 18). *Key facts about Truth Social*. Pew Research Center. https://www.pewresearch.org/fact-tank/2022/11/18/key-facts-about-truth-social-as-donald-trump-runs-for-u-s-president-again/

Fortunati, L., Sarrica, M., O'Sullivan, J., Balcytiene, A., Harro-Loit, H., Macgregor, P., Roussou, N., Salaverría, R., & De Luca, F. (2009). The influence of the Internet on European journalism. *Journal of Computer-Mediated Communication*, *14*(4), 928–963. doi:10.1111/j.1083-6101.2009.01476.x

Fortune Business Insights. (2023, April 2). *Market Research Report*. Retrieved from https://www.fortunebusinessinsights.com/industry-reports/cyber-security-market-101165

Fortune Business Insights. (2023, March 2). *Globenewswire*. Retrieved from https://www.globenewswire.com/en/news-release/2023/03/02/2619064/0/en/Cyber-Security-Market-Exhibits-13-4-CAGR-to-Hit-USD-376-32-Billion-by-2029.html

Fox, B. (2022, January 10). *UK banned Huawei because US told us to: Former minister*. EURACTIV. https://www.euractiv.com/section/politics/short_news/uk-banned-huawei-because-us-told-us-to-former-minister/

Freedom Development Institute (IDFI). (2021). *Parliament adopted the draft of the law on Information Security*. Retrieved from: https://idfi.ge/ge/the_parliament_of_the_10_convocation_adopted_the_problematic_draft_law_on_information_security

Fuster, G. G., & Jasmontaite, L. (2020). Cybersecurity Regulation in the European Union: The Digital, the Critical and Fundamental Rights. In M. Christen, B. Gordijn, & M. Loi (Eds.), *The Ethics of Cybersecurity* (pp. 97–115). Springer International Publishing. doi:10.1007/978-3-030-29053-5_5

Galeotti, M. (2014). *The 'Gerasimov Doctrine' And Russian Non-Linear War*. Retrieved from: Https://Inmoscowsshadows. Wordpress.Com/2014/07/06/The-Gerasimov-Doctrine-AndRussianNon-Linear-War/

Gao, X., & Chen, X. (2022). Role enactment and the contestation of global cybersecurity governance. *Defence Studies*, *22*(4), 689–708. doi:10.1080/14702436.2022.2110485

Garsten, B., & Jay, M. (2011). The Virtues of Mendacity: On Lying in Politics. *Modern Intellectual History*, *8*(3), 697. doi:10.1017/S1479244311000424

Gartner. (2018). *Gartner Forecasts Worldwide Information Security Spending to Exceed $124 Billion in 2019*. Retrieved from: https://www.gartner.com

Ge, T. V. (2020). *Georgian Public Broadcaster, "At the closed session of the UN Security Council, the USA, Britain and Estonia talked about Russia's cyber attacks against Georgia."* Retrieved from: https://1tv.ge/news/gaero-s-ushishroebis-sabchos-dakhurul-skhdomaze-ashsh-ma-britanetma-da-estonetma-saqartvelos-winaaghmdeg-rusetis-kibertavdaskhme-bze-isaubres/

Geers, K. (2022). *Computer Network Operations during the Russian Invasion of Ukraine*. Academic Press.

Georgetown Law Library. (2023, February 10). *International and Foreign Cyberspace Law Research Guide*. Retrieved from https://guides.ll.georgetown.edu/cyberspace/cyber-conflicts

Georgieva, I. (2020). The unexpected norm-setters: Intelligence agencies in cyberspace. *Contemporary Security Policy*, *41*(1), 33–54. doi:10.1080/13523260.2019.1677389

GFSIS. (2022). *EU's role in Russia-Ukraine War*. Retrieve from: https://gfsis.org.ge//events/live/view/1396

Gheciu, A., & Wohlforth, W. (2019). Trajectories of cyber security research. In A. Gheciu & W. C. Wohlforth (Eds.), *Oxford Handbook of international security*. Oxford University Press.

Ghiasy, R., & Rajeshwari, K. (2021). *China's Digital Silk Road and the Global Digital Order*. The Diplomat. Retrieved from: https://thediplomat.com/2021/04/chinas-digital-silk-roadand-the-global-digital-order/

Ghimire, B. K., Rawat, D. B., Liu, C., & Li, J. (2021). Sharding-Enabled Blockchain for Software-Defined Internet of Unmanned Vehicles in the Battlefield. *IEEE Network*, *35*(1), 101–107. doi:10.1109/MNET.011.2000214

Gill, D. T., & Ducheine, A. P. (2013). Anticipatory Self-Defense in the Cyber Context. *International Law Studies*, *89*, 438–471.

Ginsburg, T. (2020). Authoritarian international law? *The American Journal of International Law*, *114*(2), 221–260. doi:10.1017/ajil.2020.3

Ginsburg, T. (2020a). How Authoritarians Use International Law. *Journal of Democracy*, *31*(4), 44–58. doi:10.1353/jod.2020.0054

Girard, B. (2019). *The Real Danger of China's National Intelligence Law*. The Diplomat. Retrieved from: https://thediplomat.com/2019/02/the-real-danger-of-chinas-national-intelligence-law/

Gladicheva, V. (2016, November 9). *Privacy Shield Lawsuits in EU Court Face*. Admissibility Hurdle, MLEX. Retrieved from https://mlexmarketinsight.com/editors-picks/privacy-shield-lawsuits-eu-court-face-admissibility-hurdle/

Global Affairs Press. (2022). *NATO's Cyber Defense Evolution*. Author.

Globe News Wire. (2023, March 2). *Cyber Security Market Exhibits 13.4% CAGR to Hit USD 376.32 Billion by 2029*. Retrieved from https://www.globenewswire.com/en/news-release/2023/03/02/2619064/0/en/Cyber-Security-Market-Exhibits-13-4-CAGR-to-Hit-USD-376-32-Billion-by-2029.html

Gomez, M. A. (2019). Sound the alarm! Updating beliefs and degradative cyber operations. *European Journal of International Security, 4*.

Government of the Russian Federation. (2015). *On signing the Agreement between the Government of the Russian Federation and the Government of the People's Republic of China on cooperation in ensuring international information security*. Retrieved from https://cyber-peace.org/wp-content/uploads/2013/05/RUS-

Grauman, B. (2013). *Cyber-security: The Vexed Question of Global Rules*. Retrieved from https://www.files.ethz.ch/isn/139895/SDA_Cyber_report_FINAL.pdf

Green, N. L. (2020). Recognizing rhetoric in science policy arguments. *Argument & Computation, 11*(3), 257–268. doi:10.3233/AAC-200504

Guadagno, R. E., & Guttieri, K. (2021). Fake news and information warfare: An examination of the political and psychological processes from the digital sphere to the real world. In Research Anthology on Fake News, Political Warfare, and Combatting the Spread of Misinformation (pp. 218-242). IGI Global.

Hadji-Janev, M., & Bogdanoski, M. (2016). The swarming-based cyber defense under the framework of collective security. Security Journal, 30(1), 39-59.

Hagmann, J., Hegemann, H., & Neal, A. W. (2019). The politicisation of security: Controversy, mobilisation. *Arena Shifting. European Review of International Studies*.

Haider, A., & Schmidt, A. (2022, July). *Defining the swarm—Joint air power competence center*. https://www.japcc.org/articles/defining-the-swarm/

Hall, H. K. (2018). Restoring Dignity and Harmony to United States-European Union Data Protection Regulation. *Communication Law and Policy, 23*(2), 125–157. doi:10.1080/10811680.2018.1429773

Hambling, D. (2022). Inventor Of 'Shock & Awe' Explains How It Might Work In Ukraine. *Forbes*. Retrieved from https://www.forbes.com/sites/davidhambling/2022/02/02/inventor-of-shock--awe-explains-how-it-might-work-in-ukraine/?sh=51bb6a3013b7

Hasan, A. R., & Shah, N. A. (2020). Cyberbullying and its impact on mental health: A review of the literature. *Cureus, 12*(8), e9635. PMID:32923236

HC. (2023). *Charles Babbage Analytical Engine Explained: Everything You Need To Know*. Retrieved from: https://history-computer.com/Babbage/AnalyticalEngine.html

Healey, J. (2016). The U.S. Government and Zero-Day Vulnerabilities: From Pre-Heartbleed to Shadow Brokers. *Journal of International Affairs*. Retrieved from https://jia.sipa.columbia.edu/ online-articles/healey_vulnerability_equities_process

Hegarty, S. (2020). *The Chinese doctor who tried to warn others about coronavirus*. BBC. Retrieved from: https://www.bbc.com/news/world-asia-china-51364382

Heinegg, W. H. (2013). Territorial Sovereignty and Neutrality in Cyberspace. *U.S. Naval War College, 89*, 123–156.

Herzogenrath-Amelung, H. (2016). The new instantaneity: How social media are helping us privilege the (politically) correct over the true. *Media Culture & Society, 38*(7), 1080–1089. doi:10.1177/0163443716664855

Herzog, S. (2011). Revisiting the Estonian cyber attacks: Digital threats and multinational responses. *Journal of Strategic Security, 4*(2), 49–60. doi:10.5038/1944-0472.4.2.3

High Representative of the Union for Foreign Affairs and Security Policy. (2022). *Joint Communication to the European Parliament and the Council EU Policy on Cyber Defense*. European Commission.

History of Information. (2010). *The Creeper Worm, the First Computer Virus*. Retrieved from: https://www.historyofinformation.com/detail.php?id=2465

History. (2019). *The Invention of the Internet*. Retrieved from: https://www.history.com/topics/inventions/invention-of-the-internet

Hitchens, T., & Gallagher, N. W. (2019). Building confidence in the cyber sphere: A path to multilateral progress. *Journal of Cyber Policy Kello, L*, 2013.

Hoang, N. P., Niaki, A. A., Dalek, J., Knockel, J., Lin, P., Marczak, B., . . . Polychronakis, M. (2021). *How great is the Great Firewall? Measuring China's DNS censorship*. Retrieved from https://www.usenix.org/conference/usenixsecurity21/presentation/hoang

Hogarth, F. (1987). Dynamic Density: A Deterrent for the OMG. *RUSI Journal, 132*(2), 29–34. doi:10.1080/03071848708523163

Højsgaard, T. (2015). *Cyber-security in the European Region: Anticipatory Governance and Practices*. Academic Press.

Homeland Security. (2021, March 31). *Confronting Realities: A Vision for Cybersecurity Resilience*. Retrieved 2023, from https://www.dhs.gov/medialibrary/assets/videos/24094

Honda, K., Gibney, F., & Sandness, K. (2015). *The Nanjing Massacre: A Japanese Journalist Confronts Japan's National Shame: A Japanese Journalist Confronts Japan's National Shame*. Routledge. doi:10.4324/9781315699370

Hosang, B. J. (2017). *Rules on the Use of Force as Linchpin for the International Law of Military Operations*. Universiteit van Amsterdam.

Hosenball, M. (2020). *Top U.S. officials to spotlight Chinese spy operations, the pursuit of American secrets*. Reuters. Retrieved from: https://www.reuters.com/article/usa-china-espionage/top-u-sofficials-to-spotlight-chinese-spy-operations-pursuit-of-american-secrets-idUSL1N28S1B3

Howell O'Neill, P. (2022). Russian Hackers Tried to Bring Down Ukraine's Power Grid to Help the Invasion. *MIT Technology Review*. https://www.technologyreview.com/2022/04/12/1049586/russian-hackers-tried-to-bring-down-ukraines-power-grid-to-help-the-invasion/

Hung, H. F., & Kuo, H. Y. (2010). "One country, two systems" and its antagonists in Tibet and Taiwan. *China Information, 24*(3), 317–337. doi:10.1177/0920203X10382710

Hung, T. C., & Hung, T. W. (2022). How China's Cognitive Warfare Works: A Frontline Perspective of Taiwan's Anti-Disinformation Wars. *Journal of Global Security Studies, 7*(4), ogac016. doi:10.1093/jogss/ogac016

Huntley, S. (2023). Fog of war: how the Ukraine conflict transformed the cyber threat landscape. *Threat Analysis Group (TAG)*. Retrieved from https://blog.google/threat-analysis-group/fog-of-war-how-the-ukraine-conflict-transformed-the-cyber-threat-landscape

Huy, T. (2015). Evaluating the agility of adaptive command and control networks from a cyber complex adaptive systems perspective. *Journal of Defense Modeling and Simulation: Applications, Methodology, Technology, 12*(4), 1–18. doi:10.1177/1548512915592517

Iftikhar, N., Mustafa, A., Abbas, N., Khan, M., Raza, S., & Bashir, S. (2020). A review of cyberbullying: A new era of bullying. *Journal of Interpersonal Violence, 35*(7-8), 1687–1710.

Independent. (2017). *Ukraine cyber attack: Chaos as a national bank, state power provider, and airport hit by hackers, Russian energy firms and Danish shipping company also hit by hackers.* Retrieved from: https://www.independent.co.uk/news/world/europe/ukraine-cyber-attack-hackers-national-bank-state-power-company-airport-rozenko-pavlo-cabinet-computers-wannacry-ransomware-a7810471.html

Independent. (2023). *From war crimes to spies and cyberattacks: Ukraine's domestic spy chief on fighting Russia across all fronts.* Retrieved from: https://www.independent.co.uk/news/world/europe/ukraine-russia-war-crimes-putin-b2290489.html

Industroyer2: Industroyer Reloaded. (2022). https://www.welivesecurity.com/2022/04/12/industroyer2-industroyer-reloaded/

Insider. (2021). *What Is the SolarWinds Hack and Why Is It a Big Deal?* Retrieved from: https://www.businessinsider.com/solarwinds-hack-explained-government-agencies-cyber-security-2020-12

Insikt Group. (2021). *China's Digital Colonialism: Espionage and Repression Along the Digital Silk Road.* Retrieved from: https://go.recordedfuture.com/hubfs/reports/cta-2021-0727.pdf

International Telecommunication Union. (2019). *Measuring digital development Facts and figures.* ITU Publications. Retrieved from: https://www.itu.int/en/ITU-D/Statistics/Documents/facts/FactsFigures2019.pdf

Isachenkov, V., & Tong-hyung, K. (2023). *Xi awarded 3rd term as China's president, extending rule.* Retrieved from https://apnews.com/article/xi-jinping-china-president-vote-5e6230d8c881dc17b11a781e832accd1

ITU. (2000). *Russian Federation, "Information Security Doctrine of the Russian Federation."* Retrieved from: https://www.itu.int/en/ITU-D/Cybersecurity/Documents/National_Strategies_Repository/Russia_2000.pdf

Jafari, S., Vo-Huu, T. D., Jabiyev, B., Mera, A., & Farkhani, R. M. (2018). Cryptocurrency: A challenge to legal system. *Social Science Research Network.* doi:10.2139/ssrn.3172489

Jasanoff, S., & Kim, S.-H. (2015). Dreamscapes of modernity. Sociotechnical imaginaries and the fabrication of power. In *Dreamscapes of Modernity.* University of Chicago Press. doi:10.7208/chicago/9780226276663.001.0001

Jgharkawa, I. (2022). *Georgia's cyber security policy, challenges and opportunities.* GCSD Research.

Jiang, J., Chen, E., Yan, S., Lerman, K., & Ferrara, E. (2020). Political polarization drives online conversations about COVID-19 in the United States. *Human Behavior and Emerging Technologies*, 2(3), 200–211. doi:10.1002/hbe2.202 PMID:32838229

Johnsen, T., Zieliński, Z., Wrona, K., Suri, N., Fuchs, C., Pradhan, M., Furtak, J., Vasilache, B., Pellegrini, V., Dyk, M., Marks, M., & Krzyszton, M. (2018). Application of IoT in military operations in a smart city. In Military Communications and Information Systems Conference. doi:10.1109/ICMCIS.2018.8398690

Jones, A., Horsley, T., & Runnels, V. (2021). Exploring the Relationship Between Cyberbullying and Mental Health Among University Students: A Systematic Review. *Journal of Interpersonal Violence.* Advance online publication. doi:10.1177/08862605211004219

Josías, D., & Guerrero, V. (2022). *Ukraine Conflict: Hybrid Warfare and Conventional Military intervention.* Retrieved from: https://ceeep.mil.pe/2022/07/07/ukraine-conflict-hybrid-warfare-and-conventional-military-intervention/?lang=en

Kalathil, S. (2017). *Beyond the great firewall: How China Became a global information power.* Center for International Media Assistance.

Kamara, S., & Lauter, K. E. (2010). Cryptographic cloud storage. In *Springer ebooks* (pp. 136–149). Springer nature. doi:10.1007/978-3-642-14992-4_13

KapsokoliE. (2021, February 1). *The security challenges that the EU is facing in cyberspace.* Hellenic Association of Political Scientists (HAPSc). doi:10.2139/ssrn.3784083

KA-SAT Network Cyber Attack Overview. (2022). *Viasat.* https://news.viasat.com/blog/corporate/ka-sat-network-cyber-attack-overview

Keating, V. C., & Schmitt, O. (2021). Ideology and influence in the debate over Russian election interference. *International Politics, 58*(5), 757–771. doi:10.105741311-020-00270-4

Kello, L. (2017). *The virtual weapon and international order.* Yale University Press. doi:10.2307/j.ctt1trkjd1

Kello, L. (2021). Cyber legalism: Why it fails and what to do about it. *Journal of Cybersecurity, 7*(1), 1–15. doi:10.1093/cybsec/tyab014

Kendall-Taylor, A., Frantz, E., & Wright, J. (2020). The digital dictators: How technology strengthens autocracy. *Foreign Affairs, 99*, 103.

Kerr, J., Panagopoulos, C., & van der Linden, S. (2021). Political polarization on COVID-19 pandemic response in the United States. *Personality and Individual Differences, 179*, 110892. doi:10.1016/j.paid.2021.110892 PMID:34866723

Khan, M. A., & Salah, K. (2017b). IoT security: Review, blockchain solutions, and open challenges. *Future Generation Computer Systems, 82*, 395–411. doi:10.1016/j.future.2017.11.022

Khan, R., Khan, S. U., Zaheer, R., & Khan, S. (2012). Future Internet: The Internet of Things Architecture, Possible Applications, and Key Challenges. In *Proceedings of 2012 10th International Conference on Frontiers of Information Technology (FIT).* Institute of Electrical and Electronics Engineers. 10.1109/FIT.2012.53

Kimberly, H., & Murray, C. (2014). *China and International Law in Cyberspace.* Retrieved from https://www.uscc.gov/sites/default/files/Research/China%20International%20Law%20in%20Cyberspace.pdf

Kim, J. H., & Park, J. (2023). Perceived China threat, conspiracy belief, and public support for restrictive immigration control during the COVID-19 pandemic. *Race and Justice, 13*(1), 130–152. doi:10.1177/21533687221125818

Kitchin, R., & Dodge, M. (2019). The (in)security of smart cities: vulnerabilities, risks, mitigation, and prevention. *Journal of Urban Technology, 26*(2), 47–65. doi:10.1080/10630732.2017.1408002

Kjaersgaard, M. (2022, June 16). *Heimdal Security CEO.* Retrieved from https://heimdalsecurity.com/blog/the-role-of-cybersecurity-in-world-politics/

Klimburg, A., & Tirmaa-Klaar, H. (2011, April). *Cyber Security and Cyber Power: Concepts, Conditions and Capabilities for Cooperation for Action within EU.* TEPSA and the European Parliament. Retrieved from https://www.europarl.europa.eu/RegData/etudes/STUD/2011/433828/EXPO-SEDE_ET(2011)433828_EN.pdf

Klipstein, M., & Japaridze, T. (2022, May 16). *Collective cyber defense and attack: NATO's Article 5 after the Ukraine conflict.* Retrieved from European Leadership Network: https://www.europeanleadershipnetwork.org/commentary/collective-cyber-defence-and-attack-natos-article-5-after-the-ukraine-conflict/

Klishin, I. (2015). *Botovoysko: Why playing with soft power is not working out for the Kremlin.* Carnegie Moscow Center. Retrieved from: http://carnegie.ru/2015/07/21/ru60728/idgi

Kohler, H. (2014). The Eagle and the Hare: US-Chinese Relations, the Wolf Amendment, and the Future of International Cooperation in Space. *Geological Journal, 103*, 1135.

Kohn, K., Wright, M., & Tuffin, K. (2020). Cyberbullying in the workplace: A review of the literature. *Aggression and Violent Behavior, 50*, 101354.

Krichen, M., Ammi, M., Mihoub, A., & Almutiq, M. (2022). Blockchain for Modern Applications: A Survey. *Sensors (Basel), 22*(14), 5274. doi:10.339022145274 PMID:35890953

Krylatov, M. (2015). *Moscow launched another 'information war workshop' in Crimea*. Radio Free Europe/Radio Liberty. Retrieved from: http://ru.krymr.com/ content/article/26957545.html

Kunz, J. L. (1947). Individual and Collective Self-Defense in Article 51 of the Charter of the United Nations. *The American Journal of International Law, 41*(4), 872–879. doi:10.2307/2193095

Kuprashvili, H. (2022). *Cyberspace and terminologies: Cybersecurity*. Georgian Technical University.

Lauter, E. (2004). The advantages of elliptic curve cryptography for wireless security. *IEEE Wireless Communications, 11*(1), 62–67. doi:10.1109/MWC.2004.1269719

Lawson, S. (2012). Putting the "war" in cyberwar: Metaphor, analogy, and cybersecurity discourse in the United States. *First Monday*. Advance online publication. doi:10.5210/fm.v17i7.3848

Lee, A. (2020). What is China's social credit system and why is it controversial? *South China Morning Post*. Retrieved from: https://www.scmp.com/economy/china-economy/article/3096090/what-chinas-social-credit-system-and-why-it-controversial

Lee, A. (2021). Defense Attorneys at a Dead End: Representing Stateless Terrorist Clients Detained Indefinitely. *The Georgetown Journal of Legal Ethics, 34*, 1113.

Lee, S. (2014). China's 'Three Warfares': Origins, Applications, and Organizations. *The Journal of Strategic Studies, 37*(2), 198–221. doi:10.1080/01402390.2013.870071

Leese, M., & Hoijtink, M. (Eds.). (2019). *Technology and agency in international relations*. Routledge.

Lemelson. (2020). *Steve Jobs*. Retrieved from: https://lemelson.mit.edu/resources/steve-jobs-steve-wozniak

Lewis University. (2020). The history of cyber warfare – infographic. *The New Face of War: Attacks in Cyberspace*. Retrieved from: https://online.lewisu.edu/mscs/resources/the-history-of-cyber-warfare

Lewis, A. J. (2022). *Cyber War and Ukraine*. Center for Strategic and International Studies. https://www.csis.org/analysis/cyber-war-and-ukraine

Lewis, B. K. (2010). Social Media and Strategic Communication: Attitudes and Perceptions Among College Students. *The Public Relations Journal, 4*.

Lewis, J. A. (2015). *The Role of Offensive Cyber Operations in NATO's Collective Defence*. Tallinn Paper No.8, 1-15.

Lewis, J. A. (2015). U.S. - Japan Cooperation in Cybersecurity. Center for Strategic & International Studies (CSIS).

Lewis, J. A. (2018). *Rethinking cyber security: Strategy, mass effects, and states*. Center for Strategic and International Studies.

Liang, B., & Lu, H. (2010). Internet development, censorship, and cyber crimes in China. *Journal of Contemporary Criminal Justice, 26*(1), 103–120. doi:10.1177/1043986209350437

Liao, Y., Katz, S. J., & Stylianou, A. M. (2020). A systematic review of cyberbullying prevention programs: Research methodology and intervention frameworks. *Aggression and Violent Behavior, 50*, 101358. doi:10.1016/j.avb.2019.101358

Lilly, B., Moore, A. S., Hodgson, Q. E., & Weishoff, D. (2021). *Rand's scalable warning and resilience model (Swarm): Enhancing defenders' predictive power in cyberspace.* RAND Corporation. https://www.rand.org/pubs/research_reports/RRA382-1.html

Lin, H. (2021). Comparing the Biden administration's Interim National Security Strategic Guidance with Trump's National Cyber Strategy. Academic Press.

Lindsay, B. (2011). *Social Media and Disasters: Current Uses, Future Options, and Policy Considerations.* Congressional Research Service.

Lin, J. Y. (2011). China and the global economy. *China Economic Journal, 4*(1), 1–14. doi:10.1080/17538963.2011.609612

Li, P. (Ed.). (2017). *Japanese war crimes.* Routledge. doi:10.4324/9780203788059

Liu, Z., Guo, J., Zhong, W., & Gui, T. (2021). Multi-level governance, policy coordination and subnational responses to COVID-19: Comparing China and the US. *Journal of Comparative Policy Analysis, 23*(2), 204–218. doi:10.1080/13876988.2021.1873703

Luiijf, H., & Besseling, K. (2011). Ten National Cyber Security Strategies: compassion. *CRITIS 2001 – 6th International Conference on Critical Information Infrastructures Security.*

Ma, A., & Canales, K. (2021). China's 'social credit' system ranks citizens and punishes them with throttled internet speeds and flight bans if the Communist Party deems them untrustworthy. *Business Insider.* https://www.businessinsider.com/china-social-credit-systempunishments-and-rewards-explained-2018-4

Maass, A., Suitner, C., & Merkel, E. M. (2013). Does political correctness make (social) sense? In *Social cognition and communication* (pp. 345–360). Psychology Press.

Maftei, A., Lavric, A., Petrariu, A., & Popa, V. (2023). Massive Data Storage Solution for IoT Devices Using Blockchain Technologies. *Sensors (Basel), 23*(3), 1570. doi:10.339023031570 PMID:36772609

Magazine, C. (2021). *The History of Cybersecurity.* Retrieved from: https://cybermagazine.com/cyber-security/history-cybersecurity

Magazine, S. (2013). *The Brief History of the ENIAC Computer.* Retrieved from: https://www.smithsonianmag.com/history/the-brief-history-of-the-eniac-computer-3889120/

Maizland, L., & Albert, E. (2022). *The Chinese Communist Party.* Retrieved from https://www.cfr.org/backgrounder/chinese-communist-party

Malvenishvili, M., & Balarjishvili, N. (2022). *Cyber security reform in Georgia: current challenges, international practice, and recommendations. Institute for Development of Freedom of Information.* IDFI.

Maness, R., & Valeriano, B. (2016). The impact of cyber conflict on international interactions. *Armed Forces and Society, 42*(2), 301–323. doi:10.1177/0095327X15572997

Manson, K. (2023). WaPo: US Has Privately Attributed Hack of Viasat KA-SAT Ground Infrastructure to GRU. *Bloomberg.* Retrieved from https://payloadspace.com/wapo-us-has-privately-attributed-hack-of-viasat-ka-sat-ground-infrastructure-to-gru/

Mao, Y. (2021). Political institutions, state capacity, and crisis management: A comparison of China and South Korea. *International Political Science Review, 42*(3), 316–332. doi:10.1177/0192512121994026

Mastne. (2012). *Law of Georgia on information security.* Legislative Herald of Georgia.

Matsne. (2017). *2017-2018 National Cyber Security Strategy of Georgia. On the approval of the 2017-2018 national strategy of cyber security of Georgia and its action plan.* Legislative Herald of Georgia.

Matsne. (2021a). *2021-2024 National Cyber Security Strategy of Georgia and its Action Plan. On Approval of the National Cyber Security Strategy of Georgia for 2021-2024 and its Action Plan regarding making changes to Resolution No. 482 of the Government of Georgia.* Legislative Herald of Georgia.

Matsne. (2021b). *Georgia's Cyber Security National Strategy for 2021-2024 and its Action Plan. On the Approval of Georgia's Cyber Security National Strategy for 2021-2024 and its Action Plan on amending Resolution No. 482 of the Government of Georgia.* Legislative Herald of Georgia.

Matsne. (2021c). *Georgia's Cyber Security National Strategy for 2021-2024 and its Action Plan. On the Approval of Georgia's Cyber Security National Strategy for 2021-2024 and its Action Plan on amending Resolution No. 482 of the Government of Georgia.* Legislative Herald of Georgia.

Mcabee, A., Tummala, M., & Mceachen, J. (2019). Military intelligence applications for blockchain technology. In *Proceedings of the . . . Annual hawaii international conference on system sciences.* doi:10.24251/HICSS.2019.726

McBride, D. (2020). USA Patriot Act Boosts Government Powers While Cutting Back on Traditional Checks and Balances. In *Bioterrorism: The History of a Crisis in American Society* (pp. 307–310). Routledge. doi:10.4324/9781003123644-34

McCain, J. (2017). *John McCain says the US has no strategy to deal with Russian cyber warfare.* Retrieved from The Guardian: https://www.theguardian.com/us-news/2017/jan/27/john-mccain-says-us-has-no-strategy-to-deal-with-russian-cyber-warfare

McCarthy, D. (Ed.). (2018). *Technology and world politics: And introduction.* Routledge.

Mcdonell, S. (2020). *Ren Zhiqiang: Outspoken ex-real estate tycoon gets 18 years in jail.* BBC. Retrieved from: https://www.bbc.com/news/world-asia-china-54245327

Meiser, J. W. (2017). Ends+ ways+ means=(bad) strategy. *Jeffrey W. Meiser," Ends+ Ways+ Means=(Bad) Strategy. Parameters, 46*(4), 2016–2017.

Meltzer, J. (2013). The Internet, Cross-Border Data Flows and International Trade. SSRN *Electronic Journal.* doi:10.2139/ssrn.2292477

Michael, D. (2013). *Chinese Views on Cybersecurity in Foreign Relations. China Leadership Monitor.* http://carnegieendowment.org/2013/09/20/chinese-views-oncybersecurity-in-foreign-relations

Michael, W., & Antoniou, T. (1994). *The Laws of War: A Comprehensive Collection of Primary Documents on International Laws Governing Armed Conflict.* Academic Press.

Miller, S. (2021). Preventive detention of terrorists. In *Counter-Terrorism* (pp. 92–104). Edward Elgar Publishing. doi:10.4337/9781800373075.00014

Miloslavskaya, N., & Tolstoy, A. (2019). Internet of things: information security challenges and solutions. *Cluster Computing, 22*(1), 103–119. doi:10.1007/s10586-018-2823-6

Minárik, R., Jakschis, L., & Lindström. (Eds.). (2018). *10th international conference on cyber conflict CyCon X: Maximising effects.* Tallinn: CCDCOE.

Ministry of Defense, Government of Japan. (2015). *Joint statement of the U. S.-Japan cyber defense policy working group.* Retrieved 4 April 2023, from https://nsarchive.gwu.edu/document/21938-document-07

Ministry of Foreign Affairs MOFA. (1960, January 19). *Japan-U.S. Security Treaty: Treaty of Mutual Cooperation and Security between Japan and the United States of America*. Retrieved from Ministry of Foreign Affairs of Japan: https://www.mofa.go.jp/region/n-america/us/q&a/ref/1.html

Ministry of Foreign Affairs of Georgia. (2020a). *The concept of national security of Georgia*. Retrieved from: https://www.mfa.gov.ge/national-security-concept

Ministry of Internal Affairs of Georgia. (2020b). *Statement of the Ministry of Internal Affairs of Georgia about the cyber attack*. Retrieved from: https://police.ge/ge/saqartvelos-shinagan-saqmeta-saministros-gantskhadeba/13926

Minstreanu, S. (2018). *Life Inside China's Social Credit Laboratory*. Foreign Policy. Retrieved from: https://foreignpolicy.com/2018/04/03/life-inside-chinas-social-credit-laboratory/

Mishra, S., & Sahoo, S. (2021). Cyberbullying in Social Media and Its Impact on Mental Health: A Systematic Review. *International Journal of Mental Health and Addiction*, 1–18. doi:10.100711469-021-00540-1

Mitchell, C. (2020). *In the Age of Trump the Unraveling of America's National Security Policy*. Rowman&Littlefield.

Morgan, S. (2017). *Editor-in-Chief, "Cybersecurity Ventures", 2017 Cybercrime Report*. Retrieved from: https://cyber-securityventures.com/2015-wp/wp-content/uploads/2017/10/2017-Cybercrime-Report.pdf

Morlino, L. (2009). *Qualities of democracy: how to analyze them*. University of Aberdeen: Centre for the Study of Public Policy.

Mueller, R. S. (2012). *Combating Threats in the Cyber World: Outsmarting Terrorists, Hackers, and Spies*. RSA Cyber Security Conference San Francisco. The Federal Bureau of Investigation. Retrieved from: https://archives.fbi.gov/archives/news/speeches/combating-threats-in-the-cyberworld-outsmarting-terrorists-hackers-and-spies

Mueller, M. L. (2010). *Networks and states: The global politics of internet governance*. The MIT Press. doi:10.7551/mitpress/9780262014595.001.0001

Murgia, M., & Gross, A. (2020). Inside China's controversial mission to reinvent the Internet. *Financial Times*.

Nathaniel Fick, J. M. (2022). *Confronting Reality in Cyberspace*. Council on Foreign Relations.

National Institute of Standards and Technology (NIST). (2012, September). *Information Security*. Retrieved from https://nvlpubs.nist.gov/nistpubs/Legacy/SP/nistspecialpublication800-30r1.pdf

NATO Press conference by NATO Secretary General Jens Stoltenberg following the North Atlantic Council meeting at the level of NATO Defence Ministers. (2016, June 16). Retrieved from https://www.nato.int/cps/en/natohq/opinions_132349.htm

NATO. (2011). *NATO's new strategic concept: A comprehensive assessment*. Retrieved from: https://www.econstor.eu/bitstream/10419/59845/1/656748095.pdf

NATO. (2012, July 5). *Chicago Summit Declaration*. Retrieved from https://www.nato.int/cps/en/natohq/official_texts_87593.htm?selectedLocale=en

NATO. (2013, June 4). *Press conference by NATO Secretary General Anders Fogh Rasmussen following the NATO Defence Ministers meeting on 4 June 2013*. Retrieved from https://www.nato.int/cps/en/natolive/opinions_101151.htm

NATO. (2016, July). *Warsaw Summit Communiqué*. Retrieved from https://www.nato.int/cps/en/natohq/official_texts_133169.htm

NATO. (2018). *Brussels Summit Declaration - Issued by the Heads of State and Government participating in the meeting of the North Atlantic Council in Brussels on 11-12 July 2018*. Retrieved from: https://www.nato.int/cps/en/natohq/official_texts_156624.htm

NATO. (2022, September 20). *Collective defense and Article 5*. Retrieved from https://www.nato.int/cps/en/natohq/topics_110496.htm

NetGazeti. (2023). *Who and how the Kremlin spreads disinformation against Ukraine — research*. Retrieved from: https://netgazeti.ge/news/612725

Network Security. (2023). *Dial-up Internet Access*. Retrieved from: https://www.networxsecurity.org/members-area/glossary/d/dial-up-access.html

News, H. P. (2014). HP Study Reveals 70 Percent of Internet of Things Devices Vulnerable to Attack, *HP News*, Retrieved from: https://www8.hp.com/us/en/hp-news/press-release.html?id=1744676

News, M. (1999). *Microsoft, "Strong Holiday Sales Make Windows 98 Best-Selling Software of 1998"*. Retrieved from: https://news.microsoft.com/1999/02/09/strong-holiday-sales-make-windows-98-best-selling-software-of-1998

Nicholas, P. (2018, March 5). *The Role that Regions Can and Should Play in Critical Infrastructure Protection*. Microsoft. Retrieved from https://www.microsoft.com/security/blog/2018/03/05/the-role-that-regions-can-and-should-play-in-critical-infrastructure-protection/

Nietsche, C., & Rasser, M. (2020). *Washington's Anti-Huawei Tactics Need a Reboot In Europe Efforts to convince allies of the Chinese threat in 5G have floundered*. Foreign Policy. Retrieved from: https://foreignpolicy.com/2020/04/30/huawei-5g-europe-united-states-china/

Ning, S., & Wu, H. (2022). *Cybersecurity laws and regulations in China*. Retrieved from https://iclg.com/practice-areas/cybersecurity-laws-and-regulations/china

North Atlantic Treaty Organisation. (2016, July 8-9). *Warsaw Summit Communiqué*. Retrieved from https://www.nato.int/cps/en/natohq/official_texts_133169.htm

North Atlantic Treaty Organization. (2014, September). *Wales Summit Declaration*. Retrieved from https://www.nato.int/cps/en/natohq/official_texts_112964.htm

North Atlantic Treaty Organization. (2019, April). *The North Atlantic Treaty Washington D.C. - 4 April 1949*. Retrieved from https://www.nato.int/cps/en/natohq/official_texts_17120.htm

North Atlantic Treaty Organization. (2020, January). *Allied Joint Publication-3.20 Allied Joint Doctrine for Cyberspace Operations*. Retrieved from shorturl.at/EGNWZ

Nunes, P. F. V. (1999). *Information Warfare by Captain*. https://www.airuniversity.af.edu/Portals/10/ASPJ/journals/Chronicles/nunes.pdf

O'Neill Archive. (2022). Russia hacked an American satellite company one hour before the Ukraine invasion. *MIT Technology Review*. Retrieved from https://www.technologyreview.com/2022/05/10/1051973/russia-hack-viasat-satellite-ukraine-invasion/

Oegema, D., & Klandermans, B. (1994). Why social movement sympathizers don't participate: Erosion and nonconversion of support. *American Sociological Review*, *59*(5), 703–722. doi:10.2307/2096444

Office of the Spokesperson. (2017, July 24). *Joint Statement of the Japan-U.S. Cyber Dialogue*. Retrieved from https://2017-2021.state.gov/joint-statement-of-the-japan-u-s-cyber-dialogue/index.html

Office of the United States Trade Representative. (2020). *US-China trade facts*. Retrieved from https://ustr.gov/countries-regions/china-mongolia-taiwan/peoples-republic-china

Osawa, J. (2017). The Escalation of State-Sponsored Cyberattack and National Cyber Security Affairs: Is Strategic Cyber Deterrence the Key to Solving the Problem? *Asia-Pacific Review, 24*(2). doi:10.1080/13439006.2017.1406703

Parkirson, J., Bariyo, N., & Chin, J. (2019). Huawei Technicians Helped African Governments Spy on Political Opponents. *The Wall Street Journal*.

Peay, P. C., & Camarillo, T. (2021). No justice! Black protests? No peace: The racial nature of threat evaluations of nonviolent# BlackLivesMatter protests. *Social Science Quarterly, 102*(1), 198–208. doi:10.1111squ.12902

Perlroth, N. (2021). How China transformed Into a Prime Cyber Threat to the U.S. *The New York Times*. Retrieved from: https://www.nytimes.com/2021/07/19/technology/china-hacking-us.html

Perlroth, N., & Sanger, D. E. (2019). *Iranian hackers target Trump campaign as threats to 2020 mount*. Retrieved from The New York Times: https://www.nytimes.com/2019/10/04/technology/iranian-campaign-hackers-microsoft.html

Pernik, P. (2014). *Improving Cyber Security: NATO and the EU*. International Centre for Defence Studies.

Perot, E. (2019). The art of commitments: NATO, the EU, and the interplay between law and politics within Europe's collective defense architecture. *European Security, 28*(1), 40–65. doi:10.1080/09662839.2019.1587746

Pietromarchi, V. (2022). Russian-controlled Kherson region suffers power cuts. *Aljazeera*. Retrieved from https://www.aljazeera.com/news/liveblog/2022/11/6/live-news-us-reportedly-urging-ukraine-to-talk-to-russia

Pijpers, B. P., Boddens, J. H., & Ducheine, A. P. (2021). *Collective Cyber Defence – the EU and NATO perspective on cyber attacks*. Amsterdam Law School Legal Studies Research Paper No. 2021-37.

Pijpers, P. B. M. J., Hosang, B. H., & Ducheine, P. A. L. (2022). *A language of power? Cyber defense in the European Union* (Vol. 176). European Union Institute for Security Studies (EUISS). https://data.europa.eu/doi/10.2815/57567

Pijpers, B. P., & Arnold, L. K. (2020). Conquering the invisible battleground. *Atlantisch Perspectief, 44*(4), 10–14.

Politico. (2022). *War in Ukraine: a watershed moment for European defense policy and transatlantic security?* https://www.politico.eu/event/war-in-ukraine/

Public Television of Georgia. (2021). *Cyber Security Forum of Georgia*. Retrieved from: https://www.youtube.com/watch?v=XDKGueqfG1I&t=57s

Purvis, T., & Hunt, A. (1993). Discourse, ideology, discourse, ideology, discourse, ideology.... *The British Journal of Sociology, 44*(3), 473–499. doi:10.2307/591813

R, K. B., & Kavitha, M. (2020). Military Message Passing using Consortium Blockchain Technology. In *International Conference on Communication and Electronics Systems*. doi:10.1109/ICCES48766.2020.9138014

Radoniewicz, F. (2022). Cybersecurity in the European Union Law. In K. Chałubińska-Jentkiewicz, F. Radoniewicz, & T. Zieliński (Eds.), *Cybersecurity in Poland: Legal Aspects* (pp. 73–92). Springer International Publishing. doi:10.1007/978-3-030-78551-2_6

Rafique, M., Anwar, H. N., & Khalib, S. (2020). Perceived parenting styles and adolescent cyberbullying behaviors: The mediating role of moral disengagement. *Journal of Interpersonal Violence, 35*(21-22), 4771–4792.

Rapid 7. (2020). *Malware Attacks: Definition and Best Practices*. Retrieved from: https://www.rapid7.com/fundamentals/malware-attacks/

Reichert, C. (2020). *Europe allows Huawei for 5G through security guidelines*. CNET. Retrieved from: https://www.cnet.com/tech/mobile/europe-allows-huawei-for-5g-through-security-guidelines/

Remington, T. F. (2019). Institutional change in authoritarian regimes: Pension reform in Russia and China. *Problems of Post-Communism, 66*(5), 301–314. doi:10.1080/10758216.2018.1450154

Reporter, C. (2023). Ukraine Conflict Transformed the Cyber Threat Landscape, Says Google. *CircleID's*. Retrieved from https://circleid.com/posts/20230216-ukraine-conflict-transformed-the-cyber-threat-landscape-says-google

Reuters Staff. (2020, June 4). *UK spy chief says no threat to Five Eyes alliance over Huawei*. Reuters. https://www.reuters.com/article/us-britain-huawei-tech-five-eyes/uk-spy-chief-says-no-threat-to-five-eyes-alliance-over-huawei-idUSKBN23B2T3

Reuters. (2020). *France to invest 1 billion euros to update cyber defenses*. Retrieved from: https://www.reuters.com/article/france-cyberdefence-idUSL5N0LC21G20140207

Ria. (2020). *Cyber Security in Estonia*. Retrieved from: https://www.ria.ee/sites/default/files/cyber_aastaraamat_eng_web_2020.pdf

RIAC. (2016). *NATO's Cyber Defense Evolution - NATO's New Digital Wall*. Retrieved from: https://www.nato.int/docu/rdr-gde-prg/rdr-gde-prg-eng.pdf

Rid, T. (2012). Cyber war will not take place. *Journal of Strategic Studies, 35*(1), 5–32. doi:10.1080/01402390.2011.608939

Rieger, J., Kuhlgatz, C., & Anders, S. (2016). Food scandals, media attention and habit persistence among desensitised meat consumers. *Food Policy, 64*, 82–92. doi:10.1016/j.foodpol.2016.09.005

RMI. (2023). *Professor George Nikoladze*. Retrieved from: http://www.rmi.ge/person/nikoladze/

Robinson, N. (2013). *Cyber-Security Threat Characterization: A Rapid Comparative Analysis*. RAND Corporation.

Rosenbaum, R. (2012, April). *Richard Clarke on Who Was Behind the Stuxnet Attack*. Retrieved from https://www.smithsonianmag.com/history/richard-clarke-on-who-was-behind-the-stuxnet-attack-160630516/

Sabbah, C. (2018). *Pressing pause: A new approach for international cybersecurity norm development*. The MIT Press.

Sahin, E. (2020). An investigation of the influence of culture on cyberbullying perpetration and victimization among adolescents. *International Journal of Adolescence and Youth, 25*(1), 102–116.

Sampi. (2022). *China Cybersecurity Law: 5 Things You Should Know*. Retrieved from https://sampi.co/china-cybersecurity-law/

Sanger, D. E., & Erlanger, S. (2018). Hacked European Cables Reveal a World of Anxiety About Trump, Russia, and Iran. *The New York Times*. Retrieved from: https://www.nytimes.com/2018/12/18/us/politics/european-diplomats-cables-hacked.html

Sarah, W. (2018). *Understanding Cyberwarfare, Lessons from the Russia-Georgia War*. Modern War Institute. Retrieved from: https://mwi.usma.edu/wp-content/uploads/2018/03/Understanding-Cyberwarfare.pdf

Sari, A. (2019). The Mutual Assistance Clauses of the North Atlantic and EU Treaties: The Challenge of Hybrid Threats. *Harvard National Security Journal, 10*, 405–460.

Sarker, I. H. (2021). CyberLearning: Effectiveness analysis of machine learning security modeling to detect cyber-anomalies and multi-attacks. Elsevier.

Schaake, M., & Vermeulen, M. (2016). Towards a values-based European foreign policy to cybersecurity. *Journal of Cyber Policy*, *1*(1), 75–84. doi:10.1080/23738871.2016.1157617

Schmidt, M., Bradsher, K., & Hauser, C. (2012). U.S. Panel Calls Huawei and ZTE 'National Security Threat'. *The New York Times*.

Schmitt-Beck, R. (2015). Bandwagon effect. *The international encyclopedia of political communication*, 1-5.

Schmitt, N. M. (2013). *Tallinn Manual on the International Law Applicable to Cyber Warfare*. Cambridge Univesity Press. doi:10.1017/CBO9781139169288

Scholz, T. (2023, March 3). *Leveraging the EU-India Cybersecurity Partnership*. Observer Research Foundation. Retrieved from https://www.orfonline.org/expert-speak/leveraging-the-eu-india-cybersecurity-partnership/

Scobell, A. (2022). *Comparing Russia-Ukraine to China's Aggression Toward Taiwan*. https://www.usip.org/publications/2022/03/andrew-scobell-comparing-russia-ukraine-chinas-aggression-toward-taiwan

Security, H. (2020). *Department of Homeland Security Statement on the President's Fiscal Year 2021 Budget*. Retrieved from: https://www.dhs.gov/news/2020/02/11/department-homeland-security-statement-president-s-fiscal-year-2021-budget

Security, P. (2018). *Ransomware: Screen Lockers vs. Encryptors*. Retrieved from: https://www.pandasecurity.com/mediacenter/malware/ransomware-screen-lockers-vs-encryptors/

Segal, A. (2016). *The Hacked World Order: How Nations Fight, Trade, Maneuver, and Manipulate in the Digital Age*. Retrieved from https://www.cia.gov/static/e8955c913bf94ec5764481a03cd0f7ee/hacked-world-order.pdf

Segal, A. (2022). *How Should U.S. Cybersecurity Policy Develop?* Council on Foreign Relations.

Sen, K. (2023, March 2). *List of Cybersecurity Regulations in the European Union*. Retrieved from https://www.upguard.com/blog/cybersecurity-regulations-in-the-european-union

Shahbaz, A. (2018). *Freedom on the Net 2018: The Rise of Digital Authoritarianism*. The Freedom House. https://freedomhouse.org/report/freedom-net/2018/rise-digital-authoritarianism

Shahbaz, A., Funk, A., & Vesteinsson, K. (2022). *Countering an authoritarian overhaul of the internet*. Retrieved from https://freedomhouse.org/report/freedom-net/2022/countering-authoritarian-overhaul-internet

Shaikh, J., Nenova, M., Iliev, G., & Valkova-Jarvis, Z. (2017). Analysis of standard elliptic curves for the implementation of elliptic curve cryptography in resource-constrained e-commerce applications. In *2017 IEEE International Conference on Microwaves, Antennas, Communications and Electronic Systems (COMCAS)*. doi:10.1109/COMCAS.2017.8244805

SHAPE. (2022). *Exercise Locked Shields 2022 concludes*. Retrieved from: https://shape.nato.int/news-archive/2022/exercise-locked-shields-2022-concludes

Sharikov, P. A. (2018b). Artificial intelligence, cyberattack, and nuclear weapons—A dangerous combination. *Bulletin of the Atomic Scientists*, *74*(6), 368–373. doi:10.1080/00963402.2018.1533185

Shires, J. (2018). Enacting expertise: Ritual and risk in cybersecurity. *Politics and Governance*, *6*(2), 31–40. doi:10.17645/pag.v6i2.1329

Shires, J. (2020). Cyber-noir: Cybersecurity and popular culture. *Contemporary Security Policy*, *41*(1), 82–107. doi:10.1080/13523260.2019.1670006

Shooter, S. (2013). *Cyber Security and the EU: regulating for network security*. Bird & Bird. Retrieved from https://www.twobirds.com/-/media/PDFs/News/CybersecurityandtheEU06201300125701.pdf

Singer, P. (2011, September 20). *Deterrence in Cyberspace: Debating the Right Strategy With Ralph Langner and Dmitri Alpetrovitch*. Retrieved from https://www.brookings.edu/events/deterrence-in-cyberspace-debating-the-right-strategy-with-ralph-langner-and-dmitri-alperovitch/

Sinkkonen, E. (2021). Dynamic dictators: Improving the research agenda on autocratization and authoritarian resilience. *Democratization*, *28*(6), 1172–1190. doi:10.1080/13510347.2021.1903881

Skopik, F., Settanni, G., & Fiedler, R. (2016). A problem shared is a problem halved: A survey on the dimensions of collective cyber defense through security information sharing. *Computers & Security*, *60*, 154–176. doi:10.1016/j.cose.2016.04.003

SkyNews. (2022). *US military hackers conducting offensive operations in support of Ukraine, says head of Cyber Command*. https://news.sky.com/story/us-military-hackers-conducting-offensive-operations-in-support-of-ukraine-says-head-of-cyber-command-12625139

Slayton, R. (2017). What is the cyber offense-defense balance? Conceptions, causes, and assessment. *International Security*, *41*(3), 41. doi:10.1162/ISEC_a_00267

Sliwinski, K. F. (2014). Moving beyond the European Union's Weakness as a Cyber-Security Agent. *Contemporary Security Policy*, *35*(3), 468–486. doi:10.1080/13523260.2014.959261

So, A. Y. (2011). "One country, two systems" and Hong Kong-China national integration: A crisis-transformation perspective. *Journal of Contemporary Asia*, *41*(1), 99–116. doi:10.1080/00472336.2011.530039

Solar, C. (2020). Cybersecurity and cyber defense in emerging democracies. *Journal of Cyber Policy, 5*. https://www.tandfonline.com/doi/epdf/10.1080/23738871.2020.1820546?needAccess=true&role=button&

Song, A. K. (2019). The Digital Entrepreneurial Ecosystem—A critique and reconfiguration. *Small Business Economics*, *53*(3), 569–590. doi:10.100711187-019-00232-y

Song, S. (2021). Denial of Japan's Military Sexual Slavery and Responsibility for Epistemic Amends. *Social Epistemology*, *35*(2), 160–172. doi:10.1080/02691728.2020.1839811

Sosanya, V. (2022). *Beyond Cyber Security Tools: The Increasing Roles Of Human Factors And Cyber Insurance In The Survival of Social Media Organisations*. Research Gate. Retrieved from: https://www.researchgate.net/profile/Olutunji-Sosanya

Srinivas, J., Das, A., & Vasilakos, A. V. (2020). Designing secure lightweight blockchain-enabled rfid-based authentication protocol for supply chains in 5g mobile edge computing environment. *IEEE Transactions on Industrial Informatics, 16*(11), 7081–7093. doi:10.1109/TII.2019.2942389

Stahl, B. C. (2006). On the difference or equality of information, misinformation, and disinformation: A critical research perspective. *Informing Science*, *9*, 83. doi:10.28945/473

Steve, R. (2018). *What is cyberwar? Everything you need to know about the frightening future of digital conflict*. Retrieved from: https://www.zdnet.com/article/cyberwar-a-guide-to-the-frightening-future-of-online-conflict/

Stevens, T. (2016). *Cyber security and the politics of the time*. Cambridge University Press.

Stevens, T., & O'Brien, K. (2019). Brexit and Cyber Security. *RUSI Journal*, *164*(3), 22–30. doi:10.1080/03071847.2019.1643256

Stylianou, A., Liao, Y., & Katz, S. J. (2021). The Dark Side of Social Media: Cyberbullying and Mental Health Among Adolescents. *Journal of Youth and Adolescence*, *50*(2), 308–320. doi:10.100710964-020-01329-9

Sudhan, A., & Nene, M. J. (2017). Employability of blockchain technology in defence applications. In *International Conference Intelligent Sustainable Systems*. 10.1109/ISS1.2017.8389247

Suresh Babu, C. V. & Das, S. (2023). Impact of Blockchain Technology on the Stock Market. In K. Mehta, R. Sharma, & P. Yu (Eds.), Revolutionizing Financial Services and Markets Through FinTech and Blockchain (pp. 44-59). IGI Global. https://doi.org/10.4018/978-1-6684-8624-5.ch004

Suresh Babu, C. V. & Srisakthi, S. (2023). Cyber Physical Systems and Network Security: The Present Scenarios and Its Applications. In R. Thanigaivelan, S. Kaliappan, & C. Jegadheesan (Eds.), Cyber-Physical Systems and Supporting Technologies for Industrial Automation (pp. 104-130). IGI Global. https://doi.org/10.4018/978-1-6684-9267-3.ch006

Suresh Babu, C. V. & Yadavamuthiah, K. (2023). Precision Agriculture and Farming Using Cyber-Physical Systems: A Systematic Study. In G. Karthick (Ed.), Contemporary Developments in Agricultural Cyber-Physical Systems (pp. 184-203). IGI Global. https://doi.org/10.4018/978-1-6684-7879-0.ch010

Suresh Babu, C. V., Akshayah, N. S., et al. R. (2023). IoT-Based Smart Accident Detection and Alert System. In P. Swarnalatha & S. Prabu (Eds.), Handbook of Research on Deep Learning Techniques for Cloud-Based Industrial IoT (pp. 322-337). IGI Global. https://doi.org/10.4018/978-1-6684-8098-4.ch019

Suresh Babu, C. V., Andrew Simon, P., & Barath Kumar, S. (2023). The Future of Cyber Security Starts Today, Not Tomorrow. In S. Shiva Darshan, M. Manoj Kumar, B. Prashanth, & Y. Vishnu Srinivasa Murthy (Eds.), Malware Analysis and Intrusion Detection in Cyber-Physical Systems (pp. 348-375). IGI Global. https://doi.org/10.4018/978-1-6684-8666-5.ch016

Suresh Babu, C. V., Suruthi, G., & Indhumathi, C. (2023). Malware Forensics: An Application of Scientific Knowledge to Cyber Attacks. In S. Shiva Darshan, M. Manoj Kumar, B. Prashanth, & Y. Vishnu Srinivasa Murthy (Eds.), Malware Analysis and Intrusion Detection in Cyber-Physical Systems (pp. 285-312). IGI Global. https://doi.org/10.4018/978-1-6684-8666-5.ch013

Suresh Babu, C.V. (2023). IoT and its Applications. Anniyappa Publications.

Suresh Babu, C. V. (2022). *Artificial Intelligence & Expert System*. Anniyappa publications.

Sussan, F., & Acs, Z. J. (2017). The digital entrepreneurial ecosystem. *Small Business Economics*, *49*(1), 55–73. doi:10.100711187-017-9867-5

Svanadze, V. (2015). *Cyberspace and Cybersecurity Challenges (Collection)*. Institute of Public Affairs of Georgia.

Svanadze, V., & Gotsiridze, A. (2015). *Cyber defense. Major players in cyberspace*. Cyber Security Policy, Strategy, and Challenges. Cyber Security Bureau of the Georgian Ministry of Defense, Collection of Papers and Articles.

Tamkin, E. (2017). *10 Years After the Landmark Attack on Estonia, Is the World Better Prepared for Cyber Threats?* Foreign Policy. https://foreignpolicy.com/2017/04/27/10-years-afterthe-landmark-attack-on-estonia-is-the-world-better-prepared-for-cyber-threats/

Tang, M. (2020). Huawei versus the United States? The geopolitics of exterritorial internet infrastructure. *International Journal of Communication*, *14*, 22.

Tang, W., & Iyengar, S. (2012). *Political Communication in China: Convergence or Divergence Between the Media and Political System?* Routledge.

Teixeira, C. P., Leach, C. W., & Spears, R. (2022). White Americans' belief in systemic racial injustice and in-group identification affect reactions to (peaceful vs. destructive)" Black Lives Matter" protest. *Psychology of Violence*, *12*(4), 280–292. doi:10.1037/vio0000425

Telecommunication Standardization Sector of ITU. (2008, April). *SERIES X: Data networks, open systems, communication, and security*. Retrieved from International Communication Union: file:///C:/Users/595-424-424%20Windows/Downloads/T-REC-X.1205-200804-I!!PDF-E.pdf

The Department of Defense (DoD). (2018). *Summary Department of Defense Cyber Strategy*. Retrieved from https://media.defense.gov/2018/Sep/18/2002041658/-1/-1/1/CYBER_STRATEGY_SUMMARY_FINAL.PDF

The National Computer Network Emergency Response Technical Team. (2023). *CNCERT/CC*. Retrieved from https://www.cert.org.cn/publish/english/index.html

The New York Times. (2022). *Russia's recent aggressiveness against Ukraine has reignited the discussion about 'hybrid warfare'*. Author.

The State Council. (2014). *Ministry of Industry and Information Technology*. Retrieved from http://english.www.gov.cn/state_council/2014/08/23/content_281474983035940.htm

The White House. (2011). *International Strategy For Cyberspace, "Prosperity, Security, and Openness in a Networked World"*. Retrieved from: https://www.hsdl.org/?view&did=5665

The White House. (2017, May 11). *Presidential Executive Order on Strengthening the Cybersecurity of Federal Networks and Critical Infrastructure*. Retrieved from https://trumpwhitehouse.archives.gov/presidential-actions/presidential-executive-order-strengthening-cybersecurity-federal-networks-critical-infrastructure/

The White House. (2021). *The United States, Joined by Allies and Partners, Attributes Malicious Cyber Activity and Irresponsible State Behavior to the People's Republic of China*. Retrieved from https://www.whitehouse.gov/briefing-room/statements-releases/2021/07/19/the-united-states-joined-by-allies-and-partners-attributes-malicious-cyber-activity-and-irresponsible-state-behavior-to-the-peoples-republic-of-china/

The White House. (2021, July 19). *The United States, Joined by Allies and Partners, Attributes Malicious Cyber Activity and Irresponsible State Behavior to the People's Republic of China*. Retrieved from https://www.whitehouse.gov/briefing-room/statements-releases/2021/07/19/the-united-states-joined-by-allies-and-partners-attributes-malicious-cyber-activity-and-irresponsible-state-behavior-to-the-peoples-republic-of-china/

The White House. (2022, October). *National Security Strategy*. Retrieved from https://www.whitehouse.gov/wp-content/uploads/2022/10/Biden-Harris-Administrations-National-Security-Strategy-10.2022.pdf

The White House. (2023). *Biden-Harris Administration Announces National Cybersecurity Strategy*. Retrieved from https://www.whitehouse.gov/briefing-room/statements-releases/2023/03/02/fact-sheet-biden-harris-administration-announces-national-cybersecurity-strategy/

The White House. (2023, March 1). *US National Cybersecurity Strategy*. Author.

The White House. (2023, March). *National Cybersecurity Strategy*. Retrieved from https://www.whitehouse.gov/wp-content/uploads/2023/03/National-Cybersecurity-Strategy-2023.pdf

Thomas, T. (1996). Russian Views On Information-Based Warfare. *Airpower Journal*.

Thomas, T. L. (2004). Russia's Reflexive Control Theory And The Military. *Journal Of Slavic Military Studies*. Retrieved from: https://www.rit.edu/~w-cmmc/literature/ Thomas_2004.pdf

Thomas, E. F., & Louis, W. R. (2014). When will collective action be effective? Violent and non-violent protests differentially influence perceptions of legitimacy and efficacy among sympathizers. *Personality and Social Psychology Bulletin*, *40*(2), 263–276. doi:10.1177/0146167213510525 PMID:24311435

Thomas, R., Horton, R., Lianos, A., & Adams, C. (2020). Cyberbullying among college students: The role of online anonymity and social media use. *Journal of Interpersonal Violence*, *35*(3-4), 619–643. doi:10.1177/0886260517696874

Timberg, C. (2018). Net of Insecurity: A Flaw in the Design. *The Washington Post*. Retrieved from: https://www.washingtonpost.com/sf/business/2015/05/30/net-of-insecurity-part-1

Timmers, P. (2018). The European Union's cybersecurity industrial policy. *Journal of Cyber Policy*, *3*(3), 363–384. doi:10.1080/23738871.2018.1562560

Tong, C. (2021, October 25). *De-sinicization again in Taiwan's teaching materials*. Yazhou Zhoukan. https://theintellectual.net/zh/referrals/asia-weekly/3621-202147m.html

Transformations Through Blockchain Technology. (2022). In *Springer eBooks*. doi:10.1007/978-3-030-93344-9

U.S. Cyber Command. (2018). *Achieve and Maintain Cyberspace Superiority*. Retrieved 2023, from Cyber Command: https://www.cybercom.mil/Portals/56/Documents/USCYBERCOM%20Vision%20April%202018.pdf?ver=2018-06-14-152556-010

U.S. Embassy and Consulates in Brazil. (2020). *United States and Brazil Sign US $1 Billion Memorandum of Understanding*. Retrieved from: https://br.usembassy.gov/united-states-and-brazil-sign-us-1-billion-memorandum-of-understanding/

Ukraine Conflict: Cyberattacks, Frequently Asked Questions. (2022). CyberPeace Institute. https://cyberpeaceinstitute.org/news/ukraine-conflict-cyberattacks-frequently-asked-questions/

Unit, M. D. (2022). *An overview of Russia's cyberattack activity in Ukraine*. Microsoft. Retrieved from https://query.prod.cms.rt.microsoft.com/cms/api/am/binary/RE4Vwwd

United Nations. (n.d.). *United Nations Charter (full text)*. Retrieved from https://www.un.org/en/about-us/un-charter/full-text

University, A. N. (2022). Director GCHQ's speech on global security amid war in Ukraine. *GCHQ*. Retrieved from https://www.gchq.gov.uk/speech/director-gchq-global-security-amid-russia-invasion-of-ukraine

US Department of Defense. (2011). *Department of Defense Strategy for Operating in Cyberspace*. Arlington Country.

US Department of Education. (2022). *Science, Technology, Engineering, and Math, including Computer Science*. Retrieved from: https://www.ed.gov/stem

US Department of Justice. (2014). *US Charges Five Chinese Military Hackers for Cyber Espionage against US Corporations and a Labor Organization for Commercial Advantage*. Retrieved from https://www.justice.gov/opa/pr/2014/May/14-ag528.html

US Government. (2010). National Security Strategy 2010. Author.

Varonis. (2020). *110 Must-Know Cybersecurity Statistics for 2020*. Retrieved from: https://www.varonis.com

Vázquez, D. F., Acosta, O. P., Spirito, C., Brown, S., & Reid, E. (2012). Conceptual Framework for Cyber Defense Information Sharing within Trust Relationships. *4th International Conference on Cyber Conflict*, 429-445.

Vela, J. (2021, August 2). *The Development of the EU Cyber Security Strategy and its Importance*. FINABEL: European Army Interoperability Centre.

Venard, B. (2019). *The Cold War 2.0 between China and the US is already a virtual reality*. The Conversation. Retrieved from: https://theconversation.com/the-cold-war-2-0-between-chinaand-the-us-is-already-a-virtual-reality-125081

Vidisha, J. (2019). *America's Hidden Stories tackles the CIA's alleged involvement in the Trans-Siberian Pipeline explosion of 1982*. Retrieved from: https://meaww.com/americas-hidden-stories-busting-myth-cia-involvement-trans-siberian-pipeline-explosion-1982

Vilmer, J. B. J., & Conley, H. A. (2018). *Successfully Countering Russian Electoral Interference*. Center for Strategic & International Studies.

Volz, D., & McMillan, R. (2022). In Ukraine, a 'Full-Scale Cyberwar' Emerges. *Wall Street Journal*. https://www.wsj.com/articles/in-ukraine-a-full-scale-cyberwar-emerges-11649780203

Waever, O. (2010). Towards a political sociology of security studies. *Security Dialogue, 41*(6), 649–658. doi:10.1177/0967010610388213

Wahl, T. (2021, April 9). *Council Conclusions on Cybersecurity Strategy*. Eucrim. Retrieved from https://eucrim.eu/news/council-conclusions-on-cybersecurity-strategy/

Wang, G. (2022, November 29). *DPP finally admits their own cyber armies*. Chinatimes. https://www.chinatimes.com/newspapers/20221129000473-260109?chdtv

Weber, V. (2018). Linking cyber strategy with grand strategy: The case of the United States. *Journal of Cyber Policy, 3*.

Weiss, J. C. (2019). A world safe for autocracy? *Foreign Affairs, 98*(4), 92–108.

Wentz, L. (2009). *Cyber Warfare: Protecting the Soldier*. Retrieved from: http://Ctnsp.Dodlive. Mil/Files/2014/03/Cyberpower-I-Chap-20.Pdf

Wessel, R. A. (2015). Towards EU cybersecurity law: regulating a new policy field. In N. Tsagourias & R. Buchan (Eds.), *Research handbook on international law and cyberspace*. Edward Elgar Publishing. doi:10.4337/9781782547396.00032

Wessing, T. (2018). *Cybersecurity in Singapore and China*. Retrieved from https://www.taylorwessing.com/synapse/article-cybersecurity-singapore-china.html

White House. (2017). *United States of America, "National Security Strategy"*. Retrieved from: https://www.whitehouse.gov/wp-content/uploads/2017/12/NSS-Final-12-18-2017-0905.pdf

White House. (2017, August 18). *Statement by President Donald J. Trump on the Elevation of Cyber Command*. Retrieved from https://trumpwhitehouse.archives.gov/briefings-statements/statement-president-donald-j-trump-elevation-cyber-command/

White, K. (2015, September 24). *A Few Comments on the UN Broadband Commission's "Cyber Violence Against Women And Girls" Report*. Retrieved from https://www.popehat.com/2015/09/24/a-few-comments-on-the-un-broadband-commissions-cyber-violence-against-women-and-girls-report/

Wibisono, E. (2023). The digital entrepreneurial ecosystem in the European Union: Evidence from the digital platform economy index. *European Planning Studies, 31*(6), 1–23. doi:10.1080/09654313.2023.2202683

Wired. (2011). *July 26, 1989: First Indictment Under Computer Fraud Act*. Retrieved from: https://www.wired.com/2011/07/0726first-computer-fraud-indictment/

Wohn, D. Y., & Bowe, B. J. (2014, February). Crystallization: How social media facilitates social construction of reality. In *Proceedings of the companion publication of the 17th ACM conference on Computer supported cooperative work & social computing* (pp. 261-264). ACM.

Wolford, B. (n.d.). *What is GDPR, the EU's new data protection law?* GDPR.EU. Retrieved May 19, 2023, from Retrieved from https://gdpr.eu/what-is-gdpr/?cn-reloaded=1

Wu, Y.-S. (2022). *Ukraine and Taiwan: Comparison, Interaction, and Demonstration, Adrian Chiu Cross-Strait, History, International relations, Security, Taiwan-Ukraine.* https://taiwaninsight.org/2022/04/04/ukraine-and-taiwan-comparison-interaction-and-demonstration/

Wu, X., Xie, H., & Huang, Y. (2020). Self-disclosure and cyberbullying victimization among adolescents. *Journal of Youth Studies*, *23*(7), 921–937.

Yadav, A. (2021). Significance of elliptic curve cryptography in blockchain IoT with comparative analysis of RSA algorithm. In *2021 international conference on computing, communication, and intelligent systems (icccis)*. doi:10.1109/ICCCIS51004.2021.9397166

Yee, H., & Storey, I. (2013). *China threat: Perceptions myths.* Routledge. doi:10.4324/9780203060414

Yılmaz, Ş., & Kürşün, E. (2020). The effects of social norms and personal beliefs on cyberbullying behavior among adolescents. *Children and Youth Services Review*, *113*, 104956.

Yuchong, L., & Qinghui, L. (2021). A comprehensive review study of cyber-attacks and cyber security; Emerging trends and recent developments. Elsevier.

Yu, T., Sekar, V., Seshan, S., Agarwal, Y., & Xu, C. (2015). Handling a Trillion Flaws on a Billion Devices: Rethinking Network Security for the Internet-of-Things. *Proceedings of the 14th ACM Workshop on Hot Topics in Networks*. 10.1145/2834050.2834095

Zareen, S., Boutaba, R., & Ahmad, A. (2020). Predicting Cyberbullying in Social Media: An Ensemble Learning Approach. *IEEE Transactions on Computational Social Systems*, *7*(2), 373–384. doi:10.1109/TCSS.2019.2938796

Zeng, J. (2020). Artificial intelligence and China's authoritarian governance. *International Affairs*, *96*(6), 1441–1459. doi:10.1093/ia/iiaa172

Zenglein, M. J., & Holzmann, A. (2019). Evolving made in China 2025. *MERICS Papers on China, 8*, 78.

Zetter, K. (2022). *Viasat Hack 'Did Not' Have Huge Impact on Ukrainian Military Communications, Official Says.* Zero Day. https://zetter.substack.com/p/viasat-hack-did-not-have-huge-impact

Zetter, K. (2022). Viasat Hack "Did Not" Have Huge Impact on Ukrainian Military Communications, Official Says. *Zero Day*. Retrieved from https://zetter.substack.com/p/viasat-hack-did-not-have-huge-impact

Zheng, Z., Xie, S., Dai, H., Chen, X., & Wang, H. (2017). An overview of blockchain technology: architecture, consensus, and future trends. In *International congress on big data*. doi:10.1109/BigDataCongress.2017.85

Zhora, V. (2022). *Digital Peace Now.* https://digitalpeacenow.org/stillvulnerable-viktor-zhora/

Zhu, S., Zhang, X., Ju, Z. Y., & Wang, C. C. (2020, April 1). A study of blockchain technology development and military application prospects. *Journal of Physics: Conference Series*, *1507*(5), 052018. Advance online publication. doi:10.1088/1742-6596/1507/5/052018

About the Contributors

C. V. Suresh Babu is a pioneer in content development. A true entrepreneur, he founded Anniyappa Publications, a company that is highly active in publishing books related to Computer Science and Management. Dr. C.V. Suresh Babu has also ventured into SB Institute, a center for knowledge transfer. He holds a Ph.D. in Engineering Education from the National Institute of Technical Teachers Training & Research in Chennai, along with seven master's degrees in various disciplines such as Engineering, Computer Applications, Management, Commerce, Economics, Psychology, Law, and Education. Additionally, he has UGC-NET/SET qualifications in the fields of Computer Science, Management, Commerce, and Education. Currently, Dr. C.V. Suresh Babu is a Professor in the Department of Information Technology at the School of Computing Science, Hindustan Institute of Technology and Science (Hindustan University) in Padur, Chennai, Tamil Nadu, India. For more information, you can visit his personal blog at .

Mukesh Shankar Bharti is a research scholar with a research background in foreign policy analysis and social science research. The author holds a PhD degree in International Relations with a specialization in East and Central Europe. His research area includes democracy, political institutions, European Union and South Asia.

Tamar Karazanishvili is an invited lecturer at International Black Sea University, Tbilisi, Georgia. Mrs. Tamar successfully defended and received PhD Diploma with honor in Political Science. Furthermore, Tamar has got MA Diploma with honor in International Relations and Politics, as well as BA Diploma with honor in American Studies.

Index

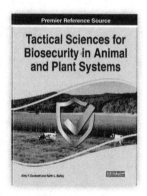

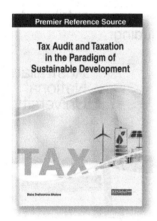

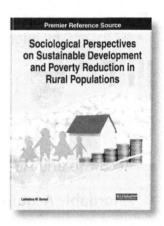

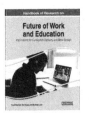

Printed in the United States
by Baker & Taylor Publisher Services